A Companion to Wace

The twelfth-century writer Wace is best known for his two influential works on the history of England [the *Roman de Brut*] and on the history of the Normans [the *Roman de Rou*], but despite this he has, until recently, been neglected. This book aims to provide a comprehensive overview of all his surviving works, including his hagiographical pieces, *La Vie de sainte Marguerite*, *La Vie de saint Nicolas* and *La Conception Nostre Dame*. Beginning with an examination of the historical and textual background necessary to an informed understanding of the poet, it moves on to discuss the manuscript tradition of each of Wace's poems, together with the sources that underlie each text, highlighting the additions, omissions and modifications made by the poet in adapting his material for new, non-Latinate audience. Particular attention is given to Wace's swan-song, the *Roman de Rou*, where his skill in combining history and romance is most clearly revealed.

F. H. M. LE SAUX is Senior Lecturer of French Studies at The University of Reading, Reading, UK.

A Companion to
Wace

F. H. M. Le Saux

D. S. BREWER

© F. H. M. Le Saux 2005

All Rights Reserved. Except as permitted under current legislation no part of this work may be photocopied, stored in a retrieval system, published, performed in public, adapted, broadcast, transmitted, recorded or reproduced in any form or by any means, without the prior permission of the copyright owner

The right of F. H. M. Le Saux to be identified as the author of this work has been asserted in accordance with sections 77 and 78 of the Copyright, Designs and Patents Act 1988

First published 2005
D. S. Brewer, Cambridge
Reprinted in paperback 2010

Transferred to digital printing

ISBN 978-1-84384-043-5 hardback
ISBN 978-1-84384-249-1 paperback

D. S. Brewer is an imprint of Boydell & Brewer Ltd
PO Box 9, Woodbridge, Suffolk IP12 3DF, UK
and of Boydell & Brewer Inc.
668 Mt Hope Avenue, Rochester, NY 14620, USA
website: www.boydellandbrewer.com

A CiP catalogue record for this book is available
from the British Library

This publication is printed on acid-free paper

Contents

Acknowledgements	vii
Abbreviations	viii
Introduction Wace: his life and times	1
Part I Wace: hagiographer	
Introduction: dates and context	11
1 *La Vie de sainte Marguerite*	13
2 *La Conception Nostre Dame*	30
3 *La Vie de saint Nicolas*	51
Conclusion	79
Part II *Le Roman de Brut*	
Introduction	81
4 Manuscripts, sources and adaptation principles	85
5 Britain, Rome and the House of Constantine	108
6 King Arthur and the passage of dominion	125
Conclusion	151
Part III *Le Roman de Rou*	
Introduction: manuscripts, sources, structure	153
7 The ancestors of William the Conqueror	160
8 William II of Normandy – the Conqueror	209
9 The aftermath of Hastings	253
Conclusion: the epilogue	275
Conclusion	279
Select bibliography	287
Index	297

Acknowledgements

This book has been a long time in the making. The initial impetus came from the realisation that more was known of the Middle English versions of Wace's *Roman de Brut* than of the work itself. My investigations into Wace's translation and adaptation technique in the *Roman de Brut* then led me to question the nature of the poet's methodology in his other works.

I have a debt of gratitude to more people than can be listed here: my colleagues of the Graduate Centre for Medieval Studies of the University of Reading, especially Professor Peter Noble, the late Professor Wolfgang van Emden, Dr Marianne Ailes, Dr Helen Roberts and Dr Vincent Moss, with whom I shared many a stimulating discussion; Dr Anthea Harris, who came to the rescue when I found that my own equipment was inadequate to the task of photographing the eastern panel of the Winchester Cathedral font (the panel in question being hidden by a column); Dr Gioia Paradisi, who kindly sent me a copy of her ground-breaking book in time for me to be able to take account of its findings; and Professor Glyn Burgess, who kept me abreast of the latest developments in *Rou* scholarship. The librarians of Durham Cathedral Library and the Palace Green Library of the University of Durham deserve a particular mention for their efficiency and helpfulness during my protracted research visits there, as does Caroline Palmer from Boydell & Brewer, whose practical advice has proved invaluable. And last but not least, all my thanks go to my husband, Dr Neil Thomas, who has helped me in a myriad of ways, and my mother, Sylvia Mary Le Saux, for her unfailing patience and support.

Abbreviations

Details of all other references can be found by reference to the Bibliography at the back of this volume.

Arnold	Wace, *Le Roman de Brut de Wace*, ed. I. Arnold, 2 vols. (Paris, 1938–40)
Burgess, *The Roman de Rou*	Wace, *The Roman de Rou*, trans. G. S. Burgess (St Helier, 2002)
Francis	Wace, *La Vie de sainte Marguerite*, ed. E. A. Francis (Paris, 1932; Classiques Français du Moyen Age 71)
Griscom	Geoffrey of Monmouth, *The Historia Regum Britanniae of Geoffrey of Monmouth with Contributions to the Study of its Place in Early British History*, ed. A. Griscom and R. E. Jones (New York, 1929)
Holden	Wace, *Le Roman de Rou de Wace*, ed. A. J. Holden, 3 vols. (Paris, 1970–3)
Keller	Wace, *La Vie de sainte Marguerite*, ed. H. E. Keller (Tübingen, 1990; Beihefte zur Zeitschrift für romanische Philologie 229)
PL	*Patrologia cursus completus, series Latina*, ed. J.-P. Migne (Paris, 1841–64)
PMLA	*Publications of the Modern Languages Association*
Ronsjö	Wace, *La Vie de saint Nicolas par Wace, poème. Poème religieux du XIIe siècle publié d'après tous les manuscrits*, ed. E. Ronsjö (Lund and Copenhagen, 1942; Etudes romanes de Lund 5)
Weiss	Wace, *Wace's Roman de Brut. A History of the British. Text and Translation*, trans. J. Weiss (Exeter, 1999)
Wright, *Burgerbibliothek MS 568*	Geoffrey of Monmouth, *The Historia Regum Britannie of Geoffrey of Monmouth, I: Bern, Burgerbibliothek MS 568*, ed. N. Wright (Cambridge, 1985)
Wright, *First Variant Version*	Geoffrey of Monmouth, *The Historia Regum Britannie of Geoffrey of Monmouth, II: The First Variant Version*, ed. N. Wright (Cambridge, 1988)

Introduction
Wace: His Life and Times

We have very few certainties regarding the life of Wace. His date of birth is unknown, and attempts to estimate it have been based essentially on extrapolations from the dates of composition of his extant works. The nineteenth-century scholar Gaston Paris concluded that the poet must have been born around the year 1100, on the grounds that by the death of Henry I, in 1135, he had already completed his studies and was established as a 'clerc lisant'.[1] Anthony Holden, the editor of the *Roman de Rou*, inclines towards 1110. A date of birth in the first half of the first decade of the twelfth century would fit with the overall picture of the poet's production; though, as Glyn S. Burgess has pointed out, Wace was still active in the mid 1170s,[2] making his career an unusually long one. His name, which also appears in the manuscripts as 'Guace' and 'Gace', is Germanic, possibly a diminutive form of Walter; it has survived to this day as a family name, including in Jersey.[3] In the case of our poet, 'Wace' must have been his Christian name, as family names were not in common usage in the early twelfth century. References to 'Robert Wace' are erroneous, based on textual misreading.[4]

What little information we have regarding Wace's long and productive life is contained in a few lines scattered in his *Roman de Rou* and a handful of legal documents. The poet was born on Jersey, was sent to school at Caen, on the Norman mainland, and pursued his studies in France before returning to Normandy, as he tells us himself in his *Roman de Rou* (*Troisième Partie*, 5305–12):

> En l'isle de Gersui fui nez,
> a Chaem fui petiz portez,
> iloques fui a letres mis,
> pois fui longues en France apris;
> quant jo de France repairai
> a Chaem longues conversai,
> de romanz faire m'entremis,
> mult en escris e mult en fis.[5]

---

[1] See G. Paris's review of H. Andresen's edition of the *Roman de Rou*, *Romania* 9 (1880), esp. pp. 594–5.
[2] *Le Roman de Rou de Wace*, ed. A. J. Holden (Paris, 1970–73), vol. 1, Introduction, p. 15. All quotes from the *Roman de Rou* will be from this edition.
[3] The family name may also have its origins in the Breton 'gwas', 'servant, vassal'. Before it was recognised that Wace was our poet's Christian name, rather than a nickname or cognomen, the late Léon Fleuriot suggested that Wace might have had Breton origins. Regrettably, Professor Fleuriot did not explore the issue in print. I wish to thank Mr Loïc Kervoas for this information.
[4] See Hans-Erich Keller, 'Le mirage Robert Wace', *Zeitschrift für Romanische Philologie* 106 (1990): 465–6.
[5] 'I was born on the island of Jersey and taken to Caen as a small child; there I went to school and was

Who paid for these long studies away from home is unknown. Presumably it was his family, as an abbey was unlikely to invest such resources in a student (however promising) who was not destined to become a monk. In the event, Wace does not appear to have received more than minor orders. He obtained the degree of 'Master', which entitled him to teach, and pursued a career as 'clerc lisant'[6] at Caen before ending his life as a canon of Bayeux cathedral, a prebend granted to him by Henry II,[7] at some time between 1166 and 1169. Wace is named as a witness in four surviving Norman charters, the first (where is he is still called 'magister Wascius', as opposed to 'canonicus') probably dating from 1166,[8] while the last dates from 1174. These documents all relate to business conducted by or involving Bishop Henry II of Bayeux (1165–1204); Wace is referred to as a canon from 1169. It is generally accepted that Wace's disappearance from legal documents after 1174 points to his having died in the mid 1170s.

Wace's lifespan covers some extremely troubled times. The political situation in Normandy at the beginning of Wace's life was difficult. The conquest of England had led to increased prosperity, with Norman families coming into new estates on the other side of the Channel, while the Norman abbeys and churches found their wealth and influence considerably increased through the donations and endowments made by the new magnates. Culturally, by 1100, it must have been difficult to distinguish between what was Norman and what was Anglo-Norman. Norman noblemen had married English heiresses, and some of the outstanding historians of the period were of mixed parentage (one may particularly mention Orderic Vitalis and William of Malmesbury). Important English prisoners from the Conquest, such as Earl Morcar, had been taken to Normandy and stayed there until a general amnesty issued by William Rufus in 1087, whilst the monastic environment offered a continuous and important forum of exchange.[9] Moreover, less than a decade after the death of King William Rufus in a hunting accident in 1100, the distinction between king of England and duke of Normandy became purely nominal. Henry I succeeded William Rufus to the throne of England while his elder brother Robert Duke of Normandy was on crusade in Jerusalem. Robert was understandably angry at having been passed over in this way, despite his seniority of birth; he rushed back and invaded England. The two brothers came to an agreement, but hostilities broke out again, on Norman soil this time, leading to Henry's victory at the battle of Tinchebray in 1106. Robert was captured and kept prisoner until his death. Thereafter, the king

---

then educated for a long time in France. When I returned from France, I stayed in Caen for a long time and set about composing works in the vernacular; I wrote and composed a good many.' Unless specified, all translations of the *Roman de Rou* are taken from Glyn S. Burgess, trans., *Wace. The Roman de Rou* (St Helier, 2002).

6 *Roman de Rou, Troisième Partie*, line 180. The exact meaning of 'clerc lisant' has been a matter for debate; see below for a discussion of the term.
7 See *Roman de Rou, Troisième Partie*, lines 5312–18.
8 The document itself is not dated. For a discussion of these charters, see Burgess, *The Roman de Rou*, pp. xvii–xix.
9 See Elisabeth M. C. van Houts, *Memory and Gender in Medieval Europe, 900–1200* (London, 1999), pp. 140–2; also Marjorie Chibnall, 'Monastic Foundations in England and Normandy, 1066–1189', pp. 37–49 in *England and Normandy in the Middle Ages*, ed. D. Bates and A. Curry (London, 1994). Cultural convergence does not of course preclude political tensions: see David Crouch, 'Normans and Anglo-Normans: A Divided Aristocracy?', pp. 51–67 in the same volume.

of England and the duke of Normandy were *de facto* one and the same person for the duration of the reign of Henry I, who spent time on both sides of the Channel attending to his business.

By the time Wace was old enough to seek employment, having returned from his studies in France (frequently understood as Paris, though Chartres would be just as likely: both were prestigious centres of learning at the time),[10] he would have found favourable conditions in his homeland. Caen, where he tells us he settled down, had two important abbeys which could have offered teaching opportunities and posts related to the management of their estates: Saint-Etienne (or Abbaye aux Hommes), founded by William the Conqueror in 1077, and Sainte Trinité (or Abbaye aux Femmes), founded by Matilda, William's queen. In addition, the fact that the duke of Normandy was of necessity frequently absent meant that the everyday running of the duchy had to be entrusted to a well-oiled administrative machinery, which would have required a qualified workforce, and potentially offered the possibility of travel and royal favour.

While we cannot state anything with certainty regarding Wace's employment, his own testimony in the *Roman de Rou* would suggest that he entered the ducal administration, as he proudly claims personal acquaintance with Henry I, Henry II and Henry the Young King (who died in 1183):

> Treis reis Henriz vi e cunui
> e clerc lisant en lur tens fui;
> des Engleis furent rei tuit trei
> e tuit trei furent duc e rei,
> rei de Engleterre la guarnie
> e duc furent de Normendie   (*Troisième Partie*, 179–84)[11]

The exact capacity in which Wace knew these kings is unclear, as the title of 'clerc lisant', which the poet himself clearly thought was self-explanatory, is now a cryptic signifier. It is possible, moreover, that Wace's privileged access to his rulers was enabled by his connections as much as his function. He may have come from an influential family that allowed him to move in aristocratic circles: one of the more obscure – and clearly corrupt – passages of the *Roman de Rou* (*Troisième Partie*, 3223–5) suggests that Wace descended on his mother's side from Turstin, chamberlain to Duke Robert the Magnificent (the father of William the Conqueror). This interpretation of the passage, requiring only minor emendations of the text as it stands, is now widely accepted.[12] At a time when personal connections were all-important (one may think of Thomas Becket, whose career took off when he entered the service of Theobald of Bec, Archbishop of Canterbury, who came from the same village as his father), a family tradition of service

---

[10] Scholarly opinion tends towards Paris, as 'France' was frequently used to refer to the actual 'Ile de France', i.e., the Paris area. See Burgess, *The Roman de Rou*, pp. xvi–xvii. On the other hand, when a prestigious tutor was required to train the future Henry II, a Chartres scholar, William of Conches, was chosen.
[11] 'I saw and knew three king Henrys; in their time I was a *clerc lisant*. All three were kings of the English and all three were dukes and kings; they were kings of England the Rich and dukes of Normandy.'
[12] For a recent discussion of Wace's possible noble origins, see Burgess, *The Roman de Rou*, pp. xix–xx.

in the ducal household would have been extremely useful, and Wace might well have been earmarked from an early age to continue such a tradition.

Another source of patronage for a young scholar in early twelfth-century Caen was one of the abbeys. Urban Tigner Holmes suggests that Wace's early patrons may have been Saint-Etienne, and the nearby abbey of Saint-Evroult, where Orderic Vitalis lived from 1085 until his death in 1143. The possibility that Wace might have been personally acquainted with Orderic is an attractive idea, though there is nothing to indicate that such was the case; there is no doubt, however, that he had knowledge of his writings. Holmes also notes that Wace's three surviving religious poems could potentially be connected with three local churches: one dedicated to St Nicholas near the abbey of Saint-Etienne, in Caen; another, in the same town, dedicated to the Virgin (Notre Dame de Froide Rue), in Caen; and a chapel dedicated to St Margaret in the cathedral of Bayeux.[13] However, as we shall see, Wace's religious commissions were rather more special than a one-off occasion piece for just the one shrine, and point to a more complex network of patronage than has generally been assumed. It is likely that the Caen abbeys, the ducal circle and the cross-Channel ecclesiastical and secular grandees knew a fairly intensive level of interaction, if only because so many of the key characters were blood relations. The boundaries between these potential patrons must have been relatively fluid.

Whether Wace started off as a teacher or directly as a 'clerc lisant', it is unlikely that he was a full-time writer. In fact, his poetical activities could be seen as having developed naturally from the duties incumbent on a 'clerc lisant'. There has been some debate about the exact meaning and implications of this title, but it would appear that the 'clerc lisant' was a sort of notary whose responsibility it was to read aloud texts in various types of assemblies. In the case of legal documents in a formal setting, it is probable that the 'clerc lisant' also had to translate the Latin into French for the benefit of the non-clerical listeners. We know that clerks in criminal cases had to translate confessions in the vernacular into Latin, when they drew up trial proceedings; the inverse process must also have been required, when passing from the written, Latin text to an oral, vernacular communicative situation. In other words, by his very status, the 'clerc lisant' was an intermediary between two cultural groups, comparable to the latimers (interpreters) whose role in diffusing Arthurian legends in Anglo-Norman England was first identified by Constance Bullock-Davies.[14] And like the latimer from the Welsh borderlands, the 'clerc lisant' probably combined his administrative responsibilities with more lighthearted activities, such as the choice of entertaining or improving texts for public readings during feast days and holidays; hence Jean-Guy Gouttebroze's image of the 'clerc lisant' as an intermediary between Latin historiography and the world of popular entertainment.[15] The holder of such an office was likely to be asked to compose occasional pieces; if he

---

[13] Urban Tigner Holmes, Jr, 'Norman Literature and Wace', pp. 46–67 in *Medieval Secular Literature: Four Essays*, ed. W. Matthews (Berkeley and Los Angeles, 1967), esp. pp. 56–61.

[14] Bullock-Davies, *Professional Interpreters and the Matter of Britain* (Cardiff, 1966).

[15] Jean-Guy Gouttebroze, 'Entre les historiographes d'expression latine et les jongleurs, le clerc lisant', pp. 215–30 in *Le clerc au Moyen Age* (Aix-en-Provence, 1995).

was gifted, one could expect him to attain a degree of recognition that might lead to more weighty commissions, for which he might (with his employer's approval) have been released from some of his administrative duties. Such was probably the career pattern of Wace.

Much of Wace's work, inevitably, has been lost. In the prologue to the Third Part (*Troisième Partie*) of his *Roman de Rou*, the poet hints at a prolific output, of 'romanz', that is, adaptations of Latin texts in French,[16] and 'serventeis', that is, short poems of a political or topical nature. The 'serventeis' would have been tightly bound to specific events and circumstances, and if any have survived at all, for example in a collection of songs like the Bayeux manuscript,[17] it will have been as anonymous pieces. Similarly, any adaptations into French of short tales comparable to Marie de France's *Lais* are unlikely to have survived if they were composed as a playful whim rather than in response to an earnest request by someone willing to invest in the dissemination of the pieces. However intensive Wace's literary activities may have been, they must have taken place on the margins of his main activity. We are told in the prologue to the *Troisième Partie* of the *Roman de Rou* that the typical response to his endeavours is: 'Mult dit bien Maistre Wace; vus devrïez tuz tens escrire/ ki tant savez bel e bien dire', 'Master Wace expresses things so nicely! You should write full-time, you know how to say things in such a beautiful and appropriate way.'[18] Wace complains that these people pay him with praise only, and that he is landed with the cost of having the texts copied by a scribe: a sure sign that he was not perceived as a professional writer dependent on his literary output for a living.

The *Roman de Rou* stands out from the rest of Wace's surviving works for its personal tone, and more especially, the narrator's bitter complaints at his patrons' lack of generosity, which begs the question of Wace's personal circumstances. If one is to believe the prologue to the *Chronique Ascendente*, generosity's hands have been so frozen by avarice that they can no longer open to distribute gifts (9–11); the poet himself is often reduced to pawning his belongings (22–23). The Second Part (*Deuxième Partie*) of the *Rou* ends with the narrator asking for some sort of recompense (4423–5):

> Qui chante boivre doit ou prendre autre loier,
> De son mestier se doit qui que peut avancier;
> Volentiers preïst grace, quer de prendre a mestier.[19]

In the last line of this passage, 'grace' is recognised as a scribal error for 'Wace'; which leads to the alternative translation: 'Wace would gladly accept anything, for he needs it.' In the *Troisième Partie*, as we have seen, the general meanness

---

[16] This word, in this particular passage of the *Rou*, is frequently translated as 'romance' by scholars (including Burgess, p. 111); but its exact meaning in Wace's day was 'text in the French language'. All of Wace's surviving works are scholarly and didactic in nature.

[17] The Bayeux manuscript gathers 100 songs, compiled in 1515 for Charles of Bourbon. The manuscript is now preserved in Paris, Bibliothèque nationale, fonds fr. 9346. See Théodore Gérold, *Le Manuscrit de Bayeux* (Strasbourg, 1921).

[18] *Roman de Rou, Troisième Partie*, 158–60; my translation.

[19] 'He who sings must drink or take some other reward. He who can should improve himself through his work; he would gladly take bounty, for he needs to take it.'

surrounding the poet is then denounced. How seriously are we to take these statements? The passage quoted above, for example, is the culmination of a section of the work composed in a style reminiscent (as we shall see in Part III of this study) of the *chanson de geste*, with a minstrel-like narrator who is totally unlike the serious, scholarly narrator of the religious poems, the *Roman de Brut*, and indeed the rest of the *Roman de Rou*. The impecunious *jongleur* asking for a drink and bemoaning his dire financial situation is a stock figure that need not bear any immediate or literal relation to Wace himself. It could however be a humorous, self-deprecatory and very heavy hint to his patrons that a little financial independence to cushion his old age would not be unwelcome.

It is of course possible that Wace experienced straitened circumstances in the course of his adult life. If the poet only took minor orders, he might have married and had the burden of a family to raise; it has indeed been suggested that Richard Wace, a canon of Bayeux towards the end of the twelfth century, could have been a son of his.[20] But by the time he was composing the *Rou*, Wace was getting on in years, and any children would presumably have grown up. There is also the possibility, raised by Burgess (p. xx), that Wace came from an impoverished or low-born family, and therefore could not fall back on inherited wealth. This, however, fails to convince. There must have been a limited fortune in Wace's background, if only to pay for his years of study in France. On the other hand, the poet must certainly have been a younger son with few or no prospects of his own: if his father witnessed the departure of William the Conqueror's fleet in 1066, he was already middle-aged when Wace was born in the 1100s. Nevertheless, Wace could have relied on the network of kinship for help, and once he received his prebend in Bayeux, he would have been financially comfortable.

To this, one may add that the indirect testimony of his surviving works points towards influential patrons. One of these, though unnamed by Wace, is probably Henry of Blois, Bishop of Winchester and Abbot of Glastonbury. While there is no indication that this grand personage – the grandson of the Conqueror by his daughter Adela – had directly commissioned poems from Wace, the extant works by our poet prior to the *Roman de Rou* may be seen as reflecting his interests in one way or another. Henry of Blois, trained at Cluny, was a prominent churchman and patron of the arts. He actively encouraged the monks of Glastonbury to have the history of the abbey written down by William of Malmesbury[21] and Caradoc of Llancarfan (though in the latter case, we are dealing with hagiography rather than historiography), and may have encouraged Geoffrey of Monmouth to write his *Historia Regum Britanniae*, in an attempt to bolster his ambitions to be archbishop, in 1138; he may also have been a patron of Chrétien de Troyes.[22] An interest in matters Arthurian ties in neatly with the interests of Glastonbury, as Caradoc of Llancarfan's *Life of Gildas* creates a link between Arthur and Glastonbury through the person of St Gildas, who was said to be buried there. It

---

[20] See Burgess, p. xix; Holmes, pp. 66–7; E. M. C. van Houts, 'Wace as Historian', pp. 103–32 in *Family Trees and the Roots of Politics*, ed. K. S. B. Keats-Rohan (Woodbridge, 1997), esp. p. 105.

[21] It is thought that William of Malmesbury and Caradoc of Llancarfan visited Glastonbury at the same time. See John Scott, ed. and trans., *The Early History of Glastonbury: an Edition, Translation and Study of William of Malmesbury's De Antiquitate Glastonie Ecclesie* (Woodbridge, 1981), pp. 3–5.

[22] See G. S. Burgess, *Chrétien de Troyes, Erec et Enide* (London, 1984), p. 97.

has been suggested that Henry of Blois might in some way be connected with the *Roman de Brut*, Wace's translation and adaptation of Geoffrey of Monmouth's *Historia Regum Britanniae*.[23] If such was the case, the link may have been through one of the Caen abbeys; however, as Henry of Blois was a close blood relative to the dukes of Normandy, he could equally have made Wace's acquaintance at the ducal court itself. Of Wace's religious poems, the *Conception Nostre Dame* in particular presupposes a very influential ecclesiastical patron who could provide access to a wide range of written sources, had strong ties with England, and could ensure the dissemination of what would have been perceived by some as a controversial work.

Henry I's death without male issue on 1 December 1135 heralded the beginning of troubled times in Normandy as in England. Henry's chosen heir, his daughter Matilda, in addition to being seen by many as unsuitable by virtue of her sex, had made an unpopular second marriage (to Geoffrey of Anjou), following the death of her first husband, Emperor Henry V; as a result, Stephen, Count of Blois (the brother of Bishop Henry of Blois), was recognised as Henry's successor and crowned king soon after Henry I's death. Matilda's attempts to overthrow Stephen were to destabilise England for over a decade; meanwhile Geoffrey of Anjou had to conquer Normandy piecemeal for his young son, the future Henry II, a process completed in 1145. During this period, the allegiance of Henry of Blois appears to have wavered somewhat, though at the outset he clearly supported his brother's claim, as did many others. *La Vie de sainte Marguerite*, possibly the oldest of Wace's poems to have come down to us, could thus be viewed as a subtle attempt to 'devalue' the prestige potential offered by her grandmother, St Margaret of Scotland, to Henry I's daughter Matilda, through a campaign aiming to bolster the popularity of St Margaret of Antioch.[24]

The political potential of the later *Roman de Brut* is less easy to discern. Wace's patron must certainly have had strong English connections, as the subject-matter of the work would not have held much interest for local Norman families. On Geoffrey of Anjou's death in 1151, Henry came into an inheritance that had been very efficiently run by his father, further enlarged by the domains that came with his new bride, Eleanor of Aquitaine. He had the means to patronise the arts and had married an intelligent and well-educated woman: the *Roman de Brut* could have been commissioned as an elegant gift for Eleanor at the beginning of their marriage. On the other hand, Henry's prospects on the English throne were still uncertain, so it is unlikely that Wace wrote the work for him directly – until, that is, 1153, when Henry was officially made Stephen's heir following the death of his son Eustace. After that date, we can well imagine a ducal commission in view of giving additional glamour to the forthcoming royal dignity. However, such a late date would imply that Wace wrote the work full-time, as it would not have been possible for him otherwise to complete so ambitious a project in so short a period of time – between (late) 1153 and 1155, when the *Roman de Brut* was finished. This raises the question of his professional status.

---

[23] See Holmes, p. 62.
[24] On the possible propagandist intent of the poem, see E. A. Francis, ed., *Wace. La Vie de sainte Marguerite* (Paris, 1932), pp. xix–xx.

It is highly probable that during the troubled years between 1135 and 1145, Wace's literary patron was a religious house or personage. The two religious poems by him that do not appear to have any secular-political agenda to them may date from this period: *La Conception Nostre Dame* and *La Vie de saint Nicolas*. The *Nicolas* is said by the narrator to have been written for a certain Robert son of Tiout, who belonged to a prominent Caen family.[25] This could indicate that the poem was composed at a time when unrest was such that only local patronage was available – yet the unusual selection of miracles recounted in the work, some of which are extremely rare and unattested in any saints' lives predating Wace, hints at an agenda going beyond personal devotion, and required access to a remarkable library. Whether by design or by coincidence, black Tournai marble fonts depicting miracles of the saint are produced after the completion of the *Vie de saint Nicolas*, at least one of which appears to have been carved following specific orders. It is still in Winchester cathedral, and was bought by Bishop Henry of Blois himself.[26]

The *Conception Nostre Dame*, for which no patron is named, is likely to have been commissioned either in the immediate aftermath to the granting of the feast of the Conception of the Virgin Mary in England (1129), or in anticipation of its official adoption in Normandy (1145). For this poem, Wace uses English sources alongside apocryphal biblical material, mediating a viewpoint that is not entirely congruent with Norman propaganda; theologically, it was composed in the middle of a polemic opposing the proponents of the newly formulated doctrine of the Immaculate Conception of Mary, and the likes of St Bernard of Clairvaux, who vigorously opposed the idea of the Immaculate Conception. Under these conditions, a patron might not wish to be named, especially if he was of some prominence and potentially called upon to work with his theological opponents in other respects. Whilst it is not unreasonable to postulate a lay patron for this work if it was composed at the earlier date (perhaps Henry I himself, who is known to have observed the feast), the poet must have received some guidance, if not actual supervision, from a senior ecclesiastical personage; after the death of Henry I, secular patronage for the *Conception Nostre Dame* becomes highly unlikely. Bishop Henry of Blois would have been in an ideal position to give Wace the support needed to access both libraries and informants, as Winchester was an important centre of Marian devotion, and had been since Anglo-Saxon times.

It has frequently been observed that Wace appears to have been familiar with the south of England by the time he wrote the *Roman de Brut*;[27] it is more than possible that part of his knowledge of England dated back to the research for the *Conception*. During his travels, Wace could also have conducted business: the Caen abbeys had property in England, and the Norman ducal administration

---

[25] See below, Part I, Introduction to Chapter 3.
[26] For a description of the Nicholas panels on the Winchester font, see below, Part I, Chapter 3.
[27] J. H. Philpot, *Maistre Wace. A Pioneer in Two Literatures* (London, 1925), p. 52, suggests that Wace visited the places mentioned by Geoffrey of Monmouth as preparation for the *Roman de Brut*, which would open the possibility that Geoffrey himself helped Wace in his work. This is an attractive hypothesis, but not especially supported by the *Roman de Brut* itself. On Wace's possible visits to England, see also Margaret Houck, *Sources of the Roman de Brut of Wace* (Berkeley and Los Angeles, 1941), pp. 219–28 and 284–7.

presumably sent occasional envoys to England to inform the king of events, ask for instructions, or liase with their English counterparts. Once again, Winchester would certainly have been on the itinerary, as the town housed the royal treasury. However, the English connection runs deeper than an isolated trip across the Channel. The evidence of the *Roman de Rou* betrays a striking readiness to adopt English versions of events against Norman ones, and Wace appears to have had some knowledge of the English language, which he is not ashamed to show off in the *Roman de Rou*.[28] This could be due to exposure to an English point of view in Normandy, but the inclusion in the *Roman de Brut* of the reference to the peasants of Cirencester as authorities in the Gurmund episode, and (more significantly still) the anachronistic prophecy of Teleusin at Christ's birth, points to a more intimate experience of England, and possibly the Marches of Wales, where he could have encountered informants with some knowledge of Welsh tradition.[29] Wace was clearly in contact with someone who could credibly claim local knowledge of the area of Cirencester, and who had a vested interest in promoting the Christian identity of the Celtic past of the land. The abbot of Glastonbury would certainly have had sympathy with such an aim.

Whoever Wace's patrons may have been – whether a religious house eager to please Bishop Henry of Blois, Henry of Blois himself, or the duke of Normandy/ king of England – one may safely infer that from the moment the poet completed his *Roman de Brut*, in 1155, his status must have changed somewhat. The work was timely, giving extra gloss to the accession to the throne of Henry II, and it was entertaining; the sheer popularity of the *Roman de Brut* would have ensured royal patronage. The *Roman de Rou* was almost certainly commissioned by the king, and the intriguing end to the *Deuxième Partie* could indicate that it was offered to Henry as an appetiser for what was to follow, in a bid to secure a prebend in Bayeux soon to be vacant. The *Troisième Partie* shows that the strategy was successful. However, throughout his career, Wace remained based in Caen; he was never a court poet, and appears to have continued his activities as 'clerc lisant' until he became a canon of the chapter of Bayeux cathedral. Writing probably took up a great deal of his time, but it never became his sole activity: hence the decade taken by the poet to complete the *Roman de Rou*.

All of the extant poems by Wace are the work of a confident and experienced writer, trained to analyse texts and give clear interpretations of them. The *Conception Nostre Dame* in particular bears the mark of a mature thinker, chosen by his patron for his moral *gravitas* as well as his intellectual ability and literary skills: a man in his mid thirties, perhaps? Which means that by the time Wace received his prebend, he was in his sixties, and that he died well into his seventies. He had managed to complete his *Roman de Rou* (even if he did not go as far as Henry II had intended, apparently), and was secure in the knowledge that his huge effort of gathering sources and testimonies had contributed to a work of

---

[28] See below Part III, Chapter 8.
[29] It may be significant that Orderic Vitalis was born near Shrewsbury, and educated from five to ten years of age in Shrewsbury itself. He would therefore have experienced some contact with neighbouring Welsh people. See M. Chibnall, *The World of Orderic Vitalis: Norman Monks and Norman Knights* (Oxford, 1984), pp. 3–16.

historiography that could not easily be bettered. If he felt strong pride in his Norman homeland, this work would have been tinged with sadness. Normandy was no longer the jewel in the English crown, but just one continental possession in the midst of the Angevin empire. The evidence of the *Roman de Rou* suggests that Wace was aware of this, and that he did not entirely approve of the policies of Henry II. Indeed, quite apart from the much-quoted passage where Henry II is gently rebuked for not having kept all his promises to the poet, there appears to be an intentional slight towards the king in the fact that Wace fails to mention his presence at the re-interment of the bones of dukes Richard I and II. Henry's entrusting of Wace's project to Benoît de Sainte-Maure is usually read as indicating Wace's fall from royal favour; but the rift appears to have been reciprocal.

It has been assumed that Wace left his *Roman de Rou* unfinished in a fit of pique. In fact, as I argue in the conclusion to Part III, Chapter 9, Wace ends his work with the end of an era; the battle of Tinchebray marked the end of Normandy as an independent narrative subject. Thanks to his prebend in Bayeux, Wace could afford to ignore his powerful patron's demands, and that, I would argue, is exactly what he did. He had experienced huge fame in his lifetime and achieved widespread recognition for his talents as both writer and scholar; he had nothing to prove, and was in possession of an income that allowed him to end his life in dignity. We do not know when, where or how his death occurred; but he died with his intellectual and personal integrity intact. Not a bad epitaph.

The present study aims to give a detailed overview of the entirety of Wace's surviving oeuvre. It is divided into three main parts, devoted to his religious works (Part I), the *Roman de Brut* (Part II) and the *Roman de Rou* (Part III). Each Part in turn is subdivided into chapters corresponding to the three hagiographical poems in Part I and to major narrative and/or structural articulations in the *Roman de Brut* and the *Roman de Rou*. Each poem is placed within its historical context, surviving manuscripts are listed and the evidence they provide regarding the reception of Wace's work is discussed. The adaptation technique of the poet is investigated, with special emphasis on the modifications made to the sources of his texts on the level of structure and content. This procedure allows us to identify agendas and interpretative issues proper to Wace: the results are not always what might have been expected from a reading of the poems in isolation from their sources. The chapters within the Parts should be read in sequence, as they follow the poet's careful build-up within each work of a nexus of themes and motifs that are essential to our appreciation of his understanding of his material. Wace comes out of this procedure as an altogether more weighty character than the somewhat frivolous writer of romances he has sometimes been held to be, and well deserving of the revival of interest he is currently enjoying.

Part I Wace: Hagiographer

INTRODUCTION: DATES AND CONTEXT

Wace's earliest extant works are three religious poems, all in octosyllabic couplets: a Life of Saint Margaret (*La Vie de sainte Marguerite*, 746 lines), an account of the Conception and Life of Our Lady (*La Conception Nostre Dame*, 1810 lines), and a Life of Saint Nicholas (*La Vie de saint Nicolas*, 1563 lines). They have not attracted the critical attention one might have expected, partly because of a scholarly bias against religious literature in general throughout the nineteenth and first half of the twentieth century,[1] and partly, one suspects, because these early poems do not correspond to the image of courtly poet prevalent among admirers of Wace's later work. Predictably, perhaps, both their authorship and literary value were questioned. The issue of authorship has now been settled, though there remains a lingering sense that these poems date back to a time when the poet was not yet in full command of his literary technique, and had not yet achieved sufficient recognition to secure commissions from prestigious patrons. Neither of these assumptions is necessarily borne out by the evidence of the texts. Like most writers of his period, Wace was first and foremost a cleric, and it is fitting that he should have made his name with pious works, the status of which, particularly in the case of hagiography, would have been no less authoritative and respectable than that of any other scholarly text. Moreover, it would be anachronistic to assume that a religious community (such as one of the Caen abbeys) or an ecclesiastical grandee would have been less desirable, prestigious or influential a patron than a lay aristocrat. Indeed, during the troubled years between the death of Henry I and the accession to the throne of England of Henry II, ecclesiastical patronage may well have been preferable on all counts. All three of Wace's surviving religious pieces appear to have been commissioned, though in one case only (*Nicolas*) are we given the name of the patron; and in all three cases it is possible to discern an underlying agenda which the poet was entrusted with advancing. This points to genuine recognition of Wace's abilities by these

---

[1] This attitude towards religious literature stemmed from expectations of 'originality' on the part of scholars, under the influence of romanticism. Religious works were largely considered derivative, and therefore inferior.

patrons, suggesting that the poet was already well established as a scholar and writer, at the very least by the time he undertook *La Conception Nostre Dame*.

We have no reliable dates of composition for Wace's three religious works, neither can we be entirely sure of the order in which they were composed. It is generally accepted is that *La Vie de sainte Marguerite* is the oldest of the three poems, on the grounds that the poet refers to himself in it as 'Wace', rather than 'maistre Wace', which could be understood as indicating that he had not yet obtained this qualification; the sequence of composition between *La Conception Nostre Dame* and *La Vie de saint Nicolas*, however, is difficult to determine. Elizabeth E. Francis, in the introduction to her edition of the *Vie de sainte Marguerite*, identifies in the prologue to the *Nicolas* echoes of the prologue to the *Conception* – but it could equally be that it is the *Conception* that echoes the *Nicolas*.[2] The historical argument appears somewhat stronger. William Ray Ashford's tentative dating of the *Conception* to the period between 1130 and 1140[3] is convincing, but the dating of the *Nicolas* to the late 1140s is purely hypothetical.[4] The poet's use of stylistic and rhetorical devices cannot be invoked in this matter, as the three works are very different in nature, and would have dictated different artistic choices for their adaptor. As we shall see, the relative absence of certain mannerisms associated with the Wace of the *Roman de Brut* or the *Roman de Rou* should rather be ascribed to the poet's versatility and his sensitivity to the texts he was handling, rather than to an as-yet undeveloped personal style.

One may nevertheless discern in these earlier poems a comparable intellectual *démarche* to that in evidence in Wace's later, major works, notably the ability to identify the characteristics of the macrostructure of the text to be translated, together with the flexibility required on the level of the microstructure to produce a successful adaptation for a new audience. The sources used for the *Conception* and the *Nicolas*, in particular, attain a level of complexity comparable to what Wace had to contend with in composing his *Roman de Rou*; but he retains narrative control, and produces coherent and highly effective renderings of his main source(s). This section will consider Wace's three religious poems in succession, giving an outline of the manuscript tradition of each text, analysing the way their sources have been approached and adapted, and exploring the agenda underlying the poet's interpretation of his material.

---

[2] E. A. Francis, ed., *La Vie de sainte Marguerite* (Paris, 1932; Classiques Français du Moyen Age 71), pp. xv–xvii.
[3] W. R. Ashford, ed., *The Conception Nostre Dame de Wace* (Chicago, 1933), pp. 13–14.
[4] See Einar Ronsjö, ed., *La Vie de saint Nicolas par Wace. Poème religieux du XIIe siècle publié d'après tous les manuscrits* (Lund and Copenhagen, 1942), pp. 15–26.

1

La Vie de sainte Marguerite

It is generally accepted that the oldest work of Wace's to have come down to us is his *Vie de sainte Marguerite*. It is preserved in three manuscripts only, none of which preserve the dialect of composition i.e., Norman French:

1. Tours, Bibliothèque municipale, 927, a paper manuscript copied in the late thirteenth century, probably in the Touraine area.[1] This manuscript, which is best known for preserving the only extant text of the twelfth-century play *Le Jeu d'Adam*, also contains Wace's *Conception Nostre Dame*. The beginning of Wace's *Marguerite* is incomplete due to damage; the poem is copied on folios 205–215v.
2. Paris, Bibliothèque de l'Arsenal, 3516, a parchment manuscript in the Picard dialect, copied in Flanders or northern Artois in the mid thirteenth century (possibly at Hesdin, the court of the counts of Artois; the manuscript was probably completed in 1267/8).[2] 'De sainte Marguerite' (fol. 125r–126v) is the twenty-seventh of sixty-three legends, which also include Wace's *Vie de saint Nicolas* and his *Conception Nostre Dame*. The manuscript contains 81 miniatures, none of which, however, appear in the 'Marguerite' section.
3. Troyes, Bibliothèque municipale 1905, was copied in north-eastern France (southern Vosges or north-eastern Franche-Comté, probably at the court of Jeanne of Burgundy) in the fourteenth century; it is lavishly illustrated, with miniatures that can be dated to 1320–1330.[3] The manuscript contains a variety of religious works in French and in Latin, predominantly hymns and prayers to the Virgin.

The Paris and the Troyes texts of *Marguerite* tend to abridge the poem slightly, and are considered by Hans-Erich Keller to be derived from a hypothetical picard 'modernisation' of Wace's work,[4] itself based on a lost Picard copy which was

---

[1] See Hans-Erich Keller, ed., *Wace. La Vie de sainte Marguerite* (Tübingen, 1990), pp. 26–7; Carin Fahlin, *Étude sur le manuscrit de Tours de la Chronique des Ducs de Normandie par Benoit* (Uppsala, 1937) and Carl Theodor Gossen, *Französische Skriptastudien. Untersuchungen zu den nordfranzösischen Urkundensprachen des Mittelalters* (Vienna, 1967), pp. 53–86.
[2] See *La Vie de sainte Marguerite*, Keller, ed., pp. 24–5. For a detailed description of this manuscript, see Jean-Charles Payen, 'Le Livre de Philosophie et de Moralité d'Alard de Cambrai', *Romania* 87 (1966): 145–50. On the date, see Einar Ronsjö's introduction to his edition of *La Vie de saint Nicolas*, pp. 18–20.
[3] For a detailed description of the manuscript and a study of the illuminations in *La Vie de sainte Marguerite*, see M. Alison Stones in the introduction to *La Vie de sainte Marguerite*, Keller, ed., pp. 185 ff.
[4] Keller, ed., *La Vie de sainte Marguerite*, pp. 28–36.

also used by the scribe of the Tours manuscript. The Tours version of the poem is therefore deemed to be closest to Wace's 'original'.

Saint Margaret was a very popular saint in the twelfth and thirteenth centuries, especially in Normandy, England and Flanders; this may to some extent account for the fact that this apparently unexceptional poem was appreciated beyond Wace's native Normandy, and still copied as late as the fourteenth century. By means of comparison, most of the medieval French poems recounting the life of Saint Margaret have come down to us in one manuscript only.[5] Elizabeth E. Francis, in the introduction to her edition of the work,[6] hints that the dissemination of Wace's poem might not have been entirely fortuitous, and could have been part of a propaganda campaign to spread the cult of Saint Margaret. In 1145, the relics of the saint were transferred to the cathedral of Montefalcone in Italy; an event that provided the initial impetus for the increase of popularity of the saint outside England and Normandy.[7] The translation of the relics of a major saint would have been negotiated and prepared well in advance, and it is possible that Wace's poem was commissioned in order to enhance the prestige of the new shrine. However, there is no mention of these relics in the poem, neither is there any suggestion in it that the reader/audience should go on pilgrimage to Montefalcone or elsewhere. The connection with 1145 must therefore remain hypothetical.

Keller suggests that Wace may have composed his *Vie de sainte Marguerite* on the request of 'un seigneur normand qui possédait aussi des terres en Angleterre' (p. 13). The idea of a patron with cross-Channel estates is interesting, though it also raises the possibility that the motivation for the poem might not entirely have been piety. One may note that the Anglo-Norman royal family had itself produced a saintly Margaret of its own, in the person of Margaret, sister of Edgar Atheling, wife of Malcolm Canmore of Scotland, and grandmother to Matilda the Empress. Following the death of Henry I's only male heir in the 'White Ship' disaster in 1120, and the lack of issue from Henry's second marriage in 1121, it is conceivable that the poem was commissioned by a patron wishing to attenuate the prestige accruing to the Scottish royal house (and Matilda herself) from such a connection, through the promotion of the older saint. If we postulate a date of composition prior to 1145, an anti-Matilda dimension to the poem is a real possibility, notably after her unpopular second marriage to Geoffrey of Anjou; moreover, until his death in 1128, William Clito, the dispossessed son of Duke Robert Curthose of Normandy, was periodically staking his claim to Normandy, with the support of France, but also some Normans.[8] There would not, therefore, have been a shortage of potential patrons for a piece of subtle propaganda under cover of religion, particularly after Henry I's death in 1135, when Matilda forcibly contested King Stephen's right to the throne.

---

[5] See Keller, *La Vie de sainte Marguerite*, pp. 13–21, for a list and discussion of the French versions of the Life of Margaret, from the twelfth to the sixteenth century.

[6] Francis, *La Vie de sainte Marguerite*, pp. ix–xii.

[7] The key event in the spread of the cult of Saint Margaret in northern France was the (much later) fall of Constantinople in 1204.

[8] See David Crouch, 'Normans and Anglo-Normans: a Divided Aristocracy', pp. 51–67 in *England and Normandy in the Middle Ages*, ed. D. Bates and A. Curry (London, 1994).

Whether Wace's poem was commissioned to deflect attention from the Anglo-Norman saint Margaret, or simply to enhance the reputation of St Margaret of Antioch, the end result was a felicitous one. Wace's handling of his sources and mastery of his poetic medium are altogether superior to the other extant French verse translations of the Margaret legend. To be sure, *La Vie de sainte Marguerite* does not display the verbal and narrative pyrotechnics of Wace's later *Roman de Brut*, but these are two very different works, based on Latin texts of very different literary qualities: whereas Geoffrey of Monmouth's *Historia Regum Britanniae* is an elegant and sophisticated piece of work, the Latin Margaret texts display the structural and rhetorical quirks one might expect of an old narrative informed by a variety of traditions. It is Wace's achievement that he translated his sources into his cultural idiom as a whole, rather than working on a literal basis.

The attribution of *La Vie de sainte Marguerite* to Wace was not always accepted, partly because of its perceived lightweight nature, partly because of the absence of an Anglo-Norman text, partly because the passage in which the author names himself is corrupt in the two manuscripts (Tours and Troyes) that preserve these lines.[9] However, Aristide Joly, in his 1879 edition of the poem, convincingly argued that 'grace' (the readings of the Tours and Troyes manuscripts), was a scribal error for 'Guace': a hypothesis reinforced by the fact that a similar error is to be found in the manuscript tradition of the *Roman de Rou*.[10] Elizabeth Francis, in her 1932 edition of the text, further suggested that *La Vie de sainte Marguerite* was an early work, by a young Wace who had not yet fully developed his poetical skills.[11] In support of this view, she points out the very simplicity of style of the poem, and the fact that *Marguerite* is the only work of Wace's where the poet does not refer to himself as 'maistre', which could indicate that he had not yet obtained the title. Any lingering doubts as to the authorship of the poem were finally dispelled in 1990, with Keller's definitive edition of the text.

Whilst the style of this short poem is undeniably unadorned, Keller identifies a number of features that may be considered as characteristic of the poet's later work:[12] symmetrical structural patterning; a strong sense of logical development; an eye for effectiveness in direct speech passages; didactic asides explaining 'scholarly' or latinate terms; and a certain 'sens de la réalité' (Keller, p. 45), with its corollary, the persona of the cautious narrator which will become Wace's trademark. We shall come back to these features. The poem is written in lines of eight syllables, rhyming two by two: that is, in octosyllabic couplets. The sense unit is clearly the line or the couplet; sentences extending over more than two lines are rare. Francis notes the occasional use of the same rhyme over four lines (rather than just two), thus giving the effect of quatrains.[13] The rhythm is regular, with a clear pause at the end of each line; only half a dozen cases of run-on lines

---

[9] Tours, 743, reads 'ce dit grace'; and Troyes, 742, reads 'Et celui doint la siue grace'. See Keller, *La Vie de sainte Marguerite*, pp. 38 and 94–5.
[10] See A. J. Holden, ed., *Le Roman de Rou de Wace*, vol. 1, p. 158 and vol. 3, p. 213.
[11] See Francis, *La Vie de sainte Marguerite*, esp. p. xvi.
[12] See Keller, *La Vie de sainte Marguerite*, pp. 40–9.
[13] See Francis, *La Vie de sainte Marguerite*, p. xxx. These quatrains are: lines 263–6, 301–4, 365–8.

(enjambement) may be found in over 740 lines, and then only between lines belonging to the same couplet.[14] In most of these cases, enjambement occurs in passages in direct speech, but the device always draws attention to the 'surplus' concept spilling over into the following line. A typical example of this may be found in Margaret's final prayer (641–2): 'Ne soit ja nez en lur maison/ Enfes, si a terme non', 'May there never be born in their house/ a child, unless it be at full term.'[15] This unobtrusively – but effectively – draws attention to the saint's attribute of protector of women in childbirth. Rhetorical effects are few, but one may note a restrained use of anaphora (the repetition of one or more words at the beginning of two or more lines) and isocolon (the repetition of a syntactical structure). An example of these devices occurs early in the poem (44–5): 'En Deu creoit omnipotent/ En Deu creoit et aoroit', 'She believed in God Almighty; she believed in God and worshipped Him.'[16] All noteworthy rhetorical and stylistic effects in *La Vie de sainte Marguerite* occur in prayers, typically in passages praising God.[17]

Sources

The legend of Saint Margaret of Antioch was available to Wace in two Latin versions: the so-called 'Mombritius' version, first published by Bonino Mombrizio in the late fifteenth century, and a version referred to as 'Caligula' by Elizabeth Francis, because one of its representatives is contained in the British Library manuscript Cotton Caligula A.VIII.[18] Francis notes in her edition (p. viii) that Wace frequently follows the Mombritius version word for word, but also that he makes minor adjustments to the order of events, feels free to expand on certain details and abridge others, and, most interestingly, that he makes use of the second, 'Caligula' version to supplement certain aspects of the general framework provided by his main source. This, as we will see below in Part II, is also what may be observed in the *Roman de Brut*, where Wace was once again working with just two main Latin sources.

The Latin text has a complex structure based on duplication of narrative motifs. The story is framed by an introduction and a conclusion in which the first-person narrator, Theotimus, establishes his credentials as eyewitness to the events recounted, and as author of the text itself. The early life of the future saint is summarily covered in some twenty lines of printed text: Margaret is the daughter of a pagan priest in Antioch. She loses her mother in infancy, and converts to Christianity; in order to escape persecution at the hands of her father,

---

[14] These are: lines 17–18, 189–90, 21–2, 512–13, 633–4, 641–2.
[15] All translations of the *Vie de sainte Marguerite* and its Latin sources and analogues are my own; all quotes of the French text are from Keller, with occasional punctuation added by myself.
[16] See also lines 548–51, where the word 'vrai' (qualifying God) is repeated 6 times.
[17] In addition to the passage mentioned above (note 16), one may mention lines 283–4: 'Voir jugierres, voire lumiere,/ Oi ma conplainte, oi ma proiere', 'True judge, true light/ Listen to my lament, listen to my prayer.'
[18] On the manuscript tradition of the Latin legend of St Margaret, see Elizabeth A. Francis, 'A Hitherto Unprinted Version of the *Passio Sanctae Margaritae* with Some Observations on Vernacular Derivatives,' *PMLA* 42 (1927): 87–105. The text of the 'Caligula' version is included pp. 97–104.

she seeks refuge with her Christian nurse, keeping her sheep. The narrative gains momentum with the account of Margaret's passion. Prefect Olybrius, who has been sent to Antioch to persecute Christians, sees Margaret keeping her sheep and falls in love with her. He determines to marry her, if she is of free birth, or take her as his concubine, if she is of servile origin. Margaret's response to his envoys is a long invocation to God to protect her from pollution. Olybrius summons her to him, and her determination in professing her faith leads him to throw her into prison. The second day, he calls Margaret in front of the tribunal, where he offers to marry her if she accepts to worship his gods; her refusal leads to her being tortured, in two successive sessions and with increasing violence. Margaret remains steadfast, praying to God all the while. She is eventually sent back to her prison cell, where her nurse tends to her and records the prayers she makes.

Margaret is then faced with another test of her faith, in that a dragon appears in her cell. It swallows her, but bursts apart through the power of the Cross, and the saint emerges unscathed. Another devil, cowering in the cell, has to submit to Margaret because of the strength of her faith; his more subtle attempts to tempt her to sin remain fruitless.

Having resisted demonic temptation, Margaret has to face a third day in front of Olybrius. She remains deaf to the entreaties of her fellow townsmen and is tortured with fire and water; but miraculously, an earthquake occurs, and a dove carrying a golden crown in its beak descends from heaven onto Margaret, whose hands and feet are miraculously unbound. Five thousand onlookers (not counting women and children) convert and are martyred on the spot by Olybrius. Margaret's executioner is unwilling to fulfil his task, but does so on Margaret's injunction, and with the guarantee that his deed will be forgiven. Before the fatal blow, another earthquake occurs, and a dove descends from heaven with the Cross, confirming Margaret's sainthood and spelling out the powers of her name for the faithful who will invoke her. Her soul is then taken to heaven by angels, while demons writhe in agony and the halt and lame who touch her body are cured.

These three sections (Days One and Two in front of Olybrius; the demonic visions in prison; and the final beheading) are characterised by the lavish use of dialogue and direct speech. In particular, Margaret's long and frequent prayers provide a near-constant reminder to the reader of the point of the story, with special emphasis on key concepts (such as Margaret's virginity and purity), through repetition. The rewards associated with acts of piety in her name are similarly stressed through the very close echoing by the divine dove of the terms of the saint's request for certain privileges for her followers. Much use is made of prolepsis, anticipating what is to come; Margaret's place among the saints of heaven is repeatedly asserted both before and during her martyrdom. The overall impression given by the Latin text is of a work designed for an oral delivery, offering plenty of scope for an entertaining, quasi-theatrical 'performance' of the text, whilst ensuring that the important points recur sufficiently often for the audience to remember them. However, these characteristics do not make for an elegant piece of literature, so it unsurprising that Wace modified his source in a number of ways.

Adaptation principles

The most striking characteristic of Wace's poem is its conciseness: just under 750 lines as compared to the 517 lines of printed Latin prose in Francis's edition. This is extremely short if one considers that not only are we passing from a synthetic language to an analytical one, with all the additional prepositions and articles this involves, but also passing from prose to verse, with the ensuing constraints of syllable-count and rhyme. This is achieved by omissions – the introduction and conclusion by Theotimus is almost entirely disregarded, for example, and much of the repetition in the Latin text is cut out – and by abbreviation. Most of Margaret's prayers are reshaped, and often quite considerably condensed in the process. But more importantly, the entire work is rethought, so that the narrative principles involved are no longer those of the Latin text.

Wace's *La Vie de sainte Marguerite* is based on a principle of narrative progression. His short 18-line introduction thus presents his material, but in a measured manner (1–8; Paris MS):

> A l'onur Deu et a s'aïe
> Dirai d'une virge la vie
> D'une damoise[le] saintime
> Qui s'amor ot vers Deu hautisme
> Et son pensé si fermement
> Que por paine ne por torment
> Ne vout onques son cuer retraire
> De Deu servir, car nel dut faire.[19]

Compared to the introduction to the Latin text, where we are promised an account of 'quomodo pugnavit contra demonem et vicit eum et coronata est', 'how [Margaret] fought against the demon and vanquished him, was crowned', the tone is less epic, and gives less away. The rest of Wace's introduction stresses Margaret's beauty, spelling out the aptness of her name ('margarita' means 'pearl') in a didactic addition to his main source-text. We are clearly about to be told the story of a virgin martyr, but none of the triumphalism of the Latin text is preserved.

The story itself is restructured. Margaret's early life is given greater emphasis: her noble origins are stressed, and her Christian faith is depicted from the outset as causing hardship for the child. She is rejected by her father, and before enduring persecution herself she is inspired by the example of the Christian martyrs around her to devote her virginity to Christ. Her merit is therefore explicit from the outset. Margaret's *passio* begins some 85 lines in the poem. Instead of her torments being presented as occurring on the three days of her trial, with a clear progression in the nature of the saint's tribulations (verbal aggression on Day One, physical torture and prison on Day Two and martyrdom on Day Three),

---

[19] 'For the honour of God and with His help, I shall tell the Life of a virgin, a most saintly damsel, who had so firmly directed her love and intent towards God the most high that despite suffering and torment she refused to divert her heart from serving God, and was not made to do so.' The emendation on line 3 (in square brackets) is my own, following Francis.

Wace attempts to introduce a neater gradation to the various tortures and temptations. Olimbrius (as Olybrius is called in the French poem) thus makes clear the choice open to Margaret from their first meeting, and her rejection of his gods and his person leads to immediate torture. The torture scene is triplicated, with increasing gravity of the violence suffered by the saint: she is first trussed up and beaten; when this has no effect, she is beaten with 'verges aspres' which tear at her flesh and make her bleed so profusely that Olimbrius and all present have to cover their face, so terrible is the sight; and finally, as Margaret persists in refusing to do Olimbrius's bidding, she is tortured so badly that her entrails hang out of her body. She is then taken to prison, where she suffers spiritual torture through the dragon and his brother, the devil. The confrontations with Olimbrius thus take place over two days rather than three: as in the Latin source, each phase of Margaret's martyrdom remains tied to one specific day, but the actual content of each phase has been redefined according to the nature of the torment rather than following the more realistic depiction of the progression of a trial.

The third phase of Margaret's *passio*, taking place at what is now her second meeting with Olimbrius, is particularly severe and ends in her triumphant death. It is distinguished from the previous phases by the appearance of miracles rewarding the saint and confirming her saintliness. The nature of the tortures devised (fire and water) are rich in Christian symbolism, and it is fitting that the torture by water, interpreted by Margaret as the purifying waters of baptism, leads to the first appearance of the divine dove and the celestial voice, and to the miraculous loosing of her bonds. The conversion and martyrdom of the bystanders indicates that the balance of power has been inverted: Margaret is now in charge. She has to command her reluctant executioner to behead her, and her martyrdom is accompanied by a whole array of signs, from an earthquake to angels, a celestial voice and the divine dove. Margaret's request to be an effective intercessor for prisoners and women in childbirth is granted. Wace then concludes with references to the authority for this story – the eyewitness Theodimus.

Wace has imposed upon the material his own sense of logical development.[20] The underlying realism of the Latin text, where the case against Margaret has to be established at a first sitting before she is made to suffer the full force of the power of the judiciary, becomes irrelevant and is discarded. The relative importance of the three phases of the *passio* is also modified. In the Latin text they occupy respectively 32%, 30% and 25% of the total work;[21] Wace radically changes this pattern, devoting 133 lines to phase 1, 225 lines to phase 2 and 213 lines to phase 3 (out of a total of 746 lines). This has as consequence a shifting of emphasis from the suffering of Margaret the helpless victim, to the authority and strength of Margaret the saint. Predictably, the material omitted by Wace is mostly to be found in phase 1 of the *passio*; and the nature of the omissions has

---

[20] Keller, *La Vie de sainte Marguerite*, pp. 40–1, views the poem differently, and discerns seven parts in the poem: Introduction (1–84); *Disputatio* on religion (85–172); First and second torture (173–278); Prison (279–506); Third and fourth tortures (507–78); Decapitation (579–719) and Epilogue (720–48). He suggests that Wace only provided one scene between Margaret and Olybrius before the tortures due to a preference for the symmetry thus achieved.

[21] The remaining 13% are accounted for by the prologue and epilogue framing the narrative.

an important impact on the characterisation of the saint. The Latin Margarita, whilst praying God for His grace and mercy, appears to be smugly aware of her own righteousness; her prayers and her speeches to her tormentors stress her own purity, and her virginity is an essential component of her self-image. By contrast, she is bluntly insulting to Olybrius and his men. In her initial prayer, when Olybrius's interest is first made known to her, she refers to herself in her prayer as 'ovem in medio luporum', 'a ewe among wolves'; 'sicut passer ab aucupe comprehensa in retia', 'like a sparrow caught in a net by the bird-catcher'; 'sicut piscis in ammo', 'like a fish in the weir'; 'in retia velut capra', 'in nets like a goat'. None of these similes, with their undertone of self-pity, are kept by Wace. He also tones down Margarita's apostrophes against Olybrius and her other tormentors; he thus translates 'O impudens canis audax', 'O shameless foolhardy dog', into a very faithful 'Tu, chiens prevos, hardis, sans honte' (231; Troyes MS), but omits her later, rhetorical 'O orribilis, O insaciabilis leo, et abominatur a Deo, confusus a Christo', 'O horrible, O insatiable lion, hateful to God, confounded by Christ', or her prayer that she be saved 'ex ore leonis', 'from the mouth of the lion', and her humility preserved 'a cornibus unicornuorum', 'from the horns of the unicorns'. However, the most important type of omission for the characterisation of Margaret at this stage of the narrative relates to her desire to become an example for other Christians by joining the throng of God's righteous virgins (140, p. 15; 176–8, p. 18). There is a warlike desire in the Latin Margarita to gain her everlasting prize by vanquishing of the powers of the devil working through Olybrius. By contrast, Wace's Margaret is depicted through her words as being less self-assured and more concerned with the basic issues at stake. Her fears for her virginity are subordinated to her fear that adversity might undermine her determination to remain steadfast in her faith, and her strength is clearly presented as a form of *imitatio Christi*: 'Bien doit on por celui morir/ Qui por nos tos vout mort soffrir', 'It is right that one should die for Him who was willing to suffer death for the sake of us all' (171–2; Paris MS).

The picture resulting from the suppression of much of Margarita's speeches and prayers is that of a young girl, not especially prone to rhetorical effects nor given to lengthy theological disquisitions, but with a clear knowledge of her faith. She is determined, but also vulnerable enough to be afraid, a trait emphasised in an addition by Wace to one of her prayers, 'Que jo ne face por paor/ Cose dont jo perde t'amor', 'That I may not do out of fear something that would make me lose your love' (185–6; Paris and Troyes MSS). As a result, the threefold torture she undergoes becomes an even more formidable test in the French text than in the Latin, and it is no coincidence that Wace chose to supplement his main source's description of the third set of tortures with additional gruesome details (the entrails hanging out of Margaret's body) taken from the Caligula version. This allows a gradation in Margaret's awareness of her own state of grace, paralleling the gradation in the phases of the *passio*.

The second phase of the *passio*, more mystical in nature, reveals to Margaret the extent of the power of prayer; but it also provides comic relief between the two harrowing torture episodes. The dragon is certainly a fearsome sight initially, but the saint dispatches it with ease; as for the wily, whining little devil remaining in the cell, there is little doubt that the readers are expected to have a good laugh at his expense. There is a sense in which these demonic temptations allow Margaret to retaliate against her human torturers. The parallels (and therefore also, the contrasts) between the saint and the demons are most obvious in the Latin texts. The dragon is thus said to have had eyes that shone 'velud margarite', literally 'like pearls', but also a clear echo of the name 'Margarita'; and its eventual fate – to split in two – is not unlike the torture exposing the entrails of the saint. But Margaret survives while the dragon dies; she is victorious in the face of adversity and sin, the dragon figuring the impotence of her human tormentors as well as the temptation of despair. It is noteworthy that while the dragon is voiceless, his brother the devil is characterised by his verbal skill, which in turn aligns him with the saint, whose utterances account for a sizeable proportion of the Latin text. Visually, he is the opposite of the dragon Rufo: he is very black ('nigerrimum') where Rufo was multicoloured, with a predominance of gold ('deauratis'); his stance is one of fear and submission ('habens manus colligatas ad genua', 'his hands bound to his knees', 252), as opposed to the iron-toothed, sword-wielding dragon; and instead of breathing fire he pleads for mercy. The temptation represented by this black devil is a particularly subtle and dangerous one. The humour of his situation, begging the saint to stop killing him with her incessant prayers (one suspects certain readers or listeners might have sympathised with him) and literally crushed under her foot, makes his onslaught all the more pernicious. At the same time that he claims to be defeated, he tries to make her succumb to pride (343–5) and to entice her into necromantic practices, following the example of King Solomon. Margaret's refusal to listen to him provides an essential confirmation of her saintly nature.

Wace recognised the importance of this second phase of the *passio*, but adapted it in such a way that the mystical dimension to Margaret's experience is considerably diminished. The parallels between the saint and the dragon are eliminated: its eyes are no longer likened to pearls, but are 'vairs conm a serpens', 'blue-green/bright like a serpent's' (312; Paris MS), and it is no longer variegated in colour but a uniform black, with the sole exception of its golden beard. Even its death is described somewhat differently, as the dragon is said by Wace to burst ('crever le fist', 338), whereas the Latin sources have it split in two ('in duas partes eum divisit', 247). The nexus of similarities and contrasts aligning the dragon with the saint and her torturers disappears, thus undermining the symbolical significance of the episode, but at the same time making it less potentially confusing for the reader or listener who might not have been trained to read these signs properly. This may also account for the omission in the French poem of the stench that pervades the cell on the appearance of the demonic dragon: its serpent-like eyes and blackness have already established its link with Satan, so there is no need to invoke smell as an additional interpretative guide.

The scene with Belgibus, the second devil, similarly underplays the more abstract and learned dimensions present in the Latin texts, making him an altogether less formidable adversary. Belgibus is said to have had his hands, feet and knees tightly bound when Margaret became aware of him, which also makes him physically less fearsome than in the Latin, where he is said to be very black in appearance, and is sitting merely *like* someone whose hands were bound to his knees.[22] The entire episode in the French poem becomes infused with situational comedy: for Belgibus to stand up to address Margaret, we must imagine him hopping along, his feet tied together and his body all contorted from his fetters. When Margaret grabs hold of him by his hair, throws him to the ground and puts her foot on his head, the devil is completely winded and almost suffocated – he has to ask Margaret to lift her foot a little so that he can catch his breath sufficiently to answer her questions. In the Latin he does not seem to suffer quite as much discomfort, as he merely asks the saint to lift her foot a little from his neck, 'ut paululum requiescam', 'that I may rest/compose myself a bit' (299).

The devil's attempts to flatter the saint and project a scholarly image of himself remain, but the simpler, less self-aware Margaret of the French poem offers fewer hints as to the potential effectiveness of his tactics. Belgibus's loaded question 'Dont as tel sens e si fort fei', 'Where did you get such good sense and such a strong faith from?' (469; Tours MS) is answered with a humble 'Ce que je sai est de Deu grace; /Son plaisir de mei fait et face', 'What I know is by the grace of God; He does as He wills with me, and may He continue to do so' (473–4; Tours MS): Wace omits the self-righteous 'Non michi licet hec tibi dicere quia non es dignus audire vocem meam', 'It is not right for me to tell you that, because you are not worthy of hearing my voice' (347–8) which opens the Latin Margaret's response and suggests that she might be open to the sin of pride. The accounts of Lucifer's fall, Solomon's imprisoning of demons in vessels and their release during the sack of Jerusalem by the Babylonians remain, but in the French text Belgibus's plea that Margaret bind him like Solomon had done meets with the saint's disbelief ('Tu ne dis se trescherie non', 'You say nothing but deception', 500; Tours MS), whereas in the Latin, the saint appears to accept that the devil is telling the truth, but recognises the temptation he is offering and is consciously rejecting it: 'iam non audiam amplius ex ore tuo', 'I will hear no more from your mouth' (368–9). The fact that the devil's account is backed up in the Latin source by the testimony of named authorities is an indication of the serious nature of the test the Latin Margaret has undergone.[23]

The consequence of these apparently minor adaptations in the French poem is that the second phase of Margaret's *passio* is more entertaining than deep. The situation is clear-cut: demons and devils have no chance of getting through to the saint, whose innocent and simple faith protects her from being deceived by the Gnostic secrets Belgibus might impart. The dragon and devil no longer represent major threats: their function is more to anticipate Margaret's ultimate triumph than to justify it.

The third phase of the *passio* is the section of the narrative in which Wace seems to follow his source-text most closely; some passages are translated almost word for word. However, here too, the detail of the Latin narrative is reshaped, to give a subtly different flavour to the account of Margaret's martyrdom. The Latin depicts this third day of Margaret's tribulations as a tripartite progression from

---

[22] That he is not actually tied up is seen in the Latin text from the fact that he takes Margaret's hand when he first addresses her (line 274).

[23] It is noteworthy that the named authorities in the Latin text ('In libris tamen Jamnee et Jambree', 351) become vague, unnamed 'livres' in the French poem (482).

torture to beheading to death, with miracles punctuating the process. The vicious, but miraculously unsuccessful, torture session culminates in the triple miracle of Margaret's bonds falling from her, the divine dove calling her to heaven and the conversion of the 5000 martyrs; the beheading scene also gives rise to the triple miracle of the earthquake, the speech of the divine dove and the apparition of the Cross. Finally, at Margaret's death, angels come to bear her soul to heaven, demons writhe in agony, while the sick, blind and lame are miraculously cured.

Wace's modifications, as in the earlier parts of the poem, bear on the selection and placing of certain details and on the speeches made by and to the heroine. On a structural level, the last phase of Margaret's martyrdom mirrors its first phase. The final torture scene, which in the Latin takes place in two stages only (fire, then water), is described in the French poem as consisting of three stages: the 'cheval fust' or 'wooden horse', on which the girl is raised in the air surrounded by blazing torches; then, after her last rebuttal of Olimbrius, the great fire lit all around her; and finally, the vat of water into which the scorched body is plunged. The temptation by the devil in prison is mirrored by Margaret's triumphant witness to the glory of God, emerging unscathed from the water, hands and feet unbound; demonic presence is replaced by the voice of the divine dove exhorting Margaret to stay firm and announcing that she is awaited in the celestial company. The witnesses in her cell have now given way to the thousands of men and women who embrace martyrdom as a result of the saint's testimony. Margaret's beheading is almost a formality and verges on self-inflicted injury. Wace's account follows his Latin sources closely. Scared by the accumulation of signs of divine approval (an earthquake, a cross appearing from the sky and a dove granting Margaret all the intercessory powers she requested), the executioner refuses to cut the saint's head off. He only does so when told that, otherwise, he will never go to heaven; and as he beheads Margaret, he prays that his sin be forgiven (by comparison, in the Latin, it is Margaret who prays that his sin in killing her be forgiven). Choirs of angels sing around the dead saint. The Tours manuscript version (the only one to preserve the full end to the poem) mentions that all the sick people who touched the corpse were healed, and that Margaret's soul, in the form of a dove, flew from the body to the sky – a detail not found in the Latin texts and evidencing a more widespread tendency in the French poem to literalise metaphorical language.

The difference in this third phase of the *passio* between Wace's sources and the French poem is most perceptible in the speeches. As elsewhere in the work, Latin direct speech tends to be abridged, as in the long monologue of the dove when Margaret is about to be beheaded, where 16 printed Latin lines shrink to 20 octosyllabic lines. Similarly, when the saint rebuts Olimbrius between having been hoisted up on the 'cheval fust' and undergone the torture of fire, her four printed Latin lines become a terse (and extremely effective) 'Non ferai', 'No, I won't' (534). However, we also find an unusually rhetorically adorned expansion in Margaret's address to God, prior to being plunged in the vat of water (549–56; Tours MS):

> Deus, qui partot as ta poissance,
> Voirs sauviere, voire esperance,

> Voirs pitez de pecheors,
> Voirs Deus voirs Sire voirs secors
> Voirs jugiere, voirs justise,
> ...
> Espant, Deus, ta beneiçon
> Sur ceste aigue par ton saint non.[24]

This use of anaphora and isocolon is a characteristic of Wace's high style in all his extant works. It is noteworthy that these rhetorical effects appear in connection with the deity, rather than in praise of Margaret herself, as is regularly the case in the Latin narrative: this reflects the necessity for doctrinal clarity in a work intended for a mixed audience. The Tours version of the poem also includes some adornment in the executioner's speech (which twice repeats 'si t'ocirai', 'I will kill you', and includes alliteration due to the repetition of 'por' and 'prie', 604–5).

On the whole, though, additions and expansions to passages in direct speech are as rhetorically unmarked as they are limited in length and scope. The material of these (very few) additions is derived from earlier speeches in the Latin version: for example, Margaret's prayer of thanksgiving to God for having preserved her virtue and chastity, 'que virgene sui et monde et pure/ Molt sui nete do tote ordure', 'as I am a virgin clean and pure; I am totally free from all pollution' (625–6; Tours MS).

The most important addition to Wace's main Latin source in this section is rhetorically unremarkable: it is Margaret's prayer that she may be a powerful intercessor in childbirth (641–50; Tours MS):

> Ne soit ja nez en lur maison
> Enfes, si a dreit terme non;
> ...
> Li enfes sainz et entiers seit
> Naturalment cum est deit.
> Se feme est en travail d'enfant
> E par besong m'ait reclamant
> Biau sire Deus, oie lur priere
> E l'un et l'autre met a vee.[25]

This passage, which is present (with some minor variations) in all the extant manuscripts of Wace's poem, is the key to the entire work. Presenting Margaret as patron saint of women in childbirth hugely increased the potential number of her devotees; whilst the saint's traditional powers remain, it marks her as a gender-specific saint in a way that runs counter to Wace's main Latin source. This suggests that Wace's systematic downplaying of Margaret's sexual fears and her overall refusal to conform to gender expectations may not only have been due to a certain distaste for repetition, but could equally be ascribed to a wider agenda,

---

[24] 'God, who holds sway everywhere, true saviour, true hope, true pity for sinners, true God, true Lord, true help, true judge, true justice, ... spread, God, Your blessing on this water, by Your holy name.'

[25] 'Grant that no child be born in their house who has not come to term ... ; may the child be healthy and unblemished as intended by nature. If a woman is in labour and calls upon me in her need, dear Lord God, listen to her prayer and grant life to both mother and child.'

aiming at extending Margaret's appeal – and, consequently, of bringing in greater revenues to her shrines.

A full conclusion to the *Vie de sainte Marguerite* has been preserved in the Tours manuscript and in a slightly abridged form in the Troyes manuscript. A short conclusion to the *passio* proper (nine lines in Troyes MS, eleven in Tours MS) introduces 'Theodimus' burying the body of the saint, and establishing his credentials as eyewitness and author of the original Life (a passage based on Theotimus's first-person postscript to the tale in the Latin); then the poet concludes the poem as a whole with an invitation to pray to God, praising Margaret and stressing the written credentials of the story, before naming himself (742–4):

> Ci faut sa vie, ce dit Grace,
> Qui de latin en romans mist
> Ce que Teheodimus escrist.[26]

The poet finally calls God's blessing on himself and his audience, praying that they be granted to live in such a way as to be safe on the day of the Last Judgment. This is a conventionally pious ending, such as would not be out of place under the pen of a cleric, and is appropriate to the subject-matter.

More notable is the way Wace presents himself: not as a poet, but as a scholar, a link in the chain of the *translatio* of knowledge by 'putting into' French the Latin Life of Margaret, itself based on Theotimus's written record. There is no false modesty here, but neither, on the surface, is Wace especially putting himself forward.[27] At the forefront is the material of the poem, its genuineness, its old and venerable written pedigree – and, in a deceptively unstudied throwaway couplet, Margaret's special relevance to women: 'Dames la devent molt amer/ E por li Damnedé loer', 'Ladies must love her very much, and praise the Lord God for her' (739–40; Tours MS only). The poet has made sure that his interpolation is suitably prominent.

The specific agenda of the work dictated a relatively discrete narrator's presence, as too strong a voice could have created an undesirable distancing effect with the traditional story. Wace's 'cautious narrator', whose trademark 'ne sai', 'I do not know', is a recurrent feature of the *Roman de Brut* and the *Roman de Rou*, should not therefore be expected to appear here. However, there is one instance, in the Troyes manuscript (lines 583–4), where the narrator's voice may be attempting to break through. When Olimbrius orders Margaret to be beheaded, we are told: 'En Armene lez fit mener/ Le chanp n'oï onques nommer', 'He had them taken to Armene; I never heard of the name of the field.' The corresponding passage in the Tours manuscript, reads: 'Hors la vile les fist mener/ Les chiés a fait a toz coper', 'He had them taken outside the city; he had them all beheaded.' We appear to be dealing with a passage that caused some scribal confusion, and the Tours text seems to have solved the problem by rewriting these lines to fit in

---

[26] 'Thus ends her life, so says Grace [i.e., Wace], who translated from Latin into Romance [i.e., French] that which Theodimus wrote.'
[27] The simple fact that he names himself is of course in itself a form of self-promotion.

with the immediate context. The Troyes version is a puzzling blend of faithful rendition of the Latin and of inexactness; for while the name of the town where the martyrs were beheaded is correct ('in Armoenia cyvitate', line 421), the statement that the exact location of the martyrdom is unknown is patently wrong, as the Latin texts explicitly say that it took place 'in campo Lymet'. The name would not have been especially difficult to work into a octosyllabic line, and if the Latin exemplar was corrupt or damaged at that point, it would have been much simpler to omit the information altogether. The sheer unlikelihood of a revising scribe or redactor making such a statement, together with the fact that the Paris manuscript has the same reading for line 584 as the Troyes manuscript, would militate in favour of it belonging to Wace's 'authorial' version: in this case, it would be the first attested instance of a disclaimer of knowledge by the Wacian narrator, designed to reinforce his status as a reliable authority. But on the whole the learned narrator does not really feature in this poem. Didactic asides are also conspicuously absent, something that may be accounted for by the principle of narrative economy which clearly drives the work. Moreover, as the areas of difficulty have been simplified or even eliminated (particularly in the exchange between Margaret and the devil), there is no need for such asides. To add them would have been a weakness.

Regarding the use of direct speech, mentioned by Keller as a characteristic of Wace's style, the first impression is that the French poem contains fewer monologues than its Latin source. Margaret's prayers, for example, are reduced in number from eleven in the Latin to nine in the French.[28] In purely quantitative terms, however, the difference is not great: excluding the introduction and conclusion to the Life, the Latin text comprises just under 70% of direct speech, while the French account totals some 66% of direct speech. The distribution patterns, though, are not identical. In the Latin text, direct speech and dialogue account for 71% of phase 1 of the *passio*, 72% of phase 2 and 64% of phase 3. By contrast, in the French text, these figures become: 67% for phase 1, 82% for phase 2 and 48% for phase 3. As may be seen in Table 1, the French poet tends to reduce the number of speech-acts in the final part of Margaret's Life: where much of the commentary and explaining in the Latin is put in the mouths of the protagonists, Wace gives more place to the narrator in phase 3, when Margaret's suffering takes on its full meaning. Phase 2, characterised by the verbal joust between Margaret and the devil, also owes its high ratio of direct speech to the fact that much of the symbolical and mystical has been streamlined and simplified, thus reducing the descriptive element present in the Latin.

Not only does Wace's poem contain fewer speech-acts than his main source (51, by various characters, against 60 in the Latin),[29] but as may be seen in Table 2, long speeches are distributed between the characters in a slightly different way to his source. In particular, the executioner Malcus is given a stronger presence in phase 3, making him an important vehicle for the didactic intent of the work: in the Latin, this function is fulfilled by the heavenly voices (particularly the dove).

---

[28] On the structural consequences of this reduction of the number of Marguerite's prayers, see Keller, pp. 42–3.

[29] By 'speech-act', I refer to a passage in uninterrupted direct speech put in the mouth of a given character.

Table 1. Number of speech-acts within the *passio*

Character	Latin Phase 1	Latin Phase 2	Latin Phase 3	Wace Phase 1	Wace Phase 2	Wace Phase 3
Olybrius	8		3	8		2
Margaret	13	9	11	11	8	8
Executioners/bystanders	3		3	1		5
Demons		5	1		5	
Dove/angels		1	3		1	2

Table 2. Length of speeches

	Latin Phase 1			Latin Phase 2			Latin Phase 3			Wace Phase 1			Wace Phase 2			Wace Phase 3		
Character	S	M	L	S	M	L	S	M	L	S	M	L	S	M	L	S	M	L
Olybrius	4	4					3			6	2					2		
Margaret	3	8	2	5	1	3	6	3	2	4	5	2	2	4	2	4	2	2
Executioners/bystanders	1	2					3			1						2	2	1
Demons				3	2		1						2	3				
Dove/angels				1			1	1	1				1			2		

S   Short speeches, up to 2 lines long
M   Medium-length speeches, up to 10 lines long
L   Long speeches, 11 lines +

It is noteworthy that in both works, many of the speech-acts are short: just under 40% of the French speeches and some 43% of the Latin speeches are two lines long or less. This reflects the element of dialogue, especially in phase 1 of the *passio*. The proportion of speeches between 3 and 10 lines in length is slightly higher in Wace's poem, accounting for 41% of the French, as compared to 38% of the Latin narrative. However, the significant difference lies in the use of very long speeches, of twenty lines and more: the Latin has two such passages, against four in the French. The longest passage in direct speech, in both the Latin and the French, is Belgibus's explaining to Margaret who he is and how he operates (38 printed lines in Latin, 48 octosyllabic lines in French). But whereas the second very long speech-act in the Latin is Margaret's prayer in prison (20 printed lines), the saint's longest speeches in the French are placed in phases 1 (one 25-line speech-act) and 3 (46 lines):[30] the first one rejecting forcefully Olimbrius's offer to spare her further torture (210–34), the latter one being her long prayer before her beheading (615–60).

One of the effects achieved by Wace's redistribution of speech-acts in his work

---

[30] The fourth speech-act in Wace of 20 lines or more is in phase 2, in the mouth of the devil Belgibus (22 lines).

is that Margaret is perceived to be interacting in a more credible manner with her human tormentors, which in turn affords greater pathos to her situation, especially in relation to Olimbrius. It also underscores the structural reworking already observed in the French poem, resulting in an ever-increasing empowering of the saint culminating in her successful request for special intercessory powers on her martyrdom: a privilege earned by her determination to remain steadfast in her faith. Furthermore, the relative silence of the saint during phase 2, where the devil is granted a total of 91 lines of speech (as compared to the saint's 53)[31] suggests that, for Wace, the focus of this stage of the *passio* is not the saint so much as her entertaining adversary.

To sum up, Wace's technique in translating his Latin source involved reshaping the original narrative on a number of levels:

He used one main source, but did not hesitate to add details borrowed from another version of the legend, Caligula; he follows the cue of Caligula in omitting the first earthquake.

The main lines and sequence of the plot remain the same, but the microstructure of the narrative undergoes important changes, through a different combination of the key elements reflecting a different logical approach. The three days of trial, with demonic temptation between Day 2 and Day 3, give way to two torture phases framing the unsuccessful onslaught by the devil, which thus takes on more prominence.

Repetition is reduced, especially in Margaret's speeches and prayers, but also through the omission of the first earthquake.

Direct speech and dialogue are used for effect, to reinforce the new microstructure, rather than predominantly as a didactic medium spelling out the meaning of the events.

A popularising intent is perceptible through the omission of arcane or scholarly detail; the intended audience is clearly not assumed to have any clerical knowledge or understanding of mystical or symbolical discourse. The remnant of realism in the Latin version (the progression of Margaret's trial) is omitted.

The narrator, though discreet in most of the work, has a stronger presence than in the Latin, particularly at the end of the poem; one instance suggests an attempt at projecting an image of reliability, through admitting to ignorance of a minor detail.

Finally, the work bears an updated message, which suggests a propagandist intent; but the new element, borrowed from the 'Caligula' text, is carefully blended in with the account of the main source and unobtrusively reinforced by the narrator in his conclusion.

The end result is a pleasant poem, with all the usual gruesome ingredients of the life of a virgin martyr, but with a lively (and probably comic) middle section

---

[31] By means of comparison, in the Latin text, the devil has 69 lines of printed text of direct speech, spread over 5 speech-acts, while Margaret totals some 59 lines over 9 speech-acts.

that sends out a reassuring signal that the particularly nasty tortures of the third phase of the *passio* need not be taken too seriously – the saint who has overcome a dragon and a devil cannot be hurt by mere fire and water. Margaret herself comes over as an unremarkable young girl, distinguished only by the extent of her faith; she has none of the self-righteousness of the Latin Margarita (until the end, when she has earned a measure of self-contentment). Her enemies are little more than cut-out figures: the spiritual threat posed by the devil is virtually eliminated by Wace, while no reason is given for the persecution visited on the Christians by Olimbrius (in the Latin, he is specifically on a state mission to quell Christianity when he meets Margarita, which explains why she has to undergo trial after publicly professing her faith). Wace's Life of Margaret is an elegant and lively poem, but the complexity of the source material is sacrificed in the process. There is no doubt, though, that it was a necessary price to pay to make this material attractive to a wide audience – in particular, to married laywomen.

If manuscript transmission is to be trusted, *La Vie de sainte Marguerite* was reasonably successful; indeed, it was remarkably successful if, as has been suggested, it was the work of a young poet whose patron might not have been very influential and was therefore unable to ensure a wide dissemination of the poem. This success was well deserved. Wace has translated his Latin source into the cultural as well as the linguistic idiom of his intended audience. Beyond the undeniable flair for words and rhythm evidenced by this poem, its most striking characteristic has to be the compromise between respect for the source text and the needs of the reader or listener, which underlies most if not all of the modifications brought to the Latin account. *La Vie de sainte Marguerite* is a translation, but it does not read that way. That is the mark of a confident scholar and a talented writer: it therefore comes as no surprise that Wace was entrusted with translating highly sensitive material, with his *Conception Nostre Dame*.

2

La Conception Nostre Dame

As we have seen, scholars tend to place the *Conception Nostre Dame* relatively early in the poet's career, before his *Vie de saint Nicolas*. The main reason for this is that in the *Nicolas* the reader can more readily discern the Wace of the *Roman de Brut*, whereas (to put things bluntly) the *Conception* was not considered to be very good literature. The first editors of the poem, G. Mancel and G.-S. Trébutien (1842), despite their more favourable opinion of Wace than many of their contemporaries, felt that he had not made the best use of his sources in this case; according to them the poet

> est loin d'avoir compris la poésie des traditions dont il s'inspirait. . . . Il retranche les détails les plus gracieux, et les remplace par d'interminables énumerations qu'il paraît affectionner particulièrement.[1]

William R. Ashford, in his 1932 critical edition of the *Conception*,[2] is especially damning: '*The Conception de Nostre Dame* has little literary merit. Its interest for modern students is almost wholly linguistic' (p. 20). This appears to reflect Ashford's own interest in philology above literary analysis, however; whilst the observations of Mancel and Trébutien alert us to the extent of Wace's reworking of his sources, suggesting hidden depths to the poem.

The *Conception Nostre Dame* is (notwithstanding the title by which the poem is now known) a Life of the Virgin from her Conception to her Dormition and Assumption. The sources on which the work is based were mainstream by medieval standards, though they were not part of the canonical corpus of Scriptures.[3] The *De nativitate Mariae*, a hybrid text combining a variety of earlier apocryphal material and dating from the Carolingian period (or possibly as late as the tenth

---

[1] *L'Établissement de la fête de la Conception Nostre Dame dite la fête des Normands par Wace trouvère anglo-normand du XIIe siècle publié pour la première fois d'après les manuscrits de la Bibliothèque du Roi*, ed. G. Mancel and G.-S. Trébutien (Caen, 1842), pp. xlii–xliii: 'was far from having understood the poetry of the traditions from which he drew his inspiration . . . He omits the most graceful details and replaces them with interminable enumerations, of which he seems to be particularly fond.'

[2] Ashford's edition is now only available in microfilm form, as a 1933 Chicago doctoral dissertation. Plans for publication had to be deferred because of the Second World War, and never came to fruition. To date, this is the only critical edition of the work available.

[3] For an overview of these sources, see Gioia Paradisi, *Le passioni della storia. Scrittura e memoria nell'opera di Wace* (Rome, 2002), pp. 39–50. A detailed analysis and identification of these sources may be found in Rita Beyers, '*La Conception Nostre Dame* de Wace: premier poème narratif sur la Vierge en ancien français', pp. 359–400 in *Serta Devota in memoriam Guillelmi Lourdaux, II. Cultura medievalis*, ed. W. Verbecke, M. Haverals et al. (Louvain, 1995).

century)[4] was used for the section devoted to the conception and birth of Mary, her own pregnancy and Joseph's misgivings. The story of the three Marys was drawn from a version of the Gospel of Pseudo-Matthew (composed in Latin between 550 and 700), the *Trinubium Annae*, known to have been in circulation from the ninth century and recounting the three marriages of Saint Anne (mother of the Virgin), the three daughters, all named Mary, she had of each marriage, and the offspring of these daughters, among whom it counts St John the Evangelist.[5] The account of the Virgin's death, burial and Assumption is based on the so-called *Gospel of Pseudo-Melito*. These texts were supplemented with details drawn from the *Protevangelium Iacobi Minoris*, which underlies all the legendary accounts of the life of the Virgin in Western Europe, including (in an edited form) the *De nativitate*. Whilst these texts are apocryphal in nature and could not therefore be considered as authorities in the full sense of the term, they were seen by medieval scholars and theologians as bearing a part of truth, and were thus acceptable sources for a work such as Wace's.[6]

The contents of these texts were popular, but the manuscripts themselves would not necessarily have been easy to find, and more so than for the *Vie de sainte Marguerite*, the *Conception* presupposes the support of a very good library. Moreover, Wace's 'minor' sources point to strong English connections; in particular, the works of Eadmer of Canterbury, a Benedictine monk who was St Anselm of Canterbury's secretary from 1093 to Anselm's death in 1109. Eadmer's writings include the *Historia novorum*, a chronicle of the major events that had happened at the time of Archbishops Lanfranc, Anselm and Raoul d'Escures, and which Wace used for his last known work, the *Roman de Rou*. Eadmer was deeply involved in the debate opposing St Bernard of Clairvaux and the supporters of the doctrine of the Immaculate Conception of the Virgin. His *Tractatus de conceptione sanctae Mariae*, written in 1141, is possibly the first clear and systematic defence in writing of the doctrine of the Immaculate Conception, whereby the Virgin Mary is believed to have been conceived free from the Original Sin.[7]

This raises the question of patronage. No patron is named in the poem, but it must have been commissioned by someone in a position of authority, as part of a campaign to promote the observance of the feast of the Conception of Our Lady some time after its official reinstatement in England in 1129. Archbishop Lanfranc's attempt to abolish many of the feasts peculiar to Anglo-Saxon England (the Conception of Our Lady among them) on his accession to the see of Canterbury in 1070 had not been entirely successful. Observance of the Conception of Mary was sufficiently well established in England for it to spread to Normandy, with a first indication of the feast in the abbey of Fécamp, in the early

---

4   See Rita Beyers, ed., *De nativitate Mariae: Kritische Voorstudie en Tekstuitgave* (PhD Leuven; Antwerp, 1980).
5   See Beyers, 'La Conception Nostre Dame de Wace', pp. 379–80.
6   On the subject, see Marielle Lamy, *L'Immaculée Conception. Étapes et enjeux d'une controverse au moyen-âge (XIIe–XVe siècle)* (Paris, 2000), esp. p. 215; also Paradisi, *Le passioni della storia*, pp. 45–6.
7   See A. Cabassut, 'Eadmer', cols. 1–5 in *Dictionnaire de Spiritualité ascétique et mystique. Doctrine et Histoire* (Paris, 1960), vol. 4, part 1; also A. W. Burridge, 'L'Immaculée Conception dans la théologie de l'Angleterre médiévale', *Revue d'Histoire Ecclésiastique* 32 (1936): 570–97.

twelfth century.[8] It was then adopted by the Normans with such fervour that the Conception of the Virgin became known as the 'fête aux Normands' (though official approval was withheld in Normandy until 1145). From Normandy, it spread eastwards, with the resistance we have noted and which our poem might have been commissioned to counter among the faithful.

Wace's patrons clearly had strong ties with England, and had the resources to provide the poet with access to relatively rare books and information, possibly even selecting for him the authority to follow in cases of conflicting versions. If the work was commissioned before the death of Henry I in December 1135, there is a possibility Wace himself might have travelled to England at this stage, before the country fell into a protracted period of unrest (though this has to remain conjectural). It is believed that he visited southern England at some time before the completion of his *Roman de Brut* in 1155: this would have been a good time, and could account for the obvious English sympathies in the *Conception*.

Manuscripts

Whoever Wace's patrons were, when the poem was completed, they ensured that it was widely disseminated. Ashcroft lists 20 extant manuscripts containing all or part of the work, mostly dating from the thirteenth and fourteenth centuries:

Thirteenth century
1. Tours, Bibliothèque municipale, 927, fols. 61r–108v. Mid-thirteenth century; South French copy of a collection originally compiled by an Anglo-Norman scribe. Contains ten items, including the twelfth-century play *Le Mystère* (or *Jeu*) *d'Adam*. Preserves Wace's *Vie de sainte Marguerite*, and all five parts of the *Conception*.[9]
2. Paris, Bibliothèque nationale, fonds fr. 818 (anc. 7208). Contains only the 'Établissement' and 'Conception' parts of the work.
3. Paris, Bibliothèque nationale, fonds fr. 1526. Central French. Contains the 'Conception', 'Histoire des Trois Maries' and 'Assomption'; the 'Conception' and 'Histoire des Trois Maries' sections are embedded in the text of *La Bible qui est compillee des .vii. estaz du monde*, by Geoffroi de Paris.
4. Paris, Bibliothèque nationale, fonds fr. 1527. Central French. Contains the 'Établissement' and 'Conception' sections, as far as line 1002, fols. 1a–10b. The manuscript also contains a long poem (4155 lines) on the lives of Jesus and Mary.
5. Paris, Bibliothèque nationale, fonds fr. 19166. Central French with traces of Picard. Contains the entire poem, fol. 186v, col. 2 – fol. 200v, col. 2.
6. Paris, Bibliothèque nationale, fonds fr. 24429. End of thirteenth century.

---

[8] See Mary Clayton, *The Cult of the Virgin in Anglo-Saxon England* (Cambridge, 1990), pp. 47–51. Clayton points out (p. 49) the defensive dimension to the story of Helsin, suggesting that it may have been used to counter objections made to the feast in the circle of the Conqueror.

[9] Ashford's base text for his edition; described in his introduction, pp. 21–42. See also Keller, *La Vie de sainte Marguerite*, pp. 21–3.

Central French. Contains the the whole poem, fols. 73a–83c; slightly modernised language.
7. Paris, Bibliothèque nationale, fonds fr. 25532. Central French. Contains the whole poem, fols. 320r–331v.[10]
8. Paris, Bibliothèque nationale, fonds fr. 25439. Eastern France/Lorraine. Does not contain the 'Établissement' or the 'Conception' sections; fragment of the 'Assomption' part, up to line 1452 (fols. 188v–193v).
9. Paris, Bibliothèque de l'Arsenal, 3516. Picard dialectal traits. Contains Wace's *Vie de sainte Marguerite*, *Vie de saint Nicolas*, and part of the *Conception Nostre Dame*. 'Établissement' and 'Conception' sections are missing; 'Assomption' up to line 1796. Mutilated folios, fols. 52v–53v.[11]
10. Carpentras, Bibliothèque municipale 473. Mid-thirteenth century. Central French. Contains the whole poem up to line 1576, fols. 126–39.
11. Oxford, University College, 100. Anglo-Norman traits. Contains the 'Histoire des Trois Maries' and the 'Assomption' sections, fols. 100r–109v.

Fourteenth century
12. London, British Library, Add. 15606. Burgundian dialect. The 'Établissement', 'Conception' (to line 1004) and 'Assomption' parts are used to frame other poems on the lives of Christ and the Virgin.[12]
13. Rome, Biblioteca Vaticana, Regina 1682. First half of the fourteenth century. Central French. Contains the whole poem in a slightly modernised language, fols. 58b–69b. Same text as MS 6.
14. Lyons, Bibliothèque municipale, 739. Some Picard traits. Contains only the 'Assomption' part. Same text as MSS 6 and 13.[13]
15. Cambridge, St John's College, B9. Central French. Contains a long poem on the lives of Jesus and Mary, of which Wace's 'Établissement' (lines 1–124) and 'Assomption' (lines 1287–1810) serve as episodes, fol. 1r, col. 1 – fol. 2r, col. 1, line 21, and fol. 48r, col. 2, line 14 – fol. 53r, col. 2, line 11.[14]
16. Paris, Bibliothèque nationale, 5002. Contains only lines 1111–56 of the poem.

Eighteenth-century copies
17. Paris, Bibliothèque nationale, fonds fr. 1504. Contains only the 'Établissement' up to line 178, fols. 417–21. Same text as MS 12.
18. Paris, Bibliothèque nationale, Moreau 1716. Contains the 'Établissement' and the 'Conception' as far as line 1004, and the 'Assomption'.

---

[10] This was the base text used by Mancel and Trébutien for their 1842 edition of the poem: see their introduction, pp. lxiii–lxv for a full description. See also Paul Meyer, 'Notice sur un MS Bourguignon (Musée Britannique Addit. 15606) suivie de pièces inédites', *Romania* 6 (1877): 1–46 and 600–4.
[11] See Keller, *La Vie de sainte Marguerite*, pp. 24–5; also E. G. R. Waters, ed., *The Anglo-Norman Voyage of St Brendan by Benedeit* (Oxford, 1928), pp. xvii–xxii.
[12] Full description by Paul Meyer, 'Notice sur un MS Bourguignon (Musée Britannique Addit. 15606) suivie de pièces inédites' and 'Notice sur un manuscrit interpolé de la *Conception* de Wace (Musée Britannique, Add. 15606)', *Romania* 16 (1887): 232–47.
[13] See Paul Meyer, review of the *Giornale di filologia romanza*, I, 3 in *Romania* 9 (1880): 162, and *Romania* 16 (1887): 54.
[14] See Paul Meyer, 'Les Manuscrits français de Cambridge, I. Saint John's College', *Romania* 8 (1879): 305–42.

Wace-based rewritten (medieval) versions:[15]

19. Rennes, Bibliothèque municipale, 593. Expanded version of Wace's 'Assomption', with a different ending, fol. 90v, col. 1 – fol. 92v, col. 3.
20. Grenoble, Bibliothèque municipale, 1137. Expanded version of Wace's 'Assomption', with a different ending; fols. 120a–129b.

One may note that only seven of these manuscripts contain, or are thought originally to have contained, the entire poem. Depending on the interests of the scribe or manuscript planner, Wace's text is abridged, whole sections are omitted, others are rewritten almost out of recognition, or bits of it are interpolated in other accounts of the life of the Virgin. The manuscripts tell a story of success, in that the work was copied widely outside of the Anglo-Norman areas of influence and was reappropriated by generations of readers; but the instability of the textual transmission also points to a work that was more valued for its subject-matter than its intrinsic qualities. The cannibalisation of Wace's work by manuscripts 19 and 20 of our list show that his *Conception* was received as a particularly successful template suitable for improvement, elaboration and adaptation, rather than as piece of literature with its own artistic integrity.

The Preface

The account of the establishment of the feast of the Conception of Our Lady prefacing the Life proper is taken from the *Miraculum de conceptione sanctae Mariae*, attributed at the time to St Anselm of Canterbury and featuring at its centre an English abbot named Helsin.[16] The significance of the choice of the *Miraculum* as authority for the validating account of the origins of the celebration of the Conception of the Virgin takes on its full meaning when one realises that it was in competition with another version of the origins of the festival, recounted in the *Sermo de Conceptione Beatae Mariae* (then also attributed to St Anselm) where the revelation of the new feast is made to an unnamed French canon saved from death and hell by the Virgin after he drowned on returning from an adulterous tryst.[17] The differences between this account and the one selected by Wace are considerable. First, the central character is named, rather than being an anonymous clergyman; the miracle is also placed at a precise time in a relatively recent past and is tied to specific historical circumstances: the immediate aftermath to Duke William's conquest of England. And crucially, the circumstances surrounding the miracle at the origin of the feast are morally less dubious; abbot Helsin has not been involved in sinful activity when the angelic vision makes him

---

[15] For a description of these two manuscripts, see Paul Meyer, 'Notice du MS 1137 de Grenoble renfermant divers poèmes sur saint Fanuel, sainte Anne, Marie et Jésus', *Romania* 16 (1887): 44–56 and 214–31.

[16] The text of this is to be found in *S. Anselmi, ex Beccensi abbate Cantuarensis archiepiscopi Opera Omnia necnon Eadmeri Monachi Historia Novotum et alia opuscula*, ed. D. G. Gerberon, vol. 2: Appendix (spuria): 'Miraculum de conceptione Beatae Mariae', cols. 325–6; 'Tractatus de conceptione Beatae Mariae Virginis', cols. 301–18. *PL* 159 (Paris, 1865).

[17] See *PL* 159, vol. 2, cols. 319–24.

promise to celebrate the Conception of the Virgin, but is returning from an entirely laudable peace-making embassy to Scandinavia. The miracle accompanying the apparition – the calming of a violent sea-storm – is not in any way prompted by the personal frailty of Helsin, who on the contrary appears to be an exemplary man of God.

The account preserved in the *Miraculum* and translated by Wace (with some significant additions and modifications) has as a further characteristic that the central figure is not only named, but was a prominent churchman of his day, attested in independent historical sources. Helsin (or Ælfsige, to give the Anglo-Saxon form of his name) was appointed abbot of St Augustine's in 1061 and acting-abbot of Ramsey in 1062; he is mentioned on several occasions in the Domesday Book, and appears to have been one of Harold's counsellors (and indeed of Edward the Confessor prior to Harold's accession to the throne) before gaining the confidence of King William. The events leading to his mission also have a ring of truth about them. The king of Denmark, we are told, on hearing of Harold's death, decides to conquer England. William wishes to pre-empt a Scandinavian invasion on his barely subdued kingdom, and chooses Helsin as his envoy. The vision at the origin of the new feast occurs on Helsin's way back to Britain, concluding his successful diplomatic mission.

The implicit position at the beginning of Wace's poem is (or appears to be, at the first reading) that the Conception of the Virgin is an accepted and well-established festival at the time of his writing, and the narrator specifically envisages the poem being read aloud as part of the celebrations (173–8):

> Quant nos la feste celebrun
> Bien est que l'estoire en diun
> Bien fait la feste a celebrer
> Bien fait l'estoire a reconter,
> E bien fait la chose a retraire
> Dunt nos devun la feste faire.[18]

The intent is openly didactic; it has as aim to explain to people what they are celebrating. An apparently unexceptional agenda: but the situation was by no means so simple. The Conception of Our Lady was in fact far from being a universally accepted feast, and while it was indeed observed 'en plusors leus', Wace's statement that it was everyone's duty to do so would have raised a number of ecclesiastical eyebrows. For the doctrine of the Immaculate Conception of Mary was a recent development in twelfth-century France, and the spread of the new feast was opposed by none other than Bernard of Clairvaux, who strongly objected to doctrine of the Immaculate Conception of the Virgin on theological grounds.[19]

---

[18] 'When we celebrate the feast, it is a good thing for us to tell its history. It is good to observe the feast, it is good to tell the story, and it is a good thing to recount what it is we must celebrate.' All translations of the *Conception* are my own.

[19] See St Bernard's letter to the canons of Lyons spelling out these reasons (*S. Bernardi Opera, VII Epistulae I*, ed. J. Leclercq and H. Rochais (Rome, 1974), pp. 387–92). St Bernard had a great devotion towards Our Lady; but he felt that it was unnecessary and pernicious to consider that she must have been conceived free from the original sin by virtue of her status of future mother of Christ. On the doctrine of the Immaculate Conception, see Marina Warner, *Alone of all her Sex. The Myth and Cult of the Virgin Mary* (London, 1989), esp. pp. 236–9; and the 'Immaculate Conception' entry in *Theotokos*.

When the *Conception Nostre Dame* was composed, the debate that opposed Eadmer of Canterbury and Bernard of Clairvaux between 1129 and 1140 was still fresh, if not actually still ongoing: the earlier one places the date of composition of the poem, the more Wace's statement that it is the duty of all listeners to observe the feast ('nus *devun* la feste faire', 'we *must* celebrate the feast')[20] becomes polemical.

The account of the 'Établissement' which prefaces Wace's poem is therefore of especial interest and demands closer attention. As mentioned above, it is based on the Latin *Miraculum de conceptione sanctae Mariae*, attributed at the time to St Anselm. In his introductory lines, Wace states that the feast of the Conception of Our Lady was first established under King William the Conqueror ('Onques n'en fu parole oïe/ Que a nul tens anceis fist on/ Feste de sa conception/ Deci al tens le rei Guillalme', 'Never has anyone heard it be said that at any time beforehand was the feast of her conception observed, up to the time of King William', 8–11). This piece of information (not to be found in the *Miraculum*) is, we know, erroneous. Mary Clayton has demonstrated that the cult of the Virgin was well-established in Anglo-Saxon England,[21] and that Winchester in particular was a centre of Marian devotion that had introduced the feast of the Conception of Our Lady well before the Norman Conquest – a feast that was actually abolished together with other Anglo-Saxon observances, following the reform of the liturgical calendar imposed by King William and implemented by Archbishop Lanfranc.[22] This re-writing of ecclesiastical history has the effect of normanising the feast; rather than being an observance suppressed by the Conqueror, the Conception of Our Lady is implicitly presented as having been established and promoted by him, and is explicitly depicted as arising from the Conquest of England (13–16):

> Par force e par bataille prist
> Viles, chastels, citez conquist.
> Homes i ot e morz e pris,
> Li reis Aralz i fu ocis.[23]

The Conquest is thus characterised by violence and bloodshed, and Harold is representative of a wider loss of Christian lives. Wace's presentation of the ensuing conflict between King Svein of Denmark and King William, markedly different to his sources, appears to hint at moral weakness on the part of the Norman king. Whilst the Danish king is said by Wace to be motivated by his friendship for Harold and his outrage at what he perceives to be an unjust invasion

---

A Theological Encyclopedia of the Blessed Virgin Mary, ed. M. O'Carroll (Wilmington, Delaware, 1986), pp. 180–2.

[20] My emphasis.

[21] It has been suggested that this early adoption of the feast (it was celebrated in England by 1030) was due to the influence of Greek monks. See Mary Clayton, *The Cult of the Virgin Mary in Anglo-Saxon England*, pp. 42–7 and 84–9. Wace's statement does however have an element of truth to it, as the doctrine of the Immaculate Conception had not yet been given a coherent formulation.

[22] For a chronology of the gradual reinstatement of the feast in post-Conquest England, see Paradisi, *Le passioni della storia*, p. 44.

[23] 'By force and battle he took towns, he conquered castles, cities. He killed and captured men there, and there King Harold was killed.'

(19–26),[24] William's reaction to Svein's threats is one of distress ('dolenz en fu') and fear ('paor en ot', 28), hinting at a troubled conscience. There is no suggestion of this in the *Miraculum*, where he is shown confidently taking due steps to counter an attack (col. 323):

> Quo audito, Guillelmus ad defendendum se praeparavit, et ex circumjacentibus regionibus milites quamplurimos congregavit, et, ut erat callidus, urbes ac castella strenuissime munivit, et omnibus necessaries opulentissime replevit.[25]

Wace's William also takes these steps, but the fact that he is acting out of fear rather than prudence detracts from the decisiveness of the action. The desire for peace smacks somewhat of despair in the French poem (35–8):

> O ses barons se conseilla
> Qu'en Danesmarche enveiera
> Saveir se ja *par nul endreit*
> As Daneis pais faire porreit.[26]

The peace with Svein negotiated by Helsin averts further military consequences, but it does not absolve William from the responsibility of bloodshed in God's eyes, neither does it provide him (and by extension, the subjects he rules) with much-needed atonement. The angelic messenger to Helsin may therefore be said to complete the abbot's mission, by offering the entire community reconciliation through the quasi-penitential observance of the feast of the Conception of the Virgin, which the narrator explicitly sees as a universal obligation: 'en plusors leus la fait hun/ E nos tuit faire la devun', 'It is observed in many places, and we must all do so' (171–2).

Helsin's undertaking to observe and promote the day of the Conception of Our Lady has a markedly formal dimension to it, making it appear part of his mission in Denmark. His exchange with the angel is that of a negotiator carefully establishing terms (in this case, the date of the feast and the liturgy to be used) before accepting an offer.[27] By association, William is as bound by Helsin's promise to the angelic apparition in Wace as he is by the abbot's promises to the Danish barons, making the observance of the new religious festival transcend the purely personal duty of Helsin. The closing lines of the 'Établissement' section – 'En plusors leus la fait hun/ E nos tuit faire la devun' – are the logical conclusion to a narrative that has been reshaped to define the feast as the collective responsibility of the Anglo-Norman people.

---

[24] One version of the *Miraculum* also offers this motivation (see Beyers, '*La Conception Nostre Dame* de Wace', p. 365), but none of the extant texts of this version (Mir. 405) predate Wace's text, and may therefore have been influenced by it.

[25] 'Having heard this, William got ready to defend himself, and assembled many soldiers from neighbouring regions, and, as he was wise, he fortified towns and castles very strongly and equipped them in great abundance with all that was necessary.'

[26] 'He decided, having consulted his barons, that he would send someone to Denmark to find out if he could ever *in any possible way* make peace with the Danes'; my emphasis.

[27] This passage is a very faithful translation of the *Miraculum*, but it stands out more in the French text as it is the only part to be in direct speech. In the Latin source, the prayers of the people on the storm-battered ship take up almost one fifth of the whole text, in direct speech. Wace replaces the whole passage with a 25-line description of the storm (69–92), just mentioning the sailors' appeals to God, Christ and Mary.

The 'Établissement' thus gives historical credentials to the feast of the Conception of the Virgin, and presents it as entirely non-problematic. Its pre-Conquest origins are occulted (and therefore also the Norman political tensions surrounding its abolition), whilst its penitential value for both England and Normandy is forcefully established. The way is paved for an easy acceptance of the material in the body of the work, the theological implications of which would have been controversial for many.

Structure and adaptation

Wace's *Conception Nostre Dame* is usually described as comprising five parts, some of which, as we have seen, were detached from the whole by various scribes and manuscript planners:

1. The 'Établissement', an introductory narrative recounting the miracle of Helsin that leads to the establishing of the festival in England (8–172)
2. The 'Conception', or account of the Virgin's Immaculate Conception, followed by her childhood and betrothal to Joseph, the Annunciation and the Nativity of Christ, followed by learned reflections on the Incarnation and the Virgin birth (173–1110)
3. A short transitional poem, where the narrator summarises what precedes and announces a new section on the Virgin's family (1111–39)
4. The 'Histoire des Trois Maries', ending with the special relationship between St John (the Evangelist) and Our Lady (1140–1292)
5. The 'Assumption', which recounts the Dormition of Our Lady and her Assumption (1293–1810)

These parts appear to have been planned from the outset to be used independently from each other, according to the liturgical needs of the moment. They are connected, in a loose but effective manner, by short transitional passages in the narrator's voice with a strong homiletic quality. The first such transitional passage occurs at the end of the 'Établissement' (173–82):

> Quant nos la feste celebrun
> Bien est que l'estoire en diun,
> Bien fait la feste a celebrer,
> Bien fait l'estoire a reconter,
> E bien fait la chose a retraire
> Dunt nos devun la feste faire.
>   Or est donc bien que je vos die
> De ma dame sainte Marie
> Coment fu conceüe e nee,
> Coment norrie e mariëe.[28]

---

[28] 'When we celebrate the feast, it is good that we tell its story, it is good to celebrate the feast, it is good to recount the story, and it is good to recall the reason why we must observe the feast. So it is right for me to tell you how My Lady Holy Mary was conceived and was born, how she was raised and married.'

La Conception Nostre Dame 39

Another transition, but more in the nature of a new start, occurs between the 'Conception' section and that of the three Marys (1111–12 and 1129–34):

> Gace a nom qui fait cest escrit
> Qui de sainte Marie a dit
> . . .
> Or dirun, o la Dé aïe,
> Coment eissi de ceste vie,
> Com Deus la fist al ciel monter.
> Mais premierement vueil conter
> Un petit de sa parenté
> Dunt mainte gent avrunt doté.[29]

The 'Histoire des Trois Maries' is thus introduced as a sort of parenthesis, ostensibly justified by the fact that this is an area many people do not know very much about; it does not flow from the preceding narrative, and draws on a specific source, the *Trinubium Annae*, distinct from the biblical and apocryphal authorities of the 'Conception' section. This would seem to be a clear invitation to users of the work to pause in the public reading of the poem at this stage, or even to excise the 'Trois Maries' part completely if time or circumstances demanded it. On the other hand, it provides important background information for an understanding of the circumstances of the Virgin at the end of her life, and in particular the family connection with St John the Evangelist, to whom she was entrusted by Christ on the Cross, and who is shown to be her nephew. This establishes a nexus of connections, both spiritual and genealogical, which gives greater resonance and verisimilitude to the bond between John and Mary in the Dormition and Assumption section, and hails back to St Anne, the Virgin's mother, who has a central role in the 'Conception' section. This 'parenthesis' functions as a pivot between the account of the early life of the Our Lady, up to and including the Nativity of Christ, and her eventual death/dormition and reunion with her son.

Common sense and verisimilitude are important to the narrator, as may be seen from other passages where he makes a first-person comment. Notably, Wace is extremely careful to make sure that the lay audience of his work do not get confused or alienated by a literal understanding of exegetical interpretation. A good example of this occurs when Joachim is said to sacrifice ten white lambs, twelve bulls and one hundred sheep as thanksgiving for the announcement that his wife is to bear him a child (392–8). These numbers are glossed in conventional exegetical manner: the lambs figure Christ; the twelve bulls figure the twelve apostles, the hundred sheep figure the celestial host, 'Quar cent cist numbres, ço savun,/ Senefië perfectiun', 'for, as we know, the number of one hundred signifies perfection' (411–12). But, the narrator hastens to add (417–20):

> Je ne di pas qu'il l'entendist
> Quant il le sacrefice fist,

---

[29] 'He is called Wace, who composed this piece of writing about holy Mary . . . Now we shall tell, with God's help, how she left this life, how God made her rise to Heaven. But first I want to say something about her family, about which many people have been uncertain.'

> Mais Sainz Espriz li enseigna,
> Qu'il deveit faire li mostra.[30]

We hear the teacher or preacher here, countering an imagined (or all too real) objection from his intended audience. Similarly, the poet refuses to get drawn into any discussion regarding the technicalities of the Virgin's Dormition and Assumption, in a passage that bears an uncanny resemblance with the later Wace's attitude towards Arthur's death in the *Roman de Brut* (1719–24):

> Sempres fu d'iluec remuëz,
> N'i fu puis veüz ne trovez,
> Ne puis dire ne afermer,
> Ne je nel vueil ci aconter
> Que hom ne feme qui vesquist
> Puis cele hore le cors veïst.[31]

This caution seems somewhat incongruous, as Wace is describing here an authoritatively attested miracle, which took place whilst the tomb was guarded by the assembled disciples; and indeed, he only adopts this pose briefly, using his stance of ignorance as a spring-board for a profession of faith (1741–6):

> Se l'om demande que je crei
> Del cors, s'il est en ciel par sei
> E l'arme par sei ensement,
> De ce respondrai je briément:
> Ce crei qu'ele est resuscitee
> E vive e mielz qu'ele n'iert nee.[32]

This is a point of faith that cannot adequately be approached with a nit-picking, earthbound mind, is the clear message. Some things simply have to be accepted, even by the most learned.[33]

Throughout this poem, there is evidence that Wace was concerned that his discourse (or to be more precise, that of his sources) might not be accessible to all, and that certain things were likely to be misconstrued by the layman. As we have seen, in the *Vie de sainte Marguerite* potentially problematic references or imagery are simply omitted; but the life of the Virgin was too elevated a subject matter for Wace to resort to systematic simplification. He therefore adopts an alternative strategy, that of signalling important events and themes through narratorial intervention, in openly didactic passages displaying a degree of rhetorical ornamentation congruent with the dignity of the topic discussed. There are

---

[30] 'I'm not saying that he was aware of this when he made the sacrifice, but the Holy Spirit instructed him and showed him what to do.'

[31] 'It [i.e., the Virgin's body] was immediately removed from there, it was not seen nor found there afterwards; I cannot tell or state, neither do I want to say here that any living man nor woman ever saw the corpse thereafter.'

[32] 'If I am asked what I believe on the subject of her body, if it is in heaven with her and together with her soul, I shall answer briefly: I believe that she is risen, and alive and better than when she was born.'

[33] The question of what happened to the Virgin's physical body at her death was still a matter for debate in the twelfth century, hence possibly Wace's relative caution in this passage. See Beyers, '*La Conception Nostre Dame* de Wace', pp. 380–95.

three high points in the narrative signalled in this way: the statement of the importance of observing the festival of the (Immaculate) Conception of Our Lady, quoted above; the closing considerations of the poem on the Virgin's corporeal assumption discussed above; and the Incarnation of Christ, lavishly adorned with anaphora and *enumeratio*, which constitutes one of the purple passages of the poem (861–78):

> Qui tot a fait, tot veit, tot ot,
> Qui mer, qui terre, qui ciel clot,
> Qui est defors, qui est dedenz,
> Qui fait les ploies e les venz,
> Qui toz tens ert e toz tens fu,
> Sainz la virgene conceü.
> Saches que por veir puet hom dire:
> Sers devint cil qui esteit sire,
> La fille est devenue mere
> E devenuz est fiz li pere.
> . . .
> Si n'iert pas de nos besoignos,
> Mais Deus por noz besoinz le fist,
> Que de la mort nos reëncist.
> De la mort, di-je, pardurable
> E de la baillie al deable.[34]

Wace is here in full predicatory mood, addressing his audience, spelling out facts, stressing their significance, in a spirit of triumphant elation. This is the key event which gives the feasts of Our Lady their significance, and the reader (or audience) is not allowed to forget it.

Within these framing interventions by the narrator, the various sections of the poem bear the mark of an author who was confident with his subject matter, familiar with a wide range of sources, and unafraid to combine, excise or elaborate on these in order to produce a clear and accessible narrative. The relation between Wace's sources and his *Conception Nostre Dame* has been investigated in detail by Rita Beyers; as noted by Gioia Paradisi, we are faced with a highly complex adaptation, walking on a constant tightrope between the narrative coherence required of a work of popularisation and the demands of accuracy and theological orthodoxy.[35] The precise extent of Wace's cutting, pasting, reformulation and commenting is difficult to assess, as the textual tradition of his sources is characterised by its diversity, and in the current state of research it is not possible to identify with confidence the exact versions of the texts that the poet might have used. However, we may note that the *Conception* was composed with three recognisable principles in mind:

---

[34] 'He who made everything; who sees all; hears all; who enclosed land, earth and sky; who is within; who is outside; who makes rains and winds; who shall always be and always has been; was conceived within the Virgin. Know that truly one can say: He who was master became a slave, the daughter has become the mother, and the father has become the son . . . And He did not need us, but God did it because of our need, so that He could redeem us from death. From death, I say: from death eternal and from the power of the devil.'

[35] Paradisi, *Le passioni della storia*, p. 47.

1. A streamlined structure. This is most perceptible at the beginning of the 'Conception' section, prior to the birth of the Virgin: where his main Latin source jumps from Joachim to Anne (to mark the simultaneity of events), Wace introduces a simpler tripartite rhythm, with the focus on Joachim (up to line 420); then on Anne (lines 421–554); and finally, on the Virgin herself.[36]
2. Narrative economy. Descriptions (for example, of the wondrous palm given to the Virgin in anticipation of her funeral) are reduced to their core elements. Passages in direct speech in the mouth of secondary characters are either omitted,[37] or reshaped to be part of a dialogue with one of the main protagonists.
3. A strong didactic intent. This is signalled by the inclusion of sometimes lengthy passages spelling out the significance of the material just presented, meaning that the balance between narrative and commentary is heavily weighted towards commentary in Wace's poem. These passages show a much greater tolerance of repetition than the narrative proper, and constitute approximately one sixth of the 'Conception' section,[38] and over one third of the 'Three Marys' section.[39] Similarly, if one includes the narrator's conclusion, the 'Assumption' section is approximately one quarter commentary.[40]

These figures clearly indicate that the overarching consideration was the didactic purpose of the poem, over and above faithfulness to any one single source-text. As pointed out by Paradisi,[41] some amount of editing on Wace's part was necessary, if only because his sources, composed well before the formulation of the doctrine of the Immaculate Conception of Our Lady, contained elements that would not have sat well in a work promoting that doctrine. This implied having to omit or edit certain details of the Pseudo-Melito B1 version, Wace's main source. In particular, it was necessary to adapt, in the 'Assumption' section, the Virgin's request to Christ (who has come to call her on her deathbed) that He deliver her from the power of darkness and preserve her from any assault of Satan; and it was impossible to keep Christ's response that 'When you see him, you shall see him according to the law of mankind whereby the end, even death, is allotted to you; but he cannot hurt you, for I am with you to help you' (Pseudo-Melito, VIII).[42] Such statements put Mary in the same situation as the rest of mankind, owing her

---

[36] Beyers ('*La Conception Nostre Dame* de Wace', p. 370) describes the way Wace combines two versions of his source (the *De nativitate* and the *Protevangelium*) to achieve this effect.

[37] A good example of this is the storm scene in the 'Établissement', where the heart-rending prayers of the people on board ship are only mentioned, thus giving greater impact to the dialogue between Helsin and the angel.

[38] These figures do not include didactic passages embedded in speeches by authoritative characters such as angels. In the 'Conception' part, these didactic asides vary from just 3 lines in length (221–3, explaining the nature of the feast that takes Joachim to the temple), to 104 lines (on the Virgin birth of Christ, 1007–110).

[39] In one 61-line eulogy of St John and virginity (1197–258).

[40] There is an element of didacticism in the speeches in this section (especially of Christ and the angel), but the account itself runs almost without interventions by the narrator (1439–48, the names of the Apostles; and 1496, a disclaimer that the narrator does not know what the angels were singing when Christ appeared to the Virgin on her deathbed). The conclusion, however, is one long homily arising from the narrative.

[41] Paradisi, *Le passioni della storia*, p. 47.

[42] Quoted from J. K. Elliott's translation of the Latin Transitus of Pseudo-Melito (also known as Transitus B1 or Tischendorf Transitus), in his *The Apocryphal New Testament* (Oxford, 1993), pp. 46–67.

immunity from the devil entirely to her son, rather than through her own privilege of having been born without the taint of the Original Sin; as such, they were incompatible with Wace's agenda. The idea that the devil is present at the moment of death is kept, but in a different context. The Virgin explains to her relatives (1373–82):

> Sachiez que quant hom deit morir
> E l'arme deit del cors eissir
> Dui angele entor le cors descendent,
> Mut ententif, qui l'arme atendent.
> Li uns de ciel est descenduz
> E li altre est d'enfer venuz.
> Chascuns a sei vuelt l'arme traire
> Mais molt est lor vie contraire,
> Quar segun ce que l'arme a fait
> En enfer chiet o en ciel vait.[43]

She makes it clear, however, that this does not apply to her (1383–6):

> Mais de mei ne seit pas dotance
> Que negune male puissance
> Me puisse faire destorbier
> Ne ja vers mei ost aprismier.[44]

Her earlier prayer 'Que nule infernal poësté/ Ne me puisse faire noisance/ Ne n'ait vers mei nule poissance', 'that no infernal power may harm me or hold any power over me' (1350–2), which echoes the Latin, thus appears as merely proof of the Virgin's humility, rather than a sign of genuine fear. As we can see, Wace goes much further than relying on repeated assertions of Mary's purity and superlative qualities to convince his reader/audience of the Virgin's special status (though he does that too, and to great effect; see especially lines 613–36).

Mary as intercessor is only mentioned twice in the poem, but at crucial moments: towards the end of the 'Conception' section, just before the narrative break brought by the 'transition poem' to the 'Three Marys' section, and at the end of the work, in a speech by Christ Himself. On her deathbed, Mary is told by her son: 'La poësté d'aidier avras/ A trestoz cels que tu voldras', 'You will have the power to help all those you will wish' (1519–20), thus giving further authority to the narrator's statement (1083–6) that

> Ja n'ert feme si pecheriz
> Ne de pechiez hom si laidiz,
> S'il reclaime sainte Marie
> O bon cuer, qu'il nen ait s'aïe.[45]

---

[43] 'Know that when one has to die, and the soul has to leave the body, two angels descend around the body, very vigilant, waiting for the soul. The one comes from Heaven, and the other from hell. Each one wants to pull the soul to him, but their aims are very different, for depending on what the soul has done, it falls in hell or goes to heaven'
[44] 'But do not fear on my account that any evil power might distress me, or even dare approach me.'
[45] 'There will never be a woman so sinful, or a man so defiled with sin that if he appeal to holy Mary with a sincere heart, he will not be helped.'

In addition to the more direct arguments put forward in the poem, Wace thus strengthens his case indirectly by tying in the doctrine of the Immaculate Conception with the already strong popular belief in the intercessory powers of the Virgin. He also depicts her in a more accessible and benign manner than his sources. In the Latin Transitus (B2) accounts,[46] which Wace appears to have used in parallel with Transitus B1, the Jews who were struck blind when they tried to desecrate her body either believe and recover their sight, or persist in their disbelief and die: Wace simply has the unbelievers remain blind, a punishment more in keeping with the image of gentleness of the Virgin. The scenes in the 'Assomption' section prior to the Virgin's death show her surrounded by loving friends and relatives, at the head of a well-run household where the disciples clearly feel at ease; a homely note, to which Wace also adds a touch of humour when he describes the disciples' confusion on finding themselves deposited in front of her house after having been whisked away from their activities by a miraculous cloud. Whereas in the Latin they loudly praise God, in our poem their first reaction is one of delight at seeing each other, then bemusement (1451–6):

> Conurent sei si s'entrevirent
> Baisierent sei, grant joie firent.
> A merveillose chose tindrent
> Qu'en tel maniere ensemble vindrent,
> E si n'en sorent l'achaison,
> Por quei vindrent ne por quei non.[47]

This is recognisably a family reunion, though admittedly with a twist, and a scene to which the audience of the poem would have been able to relate. Wace obviously had a clear grasp of his remit, and had the sufficient familiarity with his material and the issues involved to be able identify the challenges offered by his sources, and rework them into an attractive, yet acceptable form.

Stylistic strategies

Wace writes with confidence and authority; but it takes more than that to reach a popular audience successfully. The work must also be entertaining and easy to follow. In the *Conception Nostre Dame* as in *La Vie de sainte Marguerite*, one of the main devices to achieve this end is a controlled use of direct speech. As mentioned above, in the *Conception Nostre Dame*, direct speech occurs in dialogues involving the central character of a given episode; as such, it allows indirect characterisation, and in the mouth of high-status characters such as angels, may be used to introduce or reinforce points made in the narrator's

---

[46] An accessible edition of the Transitus of Pseudo-Melito (Transitus B2) is published in Appendix 2 of Mary Clayton's *The Apocryphal Gospels of Mary in Anglo-Saxon England* (Cambridge, 1998), pp. 334–43.

[47] 'They recognised each other as they caught sight of each other; they kissed each other, and were very joyful. They thought it a wondrous thing that they should have come together in such a way, without knowing the reason why they were there.'

commentaries that punctuate the text. These speech-acts are not distributed evenly throughout the poem (see Table 3).

Table 3. Distribution and length of speech-acts in direct speech, *Conception Nostre Dame*

Section	1–2 lines	3–10 lines	11–20 lines	20 lines +	Total
'Établissement'	1	4	1	–	6
'Conception'	2	12	8	2 (56 ll., 43 ll.)	24
'Trois Maries'	1	–	–	–	1
'Assomption'	2	14	4	1 (22 lines)	21

The two sections dealing directly with the Life of Our Lady, and therefore containing the core of the teaching transmitted by the poem, have a much higher incidence of direct speech than either the introductory story of Helsin or the transitional account of the Three Marys. This observation remains true if one looks at the proportion of lines in direct speech within individual sections. The 'Établissement' counts 43 lines in direct speech out of a total of 164; the 'Conception' section, some 284 lines in direct speech out of a total of 937 lines (including the commentary on the virgin birth of Christ); the so-called 'transition poem' introducing the Three Marys section has no direct speech at all in its 28 lines; the 'Three Marys' section includes just 2 lines of direct speech in 157 lines of text; and the 'Assomption' counts 179 lines of direct speech in 527 lines (including the narrator's conclusion). Even with the lengthy didactic passages closing these sections, the 'Conception' and the 'Assomption' thus have roughly one line in three in direct speech, as compared to roughly one in four for the 'Établissement', and virtual absence elsewhere. Wace appears to have planned his poem along a principle of alternation between 'lively' sections rich in direct speech, lending immediacy to the narrative and enabling a measure of identification (or empathy) with the characters on the part of the audience, and passages appealing more to their reflection and building on their relationship with the narrator/preacher.

The dialogues in the *Conception* tend to be more formal than in *La Vie de sainte Marguerite*. This is readily explained by the *dramatis personae*. Of the 52 speech-acts in direct speech in the poem, 12 (totalling 114 lines) are put in the mouth of the Virgin; 16 (totalling 220 lines) are uttered by various angels, archangels or divine voices; while Christ Himself is made to speak twice (24 lines). However, these dialogues are not lacking in psychological coherence, and have at times an almost theatrical quality that would have made them highly effective when read aloud with a minimum of voice effects. Joachim's dialogue with the High Priest (238–80) skilfully makes him go from bewilderment to dejection, while Isacar, after his harsh initial words, tries to explain – not ungently – why Joachim is not to be allowed in the temple, and ends with an encouraging 'Quant tu enfant eü avras/ Al temple vien, si ofreras', 'When you have a child, come to the temple, and then you will make your offering' (273–4). Similarly, the chirpy good humour of Uten, Anne's maid, trying to cheer up her mistress and get her in a more festive mood, turns sour all the more convincingly for the sharp snub she receives for her pains. The passage also gives an insight into Anne's mind: the reason she gives for refusing to wear her best clothes is that her husband has disappeared, which clearly is her foremost worry; and it is only when Uten throws her childlessness in her face (465–8) that Anne starts lamenting the fact that she is barren (cue for the entry of the angel announcing her pregnancy).

Longer speeches are typically made by angels,[48] and tend to transmit information of an exegetical nature. The longest speeches in the poem are put in the mouth of the angel sent to Joachim, then Anne, to reveal the impending birth of a child to them. These two speeches (56 and 43 lines) are carefully introduced by short but striking descriptions of the despair of the human protagonists. Joachim has retreated to the desert, suffering the discomfort of wind and rain, and with his shepherds as sole company – though Wace hastens to add that 'En icel tens dont nos parlun/ n'erent pas li pastor garçun/ Mais bacheler alques vaillant/ Bien fort, bien prot, bien conbatant/ Qui de larrons bien se gardassent/ E par matin ainz jor levassent', 'In those days, shepherds were not mere lads, but doughty young men, very strong, very brave, well able to fight, so that they could defend themselves from robbers, and who rose in the morning before daybreak' (307–12). Joachim's company in the desert is thus made appropriate to his rank and wealth, even if his surroundings are distinctly uncomfortable. The depiction of Joachim has overtones of Job, accused by those surrounding him of being punished for a sin which he knows he has not committed (he protests: 'N'est pas par mon pechié, ce crei', 'It's not by my fault, I believe', 280), and crying out to God for an explanation from the depths of his misery until he gets a reply. While (unlike Job) Joachim's isolation is self-inflicted and his health and fortune remain unimpaired, like Job he is determined to force God to answer him (through a form of hunger strike: 'A jeüner a proposé/ Tant que Deus l'ot revisité', 317–18); and the angel swiftly appears. His 56-line speech opens with an address to Joachim, enjoining him not to be afraid (the apparition is accompanied by a brilliant light) and stating that he is an angel of the Lord sent to reassure him that his childlessness was not due to any sin on his part. He then stresses the privileged status of the child born to older, previously barren parents (341–6):

> Quant Deus ne laist home engendrer
> Ne a sa feme enfant porter,
> Puis unt en lor veillece enfant,
> Ço est senefiance grant
> Quar cil qui naist est de dreiture
> De Deu donez, non de luxure.[49]

Such children, it is implied, are less tainted by their parents' concupiscence, and therefore more inclined to good. The angel gives the examples of Isaac and

---

[48] Only one of these long speeches is not made by an angel, in the 'Assomption' section; the speaker of this 22-line speech to Mary is Christ Himself (1499–520).

[49] 'When God does not allow a man to sire a child, or his wife to carry one, and they have a child in their old age, it is a sign of great meaning, for the child who is born has been given by God out of virtue, not lechery.'

Joseph, both born to their fathers Abraham and Jacob in their old age; and of Samuel and Samson, both born to barren women, concluding (361–4):

> Enfant qui naissent de tel gent
> Qui si tardent engendrement,
> Il suelent ester plus vaillant,
> Plus merveillos e plus sachant.[50]

In a passage reminiscent of the angel's words to Joseph in Matthew 1.20–23, the heavenly messenger then announces to Joachim that Anna will give birth to a daughter whom they will call Mary, and who will be filled with the Holy Spirit even before birth ('anceis que seit de mere nee', 371), will preserve herself from all sin and evil, and will give birth, though still a virgin, to the Saviour. Having placed the future birth within a wider eschatological plan, the angel tells Joachim to go and meet his wife at a given place.

The angel's speech to Anne follows the same general pattern. Like her husband, Anne is in a state of profound dejection, though her stance is less aggressive. She speaks rather in terms of being under a curse ('maleïçon', 489), while the child she yearns for is referred to as a blessing ('Si me done beneïçon', 480) whom she would dedicate to the Lord in thanksgiving. Anna seems to be depicted as the more pious of the two spouses, and the angel, after the usual reassurance, specifically presents the future child as a reward for her 'almosnes', 'afflictions', 'preieres' and 'oreisons' (509, 511, 512). As with Joachim, he mentions children born to old parents, giving as examples Sara and Rachel, who conceived late in life. The angel further describes Joseph, one of these wonder children, as 'd'Egipte reis e sire/ E si en osta la famire', 'who was king and lord of Egypt and who freed it of famine' (521–2), thus hinting at Mary's future regal status as Queen of Heaven, which is later explicitly stated by the narrator (1051), and confirmed by Christ in the third-longest speech of the poem (1515–18). The description of the child to Anna then includes instructions on how to raise her and how long she should stay in the temple; and the angel prophecies the Virgin birth of Christ ('Li salvere de li naistra/ Fille son pere enfantera', 'The Saviour will be born of her; the daughter will give birth to her father', 539–40) before directing Anna to the meeting-place with her husband.

The phraseology and teaching contained in these two speeches recur throughout the poem, echoed in the dialogue between the archangel Gabriel and the Virgin in the Annunciation scene (784–860) and the angel's reassurance to Joseph (975–92), and further elaborated on in the comments by the narrator (617–36, 861–78, 1007–110, 1747–60, 1797–809). The central theme, closely linked to that of Our Lady's purity, is the paradox of the daughter who gives birth to her father, which underpins the belief in Mary's intercessory powers.

Wace's handling of the octosyllabic couplet gives this poem a greater feeling of solemnity than the *Vie de sainte Marguerite*; we clearly have in the *Conception Nostre Dame* the high style demanded by the subject-matter. Enjambement

---

50 'Children born of such people who engender late in life are usually more worthy, more marvellous and wiser.'

within the couplet is not unusual, especially in passages in direct speech; the couplet, on the whole, is no longer the syntactical unit, as sentences become more complex and therefore lengthier.[51] Relative clauses are common in the *Conception Nostre Dame*, as are sentences starting with 'Quant'. One may distinguish between two levels of high style in the poem: a 'narrative' level, typically when the narrator is in his 'homiletic' mode, or when the events recounted follow biblical accounts; and a 'discursive' level, typically connected with direct speech in the mouth of an authoritative figure (angels, or Christ). The 'homiletic' high style is characterised by the length of the sentences, extending over two couplets or more; it also tends to be more rhetorically adorned than normal narrative, with key passages (such as the Incarnation of Christ) displaying a lavish use of *enumeratio* and repetition of words and syntactical structures.[52] A good example of this occurs in lines 1042–7, a single sentence (beginning in the second line of a couplet, against all the expectations one could have had from the *Vie de sainte Marguerite*) where 'virgene' + Verb recurs eight times. While the function of the couplet as sense-unit is no longer observed in this 'homiletic' high style, one may note that the rhythm of the couplet is to a great extent retained. Enjambement from one line to the following one is not common in these passages; and the rhythm is regular, based on the binary principles underlying the octosyllabic couplet.

The 'discursive' high style, by contrast, is syntactically simpler, but rhythmically more complex, thus audibly marking the special status of the speaker. The appearance of an authoritative character is regularly accompanied by abrupt breaks in the expected rhythm, as are points of especial importance within the speech of that character. Thus, the two consecutive angelic appearances to Anne, in the 'Conception' section of the work, are connected with the four following lines (548–51):

> Quant li angeles ot ce conté
> Ala s'en. Ez vos la venuz
> .ii. homes de blans dras vestuz,
> Qui unt Anna si aparlee.[53]

One may note that the couplet as sense-bearing unit is ignored. The break following 'Ala s'en' disrupts the rhythm of the octosyllabic line, creating the effect of an eleven-syllable unit (with a pause after the eighth syllable), followed by another unit of thirteen syllables (also with a pause after the eighth syllable). This emphasises the end of the first angelic apparition, and announces the second one, which will spur Anne into action. A similar sharp break in the middle of a line just before an authoritative character is about to make an utterance in direct speech occurs on lines 1317–18.

---

[51] Sentences that run over the limits of the rhyming couplet to end in the following couplet occur on average every 34 lines.
[52] For a discussion of repetition, alliteration and the use of synonyms in the *Conception*, see Ronsjö, *La Vie de saint Nicolas*, pp. 22–4.
[53] 'When the angel had said that, he left. Then, lo, two men came dressed in white clothes, who thus spoke to Anne . . .'

Rhythmical disruptions within passages in direct speech are more numerous; typically, a three- or four-syllable 'spillover' from the preceding line is following by a marked pause, thus drawing attention to the word or concept thus isolated. In one case at least, in a speech by the dying Virgin, this leads to a virtual change in metre (1407–14):

> Mais li Jüeu unt porparlé
> E de ce lor conseil fermé
> Qu'il en apres ferunt ardeir
> Mon cors s'il lu pueent aveir,
> Por sol ice que je portai
> Cume mun fil e alaitai
> Jhesum Christum, Nostre Seignor
> Qu'il teneient por seduitor.[54]

This one sentence contains two cases of enjambement followed by a marked pause, and one enjambement followed by a weaker pause. The element thus foregrounded are 'mon cors', as is relevant in a narrative recounting the Assumption of the Virgin; the name of Christ; and, less strongly but creating echoes with the extensive passages expounding the paradox of the daughter giving birth to her father, 'cume mun fil', 'as/like my son'. In rhythmical terms, these lines form six units: the initial couplet; then: 'Qu'il en après (minor pause) ferunt ardeir mon cors (ten syllables; pause after fourth syllable)/ s'il lu pueent aveir (six syllables)/ Por sol ice (minor pause) que je portai (minor pause) cume mon fil (twelve syllables, pause after the fourth and eighth syllable)/ E alaitai Jhesum Christum (minor pause) Nostre Seignor (twelve syllables, pause after the eighth syllable)/ qu'il teneient por seduitor (eight syllables)'. This passage almost slips into alexandrines.

Such a degree of flexibility (and indeed virtuosity) in the use of the octosyllabic couplet is unusual in an early twelfth-century poem,[55] and shows that Wace was in full possession of his art.

The very complexity of the task entrusted to him, and the sensitive nature of the assignment, makes it most improbable that Wace was a beginner when he composed the *Conception*. He must already have attained widespread recognition as a scholar as well as a poet to be considered for such a commission, and it is unlikely that such lofty material would have been entrusted to someone fresh from his studies and still prone to the excesses of youth. If we accept with Paradisi and others that the feast of the Conception of Our Lady was reintroduced in England in 1129 partly under the influence of Henry I (of whom we know that he personally observed the feast) it is possible that Wace's patron might have been the king himself, or a high-ranking ecclesiastic in the royal circle wishing to

---

[54] 'But the Jews have discussed and made up their mind that after [my death] they will have my body burnt, if they can get it, for the sole reason that I carried as my son and breast-fed Jesus Christ Our Lord whom they consider a deceiver.'

[55] See Paul Meyer, 'Le Couplet de deux vers', *Romania* 23 (1894): 1–35.

celebrate the event and pave the way for its acceptance in Normandy.[56] As Wace himself tells us in his *Roman de Rou*, he was personally acquainted with Henry I. But one thing is certain: the *Conception Nostre Dame* is a remarkable piece of work. It is effective propaganda, based on solid and painstaking scholarship, didactic without descending into dryness, with genuinely entertaining or touching passages, and giving throughout an impression of total conviction on the part of the poet. Of the three poems written by Wace before his celebrated *Roman de Brut*, the *Conception Nostre Dame* is the one most likely to have made his name for him in high circles – assuming, that is, that it wasn't made already.

---

[56] See Paradisi, *Le passioni della storia*, p. 50. The bishop of Winchester Henry of Blois, a close relative of the king's who presided over one of the foremost centres of Marian devotion in England, is an obvious candidate.

3

La Vie de saint Nicolas

Whether or not the composition of the *Vie de saint Nicolas* postdates the *Conception Nostre Dame*, this poem occupies an interesting intermediate position between the relatively straightforward task of adapting for a French-speaking audience the *Vie de sainte Marguerite*, from two, quite similar Latin versions, and the textual labyrinth offered by the sources relating to the life of the Virgin. Though the subject matter was less elevated than for the *Conception*, for his *Vie de saint Nicolas* Wace was working with even more popular material than that of *La Vie de sainte Marguerite*. Saint Nicholas was one of the most loved saints of the medieval Christian world; his cult was well-established in Western Europe from the eleventh century, and his miracles were celebrated in Latin Lives and hymns, as well as plays. His fame endures to this day in the popular figure of Santa Claus.

Nicholas is thought to have lived at some time in the fourth century AD. The only son of wealthy parents, so the legend tells us, he was noted from his youth for his piety and charity. At the death of his parents, he sells all his belongings and gives the money to the poor. Elected Bishop of Myra, he leads an exemplary life distinguished by numerous miracles; his legend thus credits him, amongst other marvels, with freeing three counts unjustly condemned to death by the emperor Constantine; saving some sailors threatening with shipwreck by calming a storm; averting famine from his country; and bringing back to life students murdered by an innkeeper for their money. He is said to have died on 6 December 343. As patron saint of sailors, merchants and children, Saint Nicholas met with an early popularity in Normandy, thanks to the commercial links with the Norman kingdom of Sicily. Two churches were dedicated to him in Caen alone, in the 1080s.[1] The cult was further reinforced in 1087, when Norman merchants took the relics of the saint from his tomb in Myra and transferred them to Bari, in southern Italy, which swiftly became an important pilgrimage centre. Wace's Life of Nicholas, like his Life of Margaret (or indeed the *Conception*), was thus composed in the first stages of a period of expansion in the cult of the saint; Nicolas saw his popularity spread from England, Italy and Normandy throughout twelfth-century France and western Germany.[2]

---

[1] One was a crypt under the abbey church of Sainte Trinité, the other was a Romanesque church (still standing) built by the monks of Saint-Etienne. See C. Collet, P. Leroux and J. Y. Marin, *Caen, cité médiévale. Bilan d'archéologie et d'histoire* (Caen, 1996), esp. pp. 66–72.

[2] On the chronology of the dissemination of the cult of St Nicholas, see Karl Meisen, *Nikolauskult und Nikolausbrauch im Abendlande. Eine kultgeographisch-volkskundliche Untersuchung* (Düsseldorf, 1931), esp. ch. 6, 'Die Ausbreitung und Blüte des Nikolauskultes im Mittel- und Nord-Europa', pp.

The life of the saintly bishop of Myra was first written down during the early ninth century by an anonymous Greek author, who appears to have gathered oral traditional accounts of the life and miracles of Nicholas. This first Life, known as the *Vita per Michaelem*, then served as main source for another Greek Life of Nicholas, by Methodius, Patriarch of Constantinople from 842 to 846.[3] In turn, Methodius's compilation was the main source for the first Latin version of the saint's life, by a Neapolitan cleric called Johannes Diaconus (John the Deacon) in the third quarter of the ninth century. By the tenth century, this first Latin Life was circulating in two versions. The first of these, which remains closest to Johannes Diaconus's work, is generally referred to as the Mombritius version, after Bonino Mombrizio, who first published the text in 1479. The second version contains a number of additional miracles taken from the Life of another saintly Nicholas, who was bishop of Pinara and probably died in 564; it was first published by Nicolaus Carminius Falconius in 1751, and is therefore known as the Falconius version. In addition to the prose Lives, from the tenth century onwards, an increasing number of hymns (in Latin) celebrating the saint's miracles were in circulation; and possibly from as early as the eleventh century, miracle plays were produced for performance on the saint's day (6 December).

Wace's poem is based mainly on the Mombritius version, by Johannes Diaconus, with three additional miracles from the Falconius version, and a further nine miracles derived from other sources, not all of which can be identified with certainty. We therefore have a more complex situation than with the *Vie de sainte Marguerite*, which is based on two Latin versions only. As we shall see, the structure of the poem, consisting of a prologue, an epilogue and a succession of near-independent accounts of twenty-three miracles, is also totally unlike the self-contained, linear Margaret narrative. The guidance offered to the poet by his Latin Nicholas texts is of a more fragmented nature; any internal cohesion (other than that offered by the character of Nicholas) had to be created by Wace within the episodic format dictated by the compilatory approach adopted by the Latin writers, and embraced by himself. The *Vie de saint Nicolas* is not only a translation, however brilliant, but also a new redaction based on personal research; in that respect, it is comparable to the *Conception Nostre Dame*.

Wace's tells us in the conclusion to his work that he composed the Life of Nicholas 'Ad l'oes Robert le fiz Tiout,/ Qui seint Nicholas mult amout', 'for the use of Robert son of Tiout, who greatly loved saint Nicholas' (1549–50). This Robert has been identified as a certain Robert Theoldi (or Tioudi), whose sons Roger and Robert were benefactors of the Hôtel-Dieu and of the Abbey of the Sainte Trinité at Caen in the early thirteenth century.[4] 'Robert son of Tiout'

119–71 and 177 ff. Meisen has also as annexe a useful map of Western Europe with the various medieval shrines and dedications to St Nicholas.

[3] A third Greek version of Nicholas's life (by Simeon Metaphrastes, based on the *Vita per Michaelem*) was composed during the second half of the tenth century; however, as it was not translated into Latin before the fifteenth century, it need not concern us here. Further Latin Lives of Nicholas were written in Germany, by Reginold Bishop of Eichstaett (966–91) and, in the early 1060s, by Othloh, a monk from St Emmeram's near Regensburg. See Ronsjö, *La Vie de saint Nicolas*, pp. 7–10.

[4] See Ronsjö, *La Vie de saint Nicolas*, pp. 193–4. The gift of Roger son of Robert Tioudi to the Hôtel-Dieu is mentioned in a papal bulla of Innocent III, dated 1210; his brother (?) Robert appears in three charters dated 1217, recording his donation of two houses to the abbey.

clearly belonged to an influential Caen family; an 'Alexander filius Teoldi', possibly a brother, donated a fief to the chapter of Bayeux cathedral in 1138, and is mentioned three times in the Livre Noir de Bayeux. This does not help us in the dating of the work, but it does confirm that Wace must have been based in Caen in the years prior to the accession to the throne of England of Henry II. This period, though unstable, offered good job opportunities for a competent cleric. Geoffrey of Anjou, the father of the future Henry II of England, who was engaged from the late 1130s to the mid 1140s in annexing Normandy piecemeal in the name of his son, set up a new administrative machinery in the duchy that required a qualified workforce; and when Geoffrey died in 1151, Henry left his administration in place. If, as is probable, Wace held a position within this administration, his *Vie de saint Nicolas* would be best placed either before 1146 or in the early 1150s, as the composition of a major work of scholarship would not have been especially compatible with the sustained hard work entailed by the setting up of an efficient ducal administrative system. It may be significant in this respect that the miraculous Saint Nicholas is a relatively neutral subject in terms of the politics of the time.

Ostensibly, we appear to be dealing with a clear case of lay patronage. The poem could have been commissioned by Robert in memory of his father Tiout; or it could have been commissioned in memory of Robert himself – the verb 'amout', in the imperfect, is technically open to both interpretations. As Robert's sons do not appear in charters before the first decade of the thirteenth century, it is highly probable that the verb refers to Tiout rather than his son; though the possibility remains that the poem was commissioned for Robert, rather than by him. In any case, the connections of this family with religious houses in both Bayeux and Caen make it likely that these two very important cultural centres had some part in the diffusion of Wace's poem.

Manuscripts

Wace's *Vie de saint Nicolas* has come down to us in five manuscripts, four in Anglo-Norman and one in Picard dialect, the oldest dating from the second half of the thirteenth century:

1. Paris, Bibliothèque nationale, fonds français 902, is a composite manuscript with fols. 1–162 in velum, and copied by one Anglo-Norman scribe at the end of the thirteenth century or the beginning of the fourteenth century. The second part of the manuscript, fols. 163–72, is paper, and dates from the fifteenth century; there are two 46-line columns of text per page. The Nicholas section is on fols. 117v–125v. A big letter A (with its left descending 'leg' scrolling down to the lower margin of the page) marks the beginning of the text, and each new miracle is signalled by a capital letter in red ink.
2. Oxford, Bodleian Library, 21844, Douce 270, ii + 106 folios, is a parchment manuscript which may have been produced in the late twelfth century or early thirteenth century for Durham Abbey. It contains a medley of material: a note on the manner in which children grow in their mother's womb (fol. 1);

calendars up to the reign of Edward II (fols. 2–8); glosses and sermons on various texts of the New Testament (fols. 9–84); a Lucidary (a sort of moral romance, fols. 84–91v), reputedly by St Anselm, and abruptly cut off on fol. 91v; and finally, Wace's Life of Nicholas, which occupies the rest of the manuscript. The manuscript, which has two thirty-line columns of text per page, signals the beginning of each miracle with capitals in red and/or blue ink.

3. Paris, Bibliothèque de l'Arsenal, 3516. This Picard manuscript, dated 1267 or 1268, also contains Wace's *Vie de sainte Marguerite*. The *Nicolas* section (fols. 69v–73v), copied on four fifty-line columns per page, is marked by a coloured miniature representing St Nicholas seated on a throne and holding the episcopal crozier; the text is adorned with ornamental capital letters.

4. Oxford, Bodleian Library, 1687, Digby 86, is a commonplace book dated 1272–82, probably from the Worcestershire area. This amateurish-looking little manuscript (iii + 207 + iii folios, 175 x 145mm) is an extremely important witness for our understanding of medieval English culture as, in addition to accounts and recipes, it contains poetry and prose in both English and Anglo-Norman French. The *Nicolas* section covers fols. 150–61; it is signalled by a title, 'Les miracles de seint Nicholas', and is adorned with red and black ink capitals marking the beginning of each miracle. There are no illustrations as such in this manuscript, but it does contain some doodles and the occasional ink sketch in the margin. One of these occurs in the lower margin of fol. 150v, a small head with a horn-like mitre.

5. Cambridge, Trinity College, B.14.39–40. This velum manuscript is composed of two volumes bound together: the first one dates back to the thirteenth century, the second one to the fourteenth and fifteenth centuries. The Nicholas section is preserved in the earlier of these volumes, fols. 48–57v; this version of Wace's poem lacks both the introduction and ending to the work, and (like the Digby MS, no. 4 above) has a miracle 'missing' from its account.

The interesting feature of this manuscript tradition is that the popularity of Wace's *Vie de saint Nicolas* seems to have been a predominantly Anglo-Norman, indeed English, phenomenon. The fact that three of the four Anglo-Norman witnesses (MSS 1, 4 and 5 on our list) have preserved a text that is imperfect in content and in linguistic accuracy[5] indicates that the poem had undergone considerable erosion, both in terms of multiple copying from written originals and of distortion due to copying from memory, or by dictation. The *Vie de saint Nicolas* clearly had a wide appeal, as may be seen from its inclusion in manuscripts as different as Oxford, Bodleian 21844 (Douce 270), professionally copied with great care for a monastic community, and Oxford, Bodleian 1687 (Digby 86), a gentleman's private anthology of useful or pleasant texts and titbits. It is fair to say from this evidence that Wace's *Vie de saint Nicolas* was part of the popular culture of thirteenth-century England.

The extent to which one can also postulate an enthusiastic reception of the poem on the Continent is less clear. Its very inclusion in the Arsenal 3516 luxury

---

[5] For a discussion of the imperfections and lacunae of these manuscripts, see Ronsjö, *La Vie de saint Nicolas*, pp. 46–52 and 56–8.

collection of saints' lives (manuscript 3 of our list) suggests that it was considered the 'best' Life of Nicholas available in the vernacular, whether for completeness or for literary excellence; which in turn makes it likely that the work, in its Picard or Anglo-Norman form, was also circulating in the north of France in less costly manuscripts. However, these manuscripts, if they ever existed, have not survived; one must also take into account the fact that, as the saint was already venerated in what is now France, with a feast day that was well established, Wace's poem was more likely to enter into competition with other texts – in sharp contrast with his pioneering *Conception Nostre Dame*.[6]

The narrator's stance

The composition of this poem arises from a commission ('Dit m'est et rové que jo face/ De seint Nicholas en romanz', 'I was told and requested to do in French a work on St Nicholas', 36–7), but it is also presented as an act of duty on Wace's part (1–6):

> A ces qui n'unt lectres apprises
> Ne lur ententes n'i ont mises,
> Deivent li clerc mustrer la lei,
> Parler des seinz, dire pur quei
> Chescone feste est controvee,
> Chesconë a sun jur gardee.[7]

If 'clercs' have a duty to teach (23), the laity have a duty to listen and learn (21–22); in a passage echoing the Parable of the Talents (Matthew 25.14–30, Luke 19.12–27), both groups are depicted as being morally bound to contribute to society with whatever gifts they have received from the Almighty (27–34):

> Chescon deit mustrer son saver
> Et sa bonté et son poer
> Et Deu servir, son creatur,
> Et as barons sainz pur s'amur.
> Qui ben l'aimë et ben le sert
> Bon gueredon de lui desert.
> Petit prendra qui sert petit,
> Si cum l'escriture le dit.[8]

Composing this poem is thus Wace's way of making the talent of Latin literacy granted to him fructify, in order to amass the spiritual treasure promised by the

---

6 Jehan Bodel's play, *Le Jeu de saint Nicolas*, loosely based on Miracle 15 (see Table 4 below) and dated to about 1200, shows that the material was known well enough by French audiences for the playwright to be able to manipulate it quite drastically.

7 'To those who have not learned their [Latin] letters and have not put their intent in them, clerics must teach the faith, speak of the saints, say why each feast has been established, and is observed on its own day.' All quotes of the *Vie de saint Nicolas* are from Ronsjö's edition of the text; translations are my own.

8 'Everyone must make use of his knowledge, his good heart and his strength, and serve God his creator, and for the love of Him, honour the noble saints. Whoever loves and serves Him well will earn a good reward from Him. He who gives only a small service will receive little, as Scripture tells us.'

parable. The point is given additional emphasis by its being repeated in the closing lines of the Prologue (41–4):

> En romanz voil dire un petit
> De ceo que nus le latin dit,
> Que li lai le puissent aprendre
> Qui ne poënt latin entendre.[9]

Wace's target audience, as outlined in the Prologue, is widely inclusive: all lay people, irrespective of wealth, rank, or intellectual ability may learn from his work (7–16).

> Chescon ne poet pas tut saver
> Ne tut oïr ne tut veer.
> Li un sunt lai, li un lectré,
> Li un fol, et li un senee,
> Li un petit et li un grant,
> Li un povre, li un manant.
> Si done Deus deversement
> Divers dons a diverse gent.
> Chescon deit mustrer sa bonté
> De ceo que Deus lui ad doné.[10]

Whether 'chivaler', 'burgeis', 'vilein' or 'corteis' (i.e., knight, townsman, countryman or courtier; 17–18), it is every man's duty to listen and make a contribution of their own to match that of the clerics, with their 'substance' (20).

This passage has been interpreted by Paradisi as one of the earliest formulations in the vernacular of the Three Estates model, whereby society is a unit constituted of the triad *oratores/bellatores/laboratores*, whose function is respectively to pray, to fight and to work.[11] However, this attractive (and cogently argued) reading does not take sufficient account of the polarisation between 'li clerc' and 'li lai' in the Prologue. The 'clerc', who can read Wace's Latin sources for themselves, are not part, ostensibly, of his intended readers/listeners. Conversely, no distinction is made between the knight, the townsman, the farmer or the courtier in terms of expectations: all must listen, learn, and give to the measure of their wealth to support the clerical caste who work so hard to give them reliable and authoritative guidance. Indeed, clerics, and therefore also Wace, figure as relative outsiders in the reception process of the work as depicted by the Prologue.

This sharp distinction between laity and clerics is echoed later in the work, in the narrator's interventions in Miracles 5 and 12. These are hinge episodes in the work 'signposting' the nature of the anecdotes to follow, and both feature the same rhetorical topos, where the narrator states that recounting all the wonders worked by the saint would be an impossible task (195–8 and 601–4):

---

[9] 'I will tell you a little in French of what the Latin says, so that lay people who cannot understand Latin may learn it.'

[10] 'Everyone can't know everything, or hear or see everything. Some are laymen, other are educated; some are foolish, others are wise; one is small, the other is big; one is poor, the other rich. God diversely gives different gifts to different people. Everyone must be generous in what God has given him.'

[11] Paradisi, *Le passioni della storia*, pp. 55–72.

> Gref me serreit a reconter
> E gref a vus a esculter
> Les granz miracles et les bens
> Qu'il fist a plusurs cristiens.[12]
>
> Longe chose serreit a dire
> Et mult ennuose a escrivre
> Les miracles et les socurs
> Que li seinz hom fist a plusurs.[13]

The first of these passages introduces the lifetime miracles of the saint, the second his posthumous miracles; both mark the beginning of a section describing or recounting precisely the material allegedly impossible or difficult to present. On one level, we simply have here a variation on the 'indicibility' topos favoured by medieval rhetoricians, and used to some effect in the *Conception*: Nicolas worked so many wonders that it would by impossible to tell of all of them, and even if one could, the sheer length of the narrative would make it tedious. However, these lines also emphasise the distance between Wace the learned writer and his lay audience, through the stressing of the different nature of the constraints limiting the poet and his readers. By contrast, the passage in his Latin source underlying this statement is more conventionally phrased, and does not consider the possibility that the material might bore its readers.[14] The interventions in Miracles 8 and 9 similarly imply a body of addressees distinguished from the narrator: the passage starting 'Seignurs, vus qui alez par mer', 'Lords, you who travel by sea' (227, Miracle 8), signals to a privileged group of listeners – sailors and travellers at sea – a story of especial interest to them; whilst the introduction to Miracle 9 ('Oëz, seignurs, ben fait a dire', 'Listen, lords, this is a good thing to tell', 275), though less specific, still functions on a principle of contrast between the authoritative teaching voice and the 'seignurs' whose duty it is to listen.

These two addresses to the audience both occur in the earlier section of the work, devoted to Nicholas's lifetime miracles. In the addresses by the narrator occurring in the remainder of the poem (three in the 'posthumous miracles' section, and one in the concluding miracles), the distinction between the authoritative, learned cleric and his lay addressees becomes blurred. The short (six lines) prologue to Miracle 17 retains the earlier dichotomy, with the persona of the detached moralising narrator (807–8 and 813):

> Oëz, seignurs, si apernez
> A rendre ceo que vus devez.
> ...
> Savez que seint Nicholas fist?[15]

---

[12] 'It would be difficult for me to recount, and irksome for you to listen to, the great miracles and good deeds he performed for many Christians.'
[13] 'It would take a long time to tell, and be very tedious to write down, the miracles and helpful deeds that the holy man made for many.'
[14] See Mombritius, p. 300, lines 22–5: 'Verum tempus mihi deficit: quin et sermo deserit: si de singulis eius scribere meritis contendam', 'But I would not have enough time, and words would fail me, if I undertook to write of each one his merits.'
[15] 'Listen, lords, and learn to give back what you owe. . . . Do you know what holy Nicholas did?'

However, it is framed by two addresses where the narrator includes himself in the community of listeners through the use of the first person plural. This shift is unobtrusive in Miracle 16: 'Dit vus avom de cest païen./ Or redirum d'un cristien', 'We have told you about this pagan; now we shall talk about a Christian again' (723–4). This use of the first person plural is all the more striking for its coming after two episodes where the narrator unequivocally refers to himself in the first person singular, through a thrice-repeated disclaimer of knowledge in less than one hundred lines: 'ne sai par quele acheison' (641), 'ne sai par quelle guere' (644) and 'ne sai com cil alat' (679). Ostensibly, the immediate function of the narrator's intrusion is to spell out the logical link between Miracles 15 and 16; but this link is unconvincing. Miracle 16 is not so much about the dishonest Christian as about the Jew who, like the pagan in Miracle 15, converts after witnessing Nicholas's powers. It does however pave the way for the openly inclusive addresses which appear towards the end of the work, and where the narrator establishes himself as a fellow human being rather than as a source of knowledge.

The eight-line prologue opening Miracle 20 states 'Un enemi avom mortel/ A tut le pople communel', 'We have a mortal enemy, common to all people' (1157–8); a fitting way of introducing the devil, but which also abolishes distinctions between the narrator and his addressees, as indeed between the addressees themselves (as opposed to underscoring them, as in line 227). The address opening Miracle 22 similarly has a double function. It alerts the readers or listeners that a break in the bipartite structure is about to occur (1485–6):

> Oëz que nus trovom lisant
> Que le ber fist en sun vivant.[16]

After the long section devoted to the saint's posthumous miracles, we are indeed about to return to Nicholas's lifetime: a potentially confusing state of affairs that requires some signalling. However, the way Wace does this, using the first person plural rather than, for example, the impersonal 'on', turns the listeners into co-readers with the narrator, creating the feeling of a community of knowledge as well as of faith. It also announces the tone of the conclusion where, after stating the difficulty (if not the downright impossibility) of compiling an exhaustive account of the miracles of Nicholas, the narrator ends the work with a prayer effectively abolishing the distance established in the Prologue:

> Depreom Deu, Nostre Seignur,
> Que pur cest seint et pur s'amur
> Nus doint de nos pecchez pardon
> E venir a confession
> Que nus od Deu regner poissom.
> In secula seculorum.[17]

This is a totally orthodox sentiment, couched in conventional terms; but it has a

---

[16] 'Listen to what we find in writing concerning the deeds the good man did in his lifetime.'
[17] 'Let us pray God, our Lord, that for that saint and for his love, he give us forgiveness for our sins and bring us to confession, that we may reign with God, in secula seculorum' (1557–62).

ring of sincerity to it that is in great part due to Wace's gradual distancing himself from the persona of the learned cleric, to assume that of the humble Christian soul aspiring to be part of the communion of saints in the glory of everlasting life. The *Vie de saint Nicolas*, like the *Conception Nostre Dame*, ends on a homiletic note.

Structure and contents

Wace's *Vie de saint Nicolas* contains 23 miracles (totalling 1563 octosyllabic lines), from a variety of sources, against just 11 in the Mombritius version, and 14 in the Falconius version; each miracle by Nicholas is the object of an autonomous section. These sections are of varying length, from a few lines to several pages, and are placed apparently at random within the three general parts, that is: lifetime miracles (roughly in chronological order), posthumous miracles; and concluding miracles. Table 4 gives a brief description of each miracle, together with the indication whether this miracle is also found in the Mombritius (M) or Falconius (F) collections.

Wace's main source was clearly the Johannes Diaconus text (Mombritius version), which is preserved in its entirety and with the same sequence of miracles. Within this basic framework, Wace has interpolated additional material from the Falconius version (in a different order: the two final miracles in Wace's poem correspond to chapters 16 and 17 of the 22 chapters of Falconius), and from a number of collections of Latin saints' lives, including the account of John Archdeacon of Bari about the translation of the remains of saint Nicholas from Myra to Bari.[18] This results in the loss of the loosely chronological sequence of both the Mombritius and Falconius versions, where the account begins with the infant Nicholas, continues with the miracles made by the saint during his lifetime, and ends with his posthumous miracles. Though Wace initially observes this distinction between miracles made before and after Nicholas's death, he chooses to end his work with two stories from the saint's lifetime, thus disrupting the underlying logic of his sources.

It could be argued that these final miracles are 'tagged on' rather than integrated into the relevant section of the work, due to a reluctance to juxtapose or narrate in close succession stories which are too similar (the subject-matter of Miracles 22 and 23 is very close to that of Miracles 6, 12 and 13).[19] This hypothesis would seem to have a measure of support from the narrator's conclusion to the poem, which appears to indicate a compilatory approach with a view to maximal completeness (1551–6):

> Mult avreit longes a penser
> Qui en romanz voldreit conter

---

[18] This account (which underlies Wace's Miracle 21) was frequently copied alongside the Life of St Nicholas by Johannes Diaconus (= Mombritius version) in the manuscript tradition. A painstaking research for evidence of a manuscript tradition underlying Wace's additional miracles was undertaken by Ronsjö, *La Vie de saint Nicolas*, pp. 27–45; only one of these (no. 20) appears to have been derived from oral tradition, or from a written witness now lost.
[19] See Ronsjö, *La Vie de saint Nicolas*, pp. 33–4.

Table 4. The miracles of Nicholas: contents and sources (M – Mombritius, F – Falconius)

	Lines	Miracle	M	F
1.	45–80	Early piety of the young N.	X	X
2.	81–120	Anonymous gift to the impoverished man's daughters.	X	X
3.	121–56	N. is made bishop (angelic intervention).	X	X
4.	157–94	A woman who in her joy at the news of N.'s election to the bishopric forgets her child in his bath water over the fire; the child remains miraculously unscathed in the boiling water.	—	—
5.	195–204	N.'s virtues and asceticism.	X	X
6.	205–12	N. expels a devil from a possessed child.	—	X
7.	213–26	N. resurrects three students murdered by an innkeeper.	—	—
8.	227–74	Sailors call upon N. during a storm, which subsides after an apparition of the saint.	X	X
9.	275–336	N. preserves the land from famine by multiplying a shipload of wheat.	X	X
10.	337–444	N. defeats the wiles of Diana whose idol he has destroyed (bilocation).	X	X
11.	445–600	N. releases three counts unjustly condemned to death by Constantine.	X	X
12.	601–10	N. as healer.	X	—
13.	611–32	A woman is healed by N. on his deathbed.	—	X
14.	633–50	Miraculous oil oozes from N.'s sarcophagus. The flow stops when the archbishop of the land is unjustly exiled, but starts again when he returns from exile.	—	X
15.	651–722	N. protects a pagan treasure guarded by his statue, resulting in the conversion to Christianity of the region.	X	X
16.	723–806	A Jew converts to Christianity after N. resurrects a man killed in a road accident who had refused to repay a loan secured by an image of the saint.	—	—
17.	807–934	A man who tries to replace a precious cup promised to the saint with a cheaper one loses both his son and the original cup in a storm at sea; both are restored to him after he repents. The saint then accepts his gift of the expensive cup.	—	—
18.	935–1092	A rich man called Getro, wishing for a child, goes ask N. for help, only to find him already dead. He brings home some clothes of the saint and founds a church dedicated to him. He then has a son who is abducted by thieves and bought by a pagan emperor. Ill-treated because of his devotion to N., the child is freed by the saint and brought home.	X	—

	Lines	Miracle	M	F
19.	1093–156	A merchant murdered by an innkeeper and whose dismembered body is stored like salt meat in a barrel is miraculously put together again and revived by N. Merchant and innkeeper are reconciled and go to pray at the saint's shrine.	—	—
20.	1157–376	The devil murders the son of a pious man in Lombardy while the child is left alone at home on the feast day of St N. The saint, in the form of a pilgrim, resurrects him. He is even more venerated after that, and clerics even more esteemed.	—	—
21.	1377–84	The healing oil coming from N.'s grave; an attempt to take away by stealth one of the saint's teeth is miraculously foiled.	—	—
22.	1485–518	A paralysed man is taken to N. (during the saint's lifetime) during Lent, and his health is restored after he has been rubbed with the oil of the saint's lamp.	—	X
23.	1519–45	N. frees a man possessed by an evil spirit by making the sign of the cross over him.	—	X

> Et torner en consonancie
> Ses granz miracles et sa vie.
> Ne nus ne trovom tuz escriz,
> Ne nus nes avom tuz oïz.[20]

We are given the image of a complex and superabundant narrative tradition, where oral and written sources coexist in such numbers that to merge them into one 'romanz' requires ingenuity and literary craftsmanship in addition to scholarly skills. On one level, this is a conventional 'captatio benevolentiae' aimed at enhancing the reader's appreciation of the work – indeed, Wace's Latin source uses a slightly different version of the same device at exactly the same points in the narrative. Also, the passage neatly encapsulates the nature of the problem confronting Wace. Too many miracles of a similar nature might give an impression of repetition and thus induce boredom. But the implication of the statement regarding the incompleteness of his sources – that is, that omitted miracles are due to limitations in transmission rather than to Wace's own decision – is patently misleading, as we know he did not bother to include all of the miracles present in the Falconius version.[21] Exhaustiveness of content was clearly not the main priority, despite the poet's prudent disclaimers. Moreover Wace's apparently disjointed series of anecdotes was carefully selected: a lesser-known version of Miracle 17 replaces the account preserved in most extant Latin manuscripts copied in or before the twelfth century, while Wace's version of Miracle 20 is quite different to that preserved in medieval Latin versions (the corresponding account in the *Legenda Aurea*, for example, is much shorter than Wace's, and

---

[20] 'It would take a very long time of reflection for anyone wishing to recount and turn into a rhymed narrative his great miracles and his life. We cannot find them all in writing, neither have we heard them all.'
[21] Wace thus omits Falconius, chapter 14, where the saint cures a possessed woman.

presents a number of differences in the detail).[22] Miracles 4 (the child in boiling water) and 20 (the strangled child) are extremely rare, even in later manuscripts, and no Latin source predating Wace has been identified for them.

It is important to realise that any form of joined-up, linear narrative was incompatible with the sort of material Wace had to translate and adapt. Quite apart from the fact that the exact chronology of the various miracles was impossible to determine, there was on the whole no obvious connection between any two stories beyond their miraculous nature and the personality of Nicholas himself. Moreover, as Wace would doubtless have been well aware for having submitted his own sources to such treatment, a collection of brief accounts such as these was not likely to enjoy a high degree of textual stability; the sheer mechanics of manuscript transmission meant that individual miracles might be omitted (whether intentionally or not), others might be interpolated, and the order in which they appeared would probably not remain stable. The creation of a subtle sense of progression was therefore not a realistic option. The poet had to find an alternative structuring principle, allowing flexibility whilst providing an effective vehicle for the underlying agenda of the work: to bolster the cult of the saint to whom his patron was so especially devoted.

A survey of the added miracles and their placement in relation to each other suggests that Wace's poem was carefully planned to establish the relevance of his material for as wide a section of the readership or audience of his poem as possible. By the end of the 'biographical' part of the work dealing with events which took place during the saint's lifetime (Miracles 1–13), we have seen him protecting virgins and matrons, infants and children, innkeepers, sailors and noblemen. Each successive story appeals to a different group, but with a recurrence of themes creating an overarching network of correspondences between the constitutive parts of the work as a whole. Thus, women are at the heart of Miracles 2, 4 and 13, but each reflects a different facet of the saint: his compassion and generosity, in the case of the girls who were about to be forced into prostitution; his protective powers, in the case of the child forgotten by his mother in a bath of boiling water; and his power as a healer, in the case of the woman cured on his deathbed. Children frequently benefit from the saint's protection (Miracles 4, 6, 7, 17, 18 and 20), but in narratives directed at parents from different target groups. This is true even of the three young students murdered for their money by the innkeeper (no. 7) and resurrected by the saint: as they are clerics, the parental figure here is none other than the Church.

The issues raised in the 'biographical' section of the poem recur in the posthumous section (Miracles 14–21), where the miracles added by Wace to the Mombritius and Falconius collections seem to have been chosen to mirror specific themes present in the 'lifetime' anecdotes. In the second, 'posthumous' section, accidental death, murder, illness, poverty and the devil echo the preceding narratives, but with a new focus. Framed by two miracles (14 and 21) taking place at the saint's grave, and therefore suggesting to the reader or

---

[22] In the *Legenda Aurea* (completed before 1264), the child is not left alone at home, but is enticed away from the banquet at the house by the demonic beggar, who strangles him at a crossroads. The child is brought back to life during his father's lament to Nicholas, without any miraculous apparition of the saint, or any attempt on the father's part to protect his guests from the bad news.

audience the possibility of pilgrimage, we find five tales of resurrection and/or conversion (nos 15, 16, 17, 19, 20); of these five, four (nos 16, 17, 19, 20) have been borrowed from sources other than the Mombritius or Falconius versions of the saint's life.[23] The social background of the key characters is widened further, with the inclusion of a merchant, a beleaguered archbishop, a Jew and a pagan customs officer. The supernatural element becomes more extravagantly prominent, the narration becomes more lively, and clerics and churches are repeatedly shown to profit from the piety of Nicholas's followers. There is thus a discernible movement in the poem, from a first part characterised by the simplicity of its narrative and the distance between narrator and audience, leading to a second part reinforcing certain key aspects of the first and culminating in the unusually elaborate Miracle 20, and a conclusion characterised by *sermo humilis*, like the beginning of the work, but on an inclusive, homiletic note.

Wace exploits to the full the formulaic nature of the narratives in his compendium, using the device of *repetitio cum variatio* already present in his sources to create a sense of unity between the different parts of his work. The new element in the second part – the healing oil oozing from Nicholas's sarcophagus and the refusal of the saint to allow part or all of his body to be moved – is in turn echoed in the very short final section. The presence of the holy oil is indirectly 'explained' by Miracle 22: the oil from the saint's lamp had healing properties in his lifetime already, sanctified by Nicholas's nocturnal prayers. The oil thus becomes a metaphor for the saint's asceticism and prayerfulness, a fund of good deeds and virtues that continues to flow, literally, after his death. The final miracle, where Nicholas drives out an evil spirit from a possessed man, echoes Miracle 6, and picks up the theme of demonic assaults on mankind present in Miracles 10 and 20; but it also introduces a strong visual image, that of the saint making the sign of the cross over a supplicant. On a theological level, this gesture places all the miracles within a firmly Christian context; on a more immediate level, the last glimpse of the saint afforded to the audience is that of a living bishop giving his blessing. This is an extremely shrewd move on Wace's part. The neat bipartite structure of his sources is broken, but from a didactic point of view, the work now concludes on an image of life as opposed to a somewhat earthbound emphasis on the saint's corpse, and in an attitude mirroring statues or pictorial representations of the saint.[24] Wace ensured that whatever happened to the various accounts of Nicholas's miracles in the body of the work in the course of manuscript tradition, the final image would be a familiar and reassuring one. On a more worldly level, the closing image of the bishop Nicholas blessing his people was well designed to enhance episcopal prestige in general, and could give a clue as to the upper echelons of Wace's intended audience.

---

[23] Miracles 16 and 17, which appear in the *Legenda Aurea*, are attested in a number of Latin manuscripts, added to the Mombritius version of the legend as early as the eleventh (and possibly even the tenth) century; see Ronsjö, *La Vie de saint Nicolas*, p. 36. Miracle 19, a variation on the miracle of the three students (no. 7) is also found in Latin collections of saints' lives, the earliest extant manuscripts of which date back to the twelfth century (see Ronsjö, pp. 39–42). Miracle no. 20 appears to have been derived from an oral source; no manuscripts predating Wace's *floruit* have come down to us (Ronsjö, pp. 44–5).

[24] On the iconographic representation of the saint, see Meisen, *Nikolauskult und Nikolausbrauch im Abendlande*.

Perhaps as a result of this careful planning, the manuscript tradition of the *Vie de saint Nicolas* was not as unstable as it might have been. The Paris, Bibliothèque nationale and Arsenal manuscripts preserve all the miracles, in the same order. Miracle 21 (the healing oil dripping from Nicholas's tomb and the foiled attempt to smuggle away one of his teeth) is omitted from the Cambridge and Digby manuscripts, and the Digby manuscript places the miracle of the three counts (no. 11) earlier in the collection, before Miracle 6: but otherwise, all the extant redactions of Wace's poem have preserved both the content and the sequence of the stories, variation being confined on the whole to isolated lines rather than entire sections.[25] The omission of Miracle 21 from both the Cambridge and Digby manuscripts is invoked by Ronsjö as evidence that the two manuscripts are related, sharing an 'ancestor' once removed from Digby, and twice removed from Cambridge. If such is indeed the case, it implies that the (apparently) most popular redaction circulating in non-clerical English circles in the thirteenth century had excised the only miracle explicitly stressing the unique position of Bari as sole shrine possessing bodily relics of Nicolas, and therefore implicitly encouraging the reader or listener to consider a pilgrimage there.[26] The absence of Miracle 21 gives more weight to miracles brought about by the mere invocation of the saint's name, on one's home ground. The modified sequence of miracles in MS Digby further suggests that for its copyist, Nicholas's ability to protect against abuses of power by lay authorities was of special interest: a possible indication of a widespread feeling of insecurity at a time of infighting within the royal family. It also has as consequence the placing to the forefront of the theme of Nicholas's power of bilocation (albeit through the medium of a vision), which also appears in Miracle 8; this move is entirely consistent with the omission of Miracle 21, as it characterises Nicholas as unconstrained geographically and physically even during his lifetime. His relics, though venerable, are clearly neither the only nor the best way of securing the saint's protection.

However, these two Anglo-Norman manuscripts, placed by Ronsjö farthest in transmission from Wace's original and copied (in the case of the Cambridge MS at least) by scribes with a dubious command of French,[27] cannot be said to be typical. Five surviving manuscripts, none of which are directly related to each other, implies at least double the number of prior copies now lost; all of these copies could easily have undergone the sort of reshaping observed in MS Digby, yet the manuscript tradition is remarkably stable. Wace's overall plan must have struck most of the scribes copying his poem as logical and satisfying, or at least, as not requiring too many 'improvements'. This in turn invites us to return to the

---

[25] As the final folios of MS Douce are missing, any positive statement as to its possible reading at the end of the poem can only be conjectural. However, it is clear that any modifications to the text would not have affected the sequence of the miracles. The longer lacunae in the extant manuscripts tend to affect amplificatory passages in direct speech, as in the lament of the father of the strangled child (Miracle 20; abridged in MS Douce) and the exchange between the devil and the child he is about to strangle (Miracle 20; omitted from the Cambridge manuscript).

[26] One may note that Bari's claim to exclusivity was not universally accepted: one French shrine thus claimed to have one of the saint's teeth (see M. Chibnall, *The World of Orderic Vitalis*, p. 106).

[27] Ronsjö (p. 52) goes as far as to say that the Cambridge MS text is disfigured by the 'scribe anglais'.

poem's content, in order to identify the principles underlying Wace's compendium of miracles.

Adapting the sources

The different miracles in the *Vie de saint Nicolas* vary considerably in length, both within and between the three sections of the poem. The fourteen 'lifetime' miracles are on average 45 lines long, the shortest being only eight lines in length (no. 6) and the longest totalling 156 lines (no. 11) and 108 lines (no. 10). By comparison, the average length of posthumous miracles is of 77 lines, with extremes of 15 lines (no. 18) and 220 lines (no. 20); two further sections exceed one hundred lines (no. 17, with 128 lines, and 21, with 108 lines). On the basis of these figures, it would appear that Nicholas's posthumous record was of greater interest than his achievements when alive, and that certain miracles bear more weight than others. One must of course bear in mind the fact that these variations in length may have been determined, at least in part, by the Latin sources used by Wace. It is noteworthy that the shorter miracles are typically based on the Falconius version, which can be very concise: thus Miracles 6 (8 lines), 14 (18 lines), 22 (34 lines) and 23 (27 lines).

Wace's handling of his sources in his *Nicolas* is characterised by abbreviation. This is achieved mainly by the omission of didactic or moralising comments by the Latin narrator, which are systematically excised, and a more selective use of direct speech, which typically occurs in the mouth of central characters only and then only briefly. The octosyllabic couplet is handled in a comparable way to the *Conception Nostre Dame*, though in a more restrained manner; the features noted in that poem in connection with the heightened 'homiletic' or narrative style – enjambement, the blurring of the boundaries of the couplet as a sense-unit – may also be found in the *Nicolas*.[28] Lengthy prayers or laments in the Latin sources are frequently left aside completely; even the mini-sermons delivered by Nicholas to recipients of miracles are reduced to their most minimal expression, thus limiting the need for rhetorical high style. Within these parameters the French episodes remain quite close to their Latin source, though Wace feels free to move details around, and it is not quite as easy to find long stretches of narrative that can be read alongside the Latin almost word-for-word, as is the case in the *Roman de Brut*. The most faithful episode in that respect is probably Miracle 9,[29] recounting Nicholas's miraculous multiplication of wheat during a famine. The opening address is Wace's own, and the concluding Latin commentary is omitted, but otherwise the correspondence is remarkable, including the passages in direct speech. This, however, is not representative of the poem as a whole.

A good example of the way Wace adapts his sources is Miracle 2, the

---

[28] See Ronsjö's very full analysis of these features, pp. 66–71. For a discussion of the use of repetition, synonyms and various rhetorical effects, see Ronsjö, pp. 22–5.

[29] The last miracle of the poem (no. 23, the curing of the paralytic man) is also a very close translation of the Latin, but the passage in direct speech put in the mouth of the sick man's friends is turned into reported speech by Wace.

well-known story of the saint throwing money at night through the window of an impoverished man who had determined to force his daughters into prostitution. This episode, covering just 40 octosyllabic lines in the French, is almost 100 lines long in his Latin source (and these are prose lines, in relatively small print).[30] Wace omits not only the didactic and pious asides of the narrator (amounting to some 55 Latin lines), but compresses into just fourteen lines a whole section of the account (some 40 lines long in the Latin, not counting the narrator's asides and interjections), depicting the father's reaction after each gift, his resolution to find out who his benefactor is, his vigil on the last night, his racing after Nicholas and his gratefulness (97–110):

> Treiz nuiz a lur ostel alat,
> Treiz riches dons d'or lur donat.
> Le primerain lur ad doné
> Pur relever de poverté,
> Le second lur ad fait trover
> Pur les treis filles marier,
> La terce feiz lur ad doné
> El non de Seinte Trinité.
> Par la fenestre lur getout
> Devant le lit, puis s'en alout.
> A la terce nuit cil le prist
> Qui l'out guaité si lui enquist
> Qu'il ert, dont fu, com aveit non
> Qui doné aveit si grant don.[31]

The father has disappeared from the narrative as a real character. The way in which Nicholas heard of the quandary of the man remains unmentioned (the Latin specifies that his decision to prostitute his daughters, who were unable to find husbands because of his poverty, was the gossip of the town), and none of the direct speech in the Latin is retained.

On the other hand, the four lines of direct speech in the French, put in the mouth of Nicholas: 'Jo sui Nicholas./ Va t'en, ja mar en parleras!/ Mes loë Deu ton creatur,/ E tes filles done a seignur', 'I am Nicholas. Go away, and on no account speak of it! But praise God your creator and give your daughters to husbands' (111–14) are Wace's own stylistic addition, based on an imaginative understanding of the situation and the terse statement that 'interdixit homini ut nullo modo panderet nomen eius', 'he forbade the man to mention his name in any way' (Mombritius, p. 299, lines 20–1). This is not the only example in this miracle of Wace's freedom in adapting his sources. The mention in the passage quoted in the paragraph above that each of the three gifts had a different aim, and

---

[30] Each line contains between 10 and 12 words. There are no major differences in the accounts of the Mombritius and Falconius versions for this episode.

[31] 'He went three nights running to their house, and gave them three rich gifts of gold. He gave them the first one to raise them out of poverty; the second one, to enable the girls to marry; and he gave the third time in the name of the Holy Trinity. He threw it to them through the window in front of the bed, then went away. The third night, the man who has been watching out for him caught him and asked him who he was, where he was from, what his name was, who had given so generously.'

that the third gift was actually an act of piety towards the Holy Trinity, is not to be found in the Latin, where the impression given is that this triplication is to be connected with the fact that the man has three daughters, and therefore three dowries to find. Indeed, we are told in the Latin text that he marries off his eldest daughter with the first sum of money; Wace's gloss that the first gift was to ward off poverty does not truly fit with this account. It does however impact on the way we perceive Nicholas himself; his procedure is shown to be considered, pregnant in symbolism, and shaped by his personal faith. More significantly still, Nicholas's motivations are somewhat different in the French poem, where he acts out of pure 'pitez', pity (95), whereas the Latin ascribes his generosity in equal measure to a hatred of sin and defilement: 'virginum execrans stuprum, decreuit omnino ex suis abundantiis earum supplere inopiam: ne puellae nobilibus ortae natalibus lupanari maculentur infamia', 'hating the defilement of virgins, he decided to remedy the girls' hardship with his own abundant fortune: so that girls of noble birth should not be sullied by the infamy of the brothel' (Mombritius, p. 298, lines 1–3). The resulting image of Nicholas is both more saintly (his charity becomes a sort of prayer) and more human, because of the total absence of moralising in the French account, on the part of the narrator as on the part of the saint.

The amount of direct speech within an episode varies as widely as its length. To a limited extent, Wace's use of this stylistic feature appears to have been influenced by the source used: the Falconius-based sections (Miracles 6, 13, 14, 22 and 23) thus have no direct speech at all, with the sole exception of one line in Miracle 13 – the saint's dying words. Ten of the twenty-three miracles in Wace's work (nos 1, 4, 5, 6, 7, 12, 14, 16, 22 and 23) feature no direct speech at all; in four miracles, direct speech accounts for less than ten percent of the total length of the anecdote (nos 13, 17, 19, 21); in five miracles, it accounts for between 10 and 20% of the narrative (nos 2, 3, 8, 10, 15); whilst in the four remaining miracles, direct speech takes up between 20 and 41% of the accounts, with 40% for Miracle 9, 31% for Miracle 11, just over 20% for Miracle 18, and just over 41% for Miracle 20.

As might be expected, there is a clear correlation between the length of an episode and the proportion of direct speech it contains. The two longest 'lifetime' miracles (10 and 11) thus contain 18 and 31% of direct speech respectively, and the longest account in the collection (Miracle 20) is also the one that contains the highest proportion of direct speech. However, this correlation is not perfect: Miracle 9, which is just over 60 lines long, has one of the highest ratios of direct speech in the work (40%); whilst Miracle 21 with its 108 lines only comprises seven to eight percent of direct speech. It is noticeable that episodes with a higher proportion of direct speech are always separated by one or more episodes where this feature is scarce, or even absent. This alternation of a streamlined form of narrative with more entertainingly told anecdotes would appear to be a strategy on Wace's part to avoid monotony, and the higher concentration of dialogue (and amplificatory devices in general) in the second section of the work might be an acknowledgment on his part that a mixed audience listening to a public reading of the work would need increasing encouragement as the poem progressed.

Whether an entertaining episode is more weighty in terms of content is another matter. It would be memorable, but not necessarily for the right reasons; the meaningful elements might be overshadowed by rhetoric in a way that would not occur in less elaborate narratives. A more reliable pointer to the possible importance of an episode within the general scheme of the work is the extent to which Wace modified the account of his source. Of the sixteen sections based on the versions of Mombritius and/or Falconius, two stand out for the extent of the reworking of their source-text: Miracles 11 and 18, which also happen to be among the longest of the collection. Both also include a higher than average proportion of direct speech.

Miracle 11 was one of the most popular miracles attributed to the saint in the Middle Ages; it is the story of three counts saved from an unjust death by the miraculous intervention of Nicholas. In the Latin, this miracle recounts two events, the first foreshadowing the second. The counts are sent by Constantine to suppress a rebellion. On their way, they land in Lycia, where they witness how Nicholas's intervention saves three young soldiers unjustly condemned to death by a corrupt judge, the consul Eustachius. With a great sense of suspense, we hear the saint being told to hurry, as the young men move from the prison to the place of execution; as the condemned already have their heads covered and the executioner is poised to strike, we see Nicholas running to intervene, making the sword fly out of the executioner's hand and acting as pledge for the accused. Nicholas confronts the venal consul and all ends well. The counts then continue their voyage, calm the insurrection and return to Constantinople where the Emperor gives them a triumphal welcome.

This initial part, which covers close to a third of the miracle in the Latin, is completely omitted by Wace, who reduces it to its simplest expression: three counts were sent 'ultre mer' by the Emperor, who was close to losing that overseas territory; they fulfilled their mission, and were received 'od grant honur' on their return (447–54). As a result of this omission, the parallels between the situation of the three young soldiers saved by Nicholas and the misfortune that befalls the counts are all but obliterated in the French poem. Emperor Constantine's corrupt provost Eparc condemns the counts to death on a trumped-up charge of treason; in their prison awaiting execution, one of the counts, Nepotianus, remembers Nicholas's saving of the three young men, and they appeal to the saint to help them too. Nicholas then appears in a vision to Eparc and Constantine, in their sleep, threatening them of dire retribution if they do not release the counts and restore justice. That morning, Constantine calls a meeting; the counts, initially accused of having tried to intimidate him with witchcraft, are cleared of all charges; and the Emperor sends them with many precious gifts to Nicholas, whom they thank with great devotion.

Wace follows the story-line of this second part of the miracle quite closely, but with a number of differences in points of detail. There is no suggestion that the provost actually accepted bribes to destroy the counts, as is the case in the Latin – the motivation, apparently, is just envy. Moreover, whilst the Latin goes some way towards exonerating Constantine of the full responsibility of this act of injustice, depicting him as too busy with State concerns ('in summis rei publica praeoccupatus negociis', p. 303, lines 49–50), and therefore an easy prey to the manipulative tactics of his provost, Wace unambiguously states that he 'fist prendre ces treis baronz', 'had these three lords arrested' (456). The lengthy

La Vie de saint Nicolas 69

speeches made by Eparc to the Emperor to convince him are omitted, and only the end result is considered: the counts are in prison, to be hanged in the morning, without the possibility of being ransomed.[32]

As the preliminary narrative has been omitted from the French poem, it was necessary to provide some explanation as to why the counts thought of appealing to Nicholas. Wace specifies a personal connection, 'Il l'aveient servi jadis,/ En ses preeres s'erent mis', 'They had once served him and had asked to be in his prayers' (469–70), and briefly mentions (as does the Latin at this point) his freeing of the young men (475–8):

> Veü li urent delivrer
> E tut fere quites clamer
> Treis bachelers a mort dampnez
> E ja a descoler menez.[33]

The similarity of their own plight with those of the young soldiers is reduced to its most basic element: they are about to be executed for a crime they did not commit. The culture of dishonesty revealed by the Latin text – judges can be bought at the imperial court as well as in the provinces – disappears, thus underplaying the sheer personal courage of the living Nicholas when confronting the corruption of the secular authorities. Instead, we have a rather safer situation for the saint, where he merely appears in a vision and threatens Constantine and Eparc with what they fear most: defeat and death in a decisive battle for the one, wholesale ruin and death for the other.[34] And while Constantine's gifts could be construed in the French as being made out of a spirit of repentance (in the absence of any comment on the part of the narrator, or the character himself), in the Latin the gifts are tainted with a touch of imperial displeasure, as the message accompanying them indicates: 'Eique dicite . . . non minari sed orare studeat, atque pro pace regni nostri magis totius orbis dominum poscat', 'tell him . . . to be intent on praying, not threatening, and for him to entreat the Lord of the whole world for peace for our realm' (p. 305, lines 34–6). The element of rebuke is clear.

The undercurrent of political criticism in the Latin texts, and Nicholas's less than harmonious relationship with the great and not-so-good of his world, is in effect obliterated by Wace; all that remains is Nicholas the wonder-worker. Even Nicholas the teacher, who briefly appears at the end of the Latin episode, where we are told that the counts stayed on with Nicholas for a time to be instructed in the faith by him, is reduced to the concise (and somewhat trite) 'Deu en loëz', 'Praise God for it' (600), which closes Miracle 11. The focus on the saint as worker of wonders is given particular prominence by the fact that all the passages in direct speech in the French (i.e., the visions of Constantine and Eparc, and the dialogue between Constantine and Nepocion in the tribunal) emphasise this

---

[32] This detail of the ransom is Wace's own (466).
[33] 'They had seen him free and have proclaimed innocent three young men condemned to death who were already being taken away to be beheaded.'
[34] Even in this passage, Nicholas's threats are watered down by Wace, who omits in the speech to Eparch the point that his body will be riddled with worms (Mombritius, p. 304, lines 54–5).

aspect. The achievements of Nicholas as a living person are summarily dismissed in a few lines (577–82):

> "Nicholas, dist il, conuissom,
> Mult est de grant religion."
> Si escontat qui il esteit
> E en quel liu veü l'aveit.
> Pui lur ad dit de ses bontez
> E de ses granz vertuz asez.[35]

The most striking elements in Wace's account of this miracle boil down to the defence of the innocent and Nicholas's power of bilocation (albeit in what might nowadays be called his astral body) during his lifetime – a feature also found in Miracles 8 and 10.

Nicholas's ability to appear on earth, even in a physical form, is a recurrent theme in the posthumous miracles, and is also at the core of Miracle 18, that of the abducted child, the second highly reworked episode based on a Mombritius/Falconius text. In this episode as in that of the three counts, we have in fact two miracles: first, the birth of a son to Getro and Euphrosine after years of childlessness, following their having secured a relic of St Nicholas (a piece of his clothing) and built a church dedicated to him; then the recovery of the child after his abduction by Saracen pirates. The circumstances leading to these two miracles are extensively rewritten by Wace. Initially, in the French poem, Getro is unaware of the fact that Nicholas was dying when, with his wife's consent, he sets off to visit the saint to ask him to pray for the birth of a child. It is only when he arrives in the town in mourning that he realises he has arrived too late, and therefore begs the clerics for a relic from the saint, which he duly obtains. By contrast, the Latin account opens with the saint's death and the preparations for his funeral, and only then introduces Gethro, who explains that he had come for Nicholas's blessing, but now begs for a piece of his clothing to honour. His desire for a child is mentioned only after he has obtained the relic, in a prayer addressed to the saint. The crisis leading to the loss of his young son, by contrast, is simplified in the extreme; in the Latin, instead of just the child being abducted by pirates, it is the entire congregation of worshippers at St Nicholas's feast who are captured, including the child's parents. The parents are released, but not the child. They search for him in vain; finally, the distraught Euphrosine adopts a strict ascetic lifestyle of fasting and prayer.

Euphrosine is a central character in the Latin text. It is she who suggests the building of a church to house the relic; she actively searches for the child with her husband; she prays at great length (her lament and prayers to Nicholas cover some 23 lines, in direct speech), and when the child is restored to his parents, it is Euphrosine's overwhelming joy that is depicted, kissing and clasping her lost son, and uttering the prayer of thanksgiving that closes the episode. Getro remains unmentioned in the reunion scene and the narrator himself states that Nicholas

---

[35] ' "We know Nicholas, he said, he is a very saintly man." And he said who he was, and where they had met him. Then he told them about his virtues and his very great powers.'

'reddidit illum matri suae', 'returned him [the child] to his mother' (309, 42). While Getro is clearly a beneficiary of this miracle, there is little doubt that the Latin redactor saw Nicholas's intervention primarily as a response to Euphrosine's motherly grief.

In Wace's text, however, Euphrosine all but disappears, reduced to passing mentions by the narrator or the character of Getro. She does not oppose her husband's wish to seek out Nicholas, at the beginning of the Miracle ('nel volt mie retenir', 947), and appears to be responsible for the safekeeping of the relics eventually preserved in the church she herself suggested to build;[36] but at no time do we hear her voice. Neither she nor her husband search for their missing child, and when he reappears, the insight offered into her state of mind is decidedly understated (1081–2):

> Eüfrosine en fu mult lee
> Que devant ceo iert corucee.[37]

The marginalisation of the character of Euphrosine is accompanied in Wace's adaptation of the story by a corresponding emphasis on the male characters: Getro, his son Dieudonné, the heathen emperor, St Nicholas – who is a silent but continuous presence in the narrative – and the clerics who celebrate his feast.

The clerics are especially noteworthy, in that they are mentioned three times: first, in relation to the endowment of the new church and the financial support given by Gethro and his wife for the feast of the saint to be observed with due ceremony (1007–10):

> Al miels que il unques poeient
> Feste seint Nicholas feseient
> Des clercs richement conreer,
> De fere lire e de chanter.[38]

The second mention is put in the mouth of the boy. Realising it is the anniversary of his abduction (which corresponds also to his birthday and to the feast of St Nicholas), Dieudonné lets out a heartfelt sigh that is noticed by the pagan emperor who has bought him as a slave. Asked the reason for his sadness, the child answers that it is because he remembers his family, who on this day always observed St Nicholas's feast (1039–44):

> Grant feste solt fere mis pere
> A icest jur ovec ma mere.
> Mult unt hui faite grant asemblee
> Des clercs de tote la contree

---

[36] 'Si ma femme aver les poeit/ Mult richement les gardereit', 'If my wife could have them, she would keep them very richly', Getro says to the clerics when begging for some relics (983–4). This suggests that Euphrosine's devotion to Nicholas might be greater than Wace's text otherwise indicates – unless it simply points to the division of responsibilities within the household.
[37] 'Euphrosine was very joyful, who before that had been very unhappy.'
[38] 'They observed the feast of saint Nicholas as best they could, richly equipping clerics so that they could read and sing the office.'

> Que il font chanter halt et bas
> Bien e bel pur seint Nicholas.[39]

The third mention closes the episode (1087–92):

> Chescon an puis tant qu'il vesquirent
> La feste seint Nicholas firent.
> Devant cels ne trovum nus pas
> Qui si servist seint Nicholaz
> De faire feste et d'onurer,
> De clers faire lire et chanter.[40]

If this is a hint, it is a particularly sustained one, and one that is further emphasised by the echo connecting the first two of these passages, almost verbatim, in two rhetorically marked lines (1013–14 and 1030–4):

> Mes puis en urent grant dolur,
> Grant marrement et grant tristur.[41]

> "Sire, dit il, feire le dei
> Quant me remember de ma gent,
> Qui unt pur mei grant marrement,
> E grant dolur et grant ennui,
> Car il ne sevent u jo sui."[42]

The threefold repetition of the adjective 'grant' followed by a substantive belonging to the semantic field of suffering is all the more noteworthy for the fact that, as we have seen, Wace is typically sparing with rhetorical effects in his *Vie de saint Nicolas*. The importance of this Miracle in the general pattern of significance of the poem as a whole is also indicated by Wace's adding details to his source, where he usually prunes them off. Thus, where the child only sighs in the Latin, he also cries in Wace; and where the emperor, in the Latin, gives an answer amounting to 'Well, you're here now, and there's nothing anyone can do about it', Wace has him strike the boy and forbid him ever to show such grief again. We are dealing here with a conscious effort to make the account lively and memorable.

The detail of the miracle itself is so different in the French work, as compared to the Latin text preserved by Mombritius, that it becomes a distinct version in its own right.[43] In the Latin, the boy prepares to mix his lord's drink when Nicholas seizes him by the hair ('per verticem capilli capitis sui', 309, line 42), and drops

---

[39] 'On this day, my father is in the habit of holding a great celebration with my mother. Today, they have gathered a great assembly of clerics from the whole area, whom they have commissioned to sing high and low and in a good and beautiful manner for saint Nicholas.'

[40] 'Every year thereafter for as long as they lived they observed the feast of Saint Nicholas. We cannot find anyone who more than these people served Saint Nicholas so well in celebrating and honouring him, and in getting clerics to read and sing.'

[41] 'But afterwards they [i.e. Getro and his wife] experienced great pain, great grief and great sadness on his [i.e., Dieudonné's] account.'

[42] 'Lord, he said, I must needs be sad when I remember my folk, who on my account have great grief, great pain and great distress, because they do not know where I am.'

[43] Indeed, the possibility still remains that Wace was using a source now lost for this miracle. However, this would not appear to have been the case; see Ronsjö, p. 32.

him outside the church where everyone is partaking of a feast in honour of Nicholas. Asked who he is, the child gives his name; and Euphrosine, crying for joy, rushes to embrace him. Wace omits the detail of the grasping by the hair, only stating that Nicholas took the boy to Escorande (1054). He also replaces the reunion scene by a totally different one. Gone is the festive meal outside the church doors; there is no crowd to greet Dieudonné. The boy is deposited inside the church (the closed doors of which, we are told, were not opened for him to get in), where his father is praying in solitude (1055–64). When he rises from his devotions, he notices the child standing next to him, somewhat disorientated as he thought he was still in the palace overseas. It takes the father some time to recognise his son, but when he does he is overjoyed and embraces him (1065–73). He takes the boy home where Euphrosine also rejoices in his return. Dieudonné tells them his story, making his mother cry for joy, and all then celebrate the feast of Nicholas every year thereafter. In contrast to the Latin, there is no direct speech in the account of the miracle proper. The focus is very much on the church, where the father prays and the priests and clerics, paid by him, sing the praises of the saint. We have an idyllic illustration of the respective duties of the clergy and the laity being fulfilled, in accordance with the model outlined by Wace in his Preface.

It is not possible to subject the miracles from sources other than Mombritius/Falconius to a detailed scrutiny, as the textual transmission of Wace's additional sources is uncertain. The restoring to life of a dead person is a recurrent theme in these miracles, and they have a strong missionary or baptismal element to them.[44] Of these, the most striking – and least representative of the poem as a whole – is Miracle 20, that of the strangled child. If Ronsjö is correct, it underwent considerable reshaping under the pen of Wace,[45] and therefore warrants closer attention. This miracle stands out partly because it is a basically a story about the devil, as the introductory lines to the miracle make clear (1157–64):

> Un enemi avom mortel
> A tut le pople communel.
> Ceo est diable qui d'envie
> Est tut tens plein e de boisdie.
> Quant hom plus sert son creatur
> Tant vait diables plus entur
> Pur deceiver, pur enginner,
> Pur desturber, pur desveier.[46]

Wace's devil is a more frightening character than in the Latin source identified by Ronsjö; unlike in the Latin, where he has to entice the child to a crossroads before he can harm him, in the French poem the devil strangles the boy under his parents'

---

[44] Miracle 16 appears to have been included as a companion piece to Miracle 15, which also has a missionary theme: the conversion of heathendom is thus followed by an account of the conversion within Christendom.

[45] Ronsjö, pp. 44–5.

[46] 'We have an enemy common to all: that is, the devil, who is always filled with envy and deceit. The more anyone serves his Creator, the more the devil hangs round him to deceive, trick, bewilder and corrupt him.'

roof, after gaining access to him under the guise of a beggar asking for charity. The devil is also given the longest speech in the entire work (29 lines), describing in veiled terms his fall from heaven, thus demonstrating his mastery of words, and his total impudence. However, he soon disappears from the story, and the true import of the episode seems to be of an entirely different nature.

At the heart of this story, we find the model of Christian society outlined in Wace's Prologue to the *Vie*, with a quasi-contractual dimension to lay gifts to the church. The point is not so much that Nicholas resurrected the child, but that the parents put the comfort and enjoyment of the clerics invited to their house above their natural desire to mourn their murdered son (1317–20):

> ... Ja mar nul semblant feront
> Del doel que de lur enfant unt
> Pur les clers qui s'esmaiereient
> E lor manger en guerpireient.[47]

The untypically generous space granted to the laments of the child's father and mother suggests that the grief of the parents is in this case important for our understanding of what is happening. Their merit is specifically that they put the comfort of the clerics above their personal needs or emotions, even though their heart-rending words show that their grief is extreme. Moreover, after the miraculous return to life of the child by saint Nicholas (1363–6),

> Ben iert sa feste enceis gardee
> Puis fut treis tant mels celebree.
> Ben esteient li clers servi,
> Puis furent meus et plus cheri.[48]

It is because the couple were determined to respect their part of the contract that they were worthy of a miracle; and due love and respect of the clergy is the best way of showing one's devotion to the saint. Such is the clear message.

The two miracles involving murderous innkeepers also have as underlying theme the respective duties of the clergy and the laity. Miracle 7, occurring early in the poem, appears to be directed at a clerical audience, whom the stance adopted in the Prologue had seemed to exclude. The three murdered 'clercs' are students, therefore part of the clerical class (though not necessarily in holy orders), and the concluding lines are remarkably close to Wace's description of the duties of the cleric in his Prologue (223–6):

> Pur ceo qu'as clers fit cel honur
> Funt li clers la feste a son jur
> De ben lirë et ben chanter
> Et des miracles reciter.[49]

---

[47] 'They will not in any way show the grief they feel on account of their child, because it would have upset the clerics, who would have left their meal.'

[48] 'His feast was well observed before, but afterwards it was celebrated three times better. The clerics were well looked after, but afterwards they were cherished better and more.'

[49] 'Because he did this honour to clerics, clerics observe his feast day by reading well, and singing well, and reciting miracles.'

The twin miracle (19), where an innkeeper murders a merchant, allows Wace to present the other side of the social and spiritual bargain: both the murderer and his resurrected victim go to pray at the saint's shrine, bringing not only their prayers for forgiveness, but also the 'grant aveir' (1099), the money carried by the merchant in order to 'faire offrande' (1096) to the church.

By contrast, in Miracle 17, we have a man who breaks his side of the contract, hoping to get away with donating an inferior cup to the one originally promised to the saint. As a result he loses both his son and the better cup in the sea, is exposed as someone who breaks his word, and has to make a humiliating public confession of his fault before Nicholas takes pity on him and restores his son to him. There is very little direct speech in Miracle 17 (that is also a feature of the Latin text which underlies it),[50] but it features a number of rhetorical effects that place it alongside Miracle 20 in terms of narrative ornamentation. The narrator makes use of rhetorical questions ('Savez que saint Nicholas fist?', 'Que vus fereie jo long plait?'), and the distress of the parents when they think their son has drowned is described in a way that foreshadows the Wace of the *Roman de Brut* (851–62):

> Es vus par cele mer grant plur
> Grant marrement et grant dolur
> Grant dol firent tut, mes li pere
> Le feseit greingnur et la mere.
> Crient et plurent et guaimentent,
> Compleinent sei si se dementent.
> Rumpent cheveus, depescent draz,
> Mult reclaiment seint Nicholaz.
> Empres lur fiz en mer saillessent
> Si li notiners nes tenessent.
> Sovent les veïssez lever,
> Sovent chaïr, sovent pasmer.[51]

This description, though taking its starting point from the Latin, is very much Wace's own. Moreover, the scene where the inferior cup flies off the altar when the man tries to deposit it there is retained by Wace, who carefully preserves the gradation in the three attempts: first, the cup falls to their feet; the second time, it falls into the choir; and the third time it flies beyond the choir. This suggests that we are dealing with a miracle that the poet considered more important than Miracle 2, which also features a thrice-repeated action, but was not given the same degree of narrative amplification.

The relevance of Miracle 17 is best grasped when put in parallel with Miracle 4. In both cases, the accounts are redolent of baptismal symbolism. The story of the small child forgotten in a cauldron of water left bubbling on the fire, but unscathed through the virtue of Nicholas, is strongly evocative of the waters of

---

[50] See Ronsjö's edition of the Latin version of the miracle, pp. 211–12.
[51] 'You could have seen on that sea many tears, great sadness and great grief; all were in great distress, but above all the father and the mother. They cry and weep and lament, they bemoan themselves and are in a frenzy. They pull out their hair, tear up their clothes; they repeatedly appeal to St Nicholas. They would have jumped into the sea after their son if the sailors had not restrained them; you would have seen them often rising, often collapsing, often fainting.'

the font which give new life; whilst Miracle 17 also has a child immersed (and apparently lost) in waters, but who emerges 'sanz mal, sanz dolur et sanz mort', and whose double gesture of placing the cup on the altar and of kissing that altar, places the material gift within a spiritual and sacramental context. This aspect, though discretely introduced, may be of greater historical significance than meets the eye. The many stories where Nicholas resurrects the dead show that he was already perceived as a *figura Christi* in Wace's sources; and as patron saint of sailors, he had long been associated with the sea, and therefore water. What has happened here is that this dimension to the image of the saint is taken one step further. Wace is the first writer to give us definite evidence regarding the process that made Nicholas, in addition to the patron saint of a whole range of groups, a figure emblematic of baptism.

The twelfth century sees the appearance of sculpted depictions of the miracle of the cup on baptismal fonts: a photograph of one such font, in the church of Zedelghem near Bruges, in Belgium, is reproduced in Karl Meisen's *Nikolauskult und Nikolausbrauch im Abendlande* (p. 372). A black Tournai marble font comparable to that of Zedelghem is still to be found in Winchester cathedral, with miracles of St Nicholas sculpted on two of its sides (the other two sides depicting birds and foliage). The northern face of the font depicts the legend of the maidens saved from prostitution while the eastern face appears to combine the miracle of the murdered schoolchildren and the miracle of the cup (Fig. 1). The panels are designed to be read from right to left, starting with one of Nicholas's earliest good deeds and culminating on the far left of the eastern panel with the seated Nicholas in a pose of quiet authority. At the far right of the northern panel is Nicholas's church, in front of which the saint is shown giving purses of money to the father, who is kneeling down under the gaze of his three daughters. At the far left of the northern side, beside one of the daughters, a male figure stands holding a hawk, possibly the noble suitor of the daughter, or perhaps a symbol of the rank of the impoverished father. The contiguous eastern side continues the Nicholas theme with, on the far right, the boat carrying the cheating rich man, then his son lying on the seabed clutching the precious cup. Above the child, three figures appear to be raised by Nicholas, holding his crozier and with a gesture of blessing. The eastern side of the font is curious in that Nicholas is represented on it twice: facing the children and the boat; then seated, partly turned away from the scenes at the right, and looking at the now resurrected child (recognisable by the fact that he is still holding the cup of great price). Between the two figures of Nicholas, a male character holding an axe is about to chop off the heads of the three sleeping clercs, with another (female/satanic?) figure behind him. The story of the murderous innkeeper appears to have been inserted in the panel in a sort of pictorial parenthesis, to ensure that the point of the miracle of the precious cup was fully grasped: like the students, the child is brought back to life. But the primacy of the miracle of the cup is emphasised by the fact that it frames the other miracle: a very apt decision, as it combines the themes of resurrection, but also of baptism (the child dies in the waters but is then born to a new life) and the Eucharist (as symbolised by the cup).

This font was bought for Winchester cathedral by Henry of Blois, grandson of William the Conqueror, brother of King Stephen, Bishop of Winchester from

Fig. 1. The Winchester font. The miracle of St Nicholas and the Cup appears to the right. Copyright: Anthea Harris 2002.

1129 to 1171 and Abbot of Glastonbury from 1126 to 1171. It is highly probable that Bishop Henry of Blois was familiar with Wace's work, and it is likely that the scenes on the font were carved on his own instructions: it is not usual for two miracles to be merged in the manner just described. We cannot prove that the narrative(s) depicted on the Winchester font were based on Wace's *Vie de saint Nicolas*; but the baptismal Nicholas promoted by the iconographic programme of the font is recognisably the same as in Wace's poem. To this, one may add a trivial but possibly revealing link between Wace's *Vie de saint Nicolas* and Bishop Henry of Blois. The last image we have of Nicholas in the poem is that of a bishop giving his blessing: the seal of Henry of Blois depicts him in just that attitude.[52] Mere coincidence, probably, but a highly flattering one for Henry, who one assumes would have been favourably disposed towards a work that celebrated a major saint, was at the cutting edge of the intellectual and theological trends of the time, and was very entertainingly written.

We have no certainty as to the remit entrusted to Wace by Robert son of Tiout; but the *Vie de saint Nicolas* recognisably achieves two very different effects. First, as we have seen, the Christ-like dimension to the saint is enhanced, and his miracles are endowed with a marked sacramental dimension. This made the saint a suitable

---

[52] A photograph of the seal of Henry of Blois is reproduced (p. 69) in Yoshio Kusaba, 'Henry of Blois, Winchester, and the 12th-century Renaissance', pp. 69–80 in *Winchester Cathedral. Nine Hundred Years, 1093–1993*, ed. J. Crook (Chichester, 1993).

subject for depiction on baptismal fonts. At the same time, Nicholas is turned into a much more attractive character than in the Latin sources. His image is considerably softened as compared with the French work, to the extent of turning him into something of a cut-out figure: Wace's Nicholas is no longer the outspoken Nicholas of the Latin or Greek tradition, and there is no doubt that the saint loses much of his individuality in the process. The near-absence of moralising or didactic speeches put in Nicholas's mouth leads to an impression of humility, gentleness and forgiving on the part of the saint that verges on weakness. This process, first observed in Miracle 2, is a recurrent feature in Wace's poem. It is at its most obvious in the very short transitional narratives (Miracles 5 and 12) describing the virtues of the saint. Both are savage abridgments of the Latin, which consists essentially of eulogies of the saint and his powers, introduced by the topos that a full or fitting account of them would be impossible.[53] The achievements of the saint are referred to in a more general and abstract manner by Wace; the miracles, good deeds, charity, humility, chastity, good counsel and asceticism mentioned in Miracle 8 are altogether less intimidating than in the Latin, which provides graphic illustrations of the way these qualities expressed themselves – for example the statement that he hated the company of women and avoided them 'quasi pestem', like the pest (p. 300, line 14). Not the best way of attracting female worshippers! The ailments cured by Nicholas are likewise unspecified by Wace in Miracle 12, where we simply read that 'A meinte gent dona santé/ Qui esteient en enferté', 'he gave health to many sick people' (607–8); this forestalls any attempt to turn Nicholas into a 'specialist' healer, like most other saints. However, Wace also adds two elements to the text of his source at this point: the fact that Nicholas 'plusurs delivra del diable', 'delivered many from the devil' (609), thus emphasising the spiritual dimension to the saint's powers; and his fatherly concern for all ('A tote la gent qu'il poeit/ Come bon pere socureit', 'He helped everyone he could, like a good father', 605–6). Nicholas comes over as approachable and understanding in a way that he does not in the Latin. Wace makes him an attractive character for a wider range of people, who would, if they followed the poet's instructions, enrich with their gifts the saint's shrines and the clerics attending to them. His message was disseminated far and wide, as we have seen; whoever Robert son of Tiout may have been, he had cause to be pleased.

---

[53] As we have seen, Wace preserves this aspect of his source, with some modifications.

Part I CONCLUSION

The three surviving religious poems by Wace show that he was a major poet well before he undertook the *Roman de Brut*, and a recognised scholar. It would be difficult to find three works more different from each other than the *Vie de sainte Marguerite*, the *Conception Nostre Dame* and the *Vie de saint Nicolas*: from a relatively simple, linear narrative to a tripartite exposition and commentary, and ending with an episodic compendium of miracles. However, as pointed out by Elizabeth Francis (p. xvii), all of Wace's poems have 'un intérêt d'actualité': the *Vie de sainte Marguerite* is composed at the beginning of a movement of dissemination of the cult of the saint; the *Conception Nostre Dame* was commissioned at the height of a theological dispute regarding the doctrine of the Immaculate Conception; while the *Vie de saint Nicolas* is written at a time where the cult of the saint was expanding eastwards from Normandy. In all three cases, Wace appears to have been the first writer to work on these subjects in the French language, and in all three cases, he introduces a new element to the traditional accounts. Margaret is confirmed as the protector of childbirth and women in labour; the Virgin is depicted not just as pure and good, but also free from the original sin from her conception; Nicholas receives a fresh attribute, that of the baptismal figure. Wace clearly had his finger on the intellectual and religious pulse of his time.

Even though the *Nicolas* appears to have been commissioned by a layman, it is likely that dissemination occurred through ecclesiastical channels; the patron for the *Conception* must certainly have been religious, and influential. The abbeys of Caen had close connections with England, at a time when Anglo-Norman interests spanned the Channel, and all three of Wace's religious poems have a connection with England; a very strong one in the case of the *Conception Nostre Dame*. In particular, a nexus of coincidences would seem to point to some link between Wace and Winchester, possibly in relation to the entourage of Bishop Henry of Blois.

The formal characteristics of the three poems would tend to confirm the accepted view that the *Vie de sainte Marguerite* was composed first, followed by the *Conception* and the *Nicolas*. The elegant simplicity of the *Marguerite* in itself does not suffice to place it among Wace's earlier works, but the relatively few surviving manuscripts preserving the poem suggests that less effort was put in its dissemination than was to be the case for his two other religious poems, which in turn could point to a poet who was still in the process of being recognised. The *Conception Nostre Dame* demanded a high style, the opposite of the streamlined *Marguerite*; Wace responded to this need by experimenting with the couplet. The *Vie de saint Nicolas*, in a lower register, reaps the benefit of this experience.

For all the differences between Wace's three religious poems, they all have a number of key characteristics in common:

1. Wace made use of more than one source, combining elements of each narrative according to his own discursive agenda.
2. A conscious effort is made to depict the central characters (Nicholas, the Virgin, Margaret) as less intimidating and more immediately attractive to the reader.
3. The didactic intent of the writer is perceptible through the omission of overtly scholarly details, and through narratorial explanations where these details cannot be omitted.
4. Rhetorical and stylistic adornment is used in a highly controlled manner.
5. Wace appropriates his source material to take responsibility for the overall structure of his works, as well as of their constituent episodes or sub-sections.

This points to a writer who had already elaborated a sophisticated translation/adaptation technique from the earliest of these poems. As we shall see, the fundamental principles of this technique remain constant throughout Wace's literary career.

At this stage, Wace was almost certainly composing his poems alongside his duties as 'clerc lisant'. This has implications for the way he worked. Unless he was released from his duties to research and compose a given poem (something that must have happened in the case of the delicate and complex *Conception*), he cannot have been a very fast worker. This also means that any lost works from this period are likely to have been short pieces, rather than substantial poems. The passage from relatively short religious works to long historical narratives, in the early 1150s, must therefore have been accompanied by a change in the poet's personal circumstances. Whether or not this was due to direct royal patronage, what is certain is that it allowed Wace the scope he needed to produce undisputed masterpieces.

Part II *Le Roman de Brut*

INTRODUCTION

In 1155, Wace (by then well into his forties or early fifties) completed what is generally considered among literary scholars to be his *chef d'oeuvre*: the long narrative poem now known under the title of *Roman de Brut*. Its main claim to fame for most is that it is the first vernacular piece of literature to treat of the character of Arthur, and the first work ever to mention the Round Table; as a result, the account of the reign of Arthur has all too frequently been studied in isolation from the surrounding narrative, thus distorting the way the work was perceived. Contrary to what is sometimes assumed by modern readers, this is not a romance in the current sense of the term: anyone looking here for lovelorn ladies and knights indulging in lengthy self-analysis will be disappointed. In his epilogue (14859), the poet himself refers to the work as 'la geste des Bretuns', indicating a historical narrative (or one perceived as such), focussing on the deeds of a specific nation or lineage.[1] The prevailing tone is more epic than courtly; to quote Hans-Erich Keller, 'Wace continue bien plus la tradition des chansons de geste ... qu'il n'est le précurseur de la littérature courtoise.'[2] The nature of the work is announced in the Prologue (1–8):

> Ki vult oïr e vult saveir
> De rei en rei e d'eir en eir
> Ki cil furent e dunt il vindrent
> Ki Engleterre primes tindrent,
> Quels reis i ad en ordre eü
> Ki anceis e ki puis i fu,
> Maistre Wace l'ad translaté
> Ki en conte la verité.[3]

---

[1] On the meaning and connotations of the term 'geste' in twelfth-century French vernacular historical writing, see Peter Damian-Grint, *The New Historians of the Twelfth Century Renaissance* (Woodbridge, 1999), pp. 258–60.

[2] 'Wace is far more in the tradition of the *chanson de geste* than he is a precursor of courtly literature': Keller, *Étude descriptive sur le vocabulaire de Wace* (Berlin, 1953), p. 14.

[3] 'Whoever wishes to hear and to know about the successive kings and their heirs who once upon a time were the rulers of England – who they were, whence they came, what was their sequence, who came earlier and who later – Master Wace has translated it and tells it truthfully.' Quotations of the *Roman de*

The reader or listener is approaching a work of history, based on a pattern of dynastic succession. No specific sources are acknowledged, but the implication is that they are scholarly and authoritative in nature; in particular, the stress on the correct chronological order of rulers evokes the clarity of annalistic accounts. These sources have been adapted ('translaté'),[4] with truthfulness and accuracy ('vérité')[5] as a guiding principle.

This procedure is no great departure from Wace's religious poems. Hagiography is no longer considered a sub-genre of historiography, but for a twelfth-century cleric, there would not have been any sense that a saint's life was less scholarly than a historical work, neither should one expect Wace to have approached his task in a markedly different manner from his *Conception Nostre Dame* or his *Vie de saint Nicolas*. Indeed, in many ways, the *Roman de Brut* was a simpler undertaking than either of these poems, as it is essentially based on two versions of the same work, as was the case with the *Vie de sainte Marguerite*. However, there is a difference in scale between the earlier poems and the *Brut*, whose 14866 lines dwarf the 750-odd lines of the *Marguerite*, the 1563 lines of the *Nicolas* or the 1810 lines of the *Conception*. Moreover, even though the *Roman de Brut*, being a translation from Latin into French, was technically a work of popularisation, it was addressed to a very different readership.

Wace's religious poems, by their very nature, were meant to reach a wide, mixed audience. The *Roman de Brut*, whilst also probably intended for public reading, was aimed at an aristocratic audience, and more specifically, the royal circle itself. Laȝamon, the Worcestershire priest who at the end of the twelfth century translated and adapted the *Roman de Brut* into English, claims in his prologue that Wace presented a copy of the work to Queen Eleanor (of Aquitaine).[6] That presentation copy, which one assumes Layamon worked from for his own *Brut*, is now lost, so his words remain uncorroborated; but there is no reason to doubt that Wace was aiming for the highest readership in the land.

In 1155, Henry II had only recently come to the English throne. After years of bitter infighting within the royal family, he had been recognised in 1153 as legitimate heir to the English throne by King Stephen, whom he succeeded in 1154 at the age of twenty-one. Henry had every reason to be content. Normandy was firmly in his hand, thanks to the efforts of his father, Geoffrey of Anjou, who had fought throughout the early 1140s to regain the duchy for his son and had put in place an efficient administration that allowed a smooth succession when he died in 1151. On English soil, the death in 1153 of Eustace, King Stephen's son and heir, meant that Henry had no credible rival for the crown. His marriage to

---

Brut are from Ivor Arnold's two-volume edition (Paris, 1938–40). Unless otherwise specified, all translations of the *Roman de Brut* are from Judith Weiss, *Wace's Roman de Brut: A History of the English. Text and Translation* (Exeter, 1999).

[4] On the meaning of 'translater' in French texts of this period, see Damian-Grint, *The New Historians*, pp. 16–32.

[5] This is of course a recurrent claim in medieval historiography. See Damian-Grint, *The New Historians*, pp. 114–17.

[6] See Laȝamon's *Brut*, ed. G. L. Brook and R. F. Leslie (London, 1963 and 1978), Prologue, lines 22–3: '& he heo ȝef þare æðelen Ælienor/ þe wes Henries quene þes heȝes kinges', 'and he [i.e., Wace] gave it [i.e., a presentation copy of the *Roman de Brut*] to the noble Eleanor who was the queen of Henry the high king.'

Eleanor of Aquitaine, shortly after his father's death in 1151, had made him one of the most powerful barons of France: duke of Aquitaine and Normandy, as well as count of Anjou and Maine. Moreover, the birth in August 1153 of a son, William, boded well for his own succession.[7] He was in command of huge resources, had received a thorough education (one of his teachers was the eminent William of Conches, from the school of Chartres), and was credited with mastery in many languages. Henry II was someone to be reckoned with and an eminently desirable patron.[8]

Wace's *Roman de Brut* gives the tone of the new court: elegant, learned and sophisticated. It is difficult to estimate how long it took Wace to write the poem, as we do not know what his circumstances were at the time; but if he was released from his duties as 'clerc lisant' in order to compose the work, he could have completed it within the period separating the treaty of Winchester (November 1153) and the date of 1155 mentioned in the concluding lines of the poem. If such was the case, the *Roman de Brut* is probably to be understood as a flattering gesture towards the young monarch, designed to enhance his prestige. The presentation of the work to Eleanor would then make sense: as matriarch of the new dynasty, she would have been perceived as holding an important position in the transmission of family memory to her children.[9] Moreover, a translation from the Latin into the French would have been a suitable gift to a lay woman, but not necessarily to a king with a reputation for learning. If we assume that the *Roman de Brut* was commissioned after the Treaty of Winchester specifically with the future Henry II in mind, the sponsor was clearly an experienced courtier intent on flattery, if not actually acting on behalf of Henry himself. A translation of Geoffrey of Monmouth's immensely popular *Historia Regum Britanniae* would have been ideal for propaganda purposes, lending Henry's future realm an aura of glamour and mystery. If one postulates a commission predating 1153, the motivation becomes more obscure. Could it have been meant as a gift to Eleanor? The *Historia Regum Britanniae* was after all the best-seller of its day. But if so, why does Wace fail to mention his patron? What is certain is that whoever it was must have been influential enough to have the poet released from his duties within the ducal administration.[10] At a time when work was limited to daylight hours, some release would have been essential for a poem on this scale; and this would have had to take place with the consent of Wace's employer. To this, one may add that

---

[7] For a detailed account of the events during this period, see H. W. C. Davis, *England under the Normans and the Angevins, 1066–1272* (London, 1905).

[8] On the life and policies of Henry II, see Richard Barber's recent *Henry Plantagenet* (Woodbridge, 2001). On the Plantagenet court and its patronage of the arts, see M. Aurell, 'La Cour Plantagenêt (1154–1204): entourage, savoir et civilité', pp. 9–46 in *La Cour Plantagenêt (1154–1204). Actes du colloque tenu à Thouars du 30 avril au 2 mai 1999*, ed. M. Aurell (Poitiers, 2000); also K. Broadhurst, 'Henry II of England and Eleanor of Aquitaine: Patrons of Literature in French', *Viator* 27 (1996): 53–8.

[9] See E. M. C. van Houts, *Memory and Gender in Medieval Europe, 900–1200* (London, 1999), who demonstrates that women were deeply involved in the process of remembering family history for the benefit of the younger generations.

[10] J.-G. Gouttebroze ('Pourquoi congédier un historiographe, Henry II Plantagenêt et Wace (1155–1174)', *Romania* 112 (1991): 289–311) considers (p. 292) that it is most likely that Wace worked for the Norman ducal administration, and the balance of evidence would seem to point in that direction. See above, 'Introduction: Wace: His Life and Times'.

the presentation of the work to Eleanor implies at the very least the poet's expectation of a favourable reception, and if one accepts Wace's claim in his later *Roman de Rou* that he was personally acquainted with both Henry I and Henry II, it is likely that such an expectation was founded on rather more than wishful thinking.

Whilst it was topical, the material that Wace undertook to translate, transpose and adapt for a French audience was not burningly political – from a Norman viewpoint, at least. There is some evidence that Geoffrey of Monmouth had a political agenda when writing his *Historia Regum Britanniae* (published 1135–8), though in the absence of a clear interpretative key, modern scholars vary in their reading of his work. It has been understood as a warning to the Anglo-Norman elite, by providing examples of strife within the old British royal families leading to disaster;[11] or, more recently, as being addressed to the Welsh, descendents of the Celtic rulers of Britain before the Anglo-Saxon takeover, to encourage them to present a united front against the steady Norman advance into Wales under Henry I.[12] But essentially, to Wace, it was the history of an alien people, taking place in a distant, quasi-mythical past. The distinguished pedigree given to this people by Geoffrey lent glamour to the land they once ruled and was now in Norman hands; but beyond the specific circumstances of possible Welsh rebellions, there was little direct relevance of the work to the power games at the court of the young Henry II. Wace could therefore feel free to translate his Latin source with only minor adaptations, confident that it would not blow up in his face; the only section potentially problematic in that respect – the Book of the Prophecies of Merlin – having been excluded as suitable material for his project, ostensibly on the grounds of interpretative difficulties.[13] The resulting poem appealed to a wide audience: the *Roman de Brut* is the apogee of Wace's literary career.

---

[11] See N. Wright, who in the introduction to his edition of Geoffrey of Monmouth's *Historia Regum Britanniae* (Cambridge, 1985) suggests that the work might be 'a powerful, if covert, plea for unity' (p. xv).

[12] See John Gillingham, 'The Context and Purposes of Geoffrey of Monmouth's *History of the Kings of Britain*', *Anglo-Norman Studies* 13 (1990): 99–118. By contrast, Valerie Flint ('The *Historia Regum Britanniae* of Geoffrey of Monmouth: Parody and its Purpose. A Suggestion', *Speculum* 54 (1979): 447–68) reads Geoffrey's work as an exaltation of non-monastic virtues and secular lifestyles.

[13] On the subject, see Jean Blacker, ' "Ne vuil sun livre translater"': Wace's Omission of Merlin's Prophecies from the *Roman de Brut*', pp. 49–59 in *Anglo-Norman Anniversary Essays*, ed. I. Short (London, 1993); also Paradisi, *Le Passioni della storia*, pp. 272–85.

4

Manuscripts, Sources and Adaptation Principles

The *Roman de Brut* was by far the most successful of Wace's works. Over thirty manuscripts have survived containing all or part of the poem, and further fragments continue to come to light; one was discovered as recently as 1999.[1] A full list of these manuscripts is provided by Judith Weiss in the introduction to her edition and translation of the work. Nineteen of the manuscript witnesses (eighteen of these being medieval) preserve a complete, or near-complete, text. Interest in the poem was especially great in England, as might be expected: nine of the nineteen complete or near-complete texts, and seven of the thirteen fragments known at this date, are in Anglo-Norman (A-N) manuscripts (or scraps thereof). However, it also follows from these figures that as far as we can tell, over half of the medieval manuscripts of the *Roman de Brut* were copied in Continental France (Cont.). The phenomenon was not exclusively an English one, by far. The oldest of the surviving manuscripts is Durham Cathedral Library, C iv 27, an Anglo-Norman copy dated to the end of the twelfth century; one of the extremely fragmentary fragments kept in Oxford (Bodleian, Rawl. D 913) was also originally part of a manuscript copied in the late twelfth century. Some fifteen of the extant manuscripts (eight of which are Anglo-Norman) were copied in the thirteenth century; nine of these are complete or near-complete.[2] Ten date from the late thirteenth/fourteenth century, six of them Anglo-Norman; five of the ten are complete or near-complete.[3] Three manuscripts date back to the fifteenth century,

---

[1] See Judith Weiss, 'Two Fragments from a Newly Discovered Manuscript of Wace's *Brut*', *Medium Aevum* 68 (1999): 268–77. At the latest count, we have 32 manuscripts or fragments of the *Roman de Brut*. For a full description of the manuscripts known before 1937 (in effect, all the complete or near-complete manuscripts), see Arnold, vol. 1, vii–xiv.

[2] These are: British Library, Cotton Vitellius A x (A-N); British Library, Add. 32125 (A-N); British Library, Add. 45103 (A-N); Lincoln Cathedral Library 104 (A-N); Corpus Christi College, Cambridge, 50 (A-N); Vatican Library, Otto. Lat. 1869 (A-N); Paris, Bibliothèque nationale, fonds fr. 1450 (Cont.); Paris, Bibliothèque nationale, fonds fr. 1416 (Cont.); Paris, Bibliothèque nationale, fonds fr. 794 ('Guiot' manuscript; Cont.); Montpellier, Bibliothèque Interuniv., Sect. Médecine 251 (Cont.; first 5664 lines only); National Library of the Netherlands, Royale 73 J 53 (Cont.; preserves 7348 lines of the poem); Cologny (Geneva), Bibliothèque Bodmer, 67 (A-N; lines 13642 to end); Zadar, Croatia, Archepisc. Dioc. (Cont., 13485–629 and 14287–443); Berkeley, Bancroft UCB 165 (Cont., 387–580 and 1769–954); Westminster Abbey Muniments Room, two fragments from the same A-N manuscript (from 9065 to 11534, with lacunae).

[3] These are: London, College of Arms, Arundel xiv (A-N); British Library, Harley 6508 (Cont.); British Library, Royal 13 A xxi (A-N; Wace text starts line 8729); Paris, Bibliothèque Sainte-Geneviève, 2447 (Cont.); Paris, Bibliothèque de l'Arsenal, 2981 (Cont.; much of the end missing from line 13944); Paris, Bibliothèque nationale, nouv. acq. Fr. 1415 (A-N); Paris, Bibliothèque nationale, fonds fr. 12603 (Cont.; lines 67–1950); Oxford, Bodleian Library, Rawl. D 913 (A-N; fragments); London, University Library, 574 (A-N; lines 6680–710 and 6782–812); Beinecke Library, Yale, 395, item 12 (A-N; 1–7141).

all copied on the French Continent, and all preserving a full text;[4] and finally, a copy was made in the eighteenth century of one of the fourteenth-century texts, Paris, Bibliothèque Sainte Geneviève 2447 (a Continental copy).

The scarcity of twelfth-century manuscripts is not really surprising, if only because Wace's work appears to have been used as a historical textbook by its earlier Anglo-Norman readers,[5] and such books have always suffered from wear and tear. The thirteenth century sees an explosion of interest and copying activity, on both sides of the Channel: the way in which the poem was received undergoes a clear change, with an increasingly marked interest in the narrative as a fund of stories (with an especial focus on King Arthur), particularly in Continental manuscripts. The attraction of the *Roman de Brut* then seems to wane somewhat in the fourteenth century, though it remains an important and well-copied work. Verse narrative, whether for literary or historical works, was now outmoded, and this had an impact on copying activity. Moreover, in England itself, the Matter of Britain had been appropriated by poets and historians writing in English, following in Laʒamon's footsteps: the Anglo-Normans were now anglicised.[6] By the fifteenth century, copying of the *Roman de Brut* was virtually confined to mainland France, and read as an authorising sub-text to the thriving genre of Arthurian romance.

An indication of the differing modes of reception of the *Roman de Brut* may be found in the contents of the manuscripts. The Anglo-Norman manuscripts tend to copy the poem alongside material of specifically English (and sometimes local) interest. The earliest surviving manuscript, the late-twelfth-century Durham, Cathedral Library, MS C. iv 27 (I), thus provides an overview of the history of the country, starting with Wace's *Roman de Brut*, continuing with Geffrei Gaimar's *Estoire des Engleis*, and ending with Jordan Fantosme's account of Henry II's wars in Scotland. All three works are in French verse and were clearly valued as historiography; Gaimar's work is an adaptation of various sources, foremost amongst which is the Anglo-Saxon Chronicle, whilst Jordan Fantosme's work is an eyewitness account. The manuscript tradition of Gaimar's *Estoire des Engleis* is closely bound with that of the *Roman de Brut*; all surviving copies of the work are preserved alongside Wace's poem, the others being in the thirteenth-century manuscripts Lincoln Cathedral Library, MS 104 (which also contains the only other preserved text of Fantosme), British Library, MS Add. 32125 and British Library, Royal MS 13 A XXI. These manuscripts thus provide us with a chronological sequence, with Wace's text presenting the British past of Britain, Gaimar the Anglo-Saxon past, and Fantosme the Anglo-Norman recent past and present.

The texts by Gaimar and Fantosme do not appear to have been studied with as much care by the reader(s) of the Durham manuscript as Wace's work, but it is clear that the *Roman de Brut* was being read as history, not fiction: one of the

---

[4] Paris, Bibliothèque nationale, fonds fr. 1454; Paris, Bibliothèque nationale, fonds fr. 12556. Both are Continental and identical copies.

[5] This is strongly suggested by the evidence of the oldest surviving manuscript, MS Durham Cathedral Library, C. iv 27. For a discussion of this manuscript, see F. Le Saux, pp. 29–47 in *Arthurian Studies in Honour of P. J. C. Field*, ed. Bonnie Wheeler (Cambridge, 2004).

[6] See W. R. J. Barron, ed., *The Arthur of the English: the Arthurian Legend in Medieval English Life and Literature* (Cardiff, 2001), esp. pp. 22–46 ('Dynastic Chronicles').

early owners of the manuscript painstakingly signalled every new reign in the text by a system of ink circles in the margin, in an attempt to count the total number of kings of Britain. In many cases, the roman numeral attached to a given circle is still legible; though the final count would have been inaccurate, as the manuscript has a few lacunae that have led to the 'loss' of some minor kings. That this historical interest was an enduring one is further indicated by the fact that where the original circles had grown too faint, a later reader has gone over them again in darker ink. Most of the surviving manuscripts lack such explicit evidence of a scholarly approach to the text, but the contents of the Anglo-Norman manuscripts suggest that the phenomenon lasted in England throughout the thirteenth century and beyond. British Library, MS Add. 45103 thus continues Wace's *Roman de Brut* with the statutes of King Edward I (1275–90) and the legend of Joseph of Arimathea: a combination that might not be entirely unconnected with the reburial in 1278 of the bones of Arthur and Guinevere by King Edward and his queen at Glastonbury Abbey (founded, according to legend, by Joseph of Arimathea himself). *L'Estorie de Joseph d'Arimathie* is also copied in British Library, MS Add. 32125, where it follows Wace and Gaimar.

By contrast, in Continental manuscripts, the *Roman de Brut* appears to have been valued more as an authorising narrative for the Arthurian romance. The celebrated 'Guiot' manuscript,[7] so named after the thirteenth-century scribe who copied it, thus sandwiches the *Roman de Brut* among a number of *romans antiques* such as the *Roman d'Eneas* and Benoît de Sainte Maure's *Roman de Troie*, and courtly romances by Chrétien de Troyes; the perceived affinity of Wace's work with the Matter of Antiquity as well as the Matter of Britain is further demonstrated by the copying of the *Roman d'Eneas* alongside the *Roman de Brut* in another thirteenth-century Continental manuscript, Paris, Bibliothèque Nationale Manuscrits français 1416. We therefore appear to have from an early stage a dual reception of Wace's work, one where it is read primarily to provide background for vernacular works of fiction (i.e., the French, Continental reception), and the other (in England) where it is read as independent history, with the political implications this entails.

That these two poles of interest met even for the earlier Anglo-Norman readers is revealed by the layout of the extant manuscripts.[8] Where today we would highlight the beginning of a new chapter, a new phase in a narrative or a point of special interest through typographical devices, medieval manuscript planners typically made use of capital letters, usually in coloured ink, sometimes in conjunction with more or less ornate *nota bene* symbols in the margin of the text. The distribution patterns of these capital letters give a snapshot of the way the text was read at a given time by a given reader (i.e., the manuscript planner). One may note that even in the Durham manuscript, the Arthurian section has an abnormally high density of coloured capitals as compared to the rest of the work, thus revealing an interest in the king exceeding his strictly historical dimension. Out of

---

[7] Paris, Bibliothèque nationale, fonds fr. 794.
[8] For an analysis of the distribution patterns of coloured capitals in thirteenth-century Anglo-Norman manuscripts of the work, see F. Le Saux, 'The Reception of the Matter of Britain in Thirteenth-Century England', forthcoming in *Thirteenth-Century England*, ed. Robin Frame (Woodbridge, 2005).

a total of 92 capital letters placed by the planner in Wace's text, 32 occur in the Arthurian section, predominantly highlighting amplificatory material.[9] The poem was clearly appreciated on two levels, both scholarly and as literature; and this undoubtedly accounted for its enduring success.

The testimony of the Durham manuscript shows that from an early stage in its textual transmission, the *Roman de Brut* was copied intensively, in individual sections which were then combined. The Wace section of the manuscript is clearly composite. At folio 26, though no change is apparent in the ink and layout, the hand is slightly less regular and neat, and coloured capitals become more common; the Prophecies of Merlin, translated by one Helias, are interpolated on folios 42–8, then folio 59 verso ends with a blank space of approximately 16 lines. Folio 60 recto, which continues the text where folio 59 verso had ended, and with the same layout, is in a hand both larger and less neat; the lineation is made with a wider stylus, the copyist used a thicker quill, and coloured capitals are more plentiful. The Durham manuscript is thus made up of quires copied by two scribes, and also apparently planned by different manuscript planners; while the section from folio 26 to folio 59 appears to reflect a similar copying from quires from distinct manuscripts within the 'master text'. Such a copying of quire by quire was not uncommon, especially for student texts where demand was great, turnover was swift and cost was an issue: it does however have as consequence that the textual tradition of the *Roman de Brut* is a complex one. It is virtually impossible to outline a neat 'family tree' (stemma) relating the different manuscripts to each other. Ivor Arnold's attempt to do so, in the introduction to his edition of the *Roman de Brut*, shows that manuscript groupings typically break down once or several times in the course of the poem, to recombine into fresh groupings.

Such a pattern suggests that from a relatively early stage in the work's textual history, there were at least two competing versions of the *Roman de Brut* being copied. There was no single master manuscript of which an influential patron had multiple copies made in order to disseminate the text, each copy serving as a master-copy to further scribes. It is possible that Wace himself 'published' his work in two or more sections in order to allow his patrons to observe the progress of the project. This could militate in favour of a text written under pressure of some sort of deadline, with frequent 'updates' required of the poet (as would have been the case if the *Roman de Brut* was commissioned to mark Henry's appointment as heir to the English throne). Some of the textual variants could well be Wace's own revisions on completion of his work, as we know happened with his later *Roman de Rou*. The practical consequence for the modern-day scholar, however, is that no in-depth study of the *Roman de Brut* can afford to ignore the critical apparatus of Ivor Arnold's reference edition of the text; and it is likely that

---

[9] Seventeen of these 32 capitals occur in relation to the build-up to war and its practice, such as battle arrangements, taunting, battle-speeches or single combat scenes (9977, 10113, 11503, 11741, 11881, 12041, 12083, 12263, 12305, 12397, 12655, 12743, 12813, 12967, 13953, 13143, 13167); a further five occur in the section describing the Roman embassy presenting Arthur with the Roman ultimatum and the discussions which ensue (10621, 10639, 10711, 10865, 11005). Four capitals highlight ceremonial and festivities (10147, 10303, 10385, 10437).

any future groundbreaking research on the poem will arise from the analysis of its textual transmission.

Sources

When Wace set out to write a 'geste des Bretuns', the obvious source was Geoffrey of Monmouth's *Historia Regum Britanniae* which had superseded virtually from the moment of its publication all prior histories of the British people (based on the *Historia Brittonum*, Gildas or on Bede). Geoffrey elaborates on these and other historical sources,[10] to create a full account of all the kings of Britain from the arrival of Brutus and his Trojan companions, to the glorious reign of Arthur and the eventual Celtic loss of dominion over the island. To give his history the required credibility, Geoffrey claims that he has merely translated a 'very old book' written in the British (i.e., Brythonic Celtic: Welsh, Breton or Cornish) language given to him by Walter Archdeacon of Oxford, and which contained information about a number of worthies whose absence in the histories had always surprised him: in particular, the great king Arthur. This very old book certainly did not exist, at least as Geoffrey describes it in his Dedication (i.e., 'attractively composed to form a consecutive and orderly narrative'[11]), but it fulfilled its rhetorical function. The *Historia Regum Britanniae* was widely accepted, and enjoyed a popularity that extended beyond clerical circles, partly because it gave 'serious' information regarding King Arthur, about whom tales were already being widely circulated by story-tellers. By the end of the twelfth century, the *Historia* had become an authority.[12]

The *Historia* is unconventional in a number of ways. Its tone is surprisingly secular; unusually for the history of a collective rather than an individual (typically one would expect it to be open-ended, as time does not stop), it has a clear end, with a definite sense of closure; and perhaps most strikingly of all, it displays a revisionist intent that goes against all of what was accepted at the time, in that it made Britain equal (if not superior) to Rome in its origins and achievements. The way Geoffrey manipulates his sources and handles his narrative in order to achieve his aim is analysed in some detail by Gioia Paradisi in her recent *Le passioni della storia*.[13] The end result, to quote Neil Wright,[14] is 'a narrative at once noble and tragic', giving the British 'an ancestry as ancient as any European people', with its origins in the great city of Troy. The British are depicted as related to the Romans and as their moral and military superiors. They conquer

---

[10] For an overview of what is known of Geoffrey's sources, see Barron, *The Arthur of the English*, pp. 11–18.

[11] Lewis Thorpe, trans., *Geoffrey of Monmouth, The History of the Kings of Britain* (Harmondsworth, 1966), p. 51.

[12] On the reception of Geoffrey's work, see R. W. Leckie, Jr, *The Passage of Dominion: Geoffrey of Monmouth and the Periodization of Insular History in the Twelfth Century* (Toronto, Buffalo and London, 1981), pp. 73–101.

[13] See especially chapters 8, 'L'etnogenesi nell' *Historia Brittonum* e nell' *Historia Regum Britanniae*' (pp. 123–36), and 9, 'Polisemia del paradigma troiano e riscrittura del passato romano' (pp. 137–82).

[14] *The Historia Regum Britannie of Geoffrey of Monmouth, I: Bern, Burgerbibliothek MS 568* (Cambridge, 1985), p. xix.

Rome under the brothers Belin and Brennius and give the city some of its greatest emperors (for example, Constantine is British by his mother Helen); but remain untainted by the rapaciousness and avarice of their Roman relatives (as exemplified by the image given of Julius Caesar, or by the ill-advised emperor who decided to demand tribute of Arthur). Geoffrey's unorthodox historiographical programme was not accepted by all. William of Newburgh in particular expressed his reservations in a very outspoken manner;[15] while some anonymous reader of the work reacted in an even more radical manner, by composing a new redaction (in Latin) of the *Historia Regum Britanniae*. The so-called First Variant version is thought to have been written as early as the late 1130s – virtually as soon as Geoffrey's text appeared, in 1138; and Wace had access to both versions.[16] The French poet clearly felt a greater affinity for the historiographical model upheld by the anonymous redactor of the Variant and based his own translation on it, occasionally supplementing it with Geoffrey's fuller narrative.

When much of the earlier research on the *Roman de Brut* was done, scholars were not aware of the existence of the Variant version (first published in 1951 by Jacob Hammer, and available in a critical edition only since 1998), and therefore assumed a much greater degree of adaptation and expansion by Wace than is actually the case. The First Variant version is shorter than Geoffrey's text (199 chapters against 208, 138 of which are briefer than their counterparts); it is also markedly different in terms of style.[17] In terms of content, as noted by Paradisi, the section dealing with the origins of the British is revised in the light of legendary Roman history (particularly, Landolfus Sagax), while the depiction of the Romans as the morally weaker of the two nations is strongly attenuated, bringing the account more in line with mainstream historiography. Its greater coherence at the level of narrative structure would also have attracted Wace.[18]

The most important written sources used by Wace, other than Geoffrey's *Historia* (usually referred to as the vulgate version) and the Variant version of the same work, are hagiographical in nature and appear almost exclusively in the final, post-Arthurian section; the only one that can be identified with some certainty is Goscelin of Saint Bertin's *Vita sancti Augustini*. The information added tends to be relatively minor, simply completing or amplifying a story already present in the main source. More striking is Wace's use of what must have been oral tales circulating about King Arthur: Wace is the first writer to mention the Round Table, whether in Latin or the vernacular. By so doing, he responded to two different (but, as we have seen, coexisting) expectations on the part of his audience: to learn about the past of Britain through authoritative historical discourse; and to enjoy the 'real' tale of Arthur, King of Britain.

---

[15] See William's Prologue to his *Historia rerum Anglicarum. The History of English Affairs*, ed. and trans. P. G. Walsh and M. J. Kennedy (Warminster, 1988), chapter 3. On the reasons for William's attack of Geoffrey of Monmouth, see Damian-Grint, *The New Historians*, pp. 44–8.

[16] This revised version had itself been revised at least twice by the time Wace was composing his *Roman de Brut*, but he does not appear to have made use of these later versions of the First Variant. See Neil Wright, ed., *The Historia Regum Britannie of Geoffrey of Monmouth, II: The First Variant Version* (Cambridge, 1988), esp. pp. xi–cxiv.

[17] See Wright, *First Variant Version*, pp. liii–liv.

[18] Inasmuch as the Second Variant Version of the *Historia Regum Britanniae* is not of direct interest to us here, 'Variant Version' will always refer hereafter to the First Variant Version, as edited by Wright.

Wace's poem is recognisably based on the Variant version of the *Historia Regum Britanniae* with occasional additions from other, non-Galfridian sources, up to the appearance of Merlin in the narrative.[19] Thereafter details feature which clearly indicate Wace's indebtedness to Geoffrey of Monmouth's text – or vulgate version – of the *Historia*.[20] It has been suggested that this might merely echo a characteristic of Wace's source text; but more recent research on the manuscript tradition of the Variant version shows that this hypothesis is not the most likely.[21] There remains the possibility, put forward by Hans-Erich Keller, that Wace had access to the vulgate version only at a fairly late stage of his work.[22] But this raises a number of questions; in particular, why did the French historian not interpolate at least some of the vulgate material in the earlier section of his poem? It was after all relatively easy, in a manuscript culture characterised by textual *mouvance*, to revise and modify one's work; and we know that Wace did just that for his later *Roman de Rou*. Moreover, even in the latter section of the *Roman de Brut*, it is striking that the main source remains the Variant.

Scholars who have worked on the question of Wace's relation to his sources have sometimes done so with the presupposition that Geoffrey of Monmouth's 'authorial' redaction (i.e., the vulgate version) is inherently superior to that of the anonymously scripted Variant version. Pierre Gallais contrasted 'le bon, l'authentique' (vulgate) with the 'étrange ... texte excentrique' of the Variant.[23] Before Neil Wright's authoritative work on the textual history of the *Historia Regum Britanniae*, Robert Caldwell (1956) and Hans-Erich Keller (1977) even postulated that the Variant itself might be the 'liber vetustissimus', the 'very old book' polished by Geoffrey into the elegant and fuller *Historia*. If he had had access to both versions from the outset, Wace would surely have preferred the longer, more informative text to the shorter one – such is the implicit reasoning. But the evidence of the text points in the opposite direction.

First, there are indications that Wace knew of the vulgate version of the *Historia Regum Britanniae* from the beginning of the compositional phase of his work. These echoes are mostly inconclusive, 'mere trifles', to quote Caldwell; but they are nevertheless there to be found. For instance: the short description of Corineus

---

[19] It is not my purpose here to discuss the detail of Wace's sources; one may however note the possible influence of Landolfus Sagax (see Robert A. Caldwell, 'Wace's *Roman de Brut* and the *Variant Version* of Geoffrey of Monmouth's *Historia Regum Britanniae*', *Speculum* 31 (1956), p. 677, note 12), as well as borrowings from hagiographical writings (episodes of St Ursula and St Augustine) and the occasional echo of non-learned tales (most famous of which is Wace's account of the founding of the Round Table).

[20] This was first noted by Caldwell, pp. 675–82.

[21] The possibility of Wace's source having been a composite manuscript was raised by H.-E. Keller, 'Wace et Geoffrey de Monmouth: problème de la chronologie des sources', *Romania* 98 (1977): 1–14; however, Neil Wright's work on the manuscript tradition of the Variant version of the *Historia Regum Britanniae* suggests that this is unlikely. See Wright, *First Variant Version*, Preface, pp. xci–cxv. For an example of a composite manuscript, see Daniel Huws and Brynley F. Roberts, 'Another Manuscript of the Variant Version of the *Historia Regum Britanniae*', *Bulletin of the Board of Celtic Studies* 25 (1973): 147–52.

[22] Keller, 'Wace et Geoffrey de Monmouth: problème de la chronologie des sources', *Romania* 98 (1977): 1–14, offers this possibility as an alternative to a composite version of the *Historia* underlying Wace's work.

[23] P. Gallais, 'La *Variant Version* de l'*Historia Regum Britanniae* et le *Brut* de Wace', *Romania* 87 (1966): 1–7.

(781–2) appears to be derived from the vulgate text, as do the details which fill out Wace's account of Corineus's wrestling match with Gogmagog. Godlac of Denmark returns to his country with his lady love, as in the vulgate (the Variant takes no interest in the fate of the girl after her capture by Belin); and among Conan's reasons for wanting British brides for his men is the fear of miscegenation, as in vulgate §88. The embassy of Guigelinus to Brittany follows the same pattern as the vulgate §93, and as in the vulgate, King Aldroenus explains his reason for not going to Britain in person. Finally Vortigern refuses to grant Hengist a castle, on the grounds that he is a pagan (as in the vulgate §99). Some of these details could conceivably have arisen from cues in the Variant text; however, the reason these borrowings seem to be 'trifles' is the way Wace integrates them into his poetic construction. Typically, they are blended into a more comprehensive recasting of the narrative involving further, non-Galfridian, sources of a more striking nature; notably, Helen's Invention of the Cross and the beheading in Cologne of Ursula and the 11,000 virgins. These sources are either hagiographical or learned, the vast majority of Wace's additions being (as in the latter part of his *Roman de Brut*) didactic or moralising asides: on the columns of Hercules and the sirens (729–64); on the meaning or origins of names (1276–80, on Wales: a passage echoed at the end of the *Roman*; 1310–14, on the Humber; 1437–8, on the Severn); on geographical detail (the location of the river Stour, 1424–5; the course of the Severn, 1439–40). A number of Wace's additions are obviously dictated by the demands of rhyme (in the king-list of §52, for example, the fondness of King Cherin for wine seems to have been suggested by the fact the his name rhymes with 'vin').

That Wace did not accord a privileged status to the vulgate text is confirmed by an overview of the *Roman* as a whole. The Variant text is used to the apparent exclusion of the vulgate in almost 50% of the chapters following §118. The usual pattern for the remaining material is the merging of the information and/or presentation of the two *Historia* texts, frequently accompanied by authorial adaptation. In a handful of chapters only[24] does the vulgate redaction have a major influence on the French poem, predominantly in the Arthurian section. The first episode of the *Roman de Brut* to bear a clear mark of the vulgate version of the *Historia* is that relating the execution of the defeated Hengest (§125, *Roman* 7837–7894). The differences between the two redactions of Geoffrey's work are minor, with only one truly distinctive feature: the vulgate (echoed by Wace) explicitly states that King Agag was taken prisoner by Saul, whereas the Variant omits this detail. This instance of Wace's use of the vulgate text could easily remain unnoticed, partly because of the nature of the borrowing (which under other circumstances could equally have been ascribed to the French poet's knowledge of the Scriptures), but mainly because of the extensive re-appropriation of the narrative evidenced in this passage.

Wace's handling of §125 is in many respects typical of the principles governing his work as a whole. The beginning of the passage is marked by the addition of information which firmly places the episode within a sequence of events (7837–8):

---

[24] These correspond to chapters 125, 129, 156, 157, 159, 160, 165 and 191/2 of the *Historia Regum Britanniae*.

Li reis fu lied de cele glorie
Que Deus li out duné victorie.[25]

This statement marks the end of the continuing conflict with Hengest and his Saxons, and the beginning of another phase in Aurelius's career; the addition to the Latin texts (that the victory is God-given) is so trite that there is no need to look for further sources or influences in this instance. However, it is highly significant as a structural marker. We are now shifting from the account of Aurelius's military campaigns, which are essential in establishing his royal authority over Britain, to the description of his achievements as a ruler: chapters 125 and 126 show Aurelius meting out justice, and chapters 127 to 130 describe the building work ordered by him, and particularly his greatest project, the Stonehenge memorial. Chapters 131 and 132 then recount the circumstances of his death and the transmission of power to Uther. Within the boundaries of chapter 125, Wace takes certain liberties with his sources. The Latin texts have King Aurelius ordering the dead to be buried a detail Wace chooses not to include in his verse, putting the emphasis on the tending of the wounded instead.[26] More significantly, Bishop Eldad's advice is reshaped, expanded from less than five lines in the Latin to some 36 octosyllabic lines of direct speech. This is effected by a number of didactic additions intended to clarify the biblical allusions contained in Eldad's speech such as who Agag was, and the description of his harrying of the Israelites (7855–62); his being taken prisoner by King Saul (7863–4); the great sanctity of Samuel (7868–70). Seen from this viewpoint, the inclusion of the only detail proper to the vulgate text in this section seems rather less than significant. The naming of King Saul was overdetermined from the outset. Within the text, Eldad is formally advising his own king to follow the precedent set by the holder of royal power in Samuel's day, and the vulgate reading could merely have reinforced Wace's fondness for didactic interpolations. There is little to suggest that the vulgate was viewed here as a particularly authoritative source of information.

To this, one may add that in terms of content, the differences between the two versions of the *Historia Regum Britanniae* are relatively minor. The Variant is characterised by a clear trend towards narrative compression (though certain of its paragraphs contain material not found in the vulgate: see Wright, *First Variant Version*, table 1, p. xviii), and a thorough stylistic recasting of Geoffrey's Latin prose, with a marked fondness for biblical phraseology. In terms of content, the Variant displays what Jacob Hammer terms 'a tendency to tone down or omit unpleasant details'.[27] The result of this rewriting process is described by Wright (*First Variant Version*, p. viii) as

> not devoid of literary interest. Frequent reminiscences of the bible and Classical texts (independent of the vulgate) indicate that the abbreviator was an educated man. He was also interested in historical matters, for he had recourse to Bede

---

[25] Literally: 'The king was happy at this glory, that God had granted him victory.'
[26] This is not an isolated instance. Wace appears to have had some distaste for the motif of the burial of the dead in the *Roman de Brut*, though he has no qualms about the motif in his later *Roman de Rou*.
[27] J. Hammer, ed., *The Historia Regum Britanniae: a Variant Version* (Cambridge, Mass., 1951), Preface, pp. 8–12.

and Landolfus Sagax and tried on occasion to reconcile the Galfridian version of events with these more orthodox historical authorities. Furthermore, his fondness for biblical allusion lends the First Variant in many passages (especially speeches) a tone rather more moral than that of Geoffrey's original.

Wright's sketch of the redactor of the First Variant could apply to Wace with only minor modifications. Like the Variant redactor, he is an educated man, who sees his material in a wider context of historical and literary authorities. He displays a comparable aversion to distasteful details, and a similar preference for narrative economy. And, like the Variant, his *Roman de Brut* subjects its sources to a thorough aesthetic and ideological recasting.[28]

From the Historia to the Roman

The basic structure of the material adapted by Wace is episodic. One king succeeds another, reigns and dies; his heir comes to the throne, reigns and dies; and so on. The principle is chronological and linear: going from the foundation of a great nation, to its collapse. This pattern is of course retained by Wace. To quote Margaret Houck, 'at times the *Roman de Brut* not only translates almost literally from the *Historia* . . . but more important, it follows with very little deviation the exact course of the narrative as it appears in the Latin work'.[29] On the other hand, for the specific episodes within this framework, as noted by Caldwell (p. 678), Wace felt free to make whatever adjustments he felt were needed, 'paraphrasing, expanding, and elaborating on it as best seemed to him'. The poet combines faithful, sometimes word-for-word translation with a creative selection of details from his sources, balancing lively amplification with learned soberness.

However, the salient characteristic of Wace's poem is not so much that he retained and expanded, but that he also abridged. The *Roman de Brut* is a mere 14,866 octosyllabic lines long, each of these containing on average six words, which corresponds to a ratio of between three or four French verse lines per line of Latin prose (containing some ten words each, in Neil Wright's edition of the two versions of the *Historia*). This is no mean feat. The passage from a synthetic language like Latin to an analytic one like French inevitably causes an expansion of the number of words used, simply because of the demands of the syntax of the target language. To this one must add the constraints of the octosyllabic couplet selected by Wace as a fit medium for his material. It is clear, under these circumstances, that any expansions or additions of material by the poet must have been accompanied by compressions and omissions.

The distribution of these pruned-down passages is of considerable interest. Following the rule of thumb that it took between three and four octosyllabic lines for Wace to render the concepts contained in one Latin line, one finds that Book I, relating the circumstances of Brutus's founding of Britain, appears slightly

---

[28] See Caldwell, p. 678; also Laurence Mathey-Maille, 'Traduction et création: de l'*Historia Regum Britanniae* de Geoffrey of Monmouth au *Roman de Brut* de Wace', pp. 187–93 in *Ecritures et modes de pensée au moyen âge*, ed. D. Boutet and L. Harf-Lancner (Paris, 1993).

[29] M. Houck, *The Sources of the* Roman de Brut *of Wace* (Berkeley, 1941), p. 161.

compressed;[30] the same is true of Books V,[31] VI,[32] VIII[33] and XII.[34] Book VII, containing the Prophecies of Merlin in the Latin text, is left aside with a short statement by Wace (7535–42) to the effect that he was not competent to interpret the material. By contrast, Books III (the conquests of Belin and Brennes), IX and X (Arthur) and XI (Gurmund's depredations and the Conversion of the Saxons) all display varying amounts of expansion.[35] We therefore have a pattern of marked narrative economy in the two Books framing the story, and in those relating the events occurring, in effect, between the conquest of Britain by Julius Caesar and the reign of Arthur;[36] and three high points corresponding to the two most glorious episodes in the past of the Britons, and the key event in their downfall.

Straightforward omission of material is exceedingly rare (with the obvious exception of Book VII, the prophecies of Merlin). In Book I, Brutus's 14-line verse prayer to Diana becomes a 5-line statement that Brutus prayed to her for a land in which to settle. In Book XII (§191) part of Brian's tirade reminding Cadwallan of the treachery of the Saxons is left aside, as is the storm at sea and subsequent scattering of King Cadwallan's fleet (§193), and the lament of King Cadwallader on his way to exile (§203). The only 'factual' details omitted from these two framing Books are in the much reshaped Book XII: the alliance of Penda's son with two Mercian chieftains against Oswi (§200), the civil war preceding the famine and plague under the reign of Cadwallader (§203) and the wisdom of Athelstan's rule after the demise of the Britons (§207). The bulk of Wace's omissions and compressions, throughout the *Roman de Brut*, is in fact connected with material which medieval readers and writers would have recognised as amplificatory in nature. Wace consistently recomposes speeches and battle-scenes; he tends to replace gore and severed limbs with technical military detail, particularly if the heroes of a given section are having the worse of things, and comments that could reflect negatively on the favoured ethnic group are frequently deleted. The atrocities committed by the Trojans are thus toned down in the first Book (chapters 18, 19, 20) where they are depicted as a chosen people; whilst in Book XII Wace softens the image of the now Christian Saxons who are to inherit Britain by the will of God. The poet clearly did not consider such compressions or omissions detrimental to the informative value of his work. On

---

[30] The Variant text (ed. Wright) totals 367 lines for the 22 chapters of Book I; Wace's 1251 lines divided by 3.5 gives us the slightly lower total of 367.
[31] Variant: 291 lines; Wace: 872 lines (divided by 3.5: 249).
[32] Variant: 498; Wace: 1397 lines (divided by 3.5: 399).
[33] Calculations are more delicate for the latter part of the work, where the influence of both the vulgate and the Variant is to be felt. Book VIII, in the vulgate, totals some 602 lines, and in the Variant, some 516. The equivalent section in Wace totals 1467 lines (divided by 3.5: 419).
[34] Length of vulgate text: 404 lines; length of Variant text: 309 lines; Wace: 910 lines (divided by 3.5: 260).
[35] Book III: Variant text, 332 lines; Wace: 1505 lines (divided by 3.5: 430). Book IX: Variant, 450 lines, vulgate 577 lines; Wace 2064 lines (divided by 3.5: 590). Book X: Variant, 405 lines, vulgate 510 lines, Wace 1959 lines (divided by 3.5: 560). Book XI: Variant: 186 lines, vulgate, 217 lines, Wace 929 lines (divided by 3.5: 265).
[36] The pattern of compression is already discernible in §§65–71 (i.e., Book IV); the only expansions in Book IV following Caesar's Conquest of Britain concern the birth of Christ (§64) and Arviragus's ruse in the battle against Claudius (§66).

the contrary, they keep the focus firmly on the events or features relevant for the development of the narrative, and ensure a certain ideological clarity in the depiction of power struggles: the reader has to be aware of where his sympathies should lie.

This implies that Wace himself had a firm grasp on his material, and that he expressed his personal reading, with the inevitable ideological bias that this implies, through a new weighting of the different elements in his source material, from entire episodes to isolated details. The *Roman de Brut* shows evidence that he had evolved a personal hierarchy of events, based on his understanding of his material, before he started the actual composition of his poem. Wace at times does indeed translate the Latin prose into French verse concept for concept, in the same sequence as his source-text; but he did not produce his text piecemeal, in a narrowly episodic manner. He had a strategy, which could well have remained obscured were it not for the fortunate clash in the latter part of his work between the two versions of his main source, the Variant and the vulgate versions of the *Historia Regum Britanniae*.

On the whole, Variant and vulgate follow the same narrative sequence. Wright (xxxiv ff.) identifies just sixteen chapters (out of a total of 207) in which all or part of their content is found in a different order in the vulgate and the Variant. These chapters are predominantly in the latter part of the work, from the appearance of Arthur onwards, and form two main clusters. The first (chapters 159–164) depict the reaction of Arthur and his nobles to the Roman demands, and the ensuing preparations for hostilities. The second (chapters 184–187) describes the devastation of Britain by Gurmund and its effects, in the final phase of the narrative as a whole.

The episode in the vulgate redaction of the *Historia* develops as follows: Arthur, in council, expresses his views regarding the Roman ultimatum for tribute (§159). Hoel (§160) makes a speech supporting Arthur and promising practical help, with money and men. King Angusel of Scotland (§161) thereupon expresses his eagerness for battle and also promises resources and men. Then the other kings pledge similar help, so that the entire army would be 183,300 strong excluding foot soldiers. Arthur accepts their offers and gives them instructions; he sends back the Roman messengers (§162). When Arthur's response is known, the Roman Senate orders Lucius to summon their allies in anticipation of war; the total of their manpower is 400,160 (§163). At the beginning of August the Roman troops set out for Britain (164a). Arthur hears of their coming, entrusts Britain to Modred and Guinevere, and sails to Normandy, where he will await his allies. On the way, he has a prophetic dream (§164b).

In the Variant text, §161 follows §§162a, 163 and 164a, but precedes §§162b and 164b: Arthur exposes his views relating to the Roman ultimatum (§159); he sees that he has the support of his retainers, gives them instructions and sends the messengers back to Rome (§162a). The Senate orders Lucius to instruct the Roman allies to prepare an army; the total strength of the Romans and their allies is some 430,000 men (§163). They set out for Britain at the beginning of the calends of July (§164a). Arthur is offered full support by his allies. The King of Scotland pledges his help, expressing his eagerness at the thought of battle and suggesting that they might invade Germany after having defeated the Romans

(§161). All the other kings also pledge their support; the total strength of the army is 183,300 excluding foot soldiers (§162b). Having organised the expedition, Arthur entrusts Modred and Guinevere with the task of defending Britain and sets off for Barfleur where he is to meet up with his allies. On the way, he has a prophetic dream (§164b).

The two versions of the *Historia* offer little variance in terms of contents, but in the vulgate the events are presented in chronological order with important rhetorical effects (notably direct speech), whilst in the Variant the episode is more descriptive, with fewer speeches. The overall effect is that the vulgate version of this passage reads as a build-up to the Roman campaign, with the successive speeches of Arthur, Hoel and Angusel providing a thrice-repeated justification of the British refusal to pay tribute to Rome in terms which are historical, moral and emotional. The Variant version, by contrast, reads as a more detached account of the beginning of the campaign. With fewer speeches, which are moreover scattered rather than concentrated in Arthur's council scene, the stress is shifted from the justification of the campaign to the presentation of the opponents' forces.

The *Roman de Brut* presents an interesting compromise between these two approaches. After Arthur's harangue to his councillors (10779–904), Hoel makes a speech supporting the idea of a campaign against Rome, giving an overview of the prophecies foretelling the fall of Rome, and stressing the Britons' previous successes against the eternal city (10910–54). Angusel of Scotland then expresses his approval of Hoel's words, pledges his support to Arthur, and rejoices at the idea of battle. So far, this corresponds to the sequence of the vulgate version. However, the contents of Angusel's speech bear the unmistakeable mark of the Variant, as the king suggests that the Britons march on Lorraine and Germany after having vanquished Rome:

Quant nus avrum Rome conquise,	Cumque deuictis Romanis eorum copiis
Les humes morz, la cité prise,	fuerimus ditati,
En Lohierenne trespassum	
E Loherrenne conquerum,	
E Loherregne e Alemainne,	Germanos adhuc rebelles necesse est invadamus
Que nule terre ne remainne	quatinus tota terra Cisalpina conspectui tuo
De ça les munz ki ne seit tue	pareat.
(11027–33)[37]	(Wright, p. 156)[38]

Moreover, after Angusel's speech, the French narrative echoes the Variant order rather than that of the vulgate. After the Scottish king's words, Arthur lets everyone have his say and sends off the Roman messengers with letters. As in the Variant redaction, the envoys sing the praises of Arthur throughout Rome (= §162a). When the Roman barons hear Arthur's message, they advise the Emperor to fight and Lucius orders all his allies to lend him support (= §163 of

---

[37] 'When we have taken Rome, slain the men, taken the city, we'll cross into Lorraine and conquer it, both Lorraine and Germany, so that no country remains this side of the mountains which is not yours.'

[38] 'Once we have defeated the Roman armies, we shall need to invade the hitherto rebellious Germans, so that all lands this side of the mountains obey you.'

both versions). When all is ready, they march from Rome at the beginning of August (= §164a). Arthur's allies promise the help they owe him (§162b); when he knows the exact strength of his army, Arthur arranges for all to meet at Barfleur (= §164b), and sets off after entrusting the realm to Britain and Guinevere.

This hybridisation leads to a cumulation of those features in both texts which lend added dignity and grandeur to the forthcoming campaign. Hoel's speech makes sense both aesthetically and ideologically against such an outlook, reinforcing Arthur's words and announcing those of Angusel, whose speech may be said to be the companion piece to Hoel's. No real addition is made to the Variant narrative in terms of content, and structurally, the insertion of the material in §160 did not require any major change to the narrative framework of the Variant. What is retained from Angusel's speech in the Variant, however, places Arthur's campaign into a totally different perspective; it is not merely a response to Rome's demand for tribute, it is the beginning of a world conquest. Rome is no longer the culmination of the expedition, it is, in Angusel's mouth, a mere stepping-stone. The open admiration of the Roman envoys for Arthur, as in the Variant, emphasises the prestige of the king, whilst the decision to follow the Variant's presentation of the kings and leaders on both sides ensures that the reader does not dwell too long on the fact that the Roman army outnumbers Arthur's by over two to one. By contrast, Wace chooses to end his presentation of the Briton army with a topos which allows him to evade such disquieting comparisons (11159–62):

> La gelde e les arbalastiers
> Ne les servanz ne les archiers
> Ne sai numbrer, ne cil ne firent
> Qui la grant ost ensemble virent.[39]

It is possible that the absence of precise figures for Arthur's army may be due to the Variant text used by Wace, as one of the manuscript-witnesses collated by Wright omits the last sentence of Variant §162b which states the total strength of the British army.[40] One may also venture the hypothesis that the clash of the two main sources, in forcing Wace to commit himself to a particular reading of the episode, has contributed to a greater appropriation of the narrative by the French poet, which led him to omit information that is not entirely congruent with the aura of glory surrounding Arthur's incipient campaign. Whatever the explanation for this omission, however, the pattern suggested by this passage is that of a general structure determined by the Variant, the contents of which are supplemented with information from the vulgate text.

The second structural clash between vulgate and Variant is more limited in scope than the one just discussed, but presents significant similarities to it. Like the Arthurian part, this section, which presents the arrival of Gurmund and the ensuing

---

[39] 'I cannot count the number of foot-soldiers, crossbowmen, servants or archers, nor could those who saw the great army assembled.'

[40] This is Paris, Bibliothèque de l'Arsenal, MS 982, copied in Italy or southern France in the second half of the fourteenth century (see Wright, *First Variant Version*, pp. lxxxix–xc). While this particular manuscript cannot have been Wace's source-text, it could be related to it.

build-up to St Augustine's mission to the English, comprises important material of non-Galfridian origin, such as the destruction of Cirencester through sparrows and St Augustine's punishment of the people of Dorchester. The whole episode (chapters 184–9; *Brut*, 13375–959) displays a similar merging of the contents of the two versions of the *Historia*, whilst conforming to the outline suggested by the Variant: in this case, material found in §186 of the vulgate, describing the depredations of Gurmund and his pagan followers, is inserted in §184 of the Variant. It is at this earlier stage of the narrative also that Wace introduces the theme of pagan savagery, tying it in with the description of Gurmund's invasion. (The vulgate §185 is a moralising address to the Britons by the narrator, which is not preserved in the Variant, nor re-established by Wace.) Chapter 186 of the Variant is a combination of material found in the vulgate's §186 – describing the pitiful situation of the Britons and the dire state of the Church at the hands of the pagans – and §187 (stating the Britons' inability to prevail against the Saxons). Wace not only follows the movement of the Variant, he goes one step further, concentrating all the descriptive elements relating to Gurmund's campaign in the initial section, without returning to them thereafter (as does the Variant in §187). Moreover, the underlying logic of the Variant sequence – stressing the destruction of Christianity in order to give added relief to Pope Gregory's decision to convert the English – is given greater emphasis in the French poem through the deliberate omission of information contained in §187 of the Vulgate: the divisions between the Britons, which explain their lack of success against the Saxons, go unmentioned despite their relevance to the narrative *qua* history.

Clearly, then, Wace was not aiming at completeness of information through systematic compilation. The two passages just discussed demonstrate that he interpolates material into his narrative only when his predetermined macrostructure, based on that of the Variant version of the *Historia*, allowed him to do so. The nature of this added material would appear to be determined by its congruence with the themes developed in the Variant and which form the ideological backbone of the *Roman*. This in turn confirms that the Variant was chosen as main source *not* because Wace did not know of the vulgate redaction when he started his work, but because the Variant was more compatible with his own aesthetic and historiographical principles.

The confidence with which Wace handles his sources is also perceptible at the microstructural level of the constituent episodes of his work. Like any self-respecting medieval writer, Wace followed the practice recommended by authorities of dividing long sections into shorter, more manageable units that would be easier to classify in one's mind (and thus recall when necessary).[41] These shorter units, in his Latin sources, are reflected in the 200-odd chapters of the *Historia Regum Britanniae*. Wace frequently works within the boundaries of these divisions which are occasionally highlighted in manuscripts of the *Roman de Brut* by coloured capitals and are signalled by stylistic markers within the text itself. Closure is typically achieved by factual, explanatory or didactic comments made by the narrator from his privileged vantage-point; and all new phases in the

---

[41] On the mnemonic techniques underlying medieval texts, see Mary Carruthers, *The Book of Memory: a Study of Memory in Medieval Culture* (Cambridge, 1990).

narrative begin with a new focus, signalled by deictic words (such as 'quand', 'dunc') and/or the explicit mention of the name of the central character (typically, a new ruler). However, the narrative phases thus signalled by Wace do not necessarily follow the limits of the chapters of the *Historia Regum Britanniae*.[42] Whilst they usually coincide at the beginning and end of specific reigns, there are also a number of instances in the *Roman de Brut* where the boundaries of a given phase are redefined. For example, in the French text, the reigns of Leir and Cordelia are run together in the same narrative unit (2047–55):

> Emprés les treis anz se morut;
> En Leïcestre, u li cors jut,
> Cordeïlle l'ensepeli
> En la crote el temple Jani.
> Puis ad cinc anz tenu l'enor,
> Mais ja ert vedve senz seinnor;
> Emprés cinc anz l'unt guereiee
> E la terre fort chalangiee
> Dui fil de ses serors ainz nees.[43]

There is no real break between the two reigns. This is emphasised by Wace's use of pronouns at this stage: the subject of line 2047 is the unnamed Leir who, in line 2049, becomes the (still unnamed) grammatical object, syntactically bound to the grammatical subject (Cordelia). The 'puis', 'then' (2051) introducing Cordelia's reign is likewise denied its potential value as a structural marker through the absence of an explicitly named subject of the sentence: line 2051 makes sense only in conjunction with line 2049 (which provides us with the identity of the grammatical subject, Cordelia), which itself refers back to Leir. The break occurs only after Cordelia's suicide (2065–6), the end of the section being indicated by a disapproving comment by the narrator. The reign of Cordelia is clearly presented as a continuation of Leir's. The Latin, by contrast, focuses more on the power struggles after her accession to the throne, and her death is not given any particular structural significance (it occurs in the middle of §32).

Within the account of a given reign, information may be moved around, thus changing the narrative logic of an episode; for example, Wace merges all the arguments made by the Romans to justify their retreating from Britain into one long speech, whereas the Variant version presents them in a short speech by the Senate (§90), completed by a longer passage in reported speech in the following chapter (§91). Less striking, but possibly more significant, is the way Merlin is introduced into the narrative through the linking of Vortigern's tower to his flight into Wales (7309–13):

---

[42] Comparative work based on the subdivisions of the *Historia Regum Britanniae* has of course to be handled with caution, inasmuch as we do not know how Wace's source copies presented their material. In the course of my discussion, I shall be referring routinely to the chapters as published by Wright, rather than to the book-and-chapter numbering favoured by Acton Griscom, ed., *Geoffrey of Monmouth. Historia Regum Britanniae* (London, 1929).

[43] 'After the three years, he died. Cordeille buried him in Leicester, where his body lay, in the crypt of the temple of Janus. Then she ruled the kingdom for five years. But now she was a widow, without a husband. After five years, two sons of her elder sisters made war on her and laid strong claim to the kingdom.'

Manuscripts, Sources and Adaptation Principles

> Vortiger tut lur ad guerpi,
> Ultre Saverne s'en fuï;
> Luin en Guales s'en trespassa,
> Illuec fu, illuec conversa.
> Venir fist ses sortisseürs . . .[44]

The fact that we are dealing with a new phase in the narrative has been indicated by the fact that Wace closes the previous 'chapter' with learned considerations on the names of Essex, Sussex and Middlesex (7293–308), an addition preceded by an extensively rewritten account of the Stonehenge massacre (notably, Wace has Hengist plead for Vortigern's life, on the grounds that he is his son-in-law). Vortigern's retreat to Wales, his consulting of his magicians, the decision to build a tower and the quest for the fatherless child are thus intimately bound together, where the Latin places a break (§106) between Vortigern's flight to Wales and his decision, born out of despair, to consult his wise men. In terms of content and plot, no change to the source-text is made; however, the way in which the events are viewed is subtly modified, creating in this case a link between Merlin's prophecies and Saxon treachery (as opposed merely to Vortigern's ambitions). This shift of emphasis, which makes the concluding element of a Latin section become the introductory element to the following section (or vice-versa) in the French text, but with little or no change in terms of plot-advancement, is a recurrent, if discreet, feature in the *Roman de Brut*.[45]

The tendency to view the sequence of events from a slightly different perspective to that of the *Historia Regum Britanniae* is apparent from the beginning of the *Roman de Brut*. The account of Brutus's adventures betrays a different conception of effective narration, characterised by a marked preference for a chronological sequence of events. Information is given when it becomes of immediate relevance to the plot. The name of the Greek king, mentioned at the beginning of §7 of the Latin, thus remains unknown to the reader of the French poem until the character actually takes an active role in the events. The history of the Trojan captives given in the Variant (they were brought to Greece by Pyrrhus to avenge his father's death), having no immediate bearing on the hero, is omitted. By contrast, their increase in numbers is mentioned at an earlier stage in the French text, thus making Brutus's status as rebel chief a more formidable one and his task more obviously sustainable from the outset. The nobleman Assaracus is also presented in a slightly different way, with the stress on his connection with Brutus (209–11, he is explicitly said to be instrumental in asking Brutus to lead the Trojans). The overall effect of this reworking is that the focus is more narrowly on the central character of the episode. Equally, the details added by Wace in this initial section of the poem have a direct bearing on the main protagonist: the love of Turnus for Lavinia motivates his war with Eneas, while Assaracus's pleading the cause of the Trojans convinces Brutus to accept leadership. The centre of

---

[44] 'Vortigern abandoned everything to them and fled over the Severn. He travelled deep into Wales and there he stayed. He sent for his soothsayers. . .'

[45] Among the many examples to be found, one may mention the episode of Gurguint (§46), whose death is syntactically linked with the naming of his heir and successor Guithelinus/Guincelin (3331–4). In the Latin, the introduction of Guithelin marks a new narrative phase (§47, Griscom iii.13).

interest is firmly on the ruler, and the structural unit is correspondingly the reign within a narrative that is purposefully linear.[46]

Wace's preference for a chronological sequence of events leads to minor (and not so minor) shifting of material throughout the *Roman de Brut*. Ascanius's accession to power after his father's death is mentioned before his raising of his posthumous brother. The Trojans are shown preparing for war before sending their fateful letter to King Pandrasus, rather than afterwards; and the layout of the Greek camp is described before Anacletus betrays the Greek guards, rather than being presented as explanatory material after the encounter. Similarly, Octa and Ebissa's imprisonment in London is mentioned at the same time as their capture (8531–4), rather than in the account of Uther's actions after his victory over them, as in the Latin (§137). This last example also illustrates a preference on Wace's part for a sense of closure at the end of episodes: the majority of his minor expansions or asides occur in such positions, providing a form of conclusion before moving on to something else.

Stylistic features

One of the most striking features of the *Roman de Brut* is the strong presence of the narrator, who in addition to the conventional rhetorical and narrative interjections,[47] freely provides didactic asides,[48] expresses horror or approval,[49] and generally engages with the reader in what resembles a teacher/pupil relationship. The hallmark of this narrator is the expression 'ne sai', 'I don't know', which crops up on average approximately once every 370 lines.[50] Typically used in connection with trivia that throw into relief the extent of what the narrator *does* know, 'ne sai' is widely perceived as a trademark expression of the poet's, enabling him to project a scholarly persona enhancing the authority of his discourse. The information 'not known' tends to be of a factual nature, such as the number of casualties in a given battle;[51] but sometimes, it is patently irrelevant, as when the narrator claims uncertainty as to whether King Membriz was pursuing a doe or a deer when he met with his fatal hunting accident (1486). 'Ne sai' creates the illusion of interaction between the narrator and an assumed reader, whose

---

[46] The only modification or addition at this early stage of the poem that does not reinforce the linear, forward-looking of the story is the mention why Creusa did not follow her husband and son from Troy (86–8). This is best explained by the fear on Wace's part that Aschanius's failure to succeed his father as king might be construed as an indication of illegitimacy or unworthiness, particularly since the theme of illegitimacy appears at a later stage, in the Brutus section, with Assaracus.

[47] On narrative and rhetorical interjections in the vernacular literature of the time, see Damian-Grint, *The New Historians*, pp. 143–71.

[48] For example, explaining what a legion is (3182–4), or giving a technical account of how a place-name was formed (such as Cernel, 13789–803).

[49] See for example his interjection at Judon's murder of her son (2174–5) or at the extent of Elidur's brotherly love (3523–4).

[50] For a discussion of Wace's use of 'ne sai' in the *Roman de Brut*, see F. Le Saux, 'Culture livresque et mémoire vivante dans le *Roman de Brut* de Wace', pp. 137–43 in *Temps et histoire dans le roman arthurien*, ed. J.-C. Faucon (Toulouse, 1999).

[51] For an early example of this, see line 1092, where Wace confesses he does not know how many Trojans were killed by the giants, or their names.

nit-picking questions implicitly underlie these passages. The effect is twofold. On the one hand, it softens the image of the narrator who, though a great scholar, deals with boring or impossible queries with patience and courtesy, and has the humility to admit to ignorance when answers cannot be found. On the other hand, the sheer incongruity of some of the questions posed by the fictitious implicit reader was clearly designed to foster a bond of complicity between the narrator and his readers/audience. Who cares where Eldolf found his stake at Stonehenge (7264), or what Hoel's ailment was on the eve of the battle of Bath (9266)? Through the creation of a rather childish third party, which even the less educated readers of the *Roman de Brut* could view with some condescension and amusement, Wace narrows the emotional gap between his fictional self and his addressees. In this respect, 'ne sai' may be viewed as Wace's 'secular' alternative to the homiletic strategies used in his religious poems to foster a feeling of inclusiveness. It shows that the poet was acutely aware of the necessity of engaging with his audience on more than one level if he was to maintain their interest over a long stretch of narrative, not all of which would necessarily be intrinsically entertaining. The 'ne sai' device thus points to a different intended readership for the *Roman de Brut*, as compared to Wace's earlier works: a readership that would not take kindly to being patronised and which wanted the poet's learning to be worn lightly. Consequently, Wace pulls out all the stops in his 'geste des Bretuns'.

As with his religious works, Wace composed his *Roman de Brut* in octosyllabic couplets. His choice of verse rather than prose, and of the octosyllabic couplet rather than some other metre, has been questioned by scholars at various times, partly because of our modern-day perception of verse being 'literary'. This view is now recognised as being anachronistic; as pointed out by Peter Damian-Grint, 'Verse-forms, in the eleventh, twelfth and thirteenth centuries, appear to have no direct connection with literary mode. . . . Conversely, specific verse-forms are not linked to particular genres.'[52] A wide range of texts were written in verse, including scientific textbooks such as the thirteenth-century *Novele cirurgerie*, a treatise on surgery; and of the various verse forms, notes Damian-Grint, the octosyllabic couplet was something of an all-purpose metre.[53] Wace's predecessor in historical adaptations in the vernacular, Geffrei Gaimar, also used the octosyllabic couplet, which was clearly perceived to be the best medium for works of vulgarisation. The reason for this is possibly to be found in the conventions and rhythms of Latin prose. As a discursive space, the octosyllabic couplet meets the practical requirements of the Latin period, in that it is not too long to be recited or read in a single breath; like the period, the couplet contains at least two units (*cola*) that are not necessarily self-standing semantically, but are rhythmically complete. It was therefore particularly congenial for texts written for oral delivery (as most if not all vernacular texts must have been at the time) and had the advantage of echoing the aural effect of Latin. Moreover, this was a compositional medium that Wace knew well, and mastered.

The octosyllabic couplet in the *Roman de Brut* is used in much the same way as in the *Vie de saint Nicolas*: that is, the individual line typically contains one

---

[52] Damian-Grint, *The New Historians of the Twelfth-Century Renaissance*, pp. 184–5.
[53] Damian-Grint, *The New Historians of the Twelfth-Century Renaissance*, pp. 8 and 186.

concept, the second line of the couplet providing space for elaboration or simply overspill from the first line. The second line of the couplet, and particularly the second half of that line, is frequently used by the poet to elaborate ideas or concepts by means of verbal synonyms, paraphrase or illustration, thus inscribing in the poem as a whole an aesthetics of repetition[54] that could be used as a mnemonic aid akin to the punctuating devices advocated by Quintilian in his *Institutio oratoria*.[55] In a work the length of the *Roman de Brut*, this must have been an important consideration. Enjambement is used sparingly, typically to mark the beginning of a passage in direct speech, and rarely disrupts the rhythm of the couplet. Where this happens, it occurs predominantly in passages in direct speech, to emphasise certain concepts. A good example of this is in Brutus's letter to King Pandrasus of Greece, where enjambement draws attention to 'Dardani' (229), the name of the Trojans' ancestor; 'li chaitif' (233), stressing the miserable state to which the Trojan exiles are now reduced; and 'franc' (242), indicating their aim – to be free. As in Wace's religious works, sentences do not necessarily begin or end within the boundaries of the couplets; but new narrative sections always coincide with a new couplet.

Wace is on the whole relatively sparing of rhetorical effects in his *Roman de Brut*. His favoured devices, as in his earlier works, are lists (*enumeratio*) and repetition of words at the beginning of successive lines (*anaphora*), frequently in conjunction with the repetition of syntactical structures within those lines themselves (*isocolon*). That is, effects with a strong aural appeal. He also makes a judicious use of direct speech and dialogue. Rhetorical effects are to be found mainly in descriptions, typically scenes of warfare, but also of the beauty of a land, court ceremonial, or a sea journey. Wace's description of the sailors setting sail when Arthur returns to Britain on hearing of Modred's treason (11205–38) is thus one of the most memorable of the work, with a lavish use of specialised nautical terms bound together by isolocon. Battle scenes (which account for the vast majority of descriptive passages) tend to be rather formulaic.[56] The following passage (4023–36) is representative of the more elaborate of these scenes (the exceptions being accounts of sieges, which also feature lists of siege engines):

> Dunc veïssiez chevals bien puindre,
> Hanstes brandir, chevaliers joindre,
> Escuz percier, seles voidier,
> Homes chaeir, plaies seinner.
> Chevaliers jostent, archiers traient,
> Bien s'esforcent e bien s'essaient.
> Saietes volent come pluie,
> Que plaist a cels a cez ennuie.
> Mult oïssiez testes croissir

---

[54] The regularity of a predominantly binary rhythm is occasionally broken by triads: see Domenico D'Alessandro, '*Historia Regum Britanniae* et *Roman de Brut*: une comparaison formelle', *Medioevo romanzo* 19 (1994): 37–52; esp. pp. 39–45.

[55] See M. Fabius Quintilianus, *Institutio oratoria*, ed. M. Winterbottom (Oxford, 1970), esp. IX, 4, 122–5.

[56] See for example the description of the siege of Sparatin, lines 321–44. Quite distinctive also is the account of the only naval battle in the work (2459–64), which focuses on the ships themselves rather than the fighting taking place.

> E veïssez nafrez morir;
> Tute ert de sanc l'erbe vermeille
> E ço n'esteit mie merveille,
> Kar li vif sur les mors esteient
> E sur les mors se combateient.[57]

One may note the appeal to the imagination of the reader/audience (*veïssiez/oïssiez*), which adds to the epic feel of this passage and is a regular feature of descriptive passages where the poet wishes to engage the feelings of his audience.[58]

Other descriptive passages fulfil a function that goes beyond ornamentation. Brutus's surveying of Britain thus becomes the symbolical act of foundation of a new civilisation (1209–17):

> Brutus esguarda les montainnes
> Vit les valees, vit les plainnes,
> Vit les mores, vit les boscages,
> Vit les eues, vit les rivages,
> Vit les champs, vit les praeries,
> Vit les porz, vit les pescheries,
> Vit sun pople multepleier,
> Vit les terres bien guaainier;
> Pensa sei que cité fereit.[59]

This combination of anaphora and isocolon is typical of Wace's high style. Brutus's seeing is an act of appropriation, and it is no mere coincidence that the foundation of the second Britain (i.e., Brittany) is depicted in similar terms (5917–26):

> "Cunan, dist il, en suzriant,
> Ceste contree est mult vaillant,
> Mult me semble bien guaainable,
> E plenteïve e delitable.
> Vei quels terres, vei quels rivieres,
> Vei quels forez, cum sunt plenieres;
> Grant plenté i ad de peissun
> E grant plenté de veneisun;

---

[57] 'There you could see horses being spurred on, spears brandished, knights clashing, shields pierced, saddles emptied, men fall and wounds bleed. Knights rushed together, archers shot, men struggled hard and were hard pressed. Arrows fell like rain, pleasing some, disturbing others. You could hear many heads being crushed and see the wounded die. The grass was quite red with blood, and it was not surprising, for the living were on top of the dead and fought over their bodies.'

[58] Descriptive passages introduced in such a way are especially common in the Arthurian section. D'Alessandro ('Analisi del descrittivo nell'opera romanzesca di Wace', *Annali dell'Istituto Universitario Orientale, Sez. Romanza* 33 (1991): 205–16), p. 213, counts 62% of descriptive passages in the Arthurian section opening with the verb 'veoir', as opposed to just 22% elsewhere in the poem. D'Alessandro includes in his count instances of 'Ez vos'.

[59] 'Brutus looked at the mountains, he saw the valleys, the plains, the moors, the woodland, the rivers and the river banks; he saw the fields and the meadows, the harbours and the fisheries; he saw his people multiplying and the lands growing fertile. He thought he would found a city.'

> Unches plus bel païs ne vi.
> Jo l'ai a tun ues encuvi."⁶⁰

The invitation to see the land is also an invitation to take possession of it.

Contrary to what might have been expected, there are relatively few descriptive passages in the *Roman de Brut*. Domenico D'Alessandro counts just 69 descriptions of three lines or more in the whole of the work, most of which are concentrated in the Arthurian section (which has a percentage of just over 9% of descriptive lines, as opposed to an average of less than 3% for the rest of the poem). Individual descriptions in the Arthurian section are also longer than in the rest of the work, with an average length of almost twelve lines per descriptive passage, as compared to under seven outside of the Arthurian section.⁶¹ This is of course accounted for by the presence of lavish ceremonial scenes in Wace's Latin source, but D'Alessandro notes (p. 212) Wace's obvious enjoyment of these scenes, verging on 'una sorta di autocompiacimento' found nowhere else in the work, or indeed, in any other of Wace's earlier poems, where narrative self-indulgence is far from evident. This certainly points to the importance of the reign of Arthur within the overall narrative.

Direct speech is distributed unevenly in the *Roman de Brut*. Over the entirety of the work, direct speech accounts for some 17% of the narrative, with peaks of over 30% of certain episodes in direct speech, and troughs where direct speech is entirely absent. In terms of speech-acts, that is, uninterrupted passages in direct speech put in the mouth of a given character, Wace appears to have added to his source, with about 70% more speech-acts in the French than in his Latin source; but this figure is deceptive, and is in great part due to Wace's preference for dialogue where the Variant might have direct speech followed by reported speech. Episodes with a high proportion of direct speech in the French always correspond to episodes with a high degree of direct speech in the Latin: the story of King Leir and his daughters (32% of direct speech); the rise of Vortigern and his dealings with the wily Hengist (37% of direct speech); and the reign of Aurelius (36% of direct speech), where we not only have the debate at Hengist's trial, but the strong presence of Merlin, entrusted with helping to bring the gigantic stones from Ireland to Stonehenge. By contrast, the Arthurian section has only 10% of direct speech in the pre-Roman part of the reign, and 20% from the Roman ultimatum up to Arthur's death (despite the presence of long speeches in Arthur's council scene, where they decide to wage war against Rome). These figures indicate that direct speech as a form of ornamentation was used sparingly in episodes comprising a strong descriptive element.

However, direct speech is not just an amplificatory device in the *Historia*; long pieces of public oratory (whether as a speech in a formal setting or as an official letter) also carry much of the ideological and political dimension of the work. These speeches echo each other, allowing the reader to compare, contrast and

---

60 'Cunan', he said, smiling, 'this land is most valuable; it seems to me very fertile, abundant and delightful. Look at the soil, look at the rivers, the forests – how copious they are! There are plenty of fish and plenty of game; I never saw a more beautiful land. For your benefit I have longed to have it.'
61 See D'Alessandro, 'Analisi del descrittivo', esp. pp. 209–10.

reflect on the respective situations depicted, from the wise Menbricius who advises the Trojans to leave Greece because it would be impossible to live there in peace after having been in armed conflict with the Greeks, to the wily Margadud who advises King Cadwallan to allow Penda to attack Oswi of Northumberland, thus directing the aggression of the Saxons against each other rather than against the British. In both cases we have a reflection on the difficulty of sharing a land with former enemies. Similarly, King Cassibelan's answer to Julius Caesar's demand for tribute is mirrored by Arthur's summing up of the situation in response to Lucius's demand for tribute. The importance of these speeches is recognised by Wace, who further enhances them so that the audience does not miss the point. This leads to some very long passages in direct speech: eighteen such passages (out of a total of 165) are over 35 lines in length. Of those eighteen, ten are over 50 lines long and four are over 80 lines long.[62] The two longest direct speech passages are well over one hundred lines long: Androgeus's letter to Caesar, where he offers his help to defeat King Cassibelan, and Arthur's speech reminding his barons of the glorious history of their people, thus justifying the war against Rome. In both cases, we have a British king who will be defeated by treason from within his kin group; though Androgeus has better reasons for betraying his uncle than Modred.

By means of comparison, the Variant version of the *Historia* has only three passages of direct speech extending over more than 20 printed lines: Androgeus's letter to Caesar, offering him the support that will enable the Roman conquest of Britain (§61); King Arthur's speech rehearsing the reasons why the Roman ultimatum should be rejected (§159); and King Cadwallader's lament on his way to Brittany, as he abandons a plague-ridden Britain (§203). The longest passages in direct speech in the Latin thus mark three key moments in British history, the last one being when dominion escapes the Britons for good. The sheer number of long speeches in Wace means that the symbolism underlying the placing of long speeches in his Latin source is somewhat obscured; moreover, Cadwallader's monologue is entirely omitted in the French poem. This, as we shall see, reflects the poet's own interpretation of his material. As in his religious works, Wace makes use of stylistic devices, in particular direct speech, to give additional prominence to key themes and events, but on an altogether larger scale. The very length and thematic complexity of the *Roman de Brut* mean that the poet had to rely on a network of echoes between different episodes in order to express his own reading of the British past. The next two chapters investigate Wace's handling of his material, with systematic reference to the Latin sources he reshapes.

---

[62] The longest direct-speech passages in the *Roman de Brut* are: Leir's lament and decision to go to France to his youngest daughter (1913–72); the bad advice given to Brennes (2341–404); Tonuenne's intervention (2729–816); Cassibelan's letter to Caesar (3903–60); Androgeus's letter to Caesar (4425–534); the justification for the Roman retreat from Britain (6187–251); Archbishop Guincelin's plea to Aldroen of Brittany (6345–96); the Roman ultimatum to Arthur (10639–710); Arthur's speech in the ensuing council meeting (10779–904) and King Angusel's endorsement of the decision to go to war (10958–1040).

5

Britain, Rome and the House of Constantine

The Rise and Fall of the Celtic rulers of Britain, in Wace as in his Latin sources, takes place in four phases:

1. The Foundation and early kings. This part has at its core Britain's relation with Rome, and ends with the Roman retreat from the island.
2. The House of Constantine and the advent of the Saxons.
3. Arthur, who constitutes the culmination of the House of Constantine, and whose reign faces the dual threat of Rome and the Saxons.
4. The passage of dominion to the English.

These parts are linked together by the theme of Brittany. Conquered by the Emperor Maximien in Part 1 and granted by him to Conan who founds a powerful dynasty there (at considerable expense for Britain), it becomes, in the words of Elizabeth Bryan, a 'royal nursery' for Britain.[1] King Constantine, Arthur's grandfather, is the brother of the king of Brittany, and when Vortigern usurps the power, the young princes Aurelius and Uther seek refuge there. Arthur maintains strong bonds with his Breton kinsmen, in particular his cousin Hoel who is at his side throughout his campaigns. And in the final phase, it is to Brittany that King Cadwallader flees from the plague devastating his land, and in Brittany again that he has the divine vision telling him to renounce England.

The initial phase in the history of the Celtic kings of Britain, in Wace as in his sources, revolves around the relationship between Britain and Rome. This relationship is expressed on three levels: the common origins of Britons and Romans; the military campaigns opposing Britain and Rome; and the bond of Christianity between the two nations.

The myth of origins

The myth of the Trojan origins of the Britons is of crucial importance for an understanding of the development of the plot. The French poem presents §6 (the first chapter after the prolegomena) of the Latin as follows: Eneas becomes king (9–66); length of Eneas's reign, his achievements, his posthumous son, Aschanius's regency, his pedigree, achievements and duration of his rule (67–106); the conditions of Brutus's birth (107–48); Brutus's exile to Greece and

---

[1] Elizabeth J. Bryan, 'The Afterlife of Armoriche', pp. 117–55 in *Laȝamon: Contexts, Language, and Interpretation*, ed. R. Allen, L. Perry and J. Roberts (London, 2002), quote p. 144.

his meeting the enslaved Trojans (149–60). Despite the fact that much of this section can be read in parallel with the Latin (First Variant) text, the French provides additional information on the fall of Troy: mentioning Paris and Helen (12–13), the number of Eneas's boats, and his journeying at sea (20–3, 29–36). As noted by Paradisi, Wace appears to have tried to create an echo of the *Aeneid*, particularly with the addition of sea journeys, and the mention that Turnus, Eneas's rival in Italy, was motivated by love for Lavinia. This immediately establishes within the work an alternative discourse expressing a very different viewpoint from that of Geoffrey of Monmouth, whose implicit message throughout the first section of his material appears to be the inherent superiority of the British – descended from Eneas's son Aschanius by the Trojan princess Creusa – over the Romans, descended from Eneas's son Silvius Postumus by the Italian princess Lavinia.

This bias was not shared by the redactor of the First Variant version, or indeed by Wace. An indication of this is the mention in the Variant version, maintained and slightly expanded by Wace (101–4), of Aschanius's failed attempts to move the household gods of Troy to his town of Alba, derived from Vergil's *Aeneid*. The mysterious and repeated return of the Trojan deities to his stepmother Lavinia clearly indicates that Eneas's true heir is in fact Silvius rather than Aschanius; hence its absence from Geoffrey of Monmouth's text. Within the overall context of the *Roman de Brut*, it is also significant that Aschanius is never said to be king, even though his 34-year 'regency' only comes to an end with his death. In the French poem, Brutus's pedigree is therefore slightly less impressive than in the vulgate version of the *Historia Regum Britanniae*. The regular reminder of the link between Britain and the Latium offered by the time rubrics in the Variant text, where the reader is periodically told that at a given time, such a king or prophet was active in Judea, and such a character ruled Alba, is systematically omitted by Wace, who only retains the reference to the founding of Rome (2107–10). Similarly, the only instance of Italo-British collaboration on an equal footing (King Silvius assists King Ebrauc's sons in their conquest of Germany) is omitted from the French poem, and with it, the sense of family solidarity that it implied.

The fact still remains, however, that the future founder of Britain shares with the future founding family of Rome his Trojan origins (through his father) and a common link with the royal family of the Latium (his mother is a relative of Lavinia's). Awareness of the consanguinity between the Romans and the British is reinforced throughout the narrative by frequent cases of intermarriage within their respective elites. King Ebrauc thus sends his thirty daughters to Italy, because the women of Lombardy were refusing to marry men of Trojan origin (1571–82); while Roman generals and emperors marry British princesses (Sever, Constant, Maximien), and British kings marry Roman noblewomen (Arviragus, Constantine of Brittany, Arthur). But this aspect is not given particular emphasis by Wace.

This first phase in the history of the Britons interweaves the issue of Romano-British relations with themes and situations that reappear at different stages in the work. King Locrin's love for the foreign captive Hestrild, which eventually leads to civil war, prefigures Vortigern's disastrous passion for the

Saxon Ronwen, and Uther's infatuation with Ygerne; the fear of miscegenation underlying the request by the Italian noblemen of Trojan origin of Ebrauc's thirty daughters, reappears in the account of the foundation of Brittany, with the ill-fated sending of thousands of brides to the new colonists. The tensions that may exist between two royal brothers, hinted at by Aschanius's attempt to appropriate the ancestral gods, are shown occurring in a variety of ways and with differing consequences, from violent death (Malin and Malan, Porrex and Ferrex, Bassian and Geta) to glorious collaboration (Belin and Brennes). Similarly, the quarrel between uncle and nephew that enables Julius Caesar to conquer Britain foreshadows another disastrous case of treason within the royal family, when Modred betrays his uncle Arthur. Wace attributes more importance to some of these themes than to others; and he is at his most insistent when treating the theme of linguistic change.

Whereas Rome is arguably a stable, unchanging presence, and even the city of Tours maintains its name through the ages (943–6), Britain is characterised by movement and corruption. This point is made early on in the narrative, as we are told of the names given by the newly arrived Trojans to the different regions of Britain. The statement that they called their Trojan language 'Breton' (1191) leads to the following addition by Wace to his Latin source (1192–200):

> Mais Engleis l'unt puis remué;
> La parole e li nuns dura
> Tant que Gormund i ariva;
> Gormund en chaça les Bretuns
> Si la livra a uns Saissuns
> Qui d'Angle Angleis apelé erent,
> Ki Engletere l'apelerent;
> Tuz les Bretuns si eissilierent
> Que unches puis ne redrescerent.[2]

Wace is announcing a pattern of loss before Brutus and his followers have had the time to settle. Some twenty lines later, change due to political factors is compounded by linguistic corruption due to time and ignorance. The town founded by Brutus is named by him 'Troie Nove' in honour of his ancestors, but 'ala li nuns corumpant/ Si l'apela l'om Trinovant'. King Lud subsequently renamed the town Kaerlu, we are told, which in turn was 'corompu' into Lodoïn, then (1236–46):

> Pur Lodoïn a la parfin
> Londenë en engleis dist l'um
> E nus or Lundres l'apelum.
> Par plusurs granz destruiemenz
> Que unt fait alienes genz
> Ki la terre unt sovent eüe
> Sovent prise, sovent perdue,

---

[2] 'But English has since altered it. The language and the name lasted until Gurmunt arrived: he drove out the Britons and handed it over to Saxons who, from being Angles, were called English and called the land England. They drove out all the Britons, who never returned.'

>Sunt les viles e les contrees
>Tutes or altrement nomees
>Que li anceisor nes nomerent
>Ki premierement les fonderent.³

This point is further repeated, again in connection with London, some two and half thousand lines later, in almost identical terms (3775–84):

>Par remuemenz e par changes
>Des languages as gens estranges,
>Ki la terre unt sovent conquise,
>Sovent perdue, sovent prise,
>Sunt li nun des viles changed,
>U acreü u acurcied;
>Mult en purreit l'on trover poi,
>Si come jo entent e oi,
>Qui ait tenu entierement
>Le nun qu'ele out premierement.⁴

Wace describes a process of repeated corruption by 'estrange home . . . qui le language ne saveient' (3762–3), foreigners who did not know the language; the English and the Saxons first, then the Normans and the 'Franceis/ Ki ne sourent parler Engleis' (3769–70), the French who could not speak English. Britain is placed under the sign of mutability, and the British are from the outset tainted by a form of degeneracy.

The moral connotations of such passages should not be overstressed, inasmuch as they are derived from Wace's Latin source, which makes similar observations at the same places. Moreover, the process described is a recognised linguistic phenomenon, referred to in a scholarly manner with the suitable technical terms: for example, 'bien pert par corruptiun/ Faite la compositiun' (1229–30, literally: 'the way the name was composed/constructed is clearly by corruption'); 'mais genz estranges unt le nun abregied par subtraction' (3199–200, literally: 'but foreign people have shortened the name by subtracting elements from it').⁵ Wace is showing off his learning. The most striking demonstration of philological expertise in the poem occurs in a somewhat different context, towards the end of the work, when the poet explains the meaning of the name Cernel: he refers to Latin and Hebrew, and states that 'Si est par une abscisiun/ faite la compositiun'

---

3 'Finally, people call "Lodoin", "Londene", in English, and we now call it "Lundres". Through many acts of destruction wrought by foreigners, who have often possessed the land, often seized it, often lost it, the towns and regions all now have different names from those their founders gave them, who first established them.'
4 'Through alterations and changes by the languages of foreigners, who have often conquered, lost and seized the land, the names of towns have changed, or become longer or shorter. Very few can be found, as I hear and understand, which have completely kept the name they first had.'
5 A comparable didactic passage where Wace spells out the process by which a name changed may be found in his discussion of the name of Bath (supposedly from the name of King Bladud), 1633–4. For a detailed discussion of such passages, see Paradisi, *Le passioni della storia*, pp. 211–24. On the moral connotations to these terms and Wace's attitude towards linguistic change (including in his *Roman de Rou*), see G. Paradisi, '«Par muement de languages». Il tempo, la memoria e il volgare in Wace', *Francofonia* 45 (2003): 27–45.

(13801–2, literally, 'the name is composed through an excision'). However, the repeated use of the terms 'corumpre' and 'corruptiun', in conjunction with the constant reminder that the civilisation that had first named these towns and places had been superseded,[6] may be said to pave the way for Wace's dismissal of the descendents of the old Britons, the Welsh of his day, as 'Tuit . . . mué e tuit changié/ Tuit . . . divers e forslignié/ De noblesce, d'onur, de murs/ E de la vie as anceisurs' (14851–4):[7] they are now completely different from their ancestors, in every possible way – they are degenerate. Decline is inscribed in the very foundation of Britain.

Conflict with Rome

The glorious past of the Britons, before the advent of King Arthur, is epitomised by the defeat of Rome at the hands of the brothers Belin and Brennes. The importance of this episode is indicated by Wace by the more than average degree of elaboration he brings to the account, especially in his speeches and descriptive scenes.[8] Wace adds nothing of substance here to the Latin source, but neither does he try to attenuate the salient characteristic of the episode: Rome's moral bankruptcy.

The tale starts with two royal brothers, who on their father's death divide the realm between them, the elder brother (Belin) retaining overlordship (and the crown). Bad counsellors convince the younger brother, Brennes, to challenge his brother's authority by going to Norway, marrying the king's daughter, and returning with an army. This he does; but the king of Denmark, who was due to marry the Norwegian princess, captures her at sea. His ship is caught in a storm that throws them onto the coast of Britain. Belin learns all about his brother's plans; the Norwegians are defeated, and Brennes goes into exile in France. There, he meets with the favour of the duke of Burgundy who gives him his daughter in marriage and makes him his heir. On the death of the duke, Brennes mounts an expedition against his brother. But just before they engage in battle, their elderly mother, Tonuenne, intervenes and reconciles them. The two brothers then decide to go and conquer France.

This preliminary narrative, which covers about two thirds of the episode in the Latin, is reduced to just over half of the account in the French text, which therefore gives comparatively more space to the brothers' ensuing adventures and achievements. However, this section contains a number of motifs that are congenial with a 'courtly' treatment, and Wace does to a limited extent seize this

---

[6] To this one may add that Wace adds to his source the mention of the destruction of Leicester, by a 'dissensiun', immediately after the account of its foundation (1665–6); Wace appears to be referring to post-Conquest events (see Arnold, in the note to line 1665; p. 797). Caerleon is also explicitly said (10235–6) to have deteriorated steadily from its days of glory under Arthur.

[7] '[The Welsh] have quite altered and changed, they are quite different and have quite degenerated from the nobility, the honour, the customs and the life of their ancestors.'

[8] The storm at sea (2478–90) that scatters Brennes's fleet is particularly memorable, and is thought to have influenced the depiction of a similar scenes in Thomas's *Tristan*: see Margaret M. Pelan, *L'influence du «Brut» de Wace sur les romanciers de son temps* (Strasbourg, 1931), pp. 71–97.

opportunity. The Norwegian princess remains unnamed, but her feelings for Gudlac of Denmark are made explicit; she is 'assez bele e gente', but she is unhappy at her impending marriage with Brennes because she and Godlac had long been in love, and were to have married (2439–44). Moreover, whereas the Latin text mentions only Godlac's eventual release (in exchange for an annual tribute and submission to Britain), Wace notes that 'S'amie en ad od sei menee/ Que par grant peinne out achatee' (2597–8), that he took with him his beloved whom he had bought through such effort. Brennes emerges from this incident humiliated on every count, all the more so for not having been his own bride's preference, while Belin is shown to be a forceful and canny ruler, who was able to turn the situation to his advantage. The second potentially 'courtly' scene in this section is Tonuenne's touching intervention between the two brothers. This potential is not truly exploited by Wace. He adds a few nice touches to her speech, making it psychologically more effective, but his description of the lady is anything but dignified or respectful, particularly with regards to her bared breasts which he says to be 'flaistres de viellesce e pelues' (2724), 'withered and hairy with age'. The main import of the scene is that Brennes is made to accept his position and draw a line on the past. The overall effect is that, more so than in the Latin, Brennes is clearly inferior to his brother: he is easily manipulated, listens to bad advice, does not have sufficient charisma to secure the affections of his future bride, and has a vindictive streak. The future ruler of Rome is not an attractive character.

The brothers conquer France with ease and to decide to continue on to Rome. No reasons are given, neither does the common Trojan ancestry apparently make them pause. Wace adds a list of the regions and towns they conquer (2865–74), and the increasing fear of the Romans (2875–7), who prefer to buy off the brothers rather than resist. They offer them as much as they wish, and promise an annual tribute as well. The brothers accept, and as guarantee the Romans hand over 24 noble-born children as hostages. However, they do not intend to keep their word, a fact that the narrator emphasises with proleptic remarks (2917–18, 2925–8); a situation all the more shocking because of the treachery it implies not only towards their supposed new allies, but also towards the hostages (2925–8):

> Encore unt laissied lor ostages
> Ki esteient de lor lignages,
> E l'amistied unt corumpue,
> Mult fud petit par els tenue.[9]

As a result, when the plans of the decidedly unheroic Romans to go awry, and they end up being besieged by Belin and Brennes in Rome, the horror of the scene where the brothers set up a gallows under the city walls and hang the hostages rebounds on the Romans themselves. Wace adds, in direct speech (3086–98), the insults and threats the Romans make when, after this incident, they eventually decide to fight; this makes them appear less heartless, but the ultimate responsibility for the death of the hostages remains theirs. There is only one other instance

---

[9] 'Moreover they abandoned their hostages, who came from their own families, and had damaged the friendship, paying little regard for it.'

in the *Historia* of hostages being executed as a result of the treachery of their kinsmen, in the Arthurian section (9261–2): they are Saxons.

The victory of Belin and Brennes has a taste of poetic justice to it. Brennes is left in control of the town which he treats with cruelty and fierceness (3156–8). In contrast to his brother, Belin, on his return to Britain, is characterised by the constructive and positive nature of his reign: founding towns and building marvels, maintaining law and order and promoting prosperity. The superiority of the world represented by Belin over that of the Romans is clear, but Wace does not allow the reader to dwell on it. The mention of the founding of the town of Kaerusc is used as springboard for a lengthy explanation of the reason for the change of its name to Caerleon, including a didactic aside on the number of men in a Roman legion (3171–204). The eventual Roman conquest, as in the account of the Foundation of Britain, is once again placed at the forefront by Wace.

Geoffrey of Monmouth gives the conquest of Britain by Julius Caesar a somewhat negative gloss at odds with the mainstream historiography of his time. In the vulgate version of the *Historia Regum Britanniae* as in the Variant, Caesar has his fair share of the flaws shown by his people in the Belin and Brennes episode. He is aware of his kinship with the Britons, but conceitedly assumes that they have degenerated (or, more precisely, have remained primitive), and decides to claim tribute because he thinks it will be easy to exact it from them. Wace, on the other hand, puts the decision firmly against the backdrop of the sack of Rome; Caesar wants to make the Britons know that Rome is now a power to be reckoned with (3877–84):

> De ceste ille Bretainne furent
> Belins e Brennes, ki tant crurent
> Qu'il pristrent Rome la cité
> E destrurent nostre sené.
> Bien lur devum faire saveir
> Que Rome est or d'altre poeir;
> Fortune ad sa roe tornee
> E Rome rest esviguree.[10]

As a consequence, King Cassibelan's attributing Caesar's demand for tribute to Roman avarice (an assumption implicitly validated in the Latin texts) no longer rings true, and the British no longer have the moral high ground. In addition, after the first failed invasion, Wace subtly promotes Caesar as a civilisational figure, through the addition of a description of the tower built by him at Ordres (4203–18), which becomes an item of *mirabilia* no less wondrous than Belin's tower over the Thames (Billingsgate).[11] The tower at Ordres prefigures the towers built by two other arch-enemies of Britain, Vortigern and Gurmund; it is a place of refuge, a treasure house, and Caesar's power base in France. Like the early

---

[10] 'From this island, Britain, came Belin and Brenne, who grew so great that they took the city of Rome and destroyed our senate. We must certainly let them know that now Rome wields a rather different power. Fortune has turned her wheel and Rome is strengthened again.'

[11] On Ordres and its place within the narrative, see F. Le Saux, 'Mais où sont les fenêtres? De l'*Historia Regum Britanniae* de Geoffroy de Monmouth au *Roman de Brut* de Wace et au *Brut* de Layamon', pp. 295–305 in *La fenêtre au Moyen-Age*, ed. C. Connochie-Bourgne (Aix-en-Provence, 2003).

Romans, Caesar knows the power of money, and uses it effectively to control the French; but it is of little use to him against the British, whose fatal weakness is going to be feuding in the royal family, leading to treason.

The passage where Androgeus offers his help to Caesar and the ensuing, successful conquest of the island is recounted without major modification by Wace. There are however two noteworthy features to the French account. First, Androgeus's letter to Caesar in the *Roman de Brut* is altogether longer than one would have anticipated (some 110 lines), as it recounts in detail a scene already described by the narrator (i.e., Hirelgas's death at Evelin's hands), and should typically have been abbreviated by Wace. This suggests a desire on the poet's part to exonerate Androgeus, as the gravity of the situation that has led him to take this step is emphasised through repetition. The theme of Fortune first introduced in Caesar's speech then reappears, as the narrator describes the desperate situation of the Britons besieged on their rocky hill (4665–8):

> Mais Fortune est d'altre colur
> E sa roële ad fait sun tur,
> E cil sunt el desuz turné
> Ki el desus ourent esté.[12]

The Britons have run out of luck. For the first time in their history, they will have to pay tribute to a foreign nation (4817–20); and the end of Cassibelan's reign closes, not with his achievements, but with Caesar's, as Wace adds the bit of information (4825–8) that Exeter was said to have been founded by the Roman general.

From now on, and until the Roman retreat, Rome and Britain are closely intertwined; Roman emperors become British kings, and vice-versa, as aristocratic bloodlines merge. Heirs to the throne of Britain are fostered by their relatives in Rome, leading to the gradual blurring of the distinction between Roman and Briton. And from this arises a confusion of loyalties leading to the disastrous decision by Maximien to plunder Britain of her wealth and manpower in order to overcome his rivals to the Empire. As a result of having chosen as king someone whose priority was his Roman ambitions, the British have to rely for the first time on Roman help; and the Romans will then abandon them, as being a troublesome and ruinous investment. The Britons only re-enter the scene as a military and political power after Britain has recovered from her weakness under the leadership of Arthur, thus once again offering rich pickings. But Rome's importance is not restricted to the temporal scene, and the spiritual authority invested with city through the papacy lends yet another dimension to the relations with Britain, with potentially greater implications for a twelfth-century Anglo-Norman audience.

---

[12] 'But Fortune's way is different: her wheel turned, and those who had been on top fell to the bottom.'

Rome, Britain and Christianity

As we have seen, Geoffrey of Monmouth's *Historia Regum Britanniae* is singularly secular in tone: something the First Variant redactor attempted to correct through a more moralising outlook. Wace's sympathies clearly lie with his chosen source, the Variant, though not so much in his tendency to moralise,[13] as in a shared interest in the history of the redemption of mankind. Of the entire first phase of the history of the kings of Britain, this is the only area where Wace introduces totally new material, from sources unknown.

Christianity first appears in the narrative in the account of the reign of Kimbelin, in a passage which has no counterpart in any surviving source (4855–76):

> En Bretainne aveit un devin
> Que l'on apelout Teleusin;
> Pur buen prophete esteit tenuz
> E mult esteit de tuz creüz.
> A une feste qu'il faiseient,
> U li Bretun ensemble esteient,
> Li preia li reis e requist
> Qu'alcune chose li deïst
> Del tens ki veneit en avant;
> E cil parla si dist itant:
> "Home, ne seiez en tristur;
> Atendu avum nuit e jur,
> En terre est del ciel descenduz
> Cil ki ad esté atenduz
> Ki salver nus deit, Jesu Crist"
> La prophetie que cil dist
> Fu entre Bretuns recordee;
> De lunc tens ne fu obliee.
> Il out dist veirs, pas ne menti;
> A cel tens Jesu Crist nasqui.
> Bretuns pur ço plus tost creïrent,
> Quant de Crist preeschier oirent.[14]

This passage is intriguing on several counts, not least of which is that where Wace could have got this information from is a mystery. Teleusin is readily identifiable as the Welsh poet Taliesin mentioned in the *Historia Brittonum*. He is generally accepted as an historical character, and poetry attributed to him, in Middle Welsh,

---

[13] He does make the occasional misogynistic or moralising comment (for example, Leir episode, 1883–4; Constant's coronation, 6539–40), but they are relatively unobtrusive.

[14] 'There was a soothsayer in Britain called Teleusin: he was considered a good prophet and everyone gave him much credence. At a festival, where the British were gathered together, the king begged and asked him to tell him something of the time to come. And he spoke as follows: "Man, sorrow no more. We have waited night and day: from heaven to earth has descended he whom we awaited, who will save us, Jesus Christ." The British remembered the prophecy he uttered; it was not forgotten for a long while. He told the truth and did not lie: Jesus was born at this time. For this reason the British were readier to believe when they heard people preach about Christ.'

is still extant. However, he is placed by the redactor of the *Historia Brittonum* much later in time, under the reign of King Vortigern. Taliesin also appears in Geoffrey of Monmouth's later (and less well-known) *Vita Merlini*: there as in Wace, 'Telgesinus' is a prophet; but he is a contemporary of Merlin. One can only postulate that Wace was echoing an oral source; but this is in itself surprising, as the poet is offering this information without a hint of reticence, whereas one would expect some degree of diffidence if it were not derived from an authoritative, written Latin source.[15] His informant must have been an eminently respectable and learned cleric to elicit such trust;[16] and one, it would appear, with Welsh sympathies lacking in the French poet himself.

The consequence of the addition of Taliesin's prophecy at this stage is that the Britons are shown to have an especial affinity with Christianity. They hear about the birth of Christ before anyone else, and live in expectation thereafter; they are fertile soil for the Good Word. By contrast, the conversion of Rome by Saint Peter is mentioned only in passing, some two hundred lines later. Within the narrative as a whole, the figure of Teleusin prefigures and, to some extent, counteracts that of Merlin; Wace decided not to translate Merlin's prophecies, but he has included a far more authoritative prophecy by another, older British seer. This also indirectly gives legitimacy to Merlin himself, as he is no longer an isolated phenomenon, but can be placed within a tradition of (truthful) insular prophecy at the service of kings.

The conversion of Britain under King Luces is recounted by Wace with a less spectacular, but nevertheless real modification. Luces hears about Christianity, asks Pope Eleutherius to send missionaries over to Britain to instruct the people, and gives the Pope's envoys, Fagan and Dunian, his entire support. Pagan temples are rededicated, and the pagan religious structures are replaced by Christian ones. Having established bishoprics and archbishoprics, Fagan and Dunian return to Rome, 'et cuncta que fecerant a beato papa confirmari impetraverunt' ('and they had everything they had done confirmed by the blessed pope', §72). The legitimacy of the Celtic church is thus conferred by Rome, whereas in the French poem the saintly missionaries establish parishes, bishoprics and archbishoprics 'par le rei e par sun otreiz/ Si come costume est e dreiz' (5237–8), 'Through the king and with his agreement, as is right and customary'. The Pope remains unmentioned. This procedure corresponded to Anglo-Norman practice, from William Rufus to Henry II, and it caused real tensions.[17] William Rufus in particular was perceived to be treating the English prelates like ordinary feudal tenants, and was responsible, on the death of Archbishop Lanfranc in 1089, for a lengthy vacancy of the see of Canterbury (the revenues of which were diverted into the royal treasury for that period). Lanfranc's successor, the future St Anselm, found both William Rufus and Henry I stubborn in their refusal to concede to the papacy any real authority over ecclesiastical appointments in England; his principles forced him

---

[15] Wace is no different in this respect to the other historians of his time, who are very careful to indicate to the reader the nature and quality of their sources. See van Houts, *Memory and Gender*, pp. 19–39.

[16] On the privileged position of the male clerical witness, see van Houts, *Memory and Gender*, esp. pp. 22–6.

[17] For a discussion of lay investitures in post-Conquest England, see for example Davis, *England under the Normans and Angevins*, esp. pp. 47–54, 86–102 and 125–33.

into exile twice, in 1097, under William Rufus, until the accession of Henry I, and again from 1103 to 1105. A treaty was drawn up in 1106, after the king was threatened with excommunication by the Pope; but it was a compromise that did not really solve the problem, in that the episcopate remained in a vassalic bond with the king for the temporalities attached to their position.[18] The issue of lay investiture of ecclesiastical offices returned with a vengeance, and came to a head under Henry II, with the assassination of Thomas Becket in December 1170. Jean-Guy Gouttebroze has suggested that Wace's slowness in proceeding with his *Roman de Rou* (which may have caused his fall from favour with Henry II) could have been a form of ideological protest.[19] If such was the case, however, it does not show in his *Roman de Brut*. Wace appears to side wholeheartedly with the temporal authorities in this matter, rather than with the ecclesiastical ones – perhaps with an eye to his own preferment.

Whatever the immediate reasons which might have led Wace to make this specific adjustment to his sources, it has as immediate consequence a reinforcement of the polarisation between Rome and Britain. The British church is structurally independent of Rome. The link with the Pope is always maintained (Gawain is fostered by the pope in Rome), but the bond is a loosely spiritual one rather than a hierarchical one: something of a two-edged sword, inasmuch as the independence of the British Church from the See of Peter will turn against them when St Augustine comes to evangelise the Anglo-Saxons. Augustine, in Wace, is (as we shall see) a more formidable character than in the *Historia Regum Britanniae*, due mainly to the French poet's introduction of hagiographical legends into the episode, but also because as envoy of the Pope, he is implicitly endowed with a higher degree of authority than the British bishops.

Christianity introduces a new field of rivalry with Rome, and Geoffrey of Monmouth's material is heavily weighted in favour of the British in this respect, notably with his giving Constantine, the first Christian emperor, a Briton as mother, and having him born and bred in Britain, where he is king before being implored by his Roman kinsmen to come to their help. The Pope might be in Rome, but Christianity comes to the Roman ruling classes from Britain. Despite their town being at the heart of Western Christendom, the Romans persecute the faith (under Emperor Maximianus) and have pagans as allies (a crucial point in Arthur's campaign against Emperor Lucius); whereas the Britons are persistently defined by their Christianity, to the extent that threats to Britain are also threats to her Christian identity. Wanis and Melga, the Saxons, Gurmund are all heathens who delight in the destruction of churches and the massacre of clerics, and the hallmark of the good British king is his dedication to rebuilding and strengthening the Church. Wace goes one step further, identifying Constantine's mother Helen with St Helen, who found the Cross of Christ (5720–4). He also adds a hagiographical element later, at a key point in the narrative, when Earl Dionot's daughter Ursula, sent to Brittany to be married to Conan but captured by pirates, is conflated with the figure of St Ursula of Cologne. In both cases, the royal saint

---

[18] Henry renounced the right of investing prelates with ring and staff, but continued to receive their homage for the actual lands that gave them their income. See Davis, pp. 132–3.
[19] Gouttebroze, 'Pourquoi congédier un historien', esp. pp. 291–2.

draws attention to a trend whereby Roman policy is increasingly taking precedence over British interests.

The final episode in this initial phase of the history of the British brings together all three of the thematic strands characterising Brito-Roman relations. The ill-fated reign of Maximien (Maximianus) is made possible because of the systematic intermarriage over a number of generations between the British and the Roman ruling classes. His mother is born of the Roman senatorial class and his father is the brother of Helen, queen of Britain in her own right, but also the wife of Emperor Constantine, and a saint. Patterns of loyalty become blurred: the disastrous decision to deprive Britain of her fighting men is a direct result of a process that has turned Britain into an inferior prize compared with Rome. The consequences of Maximien's imperial ambitions are compounded by his founding a second Britain, Brittany, that comes into direct competition with the motherland at a time of crisis.

The motivation for the foundation of Brittany is Maximien's awareness that in accepting the crown of Britain, he had wronged Conan, nephew of King Octave and prime contender to the throne. He therefore offers him the territory they have just conquered on the way to Rome (5927–33):

> Bretainne te fu otreiee,
> Si fust en tei bien enpleiee,
> Mais tu l'as perdue par mei
> E tu m'en sez mal gré, ço crei.
> Mais or me fai de cel pardun;
> Jo t'en rendrai tun gueredun.
> De tut cest regne te saisis.[20]

The content of this speech follows closely the corresponding passage in the Latin, with the apparently minor addition of the statement that Conan would have been a good king for Britain (5928) – something Maximien clearly fails to be. The creation of a new kingdom is thus depriving Britain of her natural leader, as well as her fighting men. From the outset, the new kingdom of Brittany, surrounded by the hostile French and threatened by miscegenation, is a drain on Britain's now scarce resources. The request to Earl Dionot to send wives to the Breton colonists echoes King Ebrauc's sending of his thirty daughters to the Trojan noblemen established in Italy; but the circumstances are very different. We are dealing now with seventy-one thousand young women of all social classes and the intent is explicitly a desire to preserve the purity of the blood-line (6009–12):

> Ne lur volt pas doner Franceises
> Ne pur force, ne pur richeises,
> Ne lur lignage entremeller
> E lur terres acomuner.[21]

---

[20] 'Britain was promised to you: it would have been in good hands, but through me you lost it and I believe you resent me for it. But now forgive me for it: I will give you your reward. I give you the whole of this land.'

[21] 'He [i.e., Conan] did not want to give them [i.e., his men] Frenchwomen, using either gifts or force, nor to intermingle their races, nor to join their countries.'

Wace's account of the foundation of Brittany varies from that of the Variant version of the *Historia* (his main source for this section) in a number of important respects. First, in the French text, Maximien slaughters the entire population of Brittany, with the intention of replacing it entirely with Britons. In the Latin only the men are massacred, thus making the threat of miscenegation a real possibility. The mention of lands (6012) by Wace links the issue not so much with concerns about ethnic purity as with territorial considerations: intermarriage with the French could be seen as weakening the Britons' exclusive claim over Brittany. Where Conan and his colonists eventually found their wives remains a mystery (in this version of the events at least),[22] for as we know, the prospective brides are all lost at sea, or captured by pirates. The hagiographical legend inserted by Wace at this point casts Britain as birth-place of martyrs, with Ursula and eleven thousand of her companions being beheaded in Cologne (6073–6).

There is little give-and-take in the relationship between Rome and Britain at this point. Britain provides Rome with power, riches and leaders, while Rome proves to be unable to give anything in exchange. Even Brittany is conquered by Conan himself, and has to be defended without help from Rome. Rome is a defective overlord in times of crisis (we had a glimpse of this in the Belin and Brennes episode), and turns out to be unable (or unwilling) to help out when the pirates Wanis and Melga take advantage of the vacuum of power in the land. Maximien sends out a competent warrior but inadequate ruler, in the person of Gratian; and Gratian's death at the hand of an enraged mob becomes yet another excuse for Rome to retreat entirely from a Britain that is no longer a profitable venture. Britain has to turn towards Brittany and the descendents of Conan for support.

The House of Constantine

Brittany, whence Britain's salvation will come, is described from the outset by Wace as a place of continuity and permanence, through an apparently throwaway remark that contrasts it sharply with Britain (5949–52):

> De cel tens, par ceste achaisun,
> Perdi Armoriche sun nun,
> Si out cest nun Bretaine e ad,
> Ne jamais, ço crei, nel perdrad.[23]

This name and, implicitly, the identity it conveys, is strongly implanted; and the kings ruling this land are depicted as endowed with the qualities of the best British rulers: powerful, wise and pious. These characteristics are at the forefront of the

---

[22] According to one medieval Welsh tradition, the female captives had their tongues cut out, so that they could not corrupt the British language by speaking a creolised version of it to their offspring with the colonists; hence the Welsh name of Llydaw (Latin: Letavia) given to Brittany, understood as meaning 'half-mute.' See Rachel Bromwich, ed. and trans., *Trioedd Ynys Prydein. The Welsh Triads* (Cardiff, 1978), pp. 316–17.

[23] 'At this moment and in this way Armorica lost its name and acquired the name of "Britain", and has it still and never, I believe, will lose it.'

episode where Archbishop Guincelin comes to beg King Aldroen for help. The scene itself is reshaped by Wace, to include more direct speech than his main source, following in this respect cues given by the vulgate text. In terms of content, however, he omits Aldroenus's negative comments on Britain contained in Geoffrey's vulgate text and his blunt attribution of the problems of the British to Roman overlordship (§92), emphasising rather the king's sorrow at Guincelin's news and his readiness to help (6401–8):

> "Si jo, dist il, vus puis valeir,
> Jo vus valdrai a mun poeir.
> Constentin, mun frere, enmerrez
> E cunestable le ferez.
> Il est chevaliers merveillus
> E de guerre mult enginnus.
> Dous mil armez li liverai
> Des plus preisez ke jo avrai."[24]

The flower of Brittany (itself descended from the flower of Britain) is thus sent to the rescue; and Guincelin's response is a delighted 'Christus vincit, Christus regnat/ Christus vincit et imperat', giving an immediate blessing not only on the new dynasty, but also on Aldroen himself. This follows the vulgate text; in the Variant, Guincelin's exclamation comes later in the narrative, after Constantine has been crowned king.

Having fulfilled his mission, Guincelin disappears from the forefront of the French poem, both at the coronation scene (which is merely mentioned, not described as in the Latin texts) and as an influential courtier. In the Latin texts, Constantine is given as bride a young woman of a noble Roman family who had been fostered by the archbishop: Wace mentions her noble origins, but not her connection with Guincelin. This could be because of a certain reluctance on the part of the poet to show ecclesiastical authorities taking too energetic a part in secular matters;[25] or, conversely, to implicitly exonerate the Church from the ill-advised decision to make the eldest son of Constantine a monk.

This new phase in the fortunes of Britain is clearly transitional in nature. It is a fresh start for Britain, free from the overlordship of Rome, but with a legacy of weakness that has not been totally overcome and will lead to the rise of the traitor Vortigern, the usurper who introduces a new enemy to the land, the pagan Saxons. Treason is the recurrent theme of this part of the *Roman de Brut*, highlighting the danger posed by the enemy within. Constantine is murdered by one of his own household knights, as is his son Constance; and Vortigern is one of the grandees of the realm. The extent of Vortigern's treachery is indicated by the fact that, whereas in the Latin texts the barons are unable to come to a decision regarding

---

[24] 'If I can be of use to you, I will help as much as I can. Take Constantine, my brother, and make him commander. He is an exceptional knight and very cunning in battle. I will give him two thousand armed men from amongst the best I have.'

[25] However, Wace retains the detail that the archbishop was made guardian of the young princes Aurelius and Uther (6453–4).

the succession of murdered King Constantine, in the French work they have chosen which of the two younger princes to make king (though no name is mentioned). Vortigern's dragging of Constance out of his monastery thus has no possible justification in terms of the common good, and Wace makes this clear in one of his rare proleptic comments (6535–40):

> Constanz la corune reçut,
> L'ordre guerpi que tenir dut;
> L'ordre Deu guerpi malement,
> Sin vint a mal definement;
> Ne deit pas huem a buen chief traire
> De faire ço qu'il ne deit faire.[26]

Moralising comments are more frequent in this part of the *Roman de Brut* than elsewhere, indicating the degree of indignation the audience should feel when told of the repeated violations of religion, decency and honour that characterise the rise to power of Vortigern.

The reigns of Constance/Vortigern, Aurelius and Uther have the highest proportion of direct speech and dialogue of the entire work (together with the Leir episode and the latter part of Arthur's reign), showcasing the various stages in the implantation of the Saxons. The arrival of Hengist reveals Vortigern as a gullible and weak man,[27] who is prepared to sacrifice both his soul and his land to satisfy his lust for Ronwen; something Wace underscores with a horrified exclamation (6993–6):

> Deus, quel hunte! Deus, quel pecchié!
> Tant l'ad Diables desveied,
> Ne l'ad pas pur ço refusee
> Que paene ert, de paiens nee.[28]

The strong Christian identity of the British established in the first part of the narrative is threatened by the king himself. When Vortimer and the Britons regain (temporary) control of the land, Christianity has been under such attack that missionaries have to be sent from Rome to re-evangelise the people. Later in the narrative, Aurelius comes in sharp contrast with Vortigern by his reliance on the advice of his ecclesiastical counsellors when it comes to deciding the fate of Hengist, then of Octa and Ebissa, his stature as Christian king being further enhanced by Wace's addition of scriptural details to the trial scene.

Merlin is a key character within the process that leads to the return of the legitimate heirs of Britain. Paradisi points out that, while the Book of the Prophecies of Merlin was not included by Wace in his work, individual prophecies are woven into the narrative, signalling the re-establishment of the House of Constantine and

---

[26] 'Constant received the crown and abandoned the vows he should have obeyed; he wrongly abandoned God's rule and thus came to a bad end. No one should succeed through doing what he should not do.'

[27] This is indicated by Wace by an clear echo between the words of Constance to Vortigern (6595–8) and those of Vortigern to Hengist (7051–2) approving what will prove to be an act of treason.

[28] 'God, what shame! God, what sin! The Devil led him so far astray, he would not refuse to marry her though she was a heathen, born of heathens.'

the eventual advent of Arthur as events of prime importance.[29] Merlin announces the impending return of Aurelius and Uther, is responsible for the building of Stonehenge, prophecies the destinies of Uther's future offspring, and provides the means for Uther to satisfy his passion for Ygerne. Merlin's importance in the episode of the conception of Arthur is thrown into greater relief in the French poem by the fact that for the first time in the work, Wace chooses to make unambiguous borrowings from the vulgate version of the *Historia*. A first, discreet instance of this may be observed in the account of Merlin and Uther's mission to Ireland, to bring back the megaliths of the Giants' Circle (corresponding to § 129 of the Latin source). The influence of the vulgate version is not to be felt so much in terms of material added, as of the order in which the material is presented, with a greater stress on the fact that this is the beginning of a military expedition. Wace's statement (8088–92) that Uther

> ... quinze mil armez merreit
> Ki as Irreis se combatreient
> S'il les pieres lur defendreient;
> Merlin ensemble od els irreit
> Ki les pieres enginnereit[30]

puts the emphasis on Uther and his army and places Merlin in a subordinate position. This contrasts with the Variant reading, where Uther and Merlin are presented virtually on an equal footing:

> Eligitur ergo Utherpendragon frater regnis ad id negotium . . . Eligitur et ipse Merlinus cuius ingenio et auxilio agenda tractentur. Parato itaque nauigio cum .xv. milibus armatorum . . .[31]

The mention of the armed men after rather than before we are told of Merlin's involvement puts the emphasis on the mission, for which both Uther and Merlin are jointly responsible, albeit in different capacities. This shift in focus follows the well-established trend throughout the *Roman de Brut*, which typically only allows for one central character within a given episode. Merlin is placed within a clear chain of command. A similar phenomenon appears to underlie the mention, in the celebrated episode of the conception of Arthur, that Merlin accompanied Uther and Ulfin to Tintagel, having also changed his appearance. This agrees with Geoffrey's vulgate version of the *Historia*, against the First Variant version where Uther and Ulfin apparently go alone. Merlin's responsibility goes beyond the simple delivering of a potion; and even though (as in the Latin sources) he refuses to indulge his royal master's frivolous desire to know the future, he is rather more of a courtier in the French poem.

The build-up to the reign of Arthur is in some respects uncharacteristic of the

---

[29] Paradisi, *Le passioni della storia*, pp. 272–85.

[30] '[would take] fifteen thousand armed men, to fight the Irish if they denied them the stones. Merlin would go with them to manoeuvre the stones.'

[31] 'So Uther Pendragon, the king's brother, was chosen for this mission . . . and Merlin himself was chosen, through whose knowledge and help the business would be conducted. Having prepared a navy with fifteen thousand men . . .'

work as a whole, and Wace appears to have wished to underline this fact. Uther's passion for Ygerne is given a 'courtly' dimension (8579–82):

> Ainz que nul semblant en feïst,
> Veire assez ainz qu'il la veïst,
> L'out il cuveitee e amee
> Kar merveilles esteit loee.[32]

This aligns Uther with the totally admirable King Aganippus of France, who also fell in love, sight unseen (with Cordeille, Leir's youngest daughter), and somewhat excuses Uther's behaviour. It is certainly significant that Wace chooses to omit from this passage the indignant reaction of the First Variant narrator who denounces 'libido insidiatrix et inimica leticie', 'lust, treacherous and inimical to happiness' (p. 132, §137), likens the situation to that of David and Bathsheba, and squarely blames Uther's desire on the Devil. This episode is the only one in the *Roman de Brut* to contain passages that are rhetorically and thematically close to the courtly romance, such as the description of Uther's behaviour at court, and the symptoms of his love-sickness, which are typically Ovidian (8659–65):

> L'amur Ygerne m'ad suspris,
> Tut m'ad vencu, tut m'ad conquis,
> Ne puis aler, ne puis venir,
> Ne puis veillier, ne puis dormir,
> Ne puis lever, ne puis culchier,
> Ne puis beivre, ne puis mangier,
> Que d'Ygerne ne me suvienge.[33]

Ulfin's response to Uther's lament – that attacking her husband and her lands was not best designed to please her (8668–74) – suggests that the passage was composed with Wace's tongue firmly in his cheek; but it does result in a whitewashing of Uther, which in turn attenuates the morally dubious overtones of the conception of Arthur. However, the courtly interlude is a brief one. Thereafter Uther is depicted as a strong ruler and general; his next (and last) major speech is a heroic celebration of his victory over the Saxons at Saint Albans.[34]

The fact that, more so than in the previous section of his poem, Wace was prepared to reshape the account of the Variant version of the *Historia*, suggests that he perceived this phase in the narrative as a preparation for the reign of Arthur, rather than a structural unit in its own right. The more explicit piety underlying Aurelius's decision to execute Hengist, the barely perceptible, but real, erosion of the independence of Merlin, the courtly excuses for Uther's pursuit of Ygerne and the concluding playing up of Uther as warrior, give Arthur a more acceptable pedigree as part of a dynasty of good, Christian kings and effective war-leaders.

---

[32] 'Before giving any sign of it, indeed, even before seeing her, he had loved and desired her, for she was exceedingly celebrated.'
[33] 'Love for Ygerne has struck me down, completely defeating and conquering me: I can neither come nor go, wake nor sleep, arise nor rest, eat nor drink, without thinking of her.'
[34] This passage shows signs of having been influenced by the vulgate version of the *Historia*, and has clearly been reshaped by Wace. The contrast between courtly/epic was certainly deliberate.

6

King Arthur and the Passage of Dominion

The reign of Arthur is the section of Wace's work where the poet takes the greatest liberties with his sources. Most notably, it is the episode where the historical stance appears to be at its weakest, with the intrusion of material that is neither didactic nor religious in origin. It is also the fullest account of any of the Celtic kings of Britain, covering two Books (Books IX and X) or 37 chapters (out of a total of 207) in the Latin sources. Wace's account of Arthur's reign is not a homogeneous, uniform whole. It develops in three stages, starting with the young king's struggle to establish his authority over Britain, during which he frees the land from the Saxon threat; continuing with his glorious mature years, which see him conquer Norway and France; and ending with the reappearance of the old enemy, Rome, and Modred's treason.

Young Arthur

Wace takes relatively little interest in the early, defensive exploits of Arthur, the high point of the Arthurian section being the foundation of the Round Table, the conquest of France and the glories of the Whitsun court at Caerleon (at which the Roman ultimatum is delivered). The account of the youthful exploits of the once and future king follows the Variant text quite closely, with only very minor, predictable additions such as the fact that the Saxon Baldulf, who has disguised himself as a jongleur to gain access to his brother through enemy lines, had been taught to sing and play the harp (9103–4). Despite the occasional rhetorical passage (for example, descriptions of Saxon débâcle, 9179–82 and 9395–406), the trend is towards compression and narrative economy. This is effected by the omission of information, albeit on a limited scale,[1] and through the subtle reshaping of certain episodes.

The focus is firmly on Arthur from the outset. The scene where Arthur arms himself before the battle of Bath remains close to the account of the First Variant version,[2] but Wace adds iron foot-protection to the young king's equipment, and

---

[1] As elsewhere in the *Roman de Brut*, the material omitted may be classified under two main headings: descriptive material, particularly in battle scenes or relating to military strategy; and features or comments that shed a negative light on the hero(es) of the moment. Wace thus omits the Saxon attempt to resist Arthur in the forest of Celidon and the resulting Briton casualties (§145) and the statement that Arthur treated the Scots and the Picts with unparalleled severity, sparing no one (§149).

[2] For an overview of the patterns of indebtedness to the Variant or the vulgate versions of the *Historia Regum Britanniae* in the Arthurian section of the *Roman de Brut*, see Table 5 (p. 152 below).

mentions that his jewel-encrusted helmet had belonged to Uther (9283–8), thus reinforcing both the scene's realism and its dynastic significance. The fight itself starts with a pre-battle speech by Arthur, where he places the encounter within a logic of revenge for the harm and treachery of the Saxons (a speech not to be found in the Variant version, and placed in the vulgate version before the arming scene), and Wace also includes a short vignette of Arthur making the first kill and shouting out his battle cry.

Having established the warlike qualities of the fifteen-year-old king, Wace subtly reshapes the following narrative to project the image of a stern but merciful ruler. The end of §149 of the Latin texts thus becomes virtually unrecognisable. Whereas his sources have the bishops and clergy of Scotland pleading for Arthur's mercy, Wace creates a pathetic scene where the ladies of the land, bare-head, bare-foot, in rags and with babies in their arms, beg for the king's pity. Wace's rewriting of the scene is interesting on two levels. First, it presents Arthur in a more favourable light. The image of bishops and clerics advancing barefoot and kneeling in front of the bloodthirsty invader is not a comfortable one; there are overtones of sacrilege in the humiliation that the holiest and best of the nation have to inflict upon themselves in order to bring a supposedly Christian king to reason. This is particularly the case in the Variant version, where the bishops' words suggest that Arthur has not even been respecting the immunity of churches: 'exorabant suppliciter ut saltem ecclesiis et populo inbelli misericordiam prestaret' (p. 143), 'they pleaded and supplicated that he show mercy at least to the churches and the non-fighting population'. Secondly, the elements contained in the women's speech are recognisably those of the clerics in the Variant version and the sequence of arguments is generally the same, with the noteworthy addition of an explicit appeal to Arthur as a Christian, as opposed to the pagan Saxons (9505–11, 9517–20):

> Li Saissun esteient paien
> E nus erium crestïen,
> De tant nus unt il plus grevez
> E plus laidement demenez.
> Mal nus unt fait, tu nus faiz pis;
> Ço ne t'iert mie enur ne pris,
> D'ocire cels ki merci querent
> . . .
> Aies merci des crestïens;
> Nus tenum la lei que tu tiens.
> Crestïenté iert abaissiede
> Se ceste terre est eisselede.[3]

The idea that Arthur is treating the Scots with more savagery than even the Saxons is clearly derived from the Latin texts, but the charge is somewhat

---

[3] 'The Saxons were heathen and were Christian; they molested us all the more for it and treated us all the more wickedly. They did us wrong; you do worse still. Neither honour nor renown will come to you from killing those who ask for mercy. . . . Have mercy on Christians: we hold the faith you hold. Christianity will be brought low if this land is ravaged.'

softened by the fact that it is made by women rather than by high-ranking ecclesiastics. Not only does their accusation carry less authority, the very fact they are at liberty to make it suggests that Arthur's ferocity did actually have limits, implying that women and children were immune from the effects of his anger – a reading not incompatible with the Variant account, though it is in contradiction with the vulgate text, which stresses that 'nulli prout reperiebatur parceret' (p. 105), 'he spared none wherever he found them'.

Wace's creative reshaping of the Scottish episode prepares us for the characterisation of Arthur as *rex iustus et pacificus* and courtly king.[4] However, the potential for additions of a courtly nature of §152, relating Arthur's marriage to Guinevere, is not exploited at all beyond positive epithets qualifying the new queen. The stress is inescapably on the dynastic implications of Arthur's marriage: Guinevere's pedigree is clarified (she is Roman on her mother's side and presumably related to Cador through her father); the union was consummated (implied by the statement of Arthur's love for his wife, 9656), but remained sterile (9657–8; a conclusion regularly drawn by Wace when a king is not succeeded by a direct heir). Arthur's marriage is therefore seen in a coldly political light and is altogether less significant than his achievements on the battlefield and as a leader of men. Similarly, the scene where Arthur describes the marvels of Britain to his nephew Hoel is relatively pedestrian (9527–86), the only difference between the Variant version and Wace's account being that the passage is transposed from reported speech to direct speech in the French.

Wace's additions to Arthur's wars of conquest in this section are minor, and do not imply the use of sources other than the Variant or vulgate versions of the *Historia Regum Britanniae*. The account of Arthur's conquest of Ireland and Iceland, which covers less than 14 lines in Wright's edition of the vulgate version and some 17 in the Variant version of chapter 153, inflates to 76 octosyllabic lines,[5] yet contains only two features that are not directly suggested by the Variant text. Arthur's presence in Ireland is first felt by the fact that he is raiding the local cattle (9669–72):

> Quant passé furent en Irlande,
> Par la terre pristrent viande;
> Vaches pristrent et pristrent bués,
> E ço que a mangier out ués.[6]

This could be seen as indicating the influence, possibly, of the Old Irish literary genre commemorating cattle-raids; or it could be construed as an echo of the

---

[4] The civilisational connotations added by Wace to the image of Arthur in chapters 151 and 152 of his source all occur in the second line of a couplet, and therefore belong to the vast group of additions due to the demands of versification. As is frequently the case, these additions (which the poet probably thought of as 'empty' fillers) are revealing. Line 9604 thus adds ruined houses to the deserted churches (9603) which prompt Arthur's rebuilding programme. Similarly, the promulgation of peace in the land (9611) is accompanied (9612) by the order that farmers till the land. This 'common touch' is shared to some extent by the Variant version, which has Arthur restore 'uiros et mulieres' (p. 144) in their ancestral rights, whereas the vulgate only mentions 'proceres' (p. 106).

[5] The expected length of the French episode would have been of between 51 and 68 octosyllabic lines.

[6] 'When they had crossed into Ireland, they seized their food from the land, taking cows and oxen and whatever was suitable to eat.'

hunting of the cattle dedicated to the Sun in the *Odyssey*. However, the mention of cattle expands on a statement (9670) that Arthur's troops land to forage, which itself seems to have been determined by the necessity to find a rhyme for 'Irlande' (8669); and in turn, the protests of the 'vilenaille' (9677) deprived of their cows and oxen motivates the hostility of the Irish King Gillomar. It is therefore more than likely that the theme of the cattle-raid, by an association of ideas, grew out of the concept of 'viande' initially introduced to meet the demands of versification. A similar phenomenon may underlie the appearance in Wace's work of a mysterious King Rummaret of Wenelande unknown to his source (9708–11):

> Gonvais, ki ert reis d'Orchenie,
> E Doldani, reis de Godlande,
> E Rummaret de Wenelande
> Orent tost la nuvele oïe.[7]

We are once again in the presence of a new feature in the second line of a couplet characterised by a difficult end-rhyme; and while it might seem surprising that Wace should make up a character *de toutes pièces*, this mysterious character and his no less mysterious realm are redundant within the episode and conspicuously absent from the rest of the work. Unsurprisingly, scholarly attempts to place Wenelande on the map have failed.[8] However, such details highlight the fact that the first phase of Arthur's rule is a total success. The land is cleared of the Saxons, and foreign kings are submitting to him and offering tribute of their own accord.

Arthur's apogee

The period between the Conquest of Scandinavia and the campaign against Rome is the highpoint of Arthur's reign. It also contains one of Wace's most celebrated additions to his Latin sources, the mention of Arthur's Round Table and of the tales circulating on it. Structurally, this addition fits neatly within the 'slot' in the Variant devoted to Arthur's greatness (§154) and may therefore be seen as an interpolation of material intended to complement the account of the main source (9747–54):

> Pur les nobles baruns qu'il out,
> Dunt chescuns mieldre estre quidout,
> Chescuns se teneit al meillur,
> Ne nuls n'en saveit le peiur,
> Fist Artur la Roünde Table
> Dunt Bretun dient mainte fable.

---

[7] 'Gonvais, king of Orkney, Doldani, king of Gotland, and Rummaret of Wenelande all [swiftly] heard the news . . .'

[8] Charles Foulon ('Two additions by Wace', *Bibliographical Bulletin of the International Arthurian Society* 24 (1972): 191) suggests that Rummaret might be derived from a Celtic name (Rummarec), and that Wenelande could be the Welsh Gwynedd. There is indeed a similarity between the names, but they take us a long way from Scandinavia.

> Illuec seeient li vassal
> Tuit chevalment e tuit egal.⁹

The interpolation is introduced in such a way that the seam is almost invisible. The suggestion of quarrels of precedence at Arthur's court appears as the logical consequence to Arthur's policy (mentioned by Wace in the lines immediately preceding this passage) of attracting the best knights to be his retainers. The Round Table is noted almost in passing, rather than as a feature in its own right. The *fables* of the *Bretuns* are not allowed to distract the reader from the point being made about Arthur's power and prestige. Indeed, the Round Table is so carefully integrated into the narrative texture that it becomes an indirect means of characterisation of Arthur himself, illustrating his ability to defuse tensions and reinforce the bond of loyalty between his men.

In view of the protracted campaigns which follow, there is nothing gratuitous to such an addition. The 'Table Roünde' is either hinted at or explicitly mentioned at each of the turning-points in Arthur's reign, until its destruction marks the end of the king himself at Camlan (13266–70):

> Dunc peri la bele juvente
> Que Arthur aveit grant nurrie
> E de plusurs terres cuillie,
> E cil de la Table Roünde
> Dunt tel los ert par tut le munde.¹⁰

The Round Table is thus an important structural marker in the account of the reign of Arthur, linking the different phases of the king's life and affording a greater cohesion and unity to the narrative. Intimately bound to Arthur, the Round Table becomes the emanation of his royal power.

The very appositeness of the anecdote of the Round Table for an understanding of the nature of Arthur's greatness may explain Wace's aside on the 'merveilles pruvees' and the 'aventures truvees' turned to fable by generations of storytellers (9787–98). The Round Table was too good to miss out, yet to mention it involved drawing upon material that would not have been deemed authoritative: hence the necessity to attribute a kernel of truth to the tales of the 'fableür': 'Ne tut mençunge, ne tut veir,/ Tut folie ne tut saveir' (9793–9), 'Not all lies, not all truth, neither total folly nor total wisdom'. The implication, of course, is that what Wace chooses to echo is 'true' and therefore in no way detracts from the integrity of his work as history; but it is striking that other obvious interpolations of extraneous material in the poem (particularly the account of the miracles of Saint Augustine) do not bring about similar efforts at self-justification, which suggests that the Round Table might be the only instance of information knowingly derived from non-written, non-Latin sources in the *Roman de Brut*.

---

⁹ 'On account of his noble barons – each of whom felt he was superior, each considered himself the best, and no one could say who was the worst – Arthur had the Round Table made, about which the British tell many a tale. There sat the vassals, all equal, all leaders.'

¹⁰ 'Then perished the flower of youth, tended and gathered by Arthur from many lands, and those of the Round Table, famous throughout the world.'

Whereas Arthur's conquests prior to the foundation of the Round Table may be termed defensive, in the broadest sense, and are initiated by the monarch himself, the campaigns which follow are to a great extent imposed upon him by circumstances. The decision to invade Norway is made in response to the fact that the Norwegians have treacherously denied the crown to Arthur's brother-in-law and vassal, Loth, who was the rightful heir of his uncle King Sichelin (9831–35):

> Quant Loth vit que sun dreit perdreit
> Se par force nel cunquereit,
> Artur sun seinnur ad requis,
> E Artur li ad bien pramis
> Que tut le regne li rendra.[11]

Arthur would not have had much leeway in such a matter; it was his duty as Loth's overlord and kinsman to support him in his just claim (which has a more than passing resemblance to that of William the Conqueror against King Harold). However, Wace introduces his decision in such a way that the campaign almost appears as the result of a whim on Arthur's part (9799–806):

> Par la bunté de sun curage
> E par le los de sun barnage
> E par la grant chevalerie
> Qu'il out afaitee e nurrie,
> Dist Artur que mer passereit
> E tute France conquerreit;
> Mais primes en Norwege ireit,
> Loth sun sururge rei fereit.[12]

The two campaigns are linked together here as they are not in the Latin texts (where we are simply told that, after subjugating Norway and Denmark, Arthur sailed to Gaul), and point to a clear plan on the king's part. Moreover, whereas Wace's sources attribute Arthur's ambitions of European conquest to reports of the fears of neighbouring kings, the French writer hints at internal pressure exercised by the Round Table itself. Arthur is surrounded by 'grant chevalerie' (9801), a crowd of ambitious warriors eager to outshine one another and who need to expend their energy. Viewed from this angle, the decision to go to Norway may be seen as a brilliant example of man-management: the wrong inflicted upon Loth is the perfect excuse to initiate military action on a larger scale. It is a just cause (a fact underlined by Wace through his statement that Sichelin had died childless and had named Loth as his heir both on his deathbed and when he was still in good health) and, being intimately bound in the nexus of feudal loyalties, one to which Arthur's 'barnage' could relate. The anticipated mention of the French campaign, the addition of legal arguments underpinning

---

[11] 'When Loth saw that he would lose his rights if he did not conquer them by force, he appealed to Arthur, his lord, and Arthur promised him that he would give him all the kingdom.'

[12] 'Prompted by his own noble disposition, the advice of his barons, and the large body of knights he had equipped and nurtured, Arthur said he would cross the sea and conquer all France. But first, he would go to Norway and make his brother-in-law Loth king there.'

Loth's claims and the explicit request for support by Loth, indirectly characterise Arthur as a good sovereign and kinsman, a skilful leader of men and competent general.

Loth's son Gawain, who is mentioned in the Latin texts at the outset of the Norwegian campaign, appears in the French narrative only after Norway has been subdued (as was to be expected, considering that Gawain plays no significant role in the campaign), as a young knight recently from Rome. The focus is thus firmly kept on Arthur, whilst a vignette describing the conquest of Denmark *sans coup férir*[13] echoes the earlier submissions of kings Gonvais and Doldani, reminding the reader of the power and prestige already gained by the British king. Arthur is shown choosing knights and archers from his new domains to take to France with him,[14] once again acting like a prudent and well-organised general: the detail also reinforces the link between the conquest of Norway and Denmark and the French campaign, allowing Wace to dispense with any further preliminaries to the account of Arthur's exploits in France.

The French campaign proper is reshaped in the *Roman de Brut*, but like the account of the conquest of Norway and Denmark, it is unmistakeably based on the structural template provided by the Variant version of the *Historia Regum Britanniae*. The bulk of the modifications to the Latin narrative in this section relates to style rather than content. The duel between Arthur and Frolle is recast in an epic mode; the main phases of the fight remain the same as in the Latin sources, but they are visualised slightly differently by the French poet, who describes the whole passage in the vein of the *chanson de geste*, with a wealth of rhetorical effects. The memorable scene where the famished Parisians call out to Frolle to make peace with Arthur is likewise based on the sober statement in the Variant text (§155) that Frolle realised that the starving populace was about to surrender and decided to resolve the matter by putting his personal safety in jeopardy.[15] The additions made by Wace are, as elsewhere, either of a didactic nature, or designed to heighten the 'realism' of the episode. Geographical verisimilitude is provided through the statement that Arthur conquers Flanders and the town of Boulogne before his first encounter with Frolle (9895), and the extended list of the French provinces conquered by Hoel (10115–16).[16] The reader is given information concerning the political status of what was then Gaul and is told that Frolle was responsible for gathering the taxes sent on to Rome. A social and emotional dimension is introduced through the mention of the many refugees in besieged Paris and their praying for peace as they observe the duel between Arthur and Frolle from the city walls; hostages are also mentioned, both before the duel and

---

[13] The Danish king Aschil and his decision to submit to Arthur are Wace's own invention. The Latin texts merely mention that Arthur submitted Dacia to his dominion.

[14] The specific mention of knights and archers is Wace's own addition. It could be seen as an instance of the poet's sense of realism (however anachronistic certain details may seem): mustering additional troops would be expected of a war leader at the outset of a hard campaign. The Latin texts (§155) only mention the 'iuuentus terrarum et insularum quas subegerat' when Arthur has initiated the hostilities with Frolle.

[15] In the vulgate text, Frolle takes this decision out of compassion for the Parisians, not because he is facing imminent mutiny.

[16] However, Wace refrains from mentioning that he did so 'ferro et igne depopulans' (Variant version, § 155). Yet another instance of the poet's 'whitewashing' his hero.

after Arthur's victory. The desire to depict the British in as positive a light as possible underlies the statement that Arthur made his army behave well and forbade plundering (this contradicts the Latin texts, §155, where we are told that Arthur laid waste the land), and the scene of Arthur's men praying that their lord be victorious in the duel with Frolle (10025–8); though, possibly in order to conciliate his French readership, Wace also adds a complimentary remark concerning the abilities of the besieged Parisians to defend their town (9977).

The French campaign ends on a note that recalls the glory of the Round Table, and foreshadows the Caerleon crown-bearing celebrations of §156. A deliberate parallel is drawn between Arthur's glorious achievement in Britain and the new society founded by him during the nine years he spends in France (10143–6):

> Es nuef anz que il France tint
> Mainte merveille li avint
> Maint orguillus home danta
> E meint felun amesura.[17]

In addition to the implicit validation this offers to Arthurian tales taking place on the Continent rather than in Britain, this emphasises the essential unity of a somewhat fragmented reign, in that wherever Arthur rules, he establishes a society based on the same principles of justice and extraordinary personal achievement. The nine years in France culminate in the distribution of lands and honours, a scene which is expanded to include the enfeoffing of such worthies as Holdin, Borel, Ligier and Richier. Having successfully expanded his realm and provided for his retainers, he can return to Britain to reap the fruits of his labour.

Arthur and Rome

The final part of Arthur's reign is subjected by Wace to a process of rhetorical amplification and addition of material that results in a fuller and longer narrative than that found in his Latin sources. Moreover, as we have seen, a major structural clash between the two versions of the *Historia* in chapters 160 to 164, resolved through the interpolation of vulgate material at a spot congenial to both the principles of linear development that underpin the narrative and the Variant's framework of events, necessitated on the poet's part an effort of reappropriation that is perceptible throughout the section.

The episode opens in a blaze of glory. Wace adds an ornate passage (10175–96), entirely of his own making, describing the joy and excitement in Britain at the return of Arthur and his army and introducing Arthur's decision to hold a great Whitsun feast in Caerleon in a formal display of royal power. This is the occasion for Wace to appropriate the narrative of chapters 156 and 157 of the *Historia Regum Britanniae*, which are predominantly descriptive in nature and therefore suitable for adaptation, expansion and rhetorical ornamentation. The very much fuller account of the vulgate version (particularly for §157, which is

---

[17] 'In the nine years he held France, many marvels happened to him, he tamed many a proud man and kept many a villain in check.'

almost double the length of its counterpart in the Variant) is quarried for information, though in a selective manner and as one source among others. In the manner familiar to him, Wace emphasises the ceremonial over the mundane (preferring the vulgate's mention of messengers bearing invitations to Arthur's celebrations at Caerleon, for example, to the Variant's stating that an abundance of merchandise was brought by sea for the festivities) and shows his fondness for didacticism (mentioning that the river Usk flows into the Severn, a detail possibly derived from personal knowledge). The stress, however, is very much on the pomp and glory of Arthur's coronation and rather less so on the institutional level evident in the ecclesiastical appointments mentioned in §157 of the Latin texts. The luxurious clothing of the Queen and her retinue is the object of a ten-line expansion in the French text (10407–16), while the descriptions of the feasting and games following the coronation are not only retained from the vulgate text, but further elaborated upon, with additional comments about the etiquette surrounding the seating arrangements (10459–62).

The key principle at work in this section of the *Roman de Brut* is very much one of repetition with increasingly specific detailing, picking up the features mentioned earlier in the narrative relative to Arthur's Round Table and weaving a network of correspondences and echoes which link the coronation at Caerleon with previous episodes in Arthur's career. There is a clear gradation in the images of glory given of the monarch: the Founding of the Round Table, where the prestige of the young king is mentioned, but not truly described; the gift-giving in Paris following the conquest of France, where Arthur acts with regal generosity towards his retainers; and the Caerleon ceremonial, where the once and future king at the top of Fortune's wheel combines glamour and power to a superlative degree. This movement is already outlined in the *Historia Regum Britanniae*, but Wace reworks it in such a way that the three scenes where Arthur is shown in the context of his court become major narrative and structural landmarks. The Caerleon festivities mark the turning point in Arthur's career. His victorious campaigns have ensured that his realm is secure and his authority unchallenged: such is the message meant to be conveyed by the Whitsun coronation. Having reached the top, however, the only possible way is now down, and the final stage of Arthur's reign displays a crumbling not only of his fortunes but of his place in the French narrative.

For the cruelty of Arthur's fate fully to be apprehended, his greatness must be shown as emphatically as possible; hence Wace's verbal pyrotechnics in this episode and his adoption of the lavish descriptions of the vulgate text, as opposed to the more restrained account of the Variant version. Wace's aesthetic and narrative convergence with what hitherto had been a relatively minor source text explains his adoption of its amplificatory material against the ambivalent (if not outrightly cynical) approach of the Variant to festivities where the excellence of the music is such that, we are told, it puts the listeners to sleep! It comes as no surprise that Wace preferred the lively vignette of the vulgate text, where people could not make up their minds as to which choir to listen to, so outstanding was the singing, and spent their time to-ing and fro-ing between the town's two main churches: the atmosphere of teeming, rejoicing crowds is an essential backdrop to the bombshell of §158, the Roman ultimatum. Similarly, the 'courtly' conventions governing the love-life of Arthur's worthies (which are not to be found in the Variant text) underscore the cultural excellence of the world about to collapse; this is a highly sophisticated society which has integrated moral values to a remarkable degree. Even Wace's remark on the avoidance of particoloured clothing among Arthur's retainers can be read as the establishment of a symbolic code akin to that of heraldry. The French text thus retains those features in his sources conducive to an image of triumphant prosperity, splendour and well-bred lightheartedness, and supplements them with details encouraging his readership to sympathetically identify with the Arthurian court. At the same time, the quasi-prelapsarian egalitarianism implicit in comments such as 'Plus erent curteis e vaillant/ Neïs li povre païsant/ Que chevalier en altres regnes/ E altresi erent les femes' (10499–502), 'Even the poor peasants were more courtly and brave than knights in other realms, and so were the women too' depicts Arthur's Britain as almost unnaturally harmonious, virtuous and prosperous. It is not right that peasants should be more courtly and valiant than knights; it goes against the order of society and undermines the hierarchical structures that ensure social stability. What seems to be an entirely positive comment could also be an ominous hint at the civil war about to break out. Such a level of perfection is not sustainable.

The Roman ultimatum borne by twelve white-haired messengers is introduced by Wace in a manner which reinforces both the element of august dignity of Arthur at his most powerful and the links between his past deeds and his present quandary. Whereas in the Latin texts (§158) the Roman envoys interrupt the distribution of gifts and benefices to the clergy, Wace opens the episode with an image of static authority: 'Artur fu assis a un deis/ Envirun lui cuntes e reis' (10621–2), 'Arthur was seated on a dais, with counts and kings around him'. The gift-giving (described by Wace in an elaborate passage characterised by the repetition of the verb *duna*, 10597–620) is apparently over; that chapter is closed, and the missive of the Roman Emperor is about to disrupt a situation of quiet, self-confident equilibrium.

Lucius's ultimatum, like most passages in direct discourse, is subjected to considerable stylistic reshaping, with the introduction, for example, of animal metaphors in the French text (10669–72). In terms of content, the missive follows the slightly fuller Variant text, with just one omission and one addition. The omission is the statement in the Latin text that the decision to issue the ultimatum came from the Senate, thus avoiding the suggestion that Lucius is not as all-powerful as his imperial title would seem to indicate. The French text skilfully fudges the issue by apparently equating the Senate and Lucius himself (my italics): 'Te sumunt *li senez* e mande...', '*The Senate* summon and order you...' (10689), 'si nel faces cum *jo* mant...', 'if you reject any of *my* commands' (10698).[18] The increased stature of Arthur's enemy adds to the heroic dimension of the following campaign, which is moreover explicitly linked to the death of Frolle (rather than merely the conquest of France as in the Latin): 'Frolle, nostre barun, as mort' (10685), 'You have slain Frollo, our baron'. The motivation for the ultimatum is therefore not mere desire for tribute, but also an overlord's duty of vengeance for

---

[18] Emphasis mine.

a faithful retainer. The whole episode is consequently ennobled with moral considerations. Arthur's defense of the envoys against the wrath of his men (a scene which grows out of the Variant's mention of the threatening behaviour of Arthur's courtiers on hearing the news) illustrates his self-restraint and respect of higher principles – in this case, the immunity of messengers – even in so extreme a situation.

The gravity of the decision to be taken – waging war against Rome itself – is indicated by the fact that, contrary to previous campaigns, the King's Council is shown at work. Wace fully grasps the importance of this episode and enhances it by changing the entire tone of the banter before Arthur's formal request for his barons' counsel, reshaping the speeches of the various barons to emphasise specific themes and underplay others.

Cador's semi-jocular praise of war is brought about in markedly dissimilar circumstances in the two Latin texts of the *Historia Regum Britanniae*. In the Variant version, Arthur leads his senior retainers to the tower where the meeting is to take place; and as they are taking their seats around the king, Cador of Cornwall breaks the silence, expressing his fear that the Britons might lose their skill at war and their bravery, mollified by too long a peace spent at playing at dice and squandering of energy with women. Arthur then asks for silence and business starts in earnest. The somewhat tense atmosphere surrounding Cador's little speech, and the quasi-formal flavour to it (everyone is seated around the king in expectant silence) all but disappear from the vulgate text. Cador's words become lightweight banter as he is climbing the stairs with Arthur and the other barons; he makes his comments within earshot of Arthur, but 'cum riso', laughing, and prompted by his merry nature ('erat leti animi', §158), in a sort of epic *insouciance*. No one takes much notice of him and his jocular mood apparently abates once seated. Wace, with his sense of decorum, understandably preferred the vulgate version, where the somewhat heretical pronouncements of Cador carry less weight. The scene thus takes place in the staircase of the Tour Gigantine, with a smiling Cador pouring scorn on 'uisdive', seen as the cause of moral and physical degeneracy (10737–64). Even within this setting, however, Cador's speech carries unwelcome connotations of trigger-happy, bellicose Britons who relished war for war's sake: Wace therefore counters Cador with Gauvain, in an addition frequently cited for its 'courtliness'.

Gauvain's eight-line speech is a systematic countering of the three arguments playfully put forth by Cador in favour of war, seen in an antinomic relationship to sloth (10737–40, 10743–49, 10763–4):

> En grant crieme ai, dist il, esté,
> E par mainte feiz en ai pensé,
> Que par oisdives e par pais
> Devenissent Bretun malveis.
> . . .
> Uisdive met hume en peresce,
> Uisdive amenuse prüesce,
> Uisdive esmuet les lecheries,
> Uisdive esprent lé drueries.
> Par lunc repos e par uisdive

> Est juvente tost ententive
> A gas, a deduit e a tables.
> ...
> Ja lunge pais nen amerai
> Ne unques lunge pais n'amai.[19]

Gawain responds by teasingly reassuring Cador that he is worrying about nothing: 'de neient estes en effrei' (10766), and advocates the virtues of peace: 'Bone est la pais emprés la guerre,/ Plus bele e mieldre en est la terre' (10767–8), 'Peace is good after war, and the land is the better and lovelier for it'. One may note however that peace is not described as an absolute good: Gawain explicitly states that it is beneficial *after war*, that is, as a period of regeneration after the hardships of fighting. Similarly, Cador's condemnation of joking and womanising is recast by Gawain in such a way as partly to answer his main objection to peace – that it softens fighting-men: 'Pur amistié e pur amies/ Funt chevaliers chevaleries' (10771–2), 'It's for love and their beloved that knights do knightly deeds'. Far from being a waste of time, these pursuits give meaning and focus to feats of arms ('chevaleries') that otherwise would be mere military exercises, and ensure that essential skills are maintained.

Gawain's words prevent the reader from forming too bellicose an image of the British: in the speeches which follow, we find a comparable underplaying by Wace of the martial element of 'defending freedom' or 'avenging opprobrium', and a corresponding emphasis on the moral aspect of the just war. Arthur stresses the weakness of the Roman cause, invoking the proverbial 'might is not right' ('force n'est mie dreiture', 10829) and constructing a case for his own claims to Rome (10875–8):

> Or poëz oïr e saveir
> Qu'altresi dei jo Rome aveir
> Cum il Bretaine, par raison,
> Se nus as anceisurs guardum.[20]

The suggestion by Hoel that Arthur's conquest of Rome is sanctioned by God is twice repeated, 'Damnedeus te vuelt exalcier' (10923), 'the Lord God wants to raise you up', and (10937–41):

> En tei sera la prophecie
> Que Sibille dist acomplie.
> Pur quei demures a saisir
> Ço que Deus te vuelt eslargir?
> Exalce tei, exalce nus.[21]

---

[19] 'I've often thought and been very afraid that the British would become weaklings through peace and idleness. . . . Idleness brings indolence, idleness lessens prowess, idleness inflames lechery and idleness kindles love affairs. Much rest and idleness makes youth give all its attention to jokes, pleasure, board games and other amusing sports. . . . I never loved a long peace, nor shall I ever do so.'

[20] 'Now you can hear and know that I have as much reasonable right to Rome as Rome to Britain, if we look at our ancestors.'

[21] 'In you the Sibyll's prophecy will be fulfilled. Why wait to seize what God wishes to grant you? Exalt yourself, exalt us.'

After Hoel's appeal to both God and old prophecies, King Angusel makes a speech focusing on the moral inadequacy of the Romans and conjures up a vision of European conquest: 'Que nule terre ne remainne/ De ça les munz ki ne seit tue' (11032–3), 'so that no country remains on this side of the mountains which is not yours'. The theme of a preordained, divinely inspired course of events is essential in defusing the hubris of words such as these, and it comes as no surprise that Wace should have chosen to follow the vulgate text of the *Historia* in this section of his work, rather than the Variant which, as we know, does not provide a speech for Hoel at all and therefore lacks the moral and providential arguments developed in it. Without the suggestion of divine approbation for the forthcoming campaign, Arthur's struggle against Rome is both foolhardy and doomed to failure: such appears to be the implication of the Variant text, which Wace obviously did not wish to retain.[22]

While the attribution of a speech to Hoel during the council is readily explained by the Latin sources, the introduction of Gawain as a prominent agent at this stage of the narrative poses a problem inasmuch as it would seem to go against the general principle in the *Roman de Brut* that the focus be always on the main protagonist (i.e., the king) of any one episode.[23] This is the first indication in the narrative that Gawain has taken his place among Arthur's close counsellors,[24] and that he, Arthur's sister's son, is confident enough to contradict (even if it is only in jest) as senior and heroic a character as Cador. Gawain is presented as someone endowed with humour and common sense, the champion of civilised – indeed, courtly – values. This is the first step in a process of gradual marginalisation of Arthur, who as the Roman campaign progresses loses much of his heroic presence to his nephew.

From the Roman ultimatum onwards, Arthur is no longer in control of his own destiny. The impetus to go to war is an external threat and Arthur is shown having to convince his barons that his decision is the right one. His departure from Britain also marks his effective loss of authority over his own kingdom. Wace announces Modred's felony in an aside that leaves no doubt as to the consequences of Arthur's decision (11177–89):

> Modret esteit de grant noblei
> Mais n'esteit pas de bone fei.
> Il aveit la reïne amee
> Mais ço esteit chose celee;
> Mult s'en celout; e ki quidast
> Que il feme sun uncle amast,
> Maïsmement de tel seinnur
> Dunt tuit li suen orent enur;
> Feme sun uncle par putage

---

[22] This is also indicated by the way Wace handles chapters 162–4 of the *Historia Regum Britanniae*, minimising the disparity of the armies being gathered.

[23] As we have seen above, this principle explains the relative downgrading of the figure of Merlin when he goes to Ireland with Uther to fetch the Giants' Circle.

[24] Gawain is mentioned twice prior to this: first, as the offspring of Arthur's sister (9639), and as a newly knighted young man, during the Norwegian campaign (9855). This is the first instance of Gawain 'in action'.

> Amat Modret si fist huntage.
> A Modret e a la reïne,
> Deus! tant mal fist cele saisine,
> Comanda tut fors la corune.[25]

In other words, Arthur has lost both his queen and his land. All that remains to him is the abstract quality of kingship, 'la corune'; and Wace's ornate vignette of Arthur's fleet leaving Southampton (11191–238) further underscores the break between the king and the tangible source of his might – Britain.

The episode of the Mont St Michel giant, in the *Roman de Brut* as in the Latin texts of the *Historia Regum Britanniae*, reintroduces in the characterisation of Arthur the mythical dimension promised by the circumstances surrounding his conception. Narratologically, it is a section dominated by oral accounts and story-telling: Arthur is told about the giant; Helen's old nurse tells Beduer about her fate and Helen's; Arthur tells his men about Ritho, another giant he defeated; the narrator tells us the full story of Ritho's collecting of kings' beards; and the companions recount their adventures, showing the giant's head on their return to camp. Coming as it does after an ominous dream of Arthur's, the episode takes us one step away from the world of human beings fighting against other human beings and leads us into the monstrous and the legendary. As if to attenuate the fabulous quality of the episode, Wace makes minor modifications and additions that lend added verisimilitude (or at least, a hint of realism) to the account: Arthur and his companions no longer manage to travel from Barfleur to the Mont St Michel within a few hours, as in the Latin texts, and we are told that the chapel founded by Hoel is dedicated to the Virgin; as many specific details relating to the geographical layout, weaponry and fighting are mentioned as possible (this section effectively combines all of the pieces of information contained in the two Latin versions); and we are even told that Arthur was not only enraged during his fight with the giant, but also frightened. Arthur's fear is mentioned first by the narrator (11531) and then by Arthur himself, in an unheroic admission that he had 'eü . . . poür' (11561). The French writer obviously felt the need to rationalise the whole episode, to the extent of adding a feature of psychological realism at odds with his sources (where Arthur is characterised by epic rage, not fear). The idealised figure of Arthur is correspondingly debased.

The account of the victorious campaign against Emperor Lucius (*Historia* chapters 166–76, *Brut* 11609–3030) evidences a shift of emphasis in the French narrative that makes Gawain the true hero of the episode. With the exception of the memorable scene (*Historia* chapter 174, *Brut* 12871–936) where Arthur throws himself into battle to give heart to his hard-pressed men, the king is depicted as a general, not as a warrior. By contrast, Wace gives particular prominence to Gawain's feats on the battlefield. He invents (11857–76) an additional confrontation during the Roman chase after Arthur's undiplomatic envoys:

---

[25] 'Modret was of noble birth, but disloyal. He was in love with the queen, but this was not suspected. He kept it very quiet; and who would have believed that he could love his uncle's wife, especially the wife of such a lord, whose kin all held him in honour? Modret loved his uncle's wife shamefully and was dishonourable. To Modret and to the queen – alas!, how unfortunate that he gave them possession! – Arthur entrusted everything but the crown.'

Gawain chops off the arm of the nameless cousin of Marcel, a prior Roman victim of his sword (and of his sarcasm). At a later stage of the same episode, during the fight with Petreius and his men, Wace explicitly attributes the merit for saving Boso of Oxford (and the attendant capture of the Roman leader) to Gawain, who is shown hacking his way through the Roman lines (12041–54, a scene not found in the Latin texts). Similarly, during the battle of Saussy, by Langres, the section describing the feats of Hoel and Gawain (who share the leadership of a Briton column; *Historia* §173) focuses in the French text on Gawain; contrary to what we find in the Latin texts, Hoel, taken in isolation, is never in the narrative spotlight. Gawain's stature is further enhanced by the statement that Lucius not only rejoiced at the thought of fighting in single combat with a warrior of Gawain's renown, but was actually looking forward to being able to boast of it: 'A Rome s'en quidot vanter' (12852). In a very real sense, the Roman campaign is Gawain's campaign.[26] One sees the point of including him in the group that decided to launch it.

By contrast, particularly at the beginning of actual hostilities with Lucius, Arthur does not appear in a very positive light: he sends a hot-blooded young man on a delicate diplomatic mission, does not have sufficient authority to make his envoys exert the necessary self-control and is generally at a disadvantage before the strategic skills and the disciplined troops of the Roman leaders. This is especially true in relation to Petreius, of whom we are told 'Bien sout d'estur, bien sout de guerre,/ Bien sout atendre et bien requerre' (11967–8), 'He was experienced in fighting and war, knowing when to wait and when to attack'. Meanwhile (11957–64),

> Bretun puineient a desrei,
> Ne vuleient estre en cunrei,
> Desirrus erent de juster
> E desirrus d'armes porter;
> Chevalerie desirroent,
> Pur ço suvent se desreoent;
> Ne lur chaleit cument qu'alast
> Mais que la guerre cumençast.[27]

Indeed, the whole episode is very nearly a disaster. The envoys, Garin of Chartres, Boso of Oxford and Gawain, only owe their life to a chance encounter with a group of 6000 of their own – a remarkable piece of good luck, which Wace (in an attempt to play down the unlikelihood of such an encounter, and possibly also to forestall any suggestion of incompetence on Arthur's part) attributes to the king's foresight. The men were sent after the messengers by him, to explore the area and, if necessary, afford them protection. Similarly, the troops that arrive under the command of Yder are explicitly said in the French text to have been sent

---

[26] After his single combat with Lucius, Gawain disappears from the narrative as an explicit presence. He is next mentioned, briefly, as a casualty when Modred attacks Arthur while disembarking (13100), and as the reason for Arthur's ensuing hatred of Modred (13143–6).

[27] 'The Britons drove forward impetuously, not caring to be organized into troops: they wanted to prove themselves in single combat and to bear weapons, they wanted knightly deeds, and so they often broke ranks. The did not care how the battle went, as long as it started.'

by a worried Arthur (the Latin text just state that they came to the rescue). Whatever their problems of discipline, the Britons have a good leader: so much is made clear by Wace. And for all his having experienced fear on the Mont St Michel, Arthur is a source of strength to his men, who model their behaviour on his own. Wace adds at the end of Arthur's pre-battle speech at Saussy a solemn oath by his men that 'tel fin cum il fera ferunt' (12450); a mimetic bond we see in action when Arthur reverses the fortune of battle by rushing to the fray and slaughtering the enemy, we are told, like a lion or a wolf, thus spurring on his men to apparently suicidal bravery. The need to cut down Arthur to human size in the giant-killing episode is not indicative of a desire on Wace's part to belittle him as a king and warrior; on the contrary.

In the account of Arthur's campaign against Lucius, Wace remains remarkably faithful to the template offered by his main Latin source, but within this preordained structure, the narrative is reshaped to a striking degree, particularly in the first six chapters of Book X (i.e., chapters 163–8). The Variant text of these chapters is consistently expanded: leaving aside the somewhat complicated §164 discussed above, involving the addition of a whole speech by Hoel, the Mont St Michel episode (§165) grows from 64 lines in the printed text of the Variant to 322 French octosyllabic lines, while Gawain's embassy and the ensuing skirmish covers 492 French lines as opposed to a mere 76 in the printed Variant. The influence of the vulgate version of the *Historia Regum Britanniae* goes some way towards explaining the fuller French text, but not to the extent one might have assumed: the printed vulgate text of the Mont St Michel episode is only some fourteen lines longer than that of the Variant, and §166 of the vulgate text is only eighteen lines longer than the Variant. In fact, here as elsewhere, the vulgate text is very much used as a secondary source, its information being merged into the narrative according to its congruence with the aesthetic or ideological outlook determined by Wace for a given episode. In a section predominantly concerned with warfare, details such as the absence of cavalry among the contingent sent by the islands to Arthur (vulgate, §162), the sinking of ships with huge rocks by the Mont St Michel giant (vulgate, §165), and specific information as to fighting arrangements (especially in chapters 167 and 168) are integrated by Wace into his text; but he also adds features which almost certainly had their only origin in what he himself, as a socially experienced twelfth-century man, would have expected under the circumstances. An example of this is Wace's totally personal addition to the description of Arthur's layout of troops before the battle at Saussy (12387–92):

> Les bons servanz, les bons archiers
> E les vaillanz arbelastriers
> Mist de dous parz defors la presse
> Pur traire bien a la traverse;
> Tuit cil furent devant lu rei,
> Il fud detriés od sun cunrei.[28]

---

[28] 'He put good servants, fine archers and brave crossbowmen outside the throng, on either side, to be able to shoot well from the flank. All these were in front of the king and he was behind with his own company.'

Moreover, even in those sections of the *Roman de Brut* which borrow quite extensively from the vulgate version of the *Historia Regum Britanniae*, the borrowing is selective, and the selected elements are more often than not rearranged according to a different internal logic. In these battle-scenes as throughout his work, Wace prefers not to disrupt the narrative flow of the high-suspense 'action' sections, and frequently anticipates material found at a later stage in the Latin texts. The pattern of borrowing from the vulgate text in the Roman campaign section is no different to that found earlier in the *Roman de Brut*, but these borrowings are more numerous. This, in conjunction with the lavish rhetorical effects to be found at this stage and Wace's many (if relatively minor) other additions to his source-text, points to the privileged status in the French work of Arthur's campaign against Rome.[29]

After the excitement and glory of the victory over Rome and the Emperor Lucius, Arthur's homecoming and the sad end to his reign (*Historia*, chapters 177–8) is a relatively jejune affair as described by Wace, covering less than 300 lines. Nevertheless, it is punctuated by scenes which parallel earlier ones in the reign of Arthur, inviting the reader to contrast past and present situations. Before he leaves for Britain, Arthur entrusts Hoel with France and Burgundy, a shadow of his glorious handing out of French estates to his barons after the conquest of France. The welcome he receives in Britain is also of a nature totally different from that of previous homecomings and signals the fact that all the achievements of Arthur's reign are now obliterated: the Saxons are back in Britain, recalled by Modred. Ironically, Arthur has to confront a similar mix of Christian and heathen in his homeland as he had on the Continent, with the culturally diverse Roman army. Gawain and Angusel of Scotland, one of the major supporters of the Roman campaign, are killed before they have properly landed. Their death may be seen as marking the end of Briton heroism.

Despite the fact that Modred is only a usurper, Wace takes pains to build up a coherent psychological profile explaining his actions. His betrayal of Arthur is motivated by his passion for Guinevere, a crime in itself, but different in nature to the lust for power underlying treason elsewhere in the work (e.g., Vortigern's betrayal of Constance). This love-motif (emphasised by the threefold repetition of the verb 'aimer', 11179–86, when Modred's treason is first revealed by the narrator) may have been suggested by the course of events, inasmuch as the *Historia Regum Britanniae* makes it clear that he was living adulterously with Guinevere. However, in the Latin text(s), this could equally be seen as a ploy on Modred's part to strengthen his claim to the throne: a consequence of his desire to rule Britain rather than its cause. Wace's foregrounding of Modred's love for Guinevere offers a measure of explanation for the traitor's behaviour, depicted as totally irresponsible. The French poem suggests (13054) that Modred could (and possibly should) have made peace overtures to Arthur when he heard of his return: but 'ne volt ne ne deigna pais faire', he refused to make peace,

---

[29] Only twice do we find comparable expansion rates in the latter part of the work (including the end of Arthur's reign): in the sections recounting the adventures of Gurmund and the mission of St Augustine of Canterbury, two key moments in the passage of dominion from the Britons to the Saxons. In neither case does Wace's additional material come from the vulgate version of the *Historia Regum Britanniae*.

compounding his treachery by calling the Saxons to his rescue. The sexual motivation underlying this decision is hinted at by Wace's reference to the land promised to the Saxons as that held by Hengist 'quant Vortiger sa fille prist' (13064), when king Vortigern married his daughter. The implication is that Modred, like Vortigern, is acting out of lust. More so than Vortigern, however, Modred is a troubled soul, acutely aware that he is in the wrong (and therefore, doomed to failure), but incapable of making amends (13073–6):

> Ne li volt pas sun dreit guerpir
> Ne querre peis, ne repentir,
> E il se set tant a culpable
> Que de pais querre serreit fable.[30]

Within the logic of the French text, it makes sense that Modred, whose primary goal was to usurp Arthur's place in the marital bed, should not be very successful as a leader of men. The intrinsic inferiority of his troups compared to Arthur's battle-hardened warriors is compounded by the fact that Modred has neither the charisma nor the strategic genius of his uncle, which leads him from humiliating defeat to humiliating defeat. Wace conjures up images of panic and deficient leadership (13127–32):

> La gent Modred s'est mise en fuie.
> Quidez que l'uns l'autre cunduie?
> Nuls n'i perneit d'altre cunrei,
> Chascun pensot de guarir sei.
> Modred s'en fuï tute nuit
> Querant recet u il s'apuit.[31]

Indeed, Modred is so overcome by his feeling of guilt that he seems to be going through the motions of resistance to Arthur, rather than genuinely doing so: when he sees his uncle's troops outside Winchester, he only *pretends* to prepare for battle ('semblant fist qu'il se cumbatreit', 13157), making instead a desperate attempt to get away: 'Mes il pensa de guarir sei;/ Mesfait ot mult si crienst lu rei' (13173–4), 'but he gave thought to saving his own skin: his misdeeds were many and he feared the king'. The salient feature of Modred's character in the Latin is persistent defiance; the vulgate text even characterises him as 'audacissimus' (§178). In the *Roman de Brut*, it is fear, to the extent that whereas in the Latin Guinevere takes the veil out of despair ('desperans', §177, both versions), in the French text it is out of shame – ostensibly shame at her sexual lapse, but in reality shame at Modred's cowardice (13201–8):

> La reïne sot e oï
> Que Modred tantes feiz fuï;

---

[30] 'He did not want to hand over his rights to him, nor seek peace, nor repent, and he knew himself to be so guilty that to seek peace would be ridiculous.'

[31] 'Modret's men fled. Did you think some of them helped to guide others? No one cared about anyone else, but each thought only of his own skin. Modret fled all night, in search of refuge on which he could rely.'

> Ne se poeit d'Arthur defendre
> Ne ne l'osot en champ atendre.
> A Everwic iert a sojor,
> En pensé fud e en tristur;
> Membra lui de la vilainie
> Que pur Modred s'esteit hunie.[32]

The loss of Guinevere under such circumstances lends added credibility to the lassitude and despair that prompts Modred to meet an honourable death at Camlan.

The reshaping of the characters of Gawain and Modred by Wace indicate that he had thought very carefully about their implication not only for the Arthurian section, but for the work as a whole. Modred is explicitly bound into a network of recurrent treason and sexual infatuation, whilst his brother Gawain is given an advisory role which anticipates another royal nephew later in the narrative (Brian) and invites comparison – and contrast – between Arthur and his successors. There is no reason to believe that these traits are due to the influence of some additional, unspecified source; they are best explained by cues given in the Variant text, developed by Wace in function of his own understanding of the Latin work. For example, Arthur's campaign against Modred closely follows the account of the Variant, which describes the events in a different sequence from the vulgate text (the siege of Winchester and Modred's flight are mentioned before Guinevere's taking the veil, §177, rather than afterwards, as in the vulgate §178); moreover, the vulgate's lengthy description of the troop formation at Camlan (§178) remains ignored by the French writer. The influx of material from chapters 156–66 of the vulgate version of the *Historia Regum Britanniae* cannot therefore be read as an indication that Wace moved from the Variant to the vulgate version in the latter part of his work. The borrowings, very much a localised phenomenon, are consistently of an amplificatory nature, included because of their appositeness to a passage to which Wace wished to give added relief. The two most memorable additions to his Latin source made by Wace – the Round Table and the mention of the Breton hope of Arthur's return – are not to be found in the vulgate text, any more than in the Variant.

The Arthurian section of the *Roman de Brut* is characterised by a circular movement whereby Arthur, mysteriously conceived through the power of Merlin, is given no less mysterious an epitaph in the guise of one of Merlin's prophecies (13275–90):

> Arthur, si la geste ne ment,
> Fud el cors nafrez mortelment;
> En Avalon se fist porter
> Pur ses plaies mediciner.
> Encore i est, Bretun l'atendent,
> Si cum il dient e entendent;

---

[32] 'The queen knew and heard that Modret had so many times been put to flight; he could neither defend himself against Arthur nor dared await him in the field. She was staying in York, melancholy and distressed. She remembered the wickedness she had done in tarnishing her honour for Modret's sake.'

> De la vendra, encor puet vivre.
> Maistre Wace, ki fist cest livre,
> Ne volt plus dire de sa fin
> Qu'en dist li prophetes Merlin;
> Merlin dist d'Arthur, si ot dreit,
> Que sa mort dutuse serreit.
> Li prophetes dist verité;
> Tut tens en ad l'um puis duté,
> E dutera, ço crei, tut dis,
> Se il est mort u il est vis.[33]

There is a sense of closure in this passage. Wace's naming himself at this stage constitutes an admission that the high point in the fortunes of the kings of Britain is now over: this is what he knows will be remembered by most of his audience and he takes advantage of this climactic phase in the development of his narrative to reaffirm his authorial status.[34] He projects an image of critical objectivity, capable of assessing his multiple sources of information: the 'geste' (i.e., the *Historia* itself); the Prophecies of Merlin that he had declined to translate because of the difficulties of interpretation they presented, but with which he now shows himself to be familiar; and first-hand information gathered among the Bretons – a mix of oral and written, of 'historical' texts and contemporary informants that we also find in the *Roman de Rou*. The sense of finality in the passage is paradoxically reinforced by the very open-endedness of Merlin's prophecy, and Wace's refusal to take sides in the matter of Arthur's possible death.

How can the British have a legitimate new king as long as Arthur is alive? Poetically, he is the last king of Celtic Britain, because as long as his death is not established, all his successors are mere regents, like Constantine of Cornwall, to whom Arthur 'Livra son regne si li dist/ Qu'il fust reis *tant qu'il revenist*' (13297–8), 'surrendered his kingdom and told him to be king *until he returned*' (my emphasis). There is no such suggestion of his return in the Latin texts (§178), though the Variant reading 'Constantino ... Britanniam regendam dimisit', 'he surrendered Britain to Constantine to rule', is perhaps more congenial to the idea than the more straightforward vulgate text, where we are told that Arthur 'diadema Britanniae concessit', 'handed over the crown of Britain'.[35] The implication, in the French text, is that Arthur's retreat to Avalon creates a vacuum of power, the inevitable consequence of which is civil war.

---

[33] 'Arthur, if the chronicle is true, received a mortal wound to his body. He had himself carried to Avalon, for the treatment of his wounds. He is still there, awaited by the Britons, as they say and believe, and will return and may live again. Master Wace, who made this book, will say no more of his end than the prophet Merlin did. Merlin said of Arthur, rightly, that his death would be doubtful. The prophet spoke truly: ever since, people have always doubted it and always will, I think, doubt whether he is dead or alive.'

[34] Wace also mentions himself by name just before Julius Caesar's conquest of Britain – another high point in the work: 'Ço testemonie e ço recorde/ Ki cest romanz fist, maistre Wace ...' (3822–3).

[35] Bern, Burgerbibliothek, MS 568 (ed. Wright) even ends §178 with an unequivocal 'Anima eius in pace quiescat' – 'May his soul rest in peace.'

After Arthur: the passage of dominion

The last 1600-odd lines of the *Roman de Brut* chart the fall of the Britons and the corresponding rise of the English. The influence of the vulgate text of the *Historia Regum Britanniae* remains perceptible, but mainly as a source of colourful background detail destined to fill in perceived gaps in the Variant narrative. The description of King Conan (virtually absent from the Variant account) is thus drawn from vulgate §181, and the earlier part of Cadwallan's reign is similarly indebted to the vulgate text for such details as the common upbringing of Cadwallan and Edwin and their knighting in Brittany (stressing their quasi-fraternal status and thus questioning the relevance of the racial factor in their ensuing conflict); the memorable scene of Cadwallan sleeping with his head on Brian's lap and being awoken by his nephew's tears falling on his face (providing some explanation for the influence over the king of this hitherto unknown character); and the gruesome account of Brian's giving his own flesh to eat to sick Cadwallan (an early indication of Brian's loyalty and physical courage). As elsewhere in the *Roman de Brut*, borrowings from the vulgate text are made selectively; and it is just one additional source among others.

Hagiography looms large, with major additions to §188 (recounting Augustine's arrival in Britain, his founding of a monastery at Canterbury, his mission to the English and the attendant miracles at Dorchester and Cernel)[36] and §189, where a totally different (spiritually and theologically more apposite) prayer is put in the mouth of Saint Oswald before the battle of Heavenfield (14459–71). Similarly, Wace reinforces the image of a saintly Cadwallader by showing him pray for a sign prior to his planned return to Britain (14781–4), thus turning the divine voice that orders him to go to Rome into a miracle in answer to a specific prayer, rather than a quasi-punitive interdiction to sail back to the homeland.[37] To hagiography, one may add in this section the influence of English historiography, which underlies additional information such as King Athelstan's moving of the boundaries of Cornwall (13935–40), his illegitimate birth and his ancestors' payment of Peter's Pence (14763–74). Wace's statement that the peace between Oswi and Cadwallan 'fud lunges guardee' (14516), which runs counter to what is suggested in the *Historia*, might also be due to access to English historical sources.

Hagiography and historiography were of course perfectly respectable sources for additional information. However, Wace's account of the final reigns of the *Historia* (where mythical time gets caught up in historical time) also betrays a readiness to accept sources that even his contemporaries would not necessarily have considered as reliable. The description of Gurmund, his royal lineage and contempt of inherited rule, the reference to a prophecy by Merlin relating to him

---

[36] A total of 112 lines (13701–812) are thus devoted to an account of Augustine's foundations and miracles, which remain unmentioned in the texts of the *Historia Regum Britanniae*. The importance of this addition for the characterisation of a saintly Augustine (who is about to cause, more or less unwittingly, the massacre of the Celtic clergy at Bangor) is of course crucial. Wace's source for this additional information, Goscelin of Saint Bertin's *Vita sancti Augustini*, is published in *PL* 80 (Paris, 1863), cols. 43–94.

[37] By contrast, the Latin texts (§203) have him pray at some length before his arrival in Brittany, interpreting the plague in Britain as a sign of divine wrath against the sinful Britons.

(13385–402) – none of these feature in the vulgate or Variant, and relating as they do to a 'literary' character, strongly suggest indebtedness to a vernacular literary source. If we are to take line 13382 seriously, some at least of this information was common knowledge (invoked, interestingly, to validate events recounted in the *Historia*, rather than some dubious addition): 'Bien en avez oï parler', 'You have certainly heard tell of them'. The description of the siege of Cirencester and the trick of the 'arsonist' sparrows (13534–608) is not to be found in the *Historia* texts either. These features, which may have been borrowed from a *chanson de geste* singing the feats of Gurmund and Isembard, are completed by learned considerations on the etymology of the name of the town, suggesting that the whole episode of the sparrows could equally have been derived from folk-etymology, relayed, one assumes, by an English informant. This is not an entirely new trend: after all, the Round Table is introduced in the Arthurian section despite the suspicious nature of its historical credentials, and linguistic change (seen as degeneration), with its consequences for place-names, is a recurrent theme in the *Roman de Brut*. But what is striking is the absence of any justification for echoing the Gurmund stories, whereas Wace had felt compelled to do so for the Round Table: he clearly has total faith in the material he is relaying.

The underlying presence of a different type of *auctoritas* in this final section of the poem is perceptible at a number of levels. Personal experience (or a trusted informant: the two are not readily distinguishable) provides 'contemporary' information validating the narrative. For example, of Cirencester we are told that 'Funt encor li païsant/ La cité as meissuns nomer' (13620–1), peasants to this day call it the city of sparrows. Extrapolations are boldly made from present-day reality and made to bear upon the distant past, with a confidence which is all the more striking for Wace's usual stance as critical narrator whose hallmark is 'ne sai . . .': the observable presence of ruins ('Encore i perent les ruines', 13631) is seen as corroborating the account of the destruction wrought by Gurmund in Britain; the ruins of the port of Aleth by the town of Dinan ('Encore i pert bien la ruine', 14228) lend verisimilitude to Cadwallan's landing there. The inhospitable island where sick King Cadwallan is served with a slice of Brian's thigh (clearly a mythic-symbolic locus in the Latin texts) is confidently identified as Guernsey, on the grounds that between Cornwall and Brittany, 'n'ad altre terrë' (14191). Wace shows here a readiness to accept as authoritative 'text' the landscape and geography of Britain (and Brittany), a non-verbal witness requiring commentary from such as the 'païsant' of Cirencester, whose words are then put on a par with those of learned Latin *auctores*.

A brief overview of Wace's additions, omissions and modifications to the final part of the poem (corresponding to Books XI and XII of the *Historia Regum Britanniae*) shows that, despite the French writer's apparently more relaxed attitude as to the origins of any supplementary material he used, the underlying principle remains that of subordination to the one main source. Most of the peculiarities of Wace's text fit neatly under the headings first formulated by Margaret Houck. The drive towards verisimilitude or 'realism' must account for the rewriting of §179, where Modred's sons are given motivation for their uprising (i.e., pride and opportunity), while their command over London and Winchester, two of England's most important towns, prompts Wace to state that 'le mielz del païs unt saisi' (13311), 'they seized the best part of the country' and that 'Issi quiderent seignur estre' (13314), 'they thought to be rulers', despite the fact that the vulgate text presents them as having failed to overthrow Constantine. On a more trivial level, here as elsewhere in the poem, Wace's 'realistic' leanings account for details such as hostages handed over to the victorious king (13353–4), the sending out of interested parties from the King's Council (all the English are made to leave the room with Penda, 14568), or the explicit eliciting or transmitting of important news by different characters (14319–24, 14363–4, etc).

This realistic strain, joined with the requirement to make the narrative emotionally engaging, may also be at the root of the far-reaching modifications brought to the account of the earlier part of the life of Cadwallan, where the Variant text is somewhat short of motivational or explanatory elements. The reason for his being sent to Brittany for his education (with Edwin) is because, 'ço me semble' of the kinship between Britons and Bretons (14023–6); he is crowned before Edwin because he is more powerful (14035–38); the reason why Cadwallan is so receptive to Brian's arguments is explained through the closeness between uncle and nephew (implicit in Cadwallan's sleeping with his head on Brian's lap), the emotional appeal of the tears that wake him up and the weakening of rational thought at such a moment of half-wakedness. The irrelevance of reasoned argumentation under these circumstances is further indicated by the extremely short (10 lines) speech where Brian explains why he is crying, as opposed to the vulgate's 20-line potted history of Britain.

What Wace chose not to borrow is revealing of the way he views the entire episode. The scene where Brian mutilates himself to restore Cadwallan to health – an indication of the resourcefulness and strength of character that will enable him to kill Edwin's astrologer – reshapes the vulgate account to make it more mundane. Cadwallan's illness is not due to a form of depression, as in the vulgate; he is 'Malade... de fievre ague/ Dunt cil returne ki bien sue' (14195–6), 'sick with acute fever, from which one can recover by profuse sweating', an illness of the body rather than the soul. The sympathetic magic at work in the vulgate account, where Brian may be said to be literally feeding his manhood to Cadwallan, is reduced to an empty whim; the king would have recovered anyway, a fact implied in Wace's statement that 'Ne sai se li reis en gusta/ Mes il guari e trespassa' (14221–2), 'I do not know if the king tasted any, but he recovered and survived.' Brian's sacrifice was not necessary; his action is turned into mere anecdote.

The drive towards realism is accompanied, as throughout the *Roman de Brut*, by the desire to spell out to the readers where their sympathies should lie. This underpins a number of comments made by the narrator, for example his condemnation of the slaying by Constantine of Modred's sons whilst under the protection of the Church (§180; *Roman*, 13320): in this instance, not to arouse sympathy for Modred's progeny as much as to indicate that the kings of Britain are no longer the heroes of the narrative, a fact reinforced by the totally dishonourable nature (duly stressed through details taken from the vulgate text) of Constantine's successor, the murderous Conan.

The shift which (in the *Historia Regum Britanniae* already) turns the Saxons into the heroes of the narrative is effected gradually by Wace, who creates a transitional period during which we sympathise totally neither with the Britons nor with their hereditary enemy. The Briton kings after Arthur are shadowy (Vortiporius), morally deficient (Constantine, Malgo) or politically inept (Cariz), whereas the pagan Gurmund, for all his bloodthirsty ways, is described admiringly both for his prowess and his regal qualities (not least, his truth to his word, 13640). It has been suggested that the passage of dominion from the Britons to the English happens in Wace's work with the conquest of the land by Gurmund,[38] whose campaign is recounted with an unusually high level of elaboration for this final part of the poem. However, the renaming of towns (13649–62) and Gurmund's establishing of English kings over the conquered land are only the first steps in a long process. The English still have to learn political maturity and (more crucially) they have to allow themselves to be enlightened by the Christian faith (13663–4, 13675–82):

> Engleis voldrent rei establir,
> Mes ne se porent assentir
> . . .
> Issi unt lungement esté
> Que il n'orent rei curuné
> Ne mustier n'i ot restoré
> Ne tenue cristïenté;
> Altel sacré ne dedié,
> Enfant levé ne baptizié.
> Cent anz e plus i ont esté
> Senz lei e senz crestïenté.[39]

The English are not yet civilised; they are therefore unable to truly assume dominion over the land handed over to them by Gurmund. Hence the importance of the mission of Saint Augustine and the stress given by Wace to his personal sanctity, which in turn produces spiritual fruit among the English: in a very real sense, the passage of dominion is the consequence of Augustine's activities, rather than of Gurmund's. The civilising effects of Christianity, however, are not immediate, and the reign of Cadwallan is to be understood as an illustration of the changing balance of powers between the two groups.

That Wace did not wish to depict a polarised, black-and-white picture of the British and the English at this stage is indicated by his handling of such scenes as Augustine's meeting with the prelates of the Celtic Church. The words of the Briton bishops are less shockingly unchristian than in the Latin texts (where they state that they have as much in common with the Saxons as with dogs), yet at the same time, the excellent reasons they have for rejecting Augustine's authority are all but omitted. As a result, the non-cooperation with Augustine appears to be derived from a selfish desire to keep the 'advantage' of Christianity to themselves, rather than a mixture of respect for ecclesiastical tradition and distrust of

---

[38] Most recently, by Paradisi, *Le passioni della storia*, pp. 233–41.
[39] 'The English wanted to appoint a king, but they could not agree. . . . For a long time matters remained this way: they had no crowned king, and they neither restored churches nor upheld Christianity. They consecrated no holy altars, brought no children to the font nor baptized them. For over a hundred years they were without creed and without Christianity.'

the hereditary enemy. The speech itself is not attributed to any single personage (in the Latin, the speaker is Abbot Dinoot), and it is noticeably shorter than in either of the Latin texts of the *Historia*. The Britons are clearly in the wrong, in that they openly declare Augustine to be their enemy for his desire to convert the English (13861–64; a statement not to be found in the Latin texts), but their hatred of the Saxons is toned down to understandable antagonism. We do not sympathise with them, but neither are we made to feel that they are total villains, and the way Wace introduces the Bangor massacre (as the direct result of Augustine complaining to King Aldeberd of Kent) tends to confirm the validity of their prejudice. But it is clear that identities are being redefined.

The friendship between Elfrid and Cadwan is a graphic illustration of the possibility of dialogue (and indeed love) between the British and the now Christian Saxons. Their holding of everything in common has overtones of the early Christian communities glimpsed in the Acts of the Apostles (certainly a deliberate echo on Geoffrey's part), and the equality between both men appears to be total (Wace follows the Variant text rather than the vulgate, where Ethelfrid/Elfrid abandons his pregnant wife, who has to seek refuge at Cadwan's court). The conflict between their sons arises out of political rivalry, without it being possible to apportion blame in a clear manner to one side or the other. Cadwallan should not have raised Edwin's hope of an agreement, only to dash it on a word of Brian's; equally, Edwin's devastation of Cadwallan's lands is unjustifiable (Wace qualifies Edwin as 'fel', 'cruel / treacherous' at this stage, 14115). However, the balance is still in favour of the British. The Saxons are not yet completely christianised, and therefore are prone to treachery (as exemplified by Penda). Moreover, though Edwin has the advantage of his astrologer's divinatory skills, Cadwallan is still connected to the mythical past of his people through Brian, who through his name and larger-than-life personality recalls heroes such as Brennes. Brian is truly the last of the old Britons, mindful of their prerogatives and glory, and full of the fighting spirit of a Gawain or a Corineus. Cadwallan, though, is no Brutus, and certainly no Arthur. His reign is very much in historical, not mythical, time; hence the manipulativeness and mediocrity, the cynical use of enemy divisions, the *Realpolitik* which allows the murder of saints. The importance given to Brian by Wace through his carefully selected borrowings from the vulgate text points to the inadequacy of Cadwallan, who without his nephew is reduced to a state of apathetic powerlessness. The absence of true leadership ultimately leads to the waste of Brian's abilities and turns him into an almost feminine figure – cradling Cadwallan's head with maternal solicitude, using tears to exert emotional pressure on him, feeding him, crying when he meets with his sister at Edwin's court (14284) and resorting to ruse rather than prowess to get rid of 'maistre Pellit'. His only act of warfare is to take Exeter, where, besieged, he waits for Cadwallan's return from Brittany.

Cadwallan's marriage to Penda's sister marks the beginning of an irreversible assimilation process between Britons and Saxons, which makes Cadwallader's renunciation of the British throne rather less momentous than it could seem. The royal house of Britain is now 'forslignié' in the most litteral sense of the term, in that the purity of its lineage is compromised; hence, perhaps, Wace's uncomplimentary opinion of the Welsh of his day (14851–4):

> Tuit sunt mué e tuit changié,
> Tuit sunt divers e forslignié
> De noblesce, d'onur, de murs
> E de la vie as anceisurs.[40]

The *Roman de Brut* ends somewhat abruptly after this statement of degeneracy. The struggle of Yvor and Yni against the English is barely hinted at and the political reasons given by the Latin texts for their lack of success (civil discord and divine punishment, according to the Variant; the combined effect of the plague and famine during Cadwallader's reign and the habit of civil war, according to the vulgate) are not even mentioned. The history of the kings of the Britons, as recounted by Wace, ends with Cadwallader's renunciation of Britain following a divine order confirmed by the prophecies of Merlin and the Sibyll.[41] The fate of the Briton remnant is of no special interest and the Latin §207 dwindles into a short, 16-line postscript. Whatever the intended readership of Geoffrey of Monmouth may have been, the Welsh are firmly excluded from that of Wace. The Celtic Britons do not just lose Britain: they are all but obliterated themselves.

---

[40] 'The Welsh have quite altered and quite changed, they are quite different and have quite degenerated from the nobility, the honour, the customs and the life of their ancestors.'

[41] And also, as in the Latin texts, the auguries of the Eagle, understood by Wace to be a prophet named Aquile (14814).

Part II CONCLUSION

It is apparent from our study that Wace was thoroughly in control of what he was doing throughout his *Roman de Brut*. His translation is based on an in-depth analysis of the themes and implications of the *Historia Regum Britanniae*, as represented by the Variant version of the text. Though the Norman writer was clearly familiar with the vulgate text and did not hesitate to borrow from it, the general framework supporting his narrative is firmly that of the Variant, with occasional interpolations. Geoffrey of Monmouth's vulgate text is not, therefore, markedly different in status to the tales mentioned in reference to the Round Table, or Goscelin of St Bertin's Life of Saint Augustine. Moreover, whereas one can find many passages (some quite extensive) where the Variant text can be read line by line alongside the French poem, it is virtually impossible to detect any evidence that Wace had the vulgate text on his work table whilst composing his *Roman de Brut*. Even in the few cases of obvious borrowing from the vulgate text, the influence is felt 'ad rem' rather than 'ad verbum' (though a striking metaphor might be adopted here or there). As with his *Vie de sainte Marguerite*, Wace's work is founded on close textual study of his source material, which he adapts to reflect his personal interpretation of the material, but also to respond to the expectations of a non-clerical audience whose interest would presumably have been mainly in the figure of Arthur. Moreover, as with the *Vie de saint Nicolas*, Wace relaxes his strict narrative control over Geoffrey's material at key points, to encourage a mixed audience to continue listening. In this, he was helped by the fact that Geoffrey of Monmouth himself followed the same strategy (this explains the presence of the memorable account of the story of Leir and his daughters after a rather dry stretch of narrative): adapting from the already polished work of a brilliant writer was undoubtedly a major advantage. This advantage was exploited to the full by Wace, and his *Roman de Brut* fully deserved its success. The superb job made of this one piece of historiography led to royal patronage and the undertaking of another major historiographical project: the adaptation in French of the history of the dukes of Normandy.

Table 5. Arthurian section: Wace's use of the Variant and vulgate versions of the *Historia Regum Britanniae*.

Paragraph, HRB	Length,* Variant	Length, vulgate	Length, Brut	Use, Variant	Use, vulgate
143	37	50	126	Main source	—
144	9	11	28	Main source	Minor add.
145	17	22	62	Merged	Merged
146	13	16	46	Main source	—
147	16	40	92	Main source	Minor add.
148	11	16	44	Main source	—
149	31	30	120	Main source	—
150	16	17	60	Var. = vulg.	Var. = vulg.
151	10	10	30	Main source	Possible
152	12	12	42	Merged	Merged
153	17	14	76	Main source	—
154	28	27	152	Main source	—
155	56	60	288	Main source	—
156	44	55	162	Minor	Main source
157	30	58	284	—	Main source
158	39	35	152	Merged	Merged
159	30	34	132	—	Main source
160	—	24	50	—	Main source
161	17	26	86	Main source	Minor
162	7 + 11	22	32	Main source	Minor
163 (Book X)	14	11	50	Main/Merge	Minor
164 a	4	22	2 + 38	Merged	Merged
b	19	—	125		
165	64	78	322	Minor	Main
166	76	94	492	Merged	Merged
167	38	40	162	Merged	Merged
168	29	35	130	Main/Merge	Minor
169	18	26	58	Main source	—
170	25	48	88	Main/Merge	Minor
171	12	28	116	Main source	Merged
172	18	20	102	Main/Merge	Minor
173	25	40	114	Merged	Merged
174	19	31	66	Merged	Merged
175	13	17	40	Main source	—
176	23	22	54	Main source	—
177 (Book XI)	34	38	192	Merged	Merged
178	21	53	76	Main source	—

* Length of the Latin texts refers to the approximate number of printed lines in Wright (10–12 Latin words per line). Length for the French poem refers to the number of octosyllabic lines.

Part III *Le Roman de Rou*

INTRODUCTION: MANUSCRIPTS, SOURCES, STRUCTURE

When Wace set out to produce his verse account of the history of the dukes of Normandy, in 1160, he was confronted by a very different set of problems from anything he had encountered before. The preparatory phase of collecting his materials would have been much more complex, and the task of selecting those suitable for inclusion in his work would have been far more delicate. The subject matter itself was heavily charged politically, and some of the events he had to deal with were still within living memory. There was no one, single work whose structure he could adopt to provide the framework for his own narrative, as the sources for the *Rou* were diverse, open-ended and compilatory. We are far from the *Roman de Brut*, where the entirety of the material was available in a compact, thought-out form; and while Wace was not inexperienced in combining disparate sources to create a logical whole (witness his *Conception Nostre Dame*), the *Roman de Rou* presented him with the problem of a subject matter that was difficult to circumscribe due to the increasingly close links between Normandy and England in the course of the period he was to present. To this, one might add that whilst the *Historia Regum Britanniae* enjoyed widespread popularity and had the advantage of recounting politically 'safe' accounts of a semi-legendary past, the chroniclers and historians of the rulers of Normandy were not granted outstanding prestige; their subject matter was too recent for it to be endowed with the authority of the Classical historians, too easily verifiable for it to be idealised with impunity, too recent to escape partisan tensions. Wace had to evolve new strategies and find a suitable narrative model.

The resulting work is unlike anything else by Wace to have come down to us. The manuscripts of the *Roman de Rou* have transmitted four poems, almost free-standing and in two different metres, that in conjunction recount the history of the dukes of Normandy from their Viking origins to Henry I of England. The *Chronique Ascendante* is a genealogy of the dukes, starting with Henry II of England and moving back in time to the founder of the dynasty, Rou. Composed in twelve-syllable lines grouped in monorhyme stanzas of varying length, it acts as a sort of Table of Contents to the work. It contains 315 lines. The *Première Partie*, in octosyllabic couplets, tells over some 751 lines of the origins of the Norman people and recounts the career of the Viking pirate Hasting. The

Deuxième Partie, in alexandrines grouped in monorhyme stanzas of varying length, like the *Chronique Ascendante*, is devoted to the early dukes, from Rou to Richard I of Normandy (more specifically, the Treaty of Jeufosse, in 965); this section contains 4425 lines. It has been suggested that the *Première Partie* might have been an early experiment on the part of Wace, a view supported by Anthony Holden, the editor of the Société des Anciens Textes Français critical edition of the work:

> La *Première Partie* est à considérer comme un premier essai, abandonné plus tard par l'auteur, sans doute lorsqu'il s'est rendu tardivement compte que le premier chapitre des sources latines restait étranger à son veritable sujet.[1]

The *Première Partie* is consequently published in an Appendix, while the *Deuxième Partie* is generally considered as the true beginning to Wace's verse history. Whether scholarly opinion will long continue to hold such a view remains to be seen. The *Troisième Partie* then finishes the account of the rule of Duke Richard I and continues up to the battle of Tinchebray, in 1106, which established Henry I of England *de facto* as duke of Normandy instead of his brother Robert Curthose. This section is the longest, with 11440 octosyllabic lines rhyming in couplets, like the Première Partie.

The mixture of metres used in the *Roman de Rou* has been variously interpreted as evidence of multiple authorship,[2] a hypothesis that Hans-Erich Keller has shown to be contradicted by the linguistic evidence of the texts;[3] a failed attempt to use a more fashionable verse form;[4] or interference by Wace's patrons.[5] It certainly indicates the extent of the poet's sensitivity to the trends evolving in Anglo-Norman intellectual circles. A number of Anglo-Norman works written towards the end of the twelfth century display a comparable (if not more complex) mix of metres: thus, Jordan Fantosme's *Chronicle* (an account of the Scottish wars in 1173–4), or Elie of Winchester's *L'Afaitement Catun*, an early to mid-thirteenth-century translation of the Distichs of Cato.[6] Though no longer a young man, Wace was clearly unafraid to be experimental. However, this daring does not appear to have paid off.

---

[1] Holden, *Le Roman de Rou de Wace*, vol. 1, p. 11: 'The *Première Partie* should be considered as a first attempt later abandoned by the author, probably when he realized, a little late, that the first chapter of his Latin sources was foreign to his real topic.' This view is shared by most scholars (see Hans-Erich Keller, *Etude descriptive sur le vocabulaire de Wace*, pp. 26–7).

[2] See P. A. Becker, 'Die Normannenchroniken: Wace und seine Bearbeiter', *Zeitschrift für Romanische Philologie* 63 (1943): 481–519, who concludes that the change of metre and the striking difference in the persona of the narrator in the *Deuxième Partie* is due to its having been penned by an 'Anonymus' who had chosen the verse form of alexandrines grouped in monorhyme stanzas after a failed attempt in octosyllabics (i.e., the *Première Partie*).

[3] See Keller, *Étude descriptive sur le vocabulaire de Wace*, pp. 16–23.

[4] See Keller, *Étude descriptive sur le vocabulaire de Wace*, pp. 25–6; this view, however, makes too much of the supposed novelty value of the alexandrine for a twelfth-century audience. See Damian-Grint, *The New Historians*, pp. 82–3.

[5] See Keller, *Étude descriptive sur le vocabulaire de Wace*, p. 26.

[6] On Jordan Fantosme, see Damian-Grint, *The New Historians*, pp. 74–6; on Fantosme's use of various metres, see the introduction to R. C. Johnston's edition of Fantosme's Chronicle (Oxford, 1981), esp. p. xxxii. On Elie of Winchester's translation of the *Distichs of Cato* (edited by T. Hunt under the title *Le Livre de Catun*), see R. J. Dean, *Anglo-Norman Literature. A Guide to Texts and Manuscripts* (London, 1999), pp. 143–4.

Introduction: Manuscripts, Sources, Structure

Only four manuscripts contain all or part of the *Roman de Rou*, three of which are medieval:

1. London, British Library, Royal 4 c xi, was copied at the beginning of the thirteenth century. It originally belonged to Battle Abbey.[7] The *Troisième Partie* of the *Roman de Rou* is copied alongside a Latin commentary of St Jerome, Geoffrey of Monmouth's *Historia Regum Britanniae* and a French version of the Pseudo-Turpin chronicle ending with a genealogy of the kings of France up to Philippe Auguste and his son Louis.
2. Paris, Bibliothèque nationale, fr. 375, dates from the end of the thirteenth century; its language displays Picard traits. It is a composite manuscript with a first section containing didactic and religious works, and a second section containing a number of romances (both Arthurian and *romans antiques*), short poems and religious works, in French verse. The *Troisième Partie* of the *Roman de Rou* comes after a genealogy of the counts of Boulogne and the romance of *Guillaume d'Angleterre*.
3. Paris, Bibliothèque nationale, nouv. acq. 718, dates from the end of the fourteenth century; it only contains the *Troisième Partie* of the *Rou*.
4. Paris, Bibliothèque nationale, Duchesne 79, is a copy of items from a number of medieval manuscripts (some now lost) by the eighteenth-century antiquarian André Duchesne, who may have intended to publish them (the items all relate to the history of Normandy). The text of the *Roman de Rou* was copied from a manuscript, now lost, that belonged to Arthur du Monstier.[8] It is followed by a fragment of Wace's *Conception Nostre Dame*, also copied from du Monstier's manuscript. The Duchesne copy is the only witness to contain all four parts of the *Roman de Rou*.

The fact that three out of the four extant manuscripts preserve only the *Troisième Partie* suggests that the four components of the poem started being copied separately early in the history of its transmission, and that the four parts of the *Rou* were not necessarily perceived to belong to the same work. It would also appear that the *Roman de Rou* was not widely disseminated outside the immediate Anglo-Norman area, as the only extant manuscript not in the Anglo-Norman dialect is from nearby northern France. Holden's study of the textual characteristics of the four manuscripts leads him to conclude that Wace himself probably added some material to the *Troisième Partie* at some stage, leading to the existence of two distinct textual 'families',[9] the characteristics of which are blended to various degrees in composite redactions, represented by MSS 3 and 4 of our list. Holden postulates the influence, at some stage, of a scriptorium or workshop 'où l'on pratiquait, à intervalles réguliers, l'échange des modèles';[10] which in turn

---

[7] For a detailed description of the *Rou* manuscripts, see Holden, *Le Roman de Rou*, pp. 19–24.
[8] Arthur du Monstier was a scholar, born in Rouen in 1586, who edited a number of Norman historical documents. See Paradisi, *Le passioni della storia*, p. 290, note 4.
[9] On the subject, see Paradisi, *Le passioni della storia*, ch. 19 'Versioni d'autore nella tradizione della parte ottosillabica lunga', pp. 309–29, who connects it with the crisis between Henry II and Thomas Becket, and the aftermath to the archbishop's murder.
[10] 'Where models were exchanged at regular intervals': Holden, *Le Roman de Rou*, p. 34.

implies a more intensive copying activity than might be surmised from the survival of just four manuscript witnesses.

The indications that Wace revised his work within his lifetime are all the more convincing because the *Roman de Rou* was written very slowly indeed. Wace tells us he started to work on it in 1160; but his *Chronique Ascendante* refers to events that took place in 1174.[11] It would appear that Wace was still working on the material some fourteen years after beginning his task. Elisabeth van Houts suggests that this slowness could be the reason why Henry II may eventually have decided to ask Benoît de Sainte-Maure to take over; and that the reason why Wace was slow was the nature of the task at hand, because 'for the last part of the *Roman de Rou*, Wace had to act as a real historian instead of as a compiler/translator'.[12] The extent of the research required for the work certainly explains much.[13]

To this, one might add that what had appeared to be a prestigious mandate in 1160 would have lost some of its gloss by the 1170s, as Normandy was increasingly just one of the continental components of the Angevin empire, rather than being the heart of a Norman empire.[14] The risks involved in writing a reasonably truthful account of the history of the Norman dukes now outweighed the advantages. The material did not offer Henry II much propaganda value, whilst providing ample scope to offend him; and that, apparently, is exactly what happened. Wace lost his royal patronage and another writer, Benoît de Sainte-Maure, was entrusted with a complete re-writing of the history of the dukes of Normandy. The practical consequence of the loss of Henry II's support for the project was that the *Roman de Rou* – the work that had cost Wace most toil and labour – did not have the dissemination of the *Roman de Brut*, or even of Wace's more successful religious pieces. It was probably copied mainly in abbeys, where it would have been valued as historiography rather than as literature. The Bayeux prebend gave Wace the financial independence to continue his work up to the point he saw fit; he completed his account of the rule of Duke Robert Curthose and left posterity to grapple with more recent events. Thereafter, Wace the Bayeux canon seems to have devoted himself entirely to his ecclesiastical duties: the *Roman de Rou* is his last known work.

Sources

We may recall that, while the self-contained nature of the *Historia Regum Britanniae* made the preliminary stage of gathering of data potentially unnecessary, Wace did nevertheless make an effort to seek out or recall additional

---

[11] One must note, however, that the description of the Siege of Rouen is usually accepted as a later interpolation. See Holden, *Le Roman de Rou*, pp. 13–14; also his 'L'Authenticité des premières parties du *Roman de Rou*', *Romania* 75 (1954): 22–53.

[12] E. M. C. van Houts, 'The Adaptation of the *Gesta Normannorum Ducum* by Wace and Benoît', pp. 115–24 in *Non nova sed nove: Mélanges de civilisation médiévale dédiés à Willem Noomen*, ed. M. Gosman and J. van Os (Groningen, 1984), p. 118.

[13] Though it does not entirely explain the full decade devoted to the project. Gouttebroze, 'Pourquoi congédier un historiographe', detects a political undercurrant in Wace's apparent lack of enthusiasm.

[14] On the Norman and Angevin 'empires', see John Le Patourel, *The Norman Empire* (Oxford, 1976), esp. pp. 116–17.

information that he felt might be useful or simply interesting for his reader/ listeners. We would therefore expect his *Rou* to have been preceded by similarly conscientious research, if only because it was so much more likely to be challenged by the Norman section of his readership if he got things wrong. This research appears to have followed the same general principles as for the *Brut*: different manuscripts were consulted, and where relevant, specific items of information were integrated into the narrative; oral tradition and contemporary informants were sought out; and the author's fund of learning was freely drawn upon to provide didactic or moralising asides, enhancing the credibility and authoritativeness of the French verse.

The material Wace had at his disposal for his new project was far from straightforward. The first known historian of the dukes of Normany, Dudo of St Quentin, whose *De Moribus et actis Normannorum* was written at the beginning of the eleventh century at the request of Duke Robert II of Normandy, was essentially a propagandist. He endowed the Normans with 'respectable' Trojan ancestry and related in a celebratory mode the rules of the first three dukes, preceded by the adventures of the Viking pirate Hasting, presented as a precursor of the founder of the ducal House of Normandy. A mix of prose and verse, the *De Moribus* has in common with the *Historia Regum Britanniae* the fact that part of its material is legendary or semi-legendary, dealing with an obscure past for which few documents remained; Holden's description of Dudo's work, 'une littérature d'ordre romanesque mais qui met en scène des personnages authentiques, et dont les évènements se déroulent sur un fond historique',[15] could almost equally be applied to Geoffrey of Monmouth's *Historia*. As in Geoffrey's work, this semi-legendary past eventually gives way to the authoritatively documented historical past.

In the mid-eleventh century, Dudo's material was taken up, in a condensed form, by William of Jumièges in his *Gesta Normannorum Ducum*, and updated with the account of the lives of later dukes, up to King William I and the Conquest of England (up to c. 1070). The work of William of Jumièges was to meet with considerable success; it was copied in abbeys throughout Normandy, but also in England and France, surviving in over forty manuscripts. The various abbeys where the *Gesta Normannorum Ducum* was recopied (in particular, the Norman abbeys of Saint-Ouen, Saint-Evroult and Bec-Hellouin) added interpolations and extensions of their own to the text. Robert of Torigni further extended the history in time, to include the reigns of William II and Henry I (of England); the Torigni continuation, however, does not appear to have been known to Wace. The material interpolated at various stages of the complex textual history of the *Gesta Normannorum Ducum* includes a number of anecdotes relating to Duke Robert the Magnificent and a description of the death of William the Conqueror, thought to have been composed by a monk of Caen (c. 1109); information concerning the rebellion of Toutain of Hiémois, the battle of Mortemer, and a number of relatively minor details relating to Duke Robert I and William the Conqueror, supplied by the Saint-Evroult monk Orderic Vitalis; and further additions by

---

[15] 'Literature that is novel-like, but with characters taken from history, and events that take place against a historical backdrop' (p. 101).

Robert de Torigni (between 1142 and 1150), most importantly about the abbey of Le Bec.[16] Other important sources of information for Wace included an eyewitness account of the life of the Conqueror, the *Gesta Guillelmi Ducis* by William of Poitiers, Orderic Vitalis's *Historia Ecclesiastica* and the *Gesta Regum Anglorum* of William of Malmesbury.

Only William of Jumièges' *Gesta Normannorum Ducum* offered a viable template for Wace's work, and the evidence suggests that the French poet used it in much the same way as he used the First Variant version of the *Historia Regum Britanniae* to determine the macrostructure of his narrative. This, as is made clear in William's Epilogue to Book vii, entailed a linear structure presenting the successive dukes of Normandy in chronological order, and an open-ended narrative allowing (indeed inviting) continuation through the addition of new accounts:

> Hactenus illustrissimos ac celeberrima annalium pagina dignissimos Willelmi regis actus quos, ut in ordine narrationis expeditum est, in ducatu plurimos, multos iam in regno merite ultionis gladio iusticie aduersarios debellando gessit, per ueritatis tramitem directo sermone prosecutus, bonis quibusdam adhortando fauentibus iuxta nostri tenuitatem ingenii conscriptos uenture etati in longum uicturos trado. Que uero eius nobilissima gesta probissimaque merita letifica spe iam tenemus, latera illius ambientibus sapientia et eloquentia preminentibus uiris honestam materiam honestis edendam factis relinquo. . . .
> Sed quia Normannorum ducum pacem atque bella cronico dirigere stilo decreuimus ad Rodbertum eiusdem regis filium, quo in presentiarum duce et aduocato gaudemus, calami uia dirigatur.[17]

William's epilogue highlights the major structural problem posed by the conquest of England for an historian of the Norman ducal house. The narrative relied on continuity of lineage and geographical locus to bind together the more or less free-standing accounts of the lives of the successive dukes. This allowed a variety of disparate information to be integrated into the work. But with William the Conqueror's accession to the throne of England, the unity of locus is called into question, whilst the splitting of the lineage into two intertwined lines, one royal, the other ducal, severely reduced its potential as a structuring principle. The answer of William of Jumièges to the new situation is to affirm the primacy of

---

[16] On the textual transmission of William of Jumièges' *Gesta Normannorum Ducum*, see E. M. C. van Houts, ed. and trans., *The Gesta Normannorum Ducum of William of Jumièges, Orderic Vitalis and Robert de Torigni* (Oxford, 1992–5), vol. 1, pp. xci–cxxviii. All quotes and translations of the *Gesta Normannorum Ducum* are from van Houts.

[17] van Houts, *The Gesta Normannorum Ducum*, vol. 2, pp. 182–5 (Epilogue: M143–M144): 'I hand down to posterity the many and noble deeds of King William, in all respects worthy to be described in the distinguished pages of annals, which he, as I have set out in my narrative, up to this moment performed in his duchy as well as in his kingdom, where with the sword of vengeance he pursued the enemies of justice, and which I have told in truthful and straightforward language, with the encouraging support of several friends, according to the simpleness of my literary talent, and in the hope that he may live long. However, I leave the composition of an honest account, based on true facts of his most noble and excellent merits we joyfully may expect from him in the future, to the men, most eminent in wisdom and eloquence who are surrounding him. . . . But since we have decided to write down the history of the peace and wars of the dukes of the Normans we shall now direct our pen to Robert, son of the king, whom at present we rejoice as duke and advocate.'

place over that of persons. The fitting material for his continuators is not the king of England, but the duke of Normandy: from the moment William the Conqueror entrusted the duchy to his son Robert, he ceased to be a Norman duke, and the historian of the Norman ducal House need not concern himself with him any more; such is the reasoning underlying the Epilogue.

This distinction, however, was itself to prove problematic, inasmuch as the history of the duchy of Normandy becomes too intimately bound to the crown of England for it to be considered in isolation. The projected outline by William of Jumièges for the continuation of his history ran counter to the lines of influence and power that determined patronage and prestige. The *Gesta Normannorum Ducum*, as it was transmitted to Wace, had no coherent overarching structuring principle beyond that of chronological order and, due to its aggregative nature, no coherent ideological or moral agenda either beyond that of enhancing the prestige of the Norman dukes. The onus of interpretation – an inevitable stage in any translation, but even more crucial in the case of a poetic adaptation – was therefore squarely on Wace's shoulders, with all the risks that this entailed. It is unfortunate, from the point of view of our poet, that he does not appear to have been aware of the continuation of the *Gesta Normannorum Ducum* by Robert de Torigni, which would not only have provided him with material he had to search for independently, but also made a clear-cut decision regarding the narrative focus for contemporary events: Robert de Torigni's continuation results in a book focused predominantly on King Henry I, whose character is eulogised to the detriment of the 'real' subject of the narrative, Duke Robert II.[18] Wace makes a very different choice, attempting to depict Robert II in as positive a manner as his sources allowed and refusing to be drawn onto the subject of King Henry's deeds (other than those that related directly to Normandy). In other words, the poet follows the programme outlined by William of Jumièges, with the consequence that his work becomes a narrative of Norman defeat. This decision alone could have cost him the patronage of Henry II.

---

[18] It is of course possible that Wace knew of Torigni's continuation, but decided not to use it for precisely that reason. On the matter, see van Houts ('Adaptation', p. 119).

7

The Ancestors of William the Conqueror

The *Roman de Rou* is made up of four different parts, distinguished by metre and style as well as by their specific function within the overall scheme of the *Roman de Rou*. The *Chronique Ascendante*, in monorhyme stanzas containing a varying number of lines (of twelve syllables), shares its formal characteristics with the *Deuxième Partie*, and the *Première Partie*, in octosyllabic couplets, announces the *Troisième Partie*, also in octosyllabic couplets. Wace seems to have planned his poem on a principle of stylistic alternation, possibly reflecting the shifting influences of his various sources, but also pointing to three main phases in the narrative: the origins of the Normans (*Première Partie*), the first dukes (*Deuxième Partie*), and the more recent rulers (*Troisième Partie*). Whatever the vagaries of manuscript transmission and later reception, these three Parts were almost certainly meant to be read in sequence when Wace started his project. The rule of Richard I is thus divided between the *Deuxième Partie*, where we are told about his childhood, and the *Troisième Partie*, where we move on to his achievements as a grown man. I shall therefore consider the constituent parts of the *Roman de Rou* in succession, as one complex narrative.

Chronique Ascendante

The *Chronique Ascendante*, a concise ascending genealogy of the present ruler with accompanying mention of some of the salient events in the lives of the different dukes, serves as a table of contents for the work proper in a format both compact and easy to memorise. The metre selected appears to be an experiment on Wace's part. The monorhyme stanzas recall strongly the *laisses* of the *chanson de geste*, with its epic-heroic stance and claims to a collectively validated authoritative voice, whilst the choice of dodecasyllabic lines with frequent enjambement, as opposed to the self-contained, predominantly decasyllabic line characteristic of the *chanson de geste*,[1] gives the poem a distinctive rhythm which would have distinguished it clearly from the *chanson* for its listeners. The implicit message is clear: this is to be a celebratory, epic piece of work, sharing with the *chanson de geste* a spirit of communal bonding through a quasi-ritual commemoration of past ancestral deeds, but nevertheless with a difference in credentials. The tone is set from the very first lines of the *Chronique* (1–7):

---

[1] Some *chansons de geste* composed in alexandrines have come down to us (see Damian-Grint, *The New Historians*, pp. 82–3), but enjambement is not a normal feature in these texts – or indeed of the decasyllabic *chansons de geste* either.

> Mil chent et soisante anz out de temps et d'espace
> puiz que Dex en la Virge descendi par sa grace,
> quant un clerc de Caen, qui out non Mestre Vace,
> s'entremist de l'estoire de Rou et de s'estrace,
> qui conquist Normendie, qui qu'en poist ne qui place,
> contre l'orgueil de France, qui encor les menasce,
> que nostre roi Henri la congnoissë et sace.[2]

This is to be a salutary warning to King Henry against the perfidy of France, depicted as the hereditary enemy of the Normans (45–61):

> Les boisdies de France ne font mie a celer,
> tout tens voudrent Franchoiz Normanz desheriter
> et tout tens se penerent d'euls vaincre et d'els grever,
> et quant Franceiz nes porent par force sormonter
> par plusors tricheries lez soulent agraver;
> forslignié sont dont l'en souloit chanter,
> faux sont et souduianz, nuz ne s'i doit fier;
> d'avoir sont covoiteuz, n'en nes peut avonder,
> de doner sont escars et demandent aver.
> Es estoires peut on et es livres trover
> qu'onques Francheiz ne voudrent as Normanz foi porter,
> ne por fiance faire ne por sur sainz jurer;
> nepoureuc bien lez seullent lez Normanz refrener,
> non pas par traïsons mez par granz cops donner.
> Se les Franceiz pooient lor pensez achever,
> ja li roiz d'Engleterre n'avrait rienz decha mer,
> a honte l'en feroient, s'il pooient, passer.[3]

This passage announces Wace's 'geste' as partaking of Dudo's propagandist outlook, but with a different aim in view. It is not only to be a celebration of the deeds of the Normans: it is a reminder to the king of England that the French hatred for the Norman people extends to him, by virtue of his ancestry. Just as they tried to dispossess Rou and his people, so will they try to dispossess the Anglo-Norman monarch of his lands. The history of the gallant resistance of the dukes of Normandy to the devious French takes on an exemplary value, in a subversive *chanson de geste*-type narrative which confiscates past French glory

---

[2] 'One thousand, one hundred and sixty years in time and space had elapsed since God in His grace came down in the Virgin when a cleric from Caen by the name of Master Wace undertook the story of Rou and his race; Rou conquered Normandy, like it or not, against the arrogance of France which still threatens them – may our King Henry recognize and be aware of this.'

[3] 'The treacherous acts of the French cannot be concealed; they are always determined to disinherit the Normans and have always taken pains to vanquish and harm them. When the French could not overcome the Normans by force, they used to employ many a trick to harm them. They are a far cry from the heroes of songs; they are treacherous and disloyal, no one should trust them. They are greedy for possessions and cannot be satisfied; when it comes to giving they are niggardly and mean with the necessities of life. In stories and books one discovers that the French were never willing to keep faith with the Normans, either with regard to promises made or oaths sworn on holy relics; nevertheless, the Normans used to hold them in check successfully, not by treachery but by dealing great blows. If the French could realize their ambitions, the King of England would own nothing on this side of the channel.'

to expose the profound degeneracy (they are literally *forslignié*) of the supposed descendants of Charlemagne or Guillaume d'Orange, 'dont l'en souloit chanter', whose feats were made into song. The deeds of Henry himself at the siege of Rouen are later cited as instances both of the essential hostility of the French and the *translatio* of prowess and nobility to the House of Normandy. Matilda's daring escape from Oxford, camouflaged in a sheet one night of thick snowfall (121–8), beyond its anecdotal appeal, may equally be read as proof of the superlative *virtus* of the Norman lineage, even in a woman. The obvious message is that contrary to the French, the Normans are emulating the glorious example of their forebears. However, the importance given to contemporary or near-contemporary events also signals that this is not only going to be an idealised account of the distant past: it is also going to be a record of more recent *gesta*, requiring the skills of the historian in equal measure to those of the translator or the poet.

The *Première Partie*

The *Première Partie* does not seem at a first glance to have a direct bearing on the subject matter of the work, recounting as it does the deeds of a forerunner of Rou, the Viking Hasting; but it is far too polished a piece of narrative verse to be dismissed as a rejected first draft. The hypothesis first formulated by Gaston Paris, that Wace composed it then realised belatedly that it was 'hors sujet',[4] also begs the question of why, when he turned his mind to the story of Rou proper, he decided to change the metre from octosyllabic couplets to alexandrines in monorhyme stanzas comparable to the 'laisses' of the French *chanson de geste*.

The *Première Partie* opens with a 94-line Prologue emphasising the necessity of books and writers to prevent people from forgetting the deeds of past generations (1–18), giving as examples the cities of Thebes, Babylon, Troy and Ninevah, which only survive through ancient writings (19–28). Similarly, the memory of great men such as King Nebuchadnezzar, Alexander or Julius Caesar would have disappeared if their achievements had not been set down in writing (29–64). This world is characterised by mutability and the only safeguards against oblivion are the books written by clerics (65–76):

> Toute rien se torne en déclin,
> tout chiet, tout meurt, tout vet a fin;
> hons meurt, fer use, fust porrist,
> tour font, mur chiet, rose flaistrist,
> cheval trebuche, drap vieillist,
> toute ovre faite o mainz porrist.
> Bien entent et connoiz et sai
> quer tuit morront et clerc et lai,
> et moult ara lor renommee
> aprés lor mort corte duree,
> se par clerc nen est mis en livre;
> ne peut par el durer ne vivre.[5]

---

[4] See Paris's 1880 review of Hugo Andresen's edition of the *Roman de Rou*.
[5] 'Everything turns to decline, everything fails, everything dies, everything comes to an end. A man dies,

This reflection on the transient nature of this world is not especially original; it is a long-established commonplace of religious literature.[6] The role of clerics as custodians of communal memory also echoes the Prologue to the *Vie de saint Nicolas*, though in this case the cleric is not so much a teacher instructing people in matters of faith, preparing them for everlasting life, as an instrument ensuring a form of survival in this life. The focus is clearly secular. The universal dimension to the phenomenon is then further exemplified by instances of countries, regions and towns that have seen their names change through time (77–94): 'Engleterre', which was once called 'Bretaingne' and 'Albion'; London, which used to be called 'Trinovant', and 'Troie Noeve'; Brittany, which was once 'Armorica'; 'Germannie', which was 'Alemaingne'; Paris, which used to be called 'Lutece'; and so on, the list including Greece, Italy, Constantinople, Scotland, Aquitaine, France, Wales, and, finally, Normandy. There is an overlap in material (and interest) with the *Roman de Brut*, but this overlap is discreet. Only four of Wace's thirteen examples relate to Britain, and the references to Scotland and Wales are sandwiched between those to Constantinople, Aquitaine and Normandy, thus diluting the British element in the passage, which reads as a random list of places leading to the key region: Normandy, once called 'Neüstrie'.

The narrator then establishes the identity of the Normans: 'Oïr devez donc Normans furent/ e dont Normanz a cest non rechurent', 'You must hear where the Normans came from and how they received this name' (95–6). The passage starts with the meaning of the name 'Norman' (97–115), referring to English to explain the sense of 'nort' and 'man', and rejecting the derogatory French folk etymology of Normandy as 'nort mendie' (120), that is, the begging northerners. The Normans are presented as Scandinavians (from Norway and Denmark) who conducted savage raids in many places, including France, until the king of France granted Neustria to Rou (141–4):

> Neüstrie, cest non osterent
> et Normendie l'apelerent;
> fierement l'ont puiz maintenue
> e de touz autres deffendue.[7]

Two elements are noteworthy here. First is the fact that Wace appears to be familiar with the English language. He quotes what seems to be an English proverb (103–6):

> Engleiz dient en leur langage
> a la guise de lor usage:

---

iron wears out, wood rots, a tower collapses, a wall falls down, a rose withers, a horse stumbles, cloth grows old; everything made by hand perishes. I understand completely and am fully aware that all men die, cleric and lay, and that after their death their fame will be short-lived, unless it is set down in a book by a cleric; it cannot survive or live on in any other way.'

6 On the *contemptus mundi* aspect of this Prologue, see Paradisi, *Le passioni della storia*, pp. 361–77; on medieval Prologues in general, see James Schultz, 'Classical Rhetoric, Medieval Poetics and the Medieval Vernacular Prologue', *Speculum* 59 (1984): 1–15 and Christiane Marchello-Nizia, 'L'historien et son prologue: forme littéraire et stratégies discursives', pp. 13–25 in *La chronique et l'histoire au moyen âge*, ed. D. Poirion (Paris, 1984).

7 'They removed the name Neustria and called it Normandy. Thereafter they kept hold of it fiercely and defended it against all others.'

"En nort alon, de nort venon,
nort fumes touz, en nort manon."[8]

He is also aware of the kinship between the languages spoken by the English and the Scandinavians (and therefore, originally, by the Normans themselves), noting that 'Mant en engleiz et en norroiz/ senefie homme en franchois', ' "Man" in English and Norse means "Homme" in French' (109–10); a detail suggesting that Wace may have had some notions of Norse (despite the fact that the language had all but died out in Normandy by his day) as well as of English. This implicit claim to linguistic abilities over and beyond mastery of Latin and French puts in a different light Wace's readiness to use English historical and hagiographical sources, from early on in his career. Whether he picked up some English whilst travelling in Britain, or through contact with English-speakers in Normandy itself (Orderic Vitalis's abbey of Saint-Evroult, for example, is not very far from Caen, and English must have been commonly heard among seafarers on Wace's native Jersey), Wace's scholarly asides reveal a definite feeling of affinity with the language and a measure of confidence in referring to it.

A second notable feature of the Prologue is that there is no attempt to attenuate the destructive nature of the Viking raids. On the contrary, lines 131–5 stress the frequency and extent of the 'persecution', 'destrucion', 'damage' and 'guere' they inflict around them. The vicious nature of these forebears of the Normans recurs again and again. Hasting's companion, Bïer (Björn), is the son of a Danish king 'qui touz temps fu de male foi', 'who was always a man of bad faith' (156); the Danes as a whole, said to be descendents of Danas of Troy, are 'de grant malice', 'very evil', with 'mains touz temps ensanglentees', 'blood constantly on their hands' (178–80), and generally 'moult diverses/ moult contraires et moult perverses', 'very hostile, perverse and wicked' (189–90). This wickedness expresses itself through human sacrifice to their god 'Tur' (i.e., Thor), in gory rituals described in some detail (191–206) with almost ethnographical detachment, and through their casting out of the land all of their children except their chosen heir (207–18), to avoid overpopulation – hence the presence of a king's son at Hasting's side. The story of Hasting shows him to be true to type: 'paeinz sorquidez,/ mout feuls et mout desmesurez', 'an arrogant pagan, very wicked and unrestrained' (229–30), a foreigner to pity and incapable of keeping his word (231–2).

Wace's sources are not backward in acknowledging the ferocious ways of the ancestors of the Normans, but this introduction to the adventures of Hasting betrays no sense of kinship on Wace's part, as if these bloodthirsty Danes were alien to him and his audience, and distasteful to boot. This appears to be part of a wider strategy on the poet's part; by emphasising the inhuman and uncivilised background from which the founder of Normandy came, the shortcomings of Rou are mitigated, whilst his qualities (in particular, his attraction to Christianity and

---

[8] 'The English say in their language, according to their usage: "We are going to the north, we come from the north, we were born in the north, we live in the north." ' This is listed as a proverb by Leger Brosnahan ('Wace's use of proverbs', *Speculum* 39 (1964): 444–73), though it sounds like the sort of sentence one might find in a primer for language learners.

eventual conversion) are all the more admirable. In this sense, the *Première Partie* is a very effective prelude to the *Deuxième Partie*. On the other hand, it still remains that these treacherous, murdering thugs are the ancestors of the Normans, and the career of Hasting presents some worrying parallels with that of Rou. Both appear to have been expelled from their homeland because of overpopulation; both fight with the king of France; both convert to Christianity when it suits them; both eventually obtain grants of land from the king of France. These parallels are obscured by the fact that the narrative of the *Première Partie* is mostly devoted to Hasting's plundering and burning of churches, monasteries and cities (including Fécamp, Rouen and Jumièges), against a backdrop of weak royal power and internecine warfare following Charlemagne's division of his empire among his sons (283–328). Moreover, the most important anecdote told of Hasting – his feigned conversion and death in order to capture the town of Luni, which he mistook for Rome – puts him in stark contrast with Rou, whose conversion is depicted as genuine.

Wace takes special pains to give authority to his account of the adventures of Hasting. He does not mention Dudo or William of Jumièges by name, following in that respect his usage in his other works, but he does invoke written authorities attesting to the extent of Hasting's depredations (447–55):

> Les livres en trai a tesmoingne
> que de Flandres sic' en Gascoingne,
> si con devers solleil couchant
> voit mer la terre avironnant,
> n'out chastel ne vieille cité
> borc ne ville d'antiquité,
> qui de Bïer ne se sentist
> et que Hastainz ne destruisist,
> ou tel raanchon ne preïst.[9]

Moreover, as in the case of Gurmund in the *Roman de Brut*, the presence of ruins in various places are mentioned as corroborative evidence, including in the poet's native Jersey (421–4):

> Em plusors liex pert la ruine
> que firent la gent sarrazine
> en Auremen et en Gernesi
> en Serc, en Erm, en Guernerui.[10]

Similarly, the ruins of the town of Luni are said to be visible: 'cen voient bien li pelerin/ qui vont a Romme le chemin', 'pilgrims on their way to Rome can clearly see them' (727–8). This account, that could easily be dismissed as the story of a

---

[9] 'I take books as my witness that from Flanders to Gascony, just as in the direction of the setting sun, where the sea runs round the edge of the land, there was no castle or old city, burg or ancient town which did not experience Björn's treatment and which Hasting did not destroy, or take such ransom as he himself sought.'

[10] 'In a number of places the ruins are visible which the Saracens [i.e., pagans] created in Alderney and Jersey, Sark, Herm and Guernsey.'

semi-legendary character of the period of the Viking raids, is given further weight through the persona of the narrator, who, as in the *Roman de Brut*, is scholarly and critical in his stance. In the Prologue, the stress on written authorities and reading goes hand in hand with learned information such as the fact that the Danube is called Ester by the 'clerc luisant' (i.e., the 'clerc lisant' such as Wace himself); whilst the charm put on Björn by his mother, protecting him against any injury by iron (149–54) is mentioned with a somewhat dismissive 'ne sai c'est voir, mez ce dit on', 'I don't know if it is true, but that's what is said' (150). Through details like these, the reader is reassured that the narrative is serious, truthful history.

The stylistics and versification of the *Première Partie* are similar to those of the *Roman de Brut*, but rhetorical effects are used with less restraint. Some of these are dictated by the nature of the material: thus, lists (typically, of places ravaged by the Danes), or the playful repetition of words derived from the same root (such as 'nort'/'Normans'). Anaphora and isocolon occurring over two lines or more are common;[11] but rhetorical adornment is at its most lavish in the episode of the capture and destruction of the town of Luni, which is also the only part of the *Première Partie* to feature direct speech. Hasting, having ravaged France, decides to conquer Rome, make Björn king over the city, and become the ruler of the whole world (459–68). They arrive outside the city of Luni, in Tuscany, which they mistake for Rome. Their arrival is described in a vignette where the young cleric reading the lessons for matins in the cathedral prophetically announces the arrival in the port of a hundred ships. His fellow clerics first think he has misread ('Que dis tu?/ Tu n'i as pas bien veü', 507–8); he repeats his statement, at which he is told to stick to the text ('Garde . . . en l'escript'); but he repeats his warning again, incapable of saying anything else (512–17). And indeed, in the morning, the town wakes up to the Viking fleet at its gates. Hasting realises it will not be possible for him to take the town by force, so decides to convince the bishop and count of Luni that he is sick and wishes to be baptized before he dies. His feigned symptoms are described with relish by Wace (573–92):

> Li cuvert malade se faint,
> sa chiere et son viaire taint,
> mout plaint le cors, moult plaint le chief,
> dist que par tout li estoit grief;
> sovent iert palle, sovent ert pers,
> sovent asdenz, sovent envers
> sovent s'endort, sovent s'ezveille,
> sovent s'estent, sovent ventraille;
> Dex, que donc nel prist paision!
> Si remainsist la traïson.
> Les bras estent, les poinz detort,
> cescun quil voit dist quil soit mort;
> qui oïst le felon crier
> et le veïst escaucherrer,
> denz reguinier, braz degeter,

---

[11] See for example 129–35, 160–4, 220–2, 255–62, 277–80, 365–8 etc.

> jambes estendre et recorber,
> sovent sangloter et baallier,
> le nes fronchir, ex rouïller,
> qui donc veïst, comment cuidast
> que li traïtres respassast?[12]

This elaborate description has as its immediate function to explain why the inhabitants of Luni, and more especially their count and their bishop, are taken in by this play-acting; but it goes on for much longer than it might have in the *Roman de Brut* (in which the closest equivalent would be some of the more elaborate battle scenes) and there is a strong entertainment value to the passage, verging on the farcical. With the requisite voice effects and facial mimicry, Hasting's feigned illness would be unambiguously comic,[13] as would, in a darker register, his plea to the bishop to be buried in the church after his baptism (614–23, 628):

> "Certes," dist il, "se je respas
> je ferai a cest lieu honor,
> e miex vous iert de moi maint jor;
> mes fieble sui et maint mal sent,
> ne cuit pas vivre longuement,
> n'ai pas le cuer sain ne delivre,
> ne cuit mie longuement vivre.
> Mez se je muir, por Dieu vous quier,
> quer me faites appareillier
> mon sepulcrë en cest moustier.
> . . .
> Sauf en serai, ce croi ge bien."[14]

There is a reynardian dimension to the character of Hasting. Like the fox, he is an unprincipled, vicious trickster, but as in the various branches of the *Roman de Renart* or the earlier Latin *Ysengrimus*,[15] we can detect a sneaking admiration for

---

[12] 'The scoundrel was feigning illness; he had stained his face and countenance and was complaining bitterly about pains in his body and his head, saying that he was hurting all over. His skin was constantly pale and livid, he was constantly lying face down or on his back, constantly falling asleep and waking up, constantly stretching and rolling on his stomach. God, if only his death agony had really taken him! In that way the trickery would have ceased. He stretched out his arms and wrung his hands; everyone who saw him thought he was on the point of death. How would anyone who heard the wretch yelling and saw his antics, how he ground his teeth and waved his arms, stretched and bent his legs, constantly sobbing and yawning, wrinkling his nose and rolling his eyes, how would anyone who had seen him thought the scoundrel would recover?'

[13] Some facial mimicry would indeed have been inevitable when reading this passage aloud, especially in the case of lines 587 and 590.

[14] 'If I recover, I will certainly do honour to this place and on many a day you will benefit because of me. But I am weak and have a great deal of pain. I do not expect to live long, my heart is not healthy or in good condition. But if I die, in God's name, I ask you to prepare a burial place for me in this church. . . . I will be saved, I feel sure.'

[15] While the earliest branches of the *Roman de Renart* postdate Wace's work (our first extant reynardian tale in French dates from 1175), Nivard's *Ysengrimus* was written in 1152, and therefore could have been known to Wace. To this, one may add that the famous portal of Modena cathedral featuring an Arthurian archivolt has a reynardian architrave, suggesting that already in the early twelfth-century, the fox was seen as a *figura diaboli*. See Jean Scheidegger, *Le Roman de Renart ou le texte de la derision* (Geneva, 1989), pp. 384–7.

his skilful play-acting, his verbal skills, and his ability to manipulate the weaknesses of his victims. In this case, the prospect of rich gifts in exchange for the burial place inside the church – a hallowed place where only the greatest and best should be interred – implicitly encourages the bishop to accede to Hasting's request; and through greed comes the downfall of the city. The disproportionate respect shown to the Viking's supposed corpse, rather sacrilegiously treated like a holy relic,[16] further underlines the disastrous error of judgment of the bishop. The scene of confusion when Hasting rises from his coffin, triggering wholesale massacre through the town, has overtones of a predator let loose in a farmyard; an aspect explicitly highlighted by the simile of a wolf slaughtering sheep 'quant il peut entrer en teit/ que li villainz ne s'aperchoit', 'when it manages to get into a fold without the peasant noticing' (707–8). The reference to the peasant eliminates any high style or epic connotations the ravening wolf could have had. The lupine or vulpine nature of Hasting recurs later in the work in the *Deuxième Partie* (line 520) when his advice to his French overlord is rejected on the grounds that 'L'en ne prant mie lou ne goupil souz son banc', literally, 'You don't invite a wolf or a fox under your bench'.[17]

After plundering the region, the Vikings, mortified that the town was not Rome after all, decide to return to France. Björn sails away to new adventures, while Hasting enters the service of the king of France and receives Chartres and its region in reward; he is still there when Rou arrives with his men, 'Normant apelé/ por ceu que de north furent né', 'called Normans because they had been born in the north' (749–50). This is a neatly circular movement, taking us back to the prologue where the meaning of the name 'Norman' was first explained; it leads us seamlessly to the story of Rou and quietly (but clearly) makes the distinction between virtuous Rou and Hasting, the diabolical leader of a heathen mob ('gent sarrazine', 422) who murdered both the bishop who christened him and the count who acted as his godfather.

The *Deuxième Partie*

The *Deuxième Partie* reads as a continuation to both the *Chronique Ascendante* and the *Première Partie*. The *Chronique* had ended with Rou, and this is where the narrative picks up the thread: 'A Rou sommes venus et de Rou vous diron,/ la commence l'estoire que nos dire devon', 'We have reached the figure of Rou and we will speak to you of Rou; the tale we have to tell begins at this point' (1–2). But it also assumes that the readers know all about Hasting, who is explicitly presented as the opposite of Rou (12–16):

> Amdui furent Danoiz, mez moult furent divers,
> Rou fist auques a droit, Hastains fist a envers,
> Rou fu amiables, Hastainz fier et divers

---

[16] Line 680, all the clerics rush to receive Hasting's corpse in the church, 'comme se ce fust un cors saint', 'as if it were for a holy relic'.

[17] The exact meaning of this line is not clear, but the implications for Hasting are obvious.

onques nen out merci ne de frans ne de sers,
ne clers ne lais n'ama, ne moigne ne convers',[18]

The octosyllabic *Première Partie* is thus part and parcel of the narrative horizon of the *Deuxième Partie*. Moreover, if we disregard the *Première Partie*, we have to face the fact that Wace, apparently, did not think it worthwhile to compose a formal prologue, beyond his praise of Henry and Eleanor in the *Chronique Ascendante*: an unusual decision for a poet with such a strong pedagogical instinct. On the other hand, the statement on line 3 of the *Deuxième Partie* that 'por l'euvre esploitier les vers abrigeron', as translated by Glyn Burgess: 'to speed our task, we will reduce the number of lines in each stanza', only makes sense by comparison with the longer stanzas of the *Chronique Ascendante*.[19] However, the stanzas do not remain short throughout the *Deuxième Partie* (the longest is some 56 lines long), so perhaps this line means, quite literally, 'we shall abridge the narrative', that is, 'we shall not indulge in lengthy anecdotes like that of Hasting at Luni'; or possibly: 'we shall not try to match Dudo's rhetorical set pieces'. All three possibilities make sense, as Wace does indeed omit all in Dudo that is not prose, prunes out much of the earlier historian's sycophantic rhetoric, and returns to a stricter principle of narrative economy.

The *Deuxième Partie* recounts the rules of three dukes, Rou, William Longsword and Richard I, over a total of 4425 lines, and in three clearly distinguished sections devoted to each duke: 1313 lines for Rou, 703 lines for William and the remaining 2400-odd lines to Richard. As in the *Chronique Ascendante*, the metre is alexandrines in monorhyme stanzas, varying from 3 to 58 lines in length. The traditional rhythm of the alexandrine, with a strong pause (caesura) after the sixth syllable, is not the norm here; the pause, though present, tends to be weak, each line typically being a sense unit.[20] There is a discernable pattern to the length of the stanzas. In the Rou section, over half of the stanzas are four lines long, and the longest covers 31 lines;[21] in the William Longsword section, the proportion of four-line stanzas dwindle to two-fifths, whilst two stanzas exceed 30 lines in length;[22] and in the Richard section, we find only two stanzas of five lines or fewer, against ten of 30 lines or more (the longest covering 58 lines). Wace obviously felt increasingly at ease with his material as he progressed in his poem, which moves from a relatively neutral, informative narrative stance (connected more especially with shorter stanzas) to the enthusiastic celebration of feats of arms and of ducal wisdom.

Dudo of St Quentin's *De moribus et actis primorum Normanniae ducum* underpins all of the accounts Wace had at his disposal for the rules of the early dukes of Normandy. William of Jumièges abbreviated this section of Dudo quite

---

[18] 'Rou and Hasting were both Danes, but very different men; Rou acted in accordance with justice, whereas Hasting did the opposite. Rou was friendly, Hasting arrogant and fickle, displaying no mercy to nobleman or serf and never showing any love for cleric or non-cleric, monk or lay brother.'
[19] This is the accepted interpretation for this line since Gaston Paris's review of Andresen's edition of the *Roman de Rou*, esp. pp. 598–9.
[20] See Holden, *Le Roman de Rou*, vol. 1, pp. 81–2.
[21] This section contains also contains five three-line 'stanzas', the shortest to be found in the work.
[22] Thirty-two and 35 lines in length, to be precise. I found no three-line stanza in the section.

savagely:[23] Wace returned to the full text of Dudo to flesh out his narrative. This may be seen from the inclusion in his work of a number of features absent from both the *Gesta Normannorum Ducum* and the Torigni interpolations drawn from Dudo, ranging from isolated details (such as the fact that Rou died in full possession of his mental faculties) to entire episodes (such as Conan's embassy to William Longsword, 1622 ff.). The way Wace uses his sources suggests that, as in the *Roman de Brut*, inclusion or exclusion of material was dictated by considerations of narrative economy tempered by a real fondness for rhetorical amplification. The focus is kept firmly on one central character, the ruling duke, and anything in Dudo (or indeed, in the *Gesta Normannorum Ducum*) that does not relate directly to him remains ignored. On the other hand, scenes involving the ruler (and such scenes in Dudo tend to be both memorable and lively, with a lavish use of direct speech and dialogue) tend to be reinstated, though usually in an abridged form. It is important to stress that this does not make Dudo Wace's main source. The sequence of events in the *Deuxième Partie* follows that of the *Gesta Normannorum Ducum*; where it does not, the new sequence is dictated by Wace's narrative agenda rather than Dudo's. Moreover, as mentioned above, the verse sections of Dudo are totally ignored; borrowings from the prose sections are extremely selective; and most of Wace's 'additional' material tends to be amplificatory in nature (speeches and descriptions, mainly) arising from cues given by his main source.

The *Deuxième Partie* is characterised by the relatively undignified persona of the narrator, who is given a patter very similar to that of a minstrel: a far cry from either Dudo or William of Jumièges and quite unlike the reliable, scholarly pose adopted in the *Roman de Brut*, or the pious narrator of the *Conception Nostre Dame*. The initial *laisse* of the *Deuxième Partie* states: 'la voie est longue et grief et le travail cremon' ('the road is long and hard and we fear the toil', 4) – not the most encouraging of *entrées en matière* – while the last *laisse* closes the narrative proper with the surprising statement (concerning the Vikings who went to Spain, 4419) that 'ne sai que puiz devindrent ne je savoir ne quier', 'I don't know and I couldn't care less',[24] which leads (4420–5) to the jongleuresque:

> Au duc de Normendie nos esteut reperrier,
> mez d'aler longue voie se peut on bien lascier
> et de beles canchons se peut il en-oisier;
> qui chante boivre doit ou prendre autre loier,
> de son mestier se doit qui que peut avancier;
> volentiers preïst grace, quer de prendre a mestier.[25]

'It's time for a break: show your appreciation to the singer': an ending, or rather, a

---

[23] Much of the material omitted by William was later re-interpolated in his text by Robert de Torigni.
[24] Burgess's more dignified translation reads: 'I do not know what became of them and I will not find out.' A similar expression appears on line 3577, where Thibaut of Chartres' motivations for attacking duke Richard are said to be envy, and 'autres achaisons que je dire ne quier', 'other reasons as well, which I do not wish to state', suggesting in this case wilful retention of information.
[25] 'We have to return to the Duke of Normandy. But one can become tired by a long journey and fine songs can become wearisome. He who sings must drink or take some other reward. He who can should progress in his profession; Wace would gladly accept bounty, for he needs to take something.'

pause in the narrative, worthy of any of the *fableürs* Wace is so dismissive of in his *Roman de Brut*. One may wonder why Wace thus 'debases' his work by this falsely non-scholarly stance. One possible explanation is that the poet is signalling a measure of discomfort with his subject matter. It is his duty to eulogise the dukes of Normandy, but in order to do so, he has to be consciously economical with the truth and ignore traditions conflicting with the prestigious image he must project. This, clearly, was no easy task, as we can see from this aside relative to Riulf's rebellion against William Longsword (1354–72):

> Entende cil qui m'ot, si me fasse escouter;
> je ne di mie fable ne je ne voil fabler,
> testemoingne m'en poent cil de Fesamp porter.
> La geste est grande, longue et grieve a translater,
> mez l'en me porroit bien mon enging aviver,
> mout m'est doux le travail quant je cuit conquester.
> Lez Normanz et lor geste m'estuet avant mener.
> A jugleours oï en m'effance chanter
> que Guillaume fist jadis Osmont essorber
> et au conte Riouf lez deus oilz crever,
> e Anquetil le prouz par enging tuer,
> e Baute d'Espaingne o un escu garder;
> ne sai noiant de ceu, n'en puiz noient trover,
> quant je n'en ai garant n'en voil noient conter.
> De la mort Anquetil ai ge oï parler,
> ochiz fu, ce soit on, n'en quier homme escouter,
> mez je ne sai comment, ne qui face a blasmer;
> n'en voil por verité la menchonge affermer
> ne le voir, se jel sai, ne voil ge pas celer.[26]

One recognises here the critical stance adopted by the narrator in the *Roman de Brut*, but the insistence on the necessity of intellectual integrity in recounting past events is new, suggesting that Wace anticipated an audience that actively expected to find certain things in his poem: things he could not include, ostensibly because of the absence of authoritative witnesses, written or oral, to confirm them. It is possible that at this early stage already, Wace realised that his work would not conform to his patron's agenda; hence the spelling out of fundamental principles that could be invoked in the event of a challenge by the king. Wace's trademark 'ne sai' appears with almost obsessive regularity in the account of the

---

[26] 'May anyone who can hear me pay attention and listen to me; I am not telling tales and do not intend to tell tales. Those in Fécamp are my witnesses. This story is a great one, long and difficult to translate. But my skill could be given encouragement; work is very sweet to me when I expect profit from it. I must continue with the Normans and their history. In my youth, I heard in the songs of the jongleurs that in the olden days William had Osmund blinded, Count Riulf's eyes put out, Anquetil the brave treacherously killed and Balzo from Spain placed in custody. I know nothing of this and can find out nothing about it. When I have no evidence, I do not wish to say anything about it. I have heard of the death of Anquetil who was killed, as we know; I do not want to exonerate anyone, but I do not know how he was killed, nor who should be blamed. I do not wish to assert lies instead of the truth, nor do I wish to conceal the truth if I know it.'

reign of William Longsword, so often that the impression given to the reader is that the poet is trying to evade having to take responsibility for his narrative.[27]

The appeal to 'cil de Fesamp' identifies authoritativeness with Norman memory,[28] but even Norman memory is not homogeneous: witness the *chansons* sung by the *jugleours*. If the short abstract provided by Wace is anything to go by, they were not particularly compatible with his task of providing King Henry with a prestigious and popular myth of lineal origins. William Longsword, supposedly a saintly figure, does not come out as a pleasant character, blinding people when he does not have them killed by ruse, as he was clearly credited with having done to the unfortunate Anquetil; and one may safely surmise that the image projected of the Normans and their rulers by neighbouring cultures was not a particularly flattering one. The collective memory of Norman raids would still have been quite vivid. 'Ne sai', under these circumstances, becomes a way of pursuing the work of propaganda initiated by Dudo whilst maintaining a mask of impartiality.

The first duke: Rou

The difficulty of conciliating the expectations of his patron and historical 'truth' was recognised by Wace from the outset, as may be seen from the way he handles the very beginning of the poem. Where Dudo presents the Viking Hasting as a precursor of Rou, Wace immediately contrasts his hero with his bloodthirsty and barbaric pagan compatriots, focusing instead on Rou's personal qualities, which are explicitly put in opposition to Hasting's cruelty (12–16; quoted above). Rou – and by extension, the Normans – is thus exonerated from the charges laid against the Vikings. This passage, which has no equivalent in the Latin sources, evidences Wace's awareness of the tension between what Rou actually was and what he must be made out to be: hence, an undeniably freer hand in dealing with his source material than what we have observed in the *Roman de Brut*. The sequence of events in individual episodes tends to follow that of William of Jumièges, but the actual contents of these episodes show that Dudo is never very far from the poet's mind. Wace not only selects the version that best suits his agenda, he also reshapes his material to give greater emphasis to certain 'desirable' aspects. Dudo's mention of civil war is turned into a struggle on the part of the younger generation to put an end to the custom of getting rid of the excess population of overcrowded Dacia through exile: this enables Wace to depict the king as unjust and heartless, and to place the brothers Rou and Garin within a generation characterised by humane aspirations unknown to their elders. The entire section preceding the brothers' arrival in Normandy is considerably abridged, thus throwing in relief Rou's prophetic dream, which reveals his vocation to Christianity and the divinely ordained nature of his subsequent conquests.

There is a clear attempt to whitewash Rou. Rembaut of Frisia's efforts to

---

[27] Almost half of the instances of the use of 'ne sai' expressions (8 out of a total of 18) in the *Deuxième Partie* occur in the 700-odd lines of the William Longsword section.

[28] This 'memory' is best understood as written, in the form of documents preserved at the abbey of Fécamp, as opposed to the oral tradition represented by the jongleurs. This passage may therefore be read as a covert dismissal of oral sources. On the use of archival documents by Norman historians, see M. Chibnall, 'Charter and Chronicle: the Use of Archive Sources by Norman Historians', pp. 1–17 in *Church and Government in the Middle Ages*, ed. C. Brooke (Cambridge, 1976).

defend his people are dismissed by the narrator as arising from an intemperate desire for vengeance, and the treatment meted out to Regnier when taken prisoner by Rou is considerably softened.[29] The reconquest of England for the beleaguered king Athelstan is also the opportunity to show a crowned king humble himself to secure Rou's assistance, and to give a flattering image of the Viking leader who refuses half of Athelstan's realm out of sheer generosity of spirit. An affinity is thereby established between the Norman ducal line and the English crown, just as the first dealings with the king of France are about to initiate a pattern of antagonism and treachery that justifies Norman destructiveness. The reason for the emphasis on French avarice and deviousness in the *Chronique Ascendante* thus goes beyond considerations of contemporary politics. It provides the work as a whole with a moral justification for virtually all of the Norman military campaigns. The fault is always, necessarily, inherently, the enemy's; and the despicable nature of the king of France and his allies is a leitmotiv in Wace's work just as it is in Dudo's.

Sizeable additions of amplificatory material appear after Rou's arrival in Normandy, a turning-point in the narrative, signalled by a digression on the meaning of the name 'Norman' (which repeats the material found in the Prologue to the *Première Partie*) 'signed' by the author and legitimised by the mention of his written source: 'cen conte Maistre Vacce qui escript a trové', 'I, Master Wace, who am telling this, found it in writing' (443). It is also the moment when Rou has to confront his evil alter ego, Hasting. They meet as Hasting is sent to the Normans by his French overlord to find out their intentions. Hasting's boasting meets with a withering put-down on Rou's part (498–501):

> "Par ma foi," ce dit Rou, "ne te congnoiz noient,
> mez de Hastain sai ge qu'il fist moult mal a gent,
> de quanque faire vout out bon commencement
> et quantqu'il commencha fina moult malement."[30]

This could have led to a confrontation; instead, Wace adds a *laisse* where Hasting tells Rou about his past (502–5):

> Dont lor a dit Hastain et conté ses fez,
> d'estranges et d'orribles et de beaux et de lez,
> et de sez granz proësces et des travaux qu'a faiz.
> "Bien devez dez or mez," ce dit Rou, "avoir paiz."[31]

There is a quasi-confessional quality to this passage, with Hasting apparently holding nothing back and Rou finally granting him 'peace', like a priest to a

---

[29] Where Dudo has Rou threaten to behead Regnier if his demands are not met, Wace mentions beheading only as the unsubstantiated fear of Regnier's wife (360–65). Wace takes advantage of this episode to add a passage in reported speech in which Regnier 'spontaneously' offers his homage to Rou.

[30] 'Upon my word', said Rou, 'I have no knowledge of you, but I do know that Hasting did a lot of harm to people. Whatever he wanted to do started well and whatever he started finished very badly.'

[31] 'Then Hasting spoke to them and related his deeds, the strange and the dreadful, the fair and the ugly, and also his great deeds of prowess and the tasks he had accomplished. "From now on", said Rou, "you shall remain at peace."'

penitent. The intrinsic moral superiority of Rou over Hasting is thus graphically illustrated, even though Rou, at this stage, has not yet been baptized.

The build-up to Rou's conversion to Christianity is given particular attention. It is announced by his prophetic dream, and repeatedly foreshadowed by the narrator; at the same time, the acts of warfare of the Norman leader are consistently presented in such a way as to minimise his violence (typically blaming the French opponent for the hostilities).[32] Rou is shown to be respectful of Church leaders such as Archbishop Franco of Rouen (who negotiates a deal with him when he first arrives in Normandy, 408–21, and later as well) and in awe of Christian ritual, to such an extent that when the clerics of Chartres carry out the relics of the town in a solemn procession (850–91), Rou flees in terror and even loses his sight for a short while (a detail drawn from William of Malmesbury, added by Wace to his main source). As explicitly stated by Wace, Rou 'n'iert mie crestïen ne baptizié n'estoit/ neporquant en son cuer amoit Dieu et cremoit', 'was not a Christian and had not been baptized, yet in his heart he loved and feared God' (404–5): he is a virtuous pagan, receptive to the Good Word, and fit material to become a Christian prince. Rou's baptism eventually occurs as a condition put on peace by the king of France and is tied in with the triple theme of vassalic submission to the French crown, marriage to a royal princess, and legitimacy of rule over Normandy and (more dubiously) Brittany. In an uncharacteristic departure from strict chronological order, these events are twice mentioned, though contrary to Dudo, Wace describes neither the baptism nor the wedding – only the homage ceremony, where the ritual kissing of the king's foot leads to his undignified fall, as Rou lifts the foot to his mouth rather than grovelling on the ground. This selectiveness is congruent with the epic tone adopted increasingly by Wace throughout the *Deuxième Partie*; *courtoisie* has little place here.

The appearance of longer stanzas characterised by direct speech and description (particularly of battle scenes, frequently described with gusto and striking rhetorical effects; see for example lines 787–91) coincides with attempts on Wace's part to mirror the phraseology and diction of the *chanson de geste* as well as its emphasis on feats of arms and ritualised male verbal interaction.[33] For example, later in the narrative, the exchange between Duke William Longsword and the abbot of Jumièges, where the duke is dissuaded from acting on his vocation to be a monk (1706ff.), has overtones of the Guillaume d'Orange cycle, as has Bernard's manipulation of Louis of France to incite him to renege on his promises to Hugh of Paris (2622ff.). More specifically, Wace seems to have tried to simulate the effect of the *laisse similaire* through the near-repetition of a given line in two different *laisses*. An example of this occurs in the Rou section in line 735, 'moult l'ont, ce dit, gabé et moult l'ont escharni',[34] which is picked up

---

[32] The campaign that leads to the offer of a wife and land to Rou by the king of France is nevertheless described as being particularly violent (following in this respect the *Gesta Normannorum Ducum*); the Normans are said to have had no more pity for the French population than a wolf would have for sheep (1061).

[33] One may mention, among the many battle scenes of the poem, the fight between Duke Richard and the German army, especially 3262–90. On the conventions of the genre, see Jean Rychner, *La chanson de geste: essai sur l'art épique des jongleurs* (Lille, 1955).

[34] 'they had mocked and insulted him greatly, he said.'

almost verbatim two lines later (737), 'mout l'ont, ce dit, Franchois escharni et gabé'.³⁵ This feature later develops into almost canonical *laisses similaires*:³⁶

Normant et li Breton ont le roi tant mené qu'il lor a hors Richart entre ses braz porté ... voiant touz ses baronz li rendi s'erité Normendie et Bretaingne et quanqu'il li a clamé emprez a Loeïs desus les sainz juré ... membre, vie et honour et paiz et loiauté a garder a Richart... (2130–40)³⁸	Normant et li Breton ont tant li roiz destroit qu'il delivra Richart et li fist tout son droit Normendie et Bretaingne et quanqu'i apendoit puiz li jura sur sainz que foi li porteroit membre, vie et honour partout li garderoit (2142–46)³⁷

These 'epic' devices give the work a peculiarly oral quality and enable the reader/listener to accept the narrator's partisan stance as a feature determined by genre. Indeed, the audience of a *chanson de geste* would have expected such a stance. By openly identifying his voice as biased (as for example on lines 806–7, where he states, 'Franchoiz ourent grant perte et Normanz grant gaaing/ ne le gaaing ne lor perte je ne plaing', literally: 'The French suffered great losses and the Normans enjoyed great gains; I deplore neither the gain nor the losses'), Wace ensures generic recognition and signals the propagandist intentions of his discourse.

The Rou section is of paramount importance, in that it provides an implicit template for what is to follow. Formally, it begins, as seen above, with very short stanzas, predominantly four lines in length, which rhythmically and stylistically may be viewed as a variation on the octosyllabic couplet of the *Roman de Brut*, giving way gradually to longer stanzas characterised by 'epic' phraseology. Structurally, Rou's rule follows the same pattern as the reigns in the *Roman de Brut*: the account of the duke's political and military achievements gives way to the mention of his record as 'culture hero', which functions as a narrative transition to his death and succession by another ruler. Rou's remarkable success in quelling theft in his territory and his acute sense of justice (exemplified in the story of the dishonest farmer and his wife) thus lead naturally to the mention of Rou's son William Longsword and the passage of power to him (1290–8), Rou's eventual death and his burial in Rouen. The final note to his life is one of piety: Wace reshapes and expands the accounts of his sources to stress that Rou ended in peace with himself and with God, after having received absolution for sins confessed with a mind free of senility. The founder of the Norman ducal house

---

35 'The French, he said, ... had reviled and mocked him a great deal.'
36 A comparable, but less striking, instance of this feature may also be found lines 3652 ff., which stress Archbishop Bruno's disgrace following his failed attempt to get Duke Richard killed by treachery.
37 'The Normans and the Bretons had harried the king until he handed Richard over to them, and gave him everything that was his right: Normandy and Brittany and everything belonging to them. Then he swore on the holy relics that he would keep faith with him and support him everywhere in life, limb and honour.'
38 'The Normans and the Bretons pressed the king until he brought Richard out to them in his arms.... In sight of all the barons he gave him back his rightful inheritance: Normandy and Brittany and everything he had claimed from him. Then Louis swore on the holy relics to maintain Richard's life, limb, honour, peace and loyalty.'

thus ends like the good, Christian prince he was destined to be; and the epitaph on his tomb in Rouen, 'qui raconte sez fez et comment il vesqui', 'which recounts his deeds and how he lived' (1313) is invoked as a validation of Wace's own account.

This reference to public monuments or artefacts preserved in religious buildings ties in once again with the conventions of the *chanson de geste*, where the weapons of a great warrior, displayed as *ex voto* in a given shrine, are presented to the audience as tangible confirmations of the truth of the story as a whole (see for example the *Moniage Guillaume*, where the hero on his retreat from the world leaves his weapons on display in church);[39] but it is also a recurrent theme in the *Roman de Brut*, where royal tombs and burial-places are regularly mentioned. Rou thus fulfills all the conditions requisite for the founder of a heroic, and indeed royal, lineage, thanks to Wace's judicious manipulation of the available sources. Strong religious feelings, or at the very least, public manifestations of piety, are therefore to be expected of the successors of Rou, the pagan convert predestined by God to a place 'la sus oveuc les angres', 'up there with the angels' (269).

Duke William I Longsword

The saintly dimension to the psyche of the new dynasty is given due emphasis in the characterisation of William Longsword, the second duke of Normandy; although as we have seen, Wace seems to have found it difficult to reconcile the ruthless leader of oral tradition with the saintly nobleman who yearned all his life to be a monk (the image Dudo strove to create). Wace's account follows his sources quite closely in what turns out to be a tale of power struggles both with the Norman nobility and the king of France. Some of the Normans, we are told, grow tired of the peace established by William and resent his marriage to a French noblewoman (1348–51). This leads to the civil war which had left conflicting accounts for Wace to contend with: 'cil de Fesamp', the 'jugleours', the 'geste' itself, and probably (though it is not mentioned by name), William of Malmesbury's *Gesta Regum Anglorum*, which gives an account of Riulf's uprising against William, his being made prisoner by his own son, Anscytel,[40] who was in turn treacherously sent to his death by William, who eventually was murdered in retaliation by one of Anscytel's surviving companions. William Longsword does not emerge from the incident very well, encouraging a son to betray his father, sending that son on a mission where he is made to deliver his own death warrant, then blinding the elderly father when in prison; a version of events clearly not only transmitted by lowly 'jugleours'. Little wonder that Wace retreats so frequently in this section behind his 'ne sai', or that he chooses at this point to present himself as a mercenary narrator (1357–9, quoted above), thus giving as many indications that the version of events he follows might not give the whole

---

[39] Guillaume's leaving his weapons to the church on his 'retirement' is also mentioned by Orderic Vitalis, vi. 3 (*The Ecclesiasical History of Orderic Vitalis*, ed. M. Chibnall (Oxford, 1969–80), vol. 3, pp. 220–1), in his section on the life of St William of Gellone, the historical personage underlying the epic hero.

[40] William of Malmesbury, *Gesta regum Anglorum. The History of the English Kings*, ed. and trans. R. A. B. Mynors, R. A. Thomson and W. Winterbottom (Oxford, 1998–9), Book ii. 125. In Wace, these names appear as 'Riouf' and 'Anquetil'.

picture. The conflict with Riulf is reduced to William's decision to go to war with his rebellious vassal and the ensuing battle, described in due epic manner (1421–1517).

William's victory on battlefield and the birth of a son strengthens the duke's position in Normandy; on the request of King Athelstan of England, he ensures that Louis, son of King Charles of France and nephew of Athelstan, is made heir to the French throne; he marries off his sister and his aunt to suitable aristocrats and generally proves to be a good ruler capable of holding prestigious court celebrations. Like his father Rou, William Longsword is a king-maker, and like Rou, he is depicted as naturally regal himself. When the king of France wishes to enter into an alliance with Henry I of Germany, he is told that no treaty would be made without the presence of William of Normandy; the negotiations that follow give Wace the opportunity (following Dudo 52 and 53) to describe William's authority, keeping the peace in the overcrowded camp and imposing the agreement on reluctant barons (1638–85). His position of power is such that Louis of France asks him to be godfather to his newborn son; and when neither Louis of France nor Hugh of Paris are willing to support their vassal Herluin in his rightful claim over Montreuil, it is to William that Herluin turns to for justice (1792–886). Yet the duke's true vocation is to the monastic life. He has to be dissuaded from entering the abbey at Jumièges by the abbot (1701–54), though he prepares for his son Richard to be recognised as his heir and raised accordingly.

William Longsword eventually dies at the hands of the count of Flanders (who had been expelled from Montreuil by William) and four accomplices, including Riulf and his nephew Balzo, during reconciliation talks. The narrator depicts the event as an act of treachery by a bunch of scoundrels. Balzo is called a mad, hostile traitor (1925: 'traïtres'; 'foux et eschis'); Riulf is a villain ('cuvert'; 1926); whilst of Arnulf of Flanders, the narrator exclaims (1895–8):

> Hernouf haï le duc, je ne m'en merveil mie,
> mez de ceu me merveil qu'il fist tel felonnie,
> miex veut ester honniz que encor ne l'ocie;
> traïson en fist laie, moult a esté honnie.[41]

Wace's focus on the way in which the duke was killed, together with the accumulation of highly charged terms to denounce his murderers, gives William Longsword the end of an innocent victim. Such a reading of the events was heavily biased (especially compared to William of Malmesbury's report that tradition, 'maiores', held that William's end was 'not undeserved', 'non immerito factum'),[42] but it had the advantage of turning William into a quasi-martyr. When his men open his personal box, it turns out that it contained no treasure, but just a monk's cowl and robe, attesting to the duke's religious vocation and saintly disposition. Like Rou, his final resting-place provides a lasting testimony to his rule: 'El mostier Nostre Dame lor seignor aporterent,/ encor i giest le cors et lez

---

[41] 'Arnulf hated the duke, which does not surprise me, but I am surprised that he committed such a crime. He preferred to be dishonoured rather than fail to kill him and he committed a wretched act of treason which caused him much shame.'

[42] William of Malmesbury, *Gesta regum Anglorum*, ii. 145.

ewres i perrent', 'They took their lord to the Church of Our Lady; the body still lies there and his deeds are still visible' (2015–16).

Richard I

With William's son, Richard I of Normandy, the pattern of the coming to power of the duke, his deeds and eventual (saintly) death is modified. Whereas the previous episodes had a hint of the Guillaume d'Orange cycle to them, this one is closer to the so-called 'epics of revolt' such as *Raoul de Cambrai*.[43] Young Richard is depicted as an innocent and vulnerable child, whom the despicable Louis of France wants to deprive of his birthright (and his life) and drives into open rebellion. Wace follows the story-line as it appears in the *Gesta Normannorum Ducum*, supplementing it with details and material from Dudo and amplificatory material of his own invention, making this section the most memorable one of the *Deuxième Partie*, with a lavish use of direct speech and dialogue. From the outset, the villain of the piece is Louis of France. He first attempts to detain the young Richard, but is forced by an outraged populace to release him and confirm him in his rights (2061–151); he then takes Richard to his court to give him the education fitting his rank, alongside his own son, but is convinced by the count of Flanders and bad advisers that the child constitutes a threat (2152–267). Richard is strictly forbidden to leave the town (2260–4). To this, Wace adds that the queen is antagonistic towards Richard because he is more handsome and refined than her own son (2271–2), for whom she covets Rouen and Normandy. Richard's only friend is his tutor and bodyguard Osmund, who observes the situation with great fear. Tensions come to a head when Richard goes hunting in the king's absence. The queen complains that he did so without her permission, and the king is enraged. He threatens to put out Richard's eyes if it happens again and holds him prisoner. Osmund warns the Normans that their young duke is in danger and organises his escape. Richard pretends to be ill and Osmund makes out that the child is dying; he then takes advantage of the fact that the guard on Richard is relaxed to smuggle him out of the town of Laon in a bundle of hay and take him to safety.

The literary potential of this anecdote is fully developed by Wace. The narrative is punctuated by proleptic remarks emphasising the inadequacy and untrustworthiness of Louis of France. When he hears that William has been murdered by Balzo on the orders of Arnulf of Flanders, 'moult l'en pesa, ce dit, mout s'en tint a honni/ mez tel semblant fist puiz que nus ne l'en creï', 'he was dismayed, he said, and felt great shame; but later he acted in such a way that no one believed this' (2055–6). Judas-like, he welcomes the fatherless Richard with a kiss, which prompts the narrator to exclaim 'Dex, porquoi l'a beisié quant foi ne li porta!/ Salua le de bouche, mez le cuer nel pensa', 'O God, why did he kiss him when he did not keep faith with him? He greeted him with his mouth, but there were different thoughts in his heart' (2065–6). Similarly, when Louis swears on oath to support and protect Richard, the narrator bursts out: 'Dex, porquoi le jura quant tenir nel vouloit!/ Puiz s'en fist il tenir por traïtor reveoit;/ bien le porroit oïr

---

[43] On the subject, see William Calin, *The Old French Epic of Revolt: Raoul de Cambrai, Renaud de Montauban, Gormond et Isembard* (Geneva, 1962).

qui l'estoire liroit', 'O God, why did he swear it when he had no intention of keeping it? Because of what he did, he was afterwards considered an outright traitor; anyone reading the story would be able to understand this clearly' (2149–51). As in the *chansons de geste*, Louis is a weak king, easily manipulated,[44] and above all, in the *Deuxième Partie* of the *Roman de Rou*, grasping. Arnulf of Flanders buys with gifts and gold the favour of the king (2176–7), who then shows himself only too willing to believe that Arnulf had nothing to do with the murder of William Longsword. The key argument that convinces Louis to treat young Richard as a potentially hostile prisoner is the revenue he will derive from so doing: 'la terre que il tient en demaigne avrïez/ mout est bonne la terre, plus fort en serïez', 'You would have the land he holds as your own property; the land is very fine and you would be the stronger for it' (2240–1). This avaricious streak will also be used by Bernard the Dane to trick Louis into reneging on his agreement with Hugh the Great of Paris, with whom he had divided Normandy (2575–717). Richard is the victim of the king's moral inadequacy, which is further shown through his giving permission to one of his retainers to abduct Bernard the Dane's wife, marry her and seize her wealth, even though her husband was alive and (ostensibly at least) the king's faithful vassal.[45] Louis fails in all the duties of an overlord.

The turning point in the fortunes of the young duke occurs with the treaty following the capture in battle of Louis, the Normans having managed to secure help from their Danish relatives. The terms of this treaty are expanded and rephrased by Wace,[46] stressing the autonomous state of Normandy: henceforth, neither Richard nor his heir owes service to the king of France (3051–8). The *chanson de geste* of the wronged child comes to an end; Richard is now fully duke of Normandy and can fend for himself. The epic tone and diction, however, remain, with some very lengthy and elaborate descriptions of battle scenes (see particularly lines 3215–369 and 3912–46); for Arnulf of Flanders will continue his mischief-making, convincing Emperor Otto to attack Normandy, and as one may have expected, neither Louis (who dies of sorrow at the defeat of the Franco-German coalition against Normandy) nor his son Lothar of France respects the treaty. Richard, despite his young age, is depicted as everything a good leader should be: pious, generous, skilled in martial arts, an adept hunter, and a stern enforcer of justice (as illustrated by his treatment of the corrupt seneschal Ralph Torta, 3090–118). In addition, we are told, 'moult iert ja de bonne entention,/ bien entendoit parole et congnoissoit raisson', 'he was already of very great purpose, understanding what was said to him and recognizing reason' (3079–80), a trait which distinguishes him sharply from Louis' successor, the hot-headed Lothar, whose response to defeat is to indulge in a tantrum (3972–77):

---

[44] See for example *Le Couronnement Louis*, or *Le Charroi de Nîmes*, in the Guillaume d'Orange cycle.
[45] The consent of the king is emphasised in the French poem by the explicit statement that 'li roiz li otrie a qui moult atalente' (2779). The sources do not make the king's collusion quite as definite.
[46] Wace draws his additional information from the *Brevis relatio de origine Willelmi Conquestoris* (ed. I. A. Giles, pp. 1–21 in *Scriptores Rerum Gestarum Willelmi Conquestoris* (London, 1855), pp. 18–19); Wace uses this anonymous minor source sporadically, especially in the section dealing with Duke William II (the Conqueror).

> Au retorner de Diepe out li roiz mout grant ire,
> l'escu jete et la lance, son gonfanon descire,
> souvent lasche sez resgnes et souvent lez retire,
> souvent tence a sez homes, souvent geint et soupire,
> souvent en jure Dieu et le baron Saint Gile
> que mort est s'il ne peut Richart prendre ou ochire.[47]

This passage, which Wace expands considerably from his sources, shows a young man who is the plaything of his emotions (encouraged, it must be said, by his evil advisor Thibaut). By contrast, when Richard realises that he will not be able to withstand a coalition with the king of France at its head and is about to lose Evreux, 'nen out talent de rire ne d'aler a gibois,/ n'atendi mie a gas n'a faire serventois', 'he had no wish to laugh or to go hunting, he spent no time on jokes or on composing *serventeis*' (4148–9), and promptly sends to King Harold of Denmark for help.

Richard's calling over to Normandy hordes of pagan Scandinavians and unleashing them on hapless Christian populations does not sit comfortably with the image of the pious young duke that Wace (following his sources) has been trying to establish up to this point. Politically it is a good move: his enemies prove to be powerless to protect their lands against the Danish invaders and are thus forced to come to an agreement with Richard at Jeufosse. But this agreement is clearly made at the expense of Christianity; Richard cynically manipulates the religious feelings of his opponents and the fears of the bishop of Chartres, to whom he declares: 'miex voil abatre eglises qu'a desonour morir/ e a paienne gent Normendie guerpir/ que li roiz par sa force m'en face a honte issir', 'I would rather demolish churches than die in dishonour, and abandon Normandy to pagans rather than be forced out of it shamefully by the king' (4287–9). Richard's priorities are starkly secular. Wace's account of the negotiation between the bishop of Chartres and Richard attenuates this somewhat, stating that 'Richart out dez povres et merci et pitié', 'Richard showed mercy and pity to the poor' (4330), and that 'vers l'evesque congnut sa coupe et pechié', 'he confessed his sin and error to the bishop' (4331): he eventually repents. Peace is reinstated, and ordinary life is resumed, a detail added by Wace to his sources (4348–50):

> Des trieues furent tuit li clerc et li loi lié,
> lez vilainz sont as viles et as bors reperrié,
> et marcheanz alerent a foire et a marchié.[48]

The normal pattern of social interaction reasserts itself. Richard then gives some lustre to his rather tarnished image of a Christian prince, by insisting that his pagan Scandinavian helpers convert to Christianity if they wish to remain in Normandy, and by rejecting their offer to conquer the whole of France for him.

---

[47] 'When he returned from Dieppe, the king was very distressed; he threw down his shield and his lance and tore up his banner, letting go his reins repeatedly and the pulling them back. He kept on quarrelling with his men and often lamented and sighed, repeatedly swearing by God and Saint Giles the good, saying that he was dead if he could not capture and kill Richard.'

[48] 'All the clerics and laymen were delighted by the truce; the peasants went back to the towns and the burgs and the merchants went to the fairs and the markets.'

The Ancestors of William the Conqueror 181

The *Deuxième Partie* of the *Roman de Rou* ends with the conversion of some Danes (though Wace does not include the mass conversion scene in Dudo) and the sailing away of the others, who destroy eighteen towns in Spain, then 'ne sai que puiz devindrent ne je savoir ne quier', 'I don't know what became of them and I will not attempt to find out' (4419). But this, clearly, is not the end of Richard's story: at the very least, the reader/listener expects a few anecdotes relating to Richard's achievements off the battlefield. As pointed out by the narrator, 'Au duc de Normendie nos esteut reperrier', 'We have to return to the Duke of Normandy' (4420). The *Deuxième Partie* thus ends on something of a cliffhanger: the best part of the story is yet to come. Wace takes due precautions to make his audience ask for more.

That the audience did ask for more is attested by the fact that the narrative continues in the so-called *Troisième Partie* – but in a different format. Despite his obvious ease with the poetic medium of the *Deuxième Partie* and the flexibility afforded by the *laisse*, Wace resumes his history of the dukes of Normandy in the same metre as the *Première Partie* of the *Rou*: the octosyllabic couplet. One can surmise a number of reasons for this apparent change of heart. Wace's favoured audience might for example have imposed it. This, on purely artistic grounds, seems unlikely. Even if they had expected something quite different, by the end of the *Deuxième Partie* listeners must surely have been won over by the vivacity and epic *souffle* of the narrative, not to mention the wit and virtuosity displayed by the poet. This is popularisation at its best. Read aloud, the alexandrine *laisses* allow a variety of rhythmical effects that are, if anything, more entertaining than the more predictable octosyllabic couplet. Nevertheless, Wace's unusual metre could have unsettled some. More seriously, there could have been political objections to the quasi-*chanson de geste* format of the work, for throughout that genre the French crown is upheld, however despicable and unjust the individual monarch. A genre in which the king of France, in effect, may be said always to win against his fractious vassals might not have been thought to be the most tactful vehicle to celebrate (Anglo-)Norman struggles against France. That objection, however, is countered by the explicitly revisionist spirit evinced in the *Chronique Ascendante* 45–61 and implies an unlikely blend of literal-mindedness and literary sophistication. Or perhaps it was felt that a narrator making statements such as 'qui chante boivre doit', 'he who sings must drink' (4423) was trivialising his material, and was at odds with the scholarly nature of the work; the jongleuresque banter could conceivably have been perceived by some as a slight on the early Norman historians. There is no doubt that the tension between the persona of the jocular jongleur and the learned, 'serious' poet is potentially disquieting; but this is more likely to have been a concern of Wace's than of his audience, as the tension between these two stances would have been increasingly difficult for him to manage as the poem progressed.

There remains the possibility that the change in metre and tone was planned by Wace from the inception of his project. It is noteworthy that the *Deuxième Partie* almost coincides with the limits of Dudo's work, on which the earlier section of the *Gesta Normannorum Ducum* is based. The different metre and narrator's persona could signal a change in narrative focus. This device would make sense in a work that, although learned, is addressed to an audience that presumably wished to be usefully entertained, but not necessarily much more – possibly at one of the 'festes' mentioned by Wace (*Troisième Partie*, 6). The straightforward naming of authorities would have been counter-productive, because potentially tedious for the general public. Clerics, or readers/listeners interested in the subject, on the other hand, might wish to be able to discern the transition from one historical discourse to another.

There are clues in *Troisième Partie* that point in this direction. Even though the narrative is picked up at exactly the point where the *Deuxième Partie* left it, it has a protracted prologue followed by a brief summary of what preceded: the *Troisième Partie* can thus be read as an autonomous piece of work, as well as a continuation. Dudo's work remains a perceptible influence on the final section of the life of Richard I of Normandy, but is no longer as pervasive as in the *Deuxième Partie*. We also observe a radical change in Wace's method. The anecdotes which take up over half of the 570-odd lines devoted to Richard I in the *Troisième Partie* are derived neither from Dudo nor from William of Jumièges, and are identified by the poet as oral traditions. How oral and popular these stories really were is a matter of debate (the anecdote of the lecherous sacristan, for example, is likely to have been connected with the abbey of Saint-Ouen,[49] even though Wace suggests the incident is at the origin of a widespread jokey proverb, 505–10). What *is* significant is that their inclusion implies on the poet's part an active search of new material and new authorities. Whereas the *Deuxième Partie* is a relatively straightforward *mise en vers* based on an abbreviative principle, the *Troisième Partie* is a far more complex endeavour. Hence, perhaps, its very different form.

The *Troisième Partie*

Wace's awareness of the importance of his contribution in the *Troisième Partie* is expressed in the Prologue, with an impassioned celebration of the role of the historian. Wace projects an image of himself as the custodian of collective memory (1–10):

> Pur remembrer des ancesurs
> les feiz e les diz e les murs,
> les felunies des feluns
> e les barnages des baruns,
> deit l'um les livres e les gestes
> e les estoires lire a festes.
> Si escripture ne fust feite
> e puis par clers litte e retraite,
> mult fussent choses ublïees
> ki de viez tens sunt trespassees.[50]

---

[49] The sacristan is said to have confessed everything to the abbot, and his tale was confirmed by the duke: 'Issi fu la chose seüe/ e la verité cuneüe' (505–6). The authority for this anecdote is therefore monastic; the tale itself contains at least one echo from the Bible (393–4).

[50] 'To remember the deeds, words and ways of our ancestors, the wicked deeds of wicked men and the brave deeds of brave men, books, chronicles and histories should be read out at festivals. If documents

The role of clerics in the transmission of knowledge, which we have already encountered in Wace's religious poems, is connected with a more historiographical concern with the importance of writing as a means of preserving the memory of things past. This aspect is stressed once again a few lines later (81–4):

> Des tresturnees de ces nuns,
> e des gestes dunt nus parluns,
> poi u nïent seüssum dire
> si l'um nes eüst feit escrire.[51]

This statement, following as it does considerations of the origin of the names 'Normant' and 'Normendie', acts as much as a justification of his subject-matter as it is a defence of historical writing, and could be understood as an implicit vindication of Dudo, whose work, whatever its shortcomings compared to the rigour of a William of Malmesbury (a major authority in this the main and final part of the *Rou*) or a William of Jumièges, deserves to be ranked among the 'bons clers', the good clerics of antiquity who 'les gestes as livres mistrent' (103–4, 'committed the deeds to books'). The very deeds of Alexander the Great and Julius Caesar would have been forgotten, argues Wace, had they not been written down ('se il ne eüssent escrit esté', 130): a consequence of the mutability of this world and the mortality of men. Empires crumble, but books remain (137–42):

> Bien entend e cunuis e sai
> que tuit murrunt e clerc e lai
> e que mult ad curte duree
> enprés la mort lur renumee,
> si par clerc nen est mis en livre;
> ne poet el durer ne vivre.[52]

Wace clearly includes himself in this blanket approval of all endeavours to defeat man's defective natural memory: he is after all the author of a number of 'estoires' read 'a festes', having undergone the strenuous process of reading and translating described in line 8. This change in pose, from story-teller to scholar, does not only coincide with the coming to an end of the influence of Dudo and the passage to a more compilatory approach. It also reflects a change in discourse.

Borrowings from Dudo do not cease completely after the *Deuxième Partie*. Wace remains indebted to the *De moribus et actis primorum Normanniae ducum* until the end of the rule of Richard I of Normandy, though for the first time major additions of new material make their appearance. What the end of the *Deuxième Partie* does coincide with, however, is the end of an epoch. The king of France in

---

were not composed, and then read and recounted by clerics, many things which transpired in times gone by would be forgotten.'

[51] 'Concerning the twists and turns of these names and deeds of which we are speaking, we would have been able to say little or nothing if someone had not had written down.'

[52] 'I understand completely and am fully aware that all men die, cleric and lay, and that after their death their fame is short-lived unless it is set down in a book by a cleric; it cannot survive or live on in any other way.'

the *Deuxième Partie* is the Carolingian Lothar. When Wace resumes the 'political' strand of his narrative in the *Troisième Partie*, Lothar is dead and a new dynasty, the Capetians, rises to the throne (thanks, following Dudo, to Norman support). The *chanson de geste*, overwhelmingly connected with the Carolingians, ceases to be historically relevant as an ideological sub-text; more crucially, with the coming to the throne of Hugh Capet, we move from the distant time of semi-myth to that of history. From now on, the heavily polarised attitudes of the *Deuxième Partie* are no longer tenable. Documents have survived, preserving the point of view and motivations of the 'other side' which cannot be ignored. Issues gain in complexity, and authorities contradict each other. More so than in the *Deuxième Partie*, Wace has to evolve strategies to determine levels of authoritativeness in his corpus of sources and actively choose one reading against another.

Because of the poet's greater responsibility in the *Troisième Partie*, authority becomes a heightened issue, which means that the propagandist dimension to the work has to be expressed through different means. The partisan stance of the lowly jongleur was no longer suitable; moreover, a history of fratricidal war, such as that which opposed Henry I of England to Robert Curthose of Normandy, did not lend itself to the black-and-white worldview of the *Deuxième Partie*. Wace therefore turns to a new narrative model, which fulfilled all the requirements of the *Troisième Partie*. It was associated with a prestigious, highly popular work, a successful French verse translation of a reputable Latin history: his own *Roman de Brut*.

The Arthurianisation of Normandy
The Prologue of the *Troisième Partie* advertises its connection with the *Roman de Brut* from the outset, not just through the use of octosyllabic couplets (a metre used by many other vernacular writers, and for a wide range of works), but also by echoing the *Roman de Brut*'s recurrent concern with onomastics and language change (11–23):

> Par lungs tens e par lungs eages
> e par muement de languages
> unt perdu lur premereins nuns
> viles plusurs e regiuns.
> Engleterre Bretainne out nun
> e primes out nun Albiun,
> e Lundres out nun Trinovant
> e Troie Nove out nun avant;
> Everwic out nun Eborac
> ki primes fu Kaer Ebrac;
> Suth Guales fu Demetia,
> North Guales Venedocia;
> Escoce out nun jadis Albaine.[53]

---

[53] 'Over time, as the years go by, through changes in language, many towns and regions have lost their original names. England was called Britain and its first name was Albion; London was called Trinovant

This list continues for another 21 lines, with examples from France, Italy and the Holy Land, leading to the change of name from Neustria to Normandy. A reader unaware of the subject-matter of the poem could be forgiven for assuming that this is a prologue to a history of Britain rather than Normandy. The material of Geoffrey of Monmouth is inescapably alluded to; the figure of Arthur looms large beneath these lines. The unspoken message is clear: the history of the dukes of Normandy is the true continuation to the history of the kings of Britain.

The impact of this Prologue is very different from that of the Prologue to the *Première Partie*, yet they are virtually identical except for the order in which their various elements are placed, leading scholars to assume that Wace had 'recycled' part of a discarded earlier poem for the Prologue to the definitive version of his work. Some 110 lines of the Prologue of the *Première Partie* (out of 124) reappear word-for-word in the Prologue of the *Troisième Partie*, with the addition of some 60 new lines. The most important shift of material occurs in relation to the theme of mutability as expressed in the names of cities and regions, leading to the discussion of the origin of the name of the Normans.[54] This material is placed at the beginning of the Prologue (*Troisième Partie*, 11–80) rather than at its end (*Première Partie*, 77–122) and the order in which names and regions are mentioned is also changed, the British elements being concentrated together in the *Troisième Partie* whereas in the *Première Partie* they are interspersed with references to Germany, Paris, Greece, Italy, Constantinople or Aquitaine. This not only places more emphasis on Britain in the *Troisième Partie*, it also attenuates the impact of the *contemptus mundi* dimension to the Prologue, as the passages describing the labile nature of this world are punctuated by statements to the effect that it can be counteracted by writing.[55] The 'recycled' section ends on this positive note; it is followed by a new passage praising the generosity shown to towards writers of old, contrasted with the meanness shown to Wace himself. The demise of generosity ('largesce', 167–8) is in turn contrasted with the liberality of Henry II (171–6), whose name serves as a transition leading to the resumption of the historical narrative. The movement in the Prologue to the *Troisième Partie* is streamlined, from negative (the transience of life and civilisations) to positive (the value of literary fame), culminating in the affirmation of the value of the present work and the praise of its patron. The glorious past, implicitly, is located in Britain, through the echo of the *Roman de Brut*; the glorious present, explicitly, is represented by Henry II alone.

The *translatio* of prestige from Britain to Normandy is further revealed by the anecdotes relative to Richard I added by Wace to Dudo and William of Jumièges.[56] The first of these depicts the duke as a knight errant in the tradition of the Arthurian romance (273–80):

---

and before that New Troy. Everwic [York] was called Eborac and firstly Kaer Ebrac. South Wales was Demetia and North Wales Venedocia. Scotland used to be called Albany.'

[54] A comparison of the two Prologues may be found in Paradisi, *Le passioni della storia*, pp. 361–77.
[55] See *Troisième Partie*, lines 81–4, 103–4, 118, 126, 129–30, 141–2.
[56] The episode contains five anecdotes of unidentified origin. The first four, recounted in succession, I shall be discussing below; the last one, relative to Richard's wife Gunnor on their wedding night, is added to the rather dry mention in the sources of their marriage after years of her being his concubine.

> Richard ama clers e clergie
> chivaliers e chevalerie;
> par nuit errout comme par jur,
> unkes de rien nen out poür,
> maint fantosme vit e trova,
> unques de rien ne s'esfreia;
> pur nule rien que il veïst
> ne nuit ne jur poür nel prist.[57]

Like Arthurian heroes, his adventures are remembered through oral tales rather than in writing: Wace insists on the popular transmission of his material, mentioning for example that people said of him ('alout la gent de lui disant', 282) that Richard could see as well at night as others could in daylight. The second anecdote, that of the lecherous sacristan of St Ouen already mentioned above, is introduced in a manner that underlines both the oral, popular nature of the tale and Wace's role in preserving it through writing (337–46):

> Autre aventure li avint
> que la gent a merveile tint,
> e ki a peine fu creüe
> se ele ne fust de tanz seüe.
> Cunter l'ai oï a plusurs,
> qui(l) le oïrent des ancesurs;
> mais mainte feiz par nunchaleir
> par perece e par nunsaveir
> remaint maint bel fait a escrire
> ki bon sereit e bel a dire.[58]

However fanciful (though it must be said that medieval writers did not view such stories with the same sweeping scorn as modern historians),[59] these tales of ghosts and devils may be said to illustrate the duke's piety and moral fibre. Anecdotes three and four, however, are the stuff of Arthurian romance at its most conventional. Both happen in the 'lande' of Corcers, near a hunting forest, in a locus that would not be out of place in Marie de France or Chrétien de Troyes (513–16):

> en la lande ad une valee
> ki n'est mult lunge ne mult lee;
> en la forest ad une plaine,
> environ est granz la champaine.[60]

---

[57] 'Richard loved clerics and learning, knights and knighthood. He travelled at night just as by day, having no fear of anything; he saw and encountered many an apparition without ever being afraid of anything. Nothing he saw, either by night or by day, caused him any fear.'

[58] 'Another adventure befell him, which was considered a marvel and would scarcely have been believed if it had not been known by so many; I have heard it related by many people who heard it from their forebears. But many a time, through lack of interest, idleness or ignorance, many a fine deed is not committed to writing which would be fine and good to relate.'

[59] See for example William of Malmesbury's story of the witch of Berkeley (*Gesta regum Anglorum*, i. 253–5), or Orderic Vitalis's account of Hellequin's hunt (*Ecclesiastical History*, Book VIII, chapter 17; Chibnall ed., vol. iv, pp. 236–51).

[60] 'In this area is a valley, neither very broad nor very long; in the forest there is an open space with fields all around it.'

The adventure that meets the duke there has all the unexplained mystery of a romance. A couple on the moor, a knight and a lady, see the duke galloping in their direction, though the terrain initially prevents him from seeing them. The knight then cuts off the lady's head, much to the duke's horror, who in due courtly manner exclaims: 'Mal faiz, mal faiz!/ Femme deit aveir partut paiz', 'Evil-doer, evil-doer! Women should live everywhere in peace' (545–6), before in turn chopping off the murderer's head. The identity of the couple, whom the duke have buried together, remains for ever unknown. The historicity of this tale is dubious, to say the least;[61] but the absence of written sources relating to the incident is neatly explained away (557–60):

> Pur le pechié que li duc fist
> del chevalier ke il ocist,
> ne fu ceo pas mis en escrit,
> mais li pere le unt as filz dit.[62]

Oral tradition is thus presented as the last bastion of truth in the face of official suppression.

The fourth anecdote does not relate to Richard directly but to one of his hunters.[63] The young man meets a 'pucelle' in the forest and seduces her. But when he wants to get up from the ground after having his wicked way with her (598–602),

> ele l'enpeinst de tel aïr,
> ne sai u od piez u od meins,
> parmi branches et parmi reims
> le fist haut cuntremunt voler
> e el furc d'un arbre encroer;[64]

and she disappears into thin air, leaving the young man in his tree, where he is eventually found by his companions. Clearly a *fée*!

Such anecdotes, which are not in the least representative of the material of the *Troisième Partie*, have as cumulative effect of depicting Normandy as an Arthurian locus. Duke Richard is a knight worthy of the Round Table, even in his failings, and *merveilleux* was rife in Neustrian woods. By contrast, Brittany, the homeland of Arthurian material, is subjected to a much-quoted attack by Wace on the magical claims of the forest of Brocéliande. This passage is added with studied negligence to a list of William the Conqueror's Breton allies (6372–96):

> e maint Breton de maint chastel,
> e cil devers Brecheliant

---

[61] To this, one may add that at one point in the story (545), the narrator seems to forget who the hero of the tale is supposed to be, and calls the duke a count. This does occur elsewhere in the *Rou*, but rarely, and generally for reasons of syllabic count or rhyme. In this line, it would have been easy to retain the duke's title.
[62] 'Because of the sin the duke committed in killing the knight, this was not set down in writing, but it has been handed down from father to son.'
[63] Once again, the duke is referred to as 'le cunte' (563) rather than by his proper title.
[64] 'She hurled him with such force, I do not know whether it was with her feet or her hands, that he flew high in the air amongst the branches and boughs and ended up perched in the fork of a tree.'

188 *Le Roman de Rou*

> donc Breton vont sovent fablant,
> une forest mult longue e lee
> qui en Bretaigne est mult loee.
> La fontaine de Berenton
> sort d'une part lez le perron;
> aler i solent veneor
> a Berenton par grant chalor,
> e a lor cors l'eve espuisier
> e le perron desus moillier;
> por ço soleient pluie aveir.
> Issi soleit jadis ploveir
> en la forest e environ,
> mais jo ne sai par quel raison.
> La seut l'en les fees veeir,
> se li Breton nos dient veir,
> e altres merveilles plusors;
> aires i selt aveir d'ostors
> e de grant cers mult grant plenté,
> mais vilain ont tot deserté.
> La alai jo merveilles querre,
> vi la forest e vi la terre,
> merveilles quis, mais nes trovai,
> fol m'en revinc, fol i alai.[65]

This parenthesis is attached to the immediate context by only the most tenuous of links: among William's supporters, some – unspecified by name – come from the area of Brocéliande. Neither can it be said to prepare the audience for some outstanding feats of arms performed by the Breton allies later in the narrative. There is no 'Breton' cameo piece in the account of the battle of Hastings and the overall image given of them is at best ambivalent, with one Breton leader reputedly ('ço fu dit', 8494–8) forfeiting his fief, whilst his overlord Alain Fergant is said to be leading a 'gent fiere e grifaigne' (8691), with all the connotations of viciousness and barbarity these adjectives can imply.[66] The description of Brocéliande itself with its wondrous spring is a masterly exercise in negative publicity. Whatever the place may once have been, it is now totally spoiled. There are no marvels there and the whole forest is virtually lifeless: the birds of prey and the deer have almost disappeared, and with them, its entertainment value for hunting noblemen. The forest has literally been reshaped – ravaged – by peasants, so that it has lost all potential for delight.

---

[65] 'and many Bretons from many castles, as well as those from the region of Brocéliande, about which the Bretons often tell stories, a very long, broad forest which is highly praised in Brittany. To one side, the fountain of Barenton emerges beside the stone slab. Hunters used to go to Barenton during great heat and scoop out the water with their horns and moisten the top of the stone; in that way they used to get rain. Thus in days gone by it would rain, in the forest and all around, but I do not know for what reason. People used to see fairies there, if the accounts of the Bretons are true, and many other marvels. There used to be hawks' nests there, and a huge quantity of stags, but peasants have destroyed everything. I went there in search of marvels; I saw the forest and the land and looked for marvels, but found none. I came back a fool and went as a fool.'

[66] Burgess translates these words as 'fierce and warlike', which are clearly desirable attributes in allies before a major military campaign; but the implications are not necessarily positive.

This passage is usually read as a self-deprecating confession of past gullibility by the sophisticated and critical narrator.[67] However, there is more to it than that. There is no suggestion on Wace's part that the *merveilles* recounted by the Bretons never happened. The only reservation he expresses relative to the rain-inducing virtues of the spring is that he cannot tell why this should have been so (6386). The *fées* seem to be viewed with more scepticism, as their existence is directly linked to Breton trustworthiness; but the anecdote concerning Richard's huntsman, which must be very close to some of the Brocéliande tales that were told at the time, is recounted with a straight face and no suggestion is made that belief in *fées* is in itself 'folie'. Wace's madness, or foolishness, appears to be that he thought the magic would still be there, not that he believed it once existed. At this key moment in the history of the dukes of Normandy, when they are about to win the throne of England, Wace is repeating the strategy we observed in the *Chronique Ascendante*. Just as the prowess of Charlemagne is shown to have left the French to endow the Normans, so has there been a *translatio* of the courtesy, prestige and glamour of Arthur from Brittany to Normandy, as exemplified positively by the anecdotes relative to the rule of Richard I, and confirmed negatively by the degeneracy of Brocéliande. The Anglo-Norman dynasty founded by William the Conqueror thus becomes the true continuation of the line of the kings of Britain, and spiritual heir to Arthur himself.

However, in order to recognise this ideological slant, it is necessary to remember anecdotes told some 6000 lines prior to this passage, and although these anecdotes are memorable both in their own right and by virtue of their position (in effect, they open the narrative), the connection might not necessarily have been made by the audience. The difficulty arises from a weakness proper to the *Troisième Partie*, as compared to the earlier *Rou* sections and the *Roman de Brut*. This weakness is structural. The template offered by William of Jumièges, though perfectly adequate for a 'straight' history in Latin, lacked focus for a work addressed to a non-clerical audience. The open-ended, chronological narrative needed internal reshaping on the level of the individual episodes to provide narrative rhythm; but Wace did not have sufficient control over contents to do this effectively.

The *Troisième Partie* covers the rules of six dukes, which constitute as many narrative units making use of different sources. The end of the rule of Richard I, which opens the *Troisième Partie* (195–654), stands out through its dependance on Dudo and unspecified sources, allegedly oral, for supplementary anecdotes. A second phase extends up to the rule of William, the Conqueror-to-be. It covers three dukes. The section on Richard II (767–2246) is based on the account of William of Jumièges with additional details from other historians (predominantly the Interpolation by Orderic Vitalis to the *Gesta Normannorum Ducum*, and William of Malmesbury's *Gesta Regum Anglorum*), though the source of one anecdote, illustrating the duke's wisdom and generosity, has not been identified. The short rule of Richard III covers a mere 42 lines (2247–88) which follow the account of the *Gesta Normannorum Ducum*, with a brief mention of the duke's

---

[67] See for example Jean Blacker, *The Faces of Time: Portrayal of the Past in Old French and Latin Historical Narrative of the Anglo-Norman Regnum* (Austin, 1994), pp. 42–3.

son (who did not succeed him, being a monk) derived from Orderic's interpolation. Duke Robert, who had first appeared in the narrative as a rebel to his brother Richard, rules in lines 2289–3240; as ever, the account of his rule follows the lines established in the *Gesta Normannorum Ducum*, with the occasional omission or abridgment, many expansions of a rhetorical nature and the occasional addition of material, mainly anecdotal in nature. The anecdotes in this third section prepare the reader for the fourth section, the high point of the work, devoted to William, the Conqueror-to-be: the *Gesta Normannorum Ducum* is increasingly supplemented by other written sources such as the *Gesta Guillelmi*, by William of Poitiers, the *Carmen de Hastingae proelio* by Guy of Amiens and Eadmer's *Historia Novorum*, but also by what can only have been personal investigative research. This section evidences some loss of narrative control, as Wace was clearly under pressure to produce an image of the past that corresponded to the memories – and interests – of the Norman families surrounding him. The fifth and final section relates the ill-fated rule of Duke Robert Curthose; the narrative leans heavily on Orderic Vitalis's *Historia Ecclesiastica*, with occasional borrowing from William of Malmesbury and Eadmer of Canterbury. In marked contrast to the preceding section, Wace now tends to abbreviate his sources, with only rare additions of his own.

Duke Richard I

After the helpless child of the *Deuxième Partie*, the image of Richard I in the *Troisième Partie* is altogether more glamorous. It follows Dudo and the *Gesta Normannorum Ducum* closely, with, as we have seen above, the addition of five successive anecdotes not to be found in Wace's main sources. These give Richard and his land an aura of Arthurian romance; his wisdom and virtue are such that demons and angels appeal to his arbitration and his bravery is so great that he is unafraid of the ghosts and devils he encounters in his nightly wanderings. In this respect, as in the *Deuxième Partie*, we are still dealing with a character with a strong literary colouring. The fifth and final anecdote recounted at the beginning of this section, however, has a more homely feel to it, and brings the reader back to reality: it is the account of Richard's wedding night with Gunnor. By this stage, they have been a couple for many years and had had five sons and three daughters together, but the liberating effect of marriage on Gunnor and her delight at being Richard's equal rather than his mistress, are rendered with sensitivity and humour. Once they go to bed, she turns her back on Richard, who is very surprised – she's never done that before. At which Gunnor laughingly answers that now she is a lady, she can do as she likes, and can sleep in whatever way she likes; at last, she feels secure (641–5):

> Çanariere fu le lit vostre,
> mais est il e mien e vostre:
> unkes mais aseüre n'i jui,
> ne sanz pour od vus ne fui,
> ore sui aukes aseüree.[68]

---

[68] 'Hitherto, the bed was yours, but now it is mine and yours. I never lay in it with confidence and was never with you without fear. Now I have some security.'

If Wace is to be believed, this anecdote (inserted before a few lines of praise of Gunnor taken from Dudo) was common knowledge: 'Asez fu puis lunges retrait/ ceo ke Gunor ot dit e fait', 'for a long time afterwards, the story of what Gunnor had said and done was recounted' (649–50). The intimacy of this scene and the fact that it relates to the duke's consort, not the duke himself, makes it quite unlike anything in the previous 'Parties' of the *Roman de Rou* (with the exception, possibly, of the vignette of Matilda escaping under her sheet in the *Chronique Ascendante*); Wace shows here a willingness to depict Gunnor as an individual in her own right. The *Troisième Partie* contains another striking anecdote involving a duke and his mistress (also supplementing the material of the *Gesta Normannorum Ducum*): that of Arlette, the mother of the future William the Conqueror, who when she was taken to Duke Robert's bed for the first time is said to have torn her shift down to her feet, because it was not right for cloth that had been in contact with her legs and feet to be thrust in his face (2831–45). These two anecdotes suggest that Wace had access to a fund of stories relative to the intimacy of the dukes, that he exploited in order to enhance the dignity of these two matriarchs of the Norman ducal house, both of whom had produced their offspring out of wedlock.

In the case of Gunnor, the anecdote also brings the focus back onto the hard facts of Richard's rule. Lothar has died, Hugh Capet has succeeded him to the French throne thanks to the support of Richard (who had married Hugh's sister Emma), and reconciliation had been made with the count of Flanders. Richard's virtues as overlord are extolled, as is his support of the Church (in particular his building of Rouen cathedral, of the Mont St Michel and of the abbey of Holy Trinity at Fécamp). He is then shown putting his affairs in order on his deathbed and, in an echo of the ends of the previous dukes, dies like a good Christian after having confessed his sins and received the Holy Sacrament. This pious end, it should be noted, is Wace's own addition to his sources, thus indicating the importance of religious piety in the image he constructs of Rou's lineage. As with the other dukes, we are told where Richard is buried and what monuments preserve his memory (in this case, a chapel dedicated to St Thomas). The honour then passes to his heir, Richard II of Normandy, following both the Latin sources and the pattern of lifetime achievements/death/succession first established in the *Roman de Brut*.

Duke Richard II
The rule of Richard II resembles that of his father in that it is marked by rebellion and warfare: a peasants' revolt, mercilessly quashed; the rebellion of his illegitimate brother William (with whom he is eventually reconciled); an English invasion of Normandy; and armed conflict with his brother-in-law, Odo Count of Chartres (on a matter of dowry). Like Richard I, Richard II does not hesitate to appeal to his heathen Scandinavian allies, and the enduring bond between the Danes and the Normans is one of the most striking features of Book v. of the *Gesta Normannorum Ducum*. William of Jumièges, who from the beginning of the reign of Richard II onwards is a contemporary of the events he recounts, gives a horrified account of the massacre of the Danish settlers in England by King Ethelred (v. 6) and mentions a treaty between the Norman duke and King Svein of

Denmark allowing the Danish king to use Normandy as a base for his campaign of retaliation. The entanglement with England becomes more complex. King Ethelred, married to Richard II's sister Emma, tries to invade Normandy, but matrimonial policy also makes the Norman dukes and the English kings natural allies; when King Svein conquers London, Ethelred seeks refuge with his wife and sons (and the royal treasure) at Richard's court in Rouen.[69] Richard thus becomes the protector of his nephews Edward and Alfred, the heirs to the English throne. The relationship with France under Richard II does not seem to have been as tense as under his predecessors. The king of France is not depicted as an enthusiastic supporter of Richard (he only intervenes to settle the feud between Richard and Odo of Chartres out of fear that Richard's vicious pagan allies might set their sights on his territories, after having massacred the inhabitants of Dol, in Brittany); but neither is there any evidence of antagonism between Normandy and France under Richard II. Moreover, the duke of Normandy is shown to be supportive of King Robert the Pious of France, helping him to restore Melun to a wronged vassal (*Gesta Normannorum Ducum* v. 14), and supporting his claim to the duchy of Burgundy (*Gesta Normannorum Ducum* v. 15).

Wace's account follows the sequence of events of his main source closely, with only one significant modification: the marriage of Geoffrey of Brittany, placed by William of Jumièges between the failed English invasion of Normandy and the English massacre of the Danes, is mentioned by Wace after Svein's seizing of Aethelred's throne. This allows the poet to deal with all the 'English' events as a sequence, Geoffrey of Brittany's marriage to Richard's sister Hawise then serving as a transition to introduce the marriage of Odo of Chartres with another of Richard's sisters, Matilda. The juxtaposition of these two unions highlight the contrast between the fruitful marriage of Geoffrey and Hawise and that of Matilda and Odo: Matilda dies childless, Odo refuses to relinquish the town of Dreux that was part of her dowry, and the land is engulfed in war. In terms of content, Wace omits a great deal of important information, such as the treaty between the Normans and King Svein and the entirety of the material in chapters 14 and 15 of Book v. of the *Gesta Normannorum Ducum*: that is, the two episodes where Richard displays his support of King Robert (the Pious) of France, first in restoring Melun to its rightful owner (a vassal of the king of France), and then in supporting the King of France's claim to Burgundy. These omissions suggest that Wace was not happy with Richard's image of faithful vassal of the king of France projected by such material, either for political reasons, or because it disrupted the neat polarisation between (good) Normans and (bad) French established from the beginning of the *Rou*. Most of Wace's additions are amplificatory in nature (speeches in the peasants' revolt passage, for example, and the highly elaborate description of the battle opposing Odo and Richard, 1493–1626). We do however find the occasional borrowing from William of Malmesbury's *Gesta Regum* and a number of additions from minor sources such as the *Life of Saint Edmund* (mentioned explicitly, 1313–15), local common knowledge and, probably, family

---

[69] The *Anglo-Saxon Chronicle* gives a slightly different version of these events, which William of Jumièges is clearly recounting from a Norman perspective. See van Houts, notes to *Gesta Normannorum Ducum* v. 7–8.

traditions. Richard's piety is thus exemplified and illustrated by the foundation of the Abbey of Fécamp (a piece of information not in the *Gesta Normannorum Ducum*), while his natural nobility is stressed by a 12-line, rhetorically marked statement by Wace that the duke only allowed men of noble birth to serve in his household, from the chaplain to the ushers (797–808).[70] This stress on the noble origins of all the duke's entourage could have been derived from family lore, as Wace may have counted among his ancestors the chamberlain of Duke Robert the Magnificent, Richard II's son (a suggestion first made by Gaston Paris, and now widely accepted).[71]

The first challenge to Richard II occurs when the peasants of Normandy revolt because of the excessive burden of customary dues. Wace expands on the motivation of the peasants to such an extent that he seems to be sympathetic to their claims. Whereas William of Jumièges (v. 2) suggests that the revolt arose from restrictions in rights of way through forests ('in siluarum compendiis') and in traffic on rivers ('in aquarum commerciis'), Wace provides a list of the sorts of lawsuits the peasants have to face relative to taxes, dues and customs: the passage extends over seven lines, the word 'plaiz' ('lawsuit') recurring twelve times (844–50). The peasants conclude that they would be better off without their lords; Wace gives voice to their reasoning in a long passage in direct speech (864–94), where they affirm their equal human status as their overlords ('Nus sumes humes cum il sunt', 'We are men as they are', 867). They consider their superior numbers – thirty or forty to one – and come to the conclusion that they would have the upper hand in a confrontation. Whether this passage really betrays sympathy for the peasants is debatable. As pointed out by Dolores Buttry, Wace does not condemn the peasants, which could be read as indicating some compassion or understanding on his part, although he stops short of wishing to see the social order overturned.[72] On the other hand, there is a real possibility that this passage was meant to be burlesque. The peasants are hopelessly unrealistic, and the list made by their leaders of the weapons at their disposal shows clearly that we are dealing with an untrained, unarmed mob (883–8):

> As maçues e as granz peus,
> as saietes e as tineus,
> as haches, as arcs, as gisarmes
> e as pieres, ki n'avra armes,
> od la grant gent ke nus avum
> des chevaliers nus defendum.[73]

This belief in the power of superior numbers is not entirely illusory; the attempted invasion of Normandy by Ethelred will be rebuffed by a force made up

---

[70] This passage repeats the word 'gentil' ('noble') eight times, with the construction 'gentil furent li + Noun' repeated seven times.
[71] This requires the emendation of line 3225, which as it stands makes little sense. See Paris in *Romania* 9 (1880): 526–7.
[72] See Dolores J. Buttry, 'Contempt or Empathy? Master Wace's Depiction of a Peasant Revolt', *Romance Notes* 37 (1996): 31–8.
[73] 'With clubs and large stakes, arrows and staffs, axes, bows and pikes, and stones for those who have no arms, let us defend ourselves against knights with the large number of men we have.'

of men and women of all social classes, similarly armed with improvised weapons (1095–8):

> Neis les veilles i sunt curues
> od pels, od tinels, od maçues,
> escorcies e rebracies,
> de bien ferir aparaillies.[74]

However, there is a major difference between the circumstances surrounding these two passages: all estates are working together in the passage just quoted, in the communal interest, whereas the rebellious peasants are attempting to destroy the social fabric. Moreover, even the old women know better than to go to battle armed just with stones: the peasant leaders, who could have been depicted as so many Davids against the knightly Goliaths, come over as plain stupid, sending their weaponless followers against trained, armed knights. Their motivations are also less than admirable: whereas Wace's list of the strictures placed on the everyday life of the farmers could conceivably be construed as suggesting that their grievances were not unfounded, the note on which the speech of the ringleaders ends reveals the extent of their selfishness and irresponsibility (889–94):

> Ensi poüm aler el bois,
> arbres trenchier e prendre a chois,
> es vivers prendre les peissuns
> e es forez les veneisuns;
> de tut ferum nos voluntez,
> des bois, des eaues e des prez.[75]

There is no awareness of the necessity of regulating the use of natural resources, and the passage brings to mind Wace's parenthesis on the forest of Brocéliande, once lush and wondrous, but now turned into a desert by the 'vilain' (*Deuxième Partie*, 6392). The almost childlike glee at the thought of a world without rules, coming immediately after the ludicrous image of peasants trying to fight knights with stones, would at the very least have raised a superior smile (if not a contemptuous laugh) in educated and aristocratic circles.

The repression following the uprising is described by Wace with a wealth of gruesome details not found in the *Gesta Normannorum Ducum*. News of the revolt come to the ears of Richard because the peasants are unable to keep their preparations secret (905–11); Richard's uncle Ralph offers to deal with the problem,[76] and does so with exemplary cruelty. Whereas in the *Gesta Normannorum Ducum* the count has the hands and feet of the peasant envoys chopped off, thus immediately putting an end to the problem, in Wace, he captures the ringleaders and inflicts a variety of tortures on them: teeth are pulled

---

[74] 'Even the old women came running up with stakes, cudgels and clubs and their skirts and sleeves rolled up, ready to deal good blows.'

[75] 'In this way we can go into the woods, cut down trees and take what we will, catch fish in the rivers and venison in the forests. We will do as we wish with everything, with the woods, the ponds and the meadows.'

[76] Wace mistakenly states that he was count of Evreux: see Holden, note to line 917.

out, limbs branded with hot irons, eyes torn out of their sockets, as well as hands and feet being cut off the unfortunate rebels. Some, Wace tells us, are roasted alive; others are boiled alive; while those with money pay all they have to be ransomed from their punishment (953–6).

Two questions arising from this passage are, first, where did Wace find this information; and secondly, why did he include it. It could be that the count of Ivry's treatment of the peasants was kept alive by oral tradition – possibly with some 'embellishments', and with the support of the Norman nobility – as a cautionary tale; with a writer other than Wace, one might also suspect that the description could have been due at least in part to literary licence, as these details make the episode much more memorable. The most important effect of the inclusion of this list of horrors, however, lies in the reader's perception of the young duke. At no time is Richard II directly involved in the events in Wace's version; indeed, when his uncle offers to take care of the problem, he explicitly forbids him to do so: 'ja mar en moverez voz piez', literally, 'You'd better not move a foot' (921), and more elegantly translated by Burgess as 'You would only regret taking action yourself.' The ruthless violence with which the peasants are treated throws into greater relief the mercy with which Richard treats other rebels – in particular, his illegitimate half-brother William, in the episode immediately following the peasant revolt. The additions made by Wace to this section (corresponding to *Gesta Normannorum Ducum* v. 3) are relatively minor, but all contribute to a highly positive image of the young duke: first, that he gave all his siblings lands and titles (961–2); a proleptic comment by the narrator that William did not keep his oath of fealty for long (965–6), firmly putting Richard in the right in the ensuing conflict; the counsellors responsible for leading William astray are castrated and blinded by Richard (985–6),[77] showing that the young duke is capable of being harsh when necessary; and when the brothers are eventually reconciled, Wace underscores Richard's generosity through his praise of the rich, well-connected and virtuous bride he gives the now repentant William. The praise of Lieceline also allows Wace to insert a piece of information of local interest, through the mention that she founded an abbey dedicated to the Virgin on the Dive. Strangely, Wace diverges from the *Gesta Normannorum Ducum* in stating (erroneously) that her son Hugh, who was bishop of Lisieux from 1049 (or 1050) to 1077, was called John; an indication, perhaps, that Wace was drawing on information from the family, or – more likely, inasmuch as he also erroneously states that Lieceline was an only child – that he was under some pressure to reflect local traditions, possibly transmitted by the abbey founded by the lady. Pressure of this nature becomes increasingly obvious as the *Troisième Partie* unfolds, culminating in the account of the rule of Richard II's grandson, the future William the Conqueror.

The second challenge to Richard's authority comes from England. Aethelred's decision to send a force to Normandy to capture Richard, said by William of Jumièges (v. 4) to have been motivated by unspecified points of dissension, is presented in a somewhat dismissive way by Wace: 'ne sai par ire u par envie', 'I do not know whether [it was caused] by anger or envy' (1058). The negative

---

[77] In the *Gesta Normannorum Ducum* they are killed in battle or exiled.

colouring brought to Ethelred's reasons for wishing Richard ill is further emphasised by Wace's statement that the English king was not even restrained by the fact that he was married to Richard's sister (1059–60), an explicit moral judgment on his actions. The invasion, as we have seen, is a failure, due to the determined resistance of the inhabitants of the Cotentin peninsula. The incident closes with the laments of the English women for their dead fathers, husbands, sons, brothers and lovers, and the rejoicing of Duke Richard (an addition of Wace's, 1185–90). This instance of Ethelred's lack of moral direction is then followed directly in the *Troisième Partie* by an especially revolting example of English cruelty, with the massacre of all the Danes living in the land on St Brice's Day (13 November 1002) that prompts King Svein of Denmark to mount an expedition to avenge his kinsmen which results in Ethelred losing his throne. Wace's handling of this section differs from that of William of Jumièges mainly in the way he presents Svein and Ethelred. Whereas in the *Gesta Normannorum Ducum*, Ethelred is unequivocally said to have ordered the massacre himself 'subito furore', 'in a sudden fury' (v. 6), Wace presents the decision as a collective one, a 'felun conseil', 'wicked decision' (1209) taken by the English rather than their king, who indeed is not mentioned at all in the French text. By contrast, King Svein of Denmark is depicted in even more negative terms than in the *Gesta Normannorum Ducum*. Wace omits any mention of the council which advises Svein to mount a punitive expedition; his merciless behaviour is repeatedly mentioned; and his death is announced quoting the down-to-earth proverb 'Chiens esragiez lunges ne vit', 'A mad dog does not live long' (1310). He is further said to have been punished by St Edmund (1313–15). Significantly, Wace omits entirely the treaty passed between Richard and Svein (*Gesta Normannorum Ducum* v. 7), whereby the Danes are allowed to use Normandy as a safe haven and would sell any English booty there. The Norman duke thus remains unsullied by any alliance with this bloodthirsty pagan and stands on moral high ground: despite Ethelred's act of hostility towards him, we do not see him (as in the Latin source) encouraging his enemies. When Ethelred and his family arrive in Rouen as refugees, Richard's welcome appears to be entirely in character, and his accepting to foster his two nephews places him in the tradition of king-makers established by his ancestor Rou.

The third challenge to Richard's rule comes with the refusal of Odo of Chartres to relinquish Dreux following the death of his wife Matilda. Wace expands this section considerably, particularly the battle outside Tillières (1493–626), which appears to have been created in an entirely literary manner using the fund of motifs derived from Arthur's Roman campaign in the *Roman de Brut*. Efforts are clearly made to make this episode more epic and memorable, with the addition of details such as Hugh of Maine's horse dying of exhaustion (1637–43), the count's fear of being captured for ransom (1654) and the short dialogue where he misleads his pursuers (who think he is a shepherd). Wace further adds an explicit mention of continuing guerrilla warfare between Odo and Richard (1677–702) as justification for the duke's appeal to the two pagan kings Olaf of Norway and Lacman of Sweden for help, resulting in the devastation of Brittany. King Robert of France then intervenes, reconciles Richard and Odo, and King Olaf, having received baptism, returns to Norway where he becomes a martyr for his faith. All ends well; Richard marries the sister of Geoffrey of Brittany, who gives him three sons and three daughters, then dies at an early age. Wace adds to the *Gesta Normannorum Ducum* that Richard remarried and had two further sons, William Count of Taillou and Maugier, who eventually became an archbishop.

At this point, Wace includes two anecdotes relative to Richard's generosity and piety not found in William of Jumièges' redaction of the *Gesta Normannorum Ducum*. The first one has no known source; it is the story of a knight who stole a spoon from the duke's table in order to fund his love of entertaining (1863–974). Richard, who has noticed what the knight has done, does not allow his chamberlain to confront him in public but secretly sends him to pay the man's debts by redeeming his pledges. The spoon is among the pledges. The knight is mortified that his theft was discovered and decides to leave the court. The duke finds this out, rides after him, makes him return and publicly gives him enough money to support himself without stealing other people's property; the knight was never reproached for his action. A brilliant example of the duke's ability to defuse what could have turned into a scandal, as well as an instance of great forgiveness and generosity. The second anecdote was interpolated in Wace's copy of the *Gesta Normannorum Ducum* (v. 13a) and originated in Saint-Etienne of Caen. A certain Bernard the Philosopher wishes to meet Richard; in order to catch his attention, he pretends to aim an arrow at the duke as he appears at his window. Bernard is arrested, brought to Richard, and becomes a member of his household. He is eventually buried in Cherbourg, on the very site where Richard was in the habit of praying (something he requested three days before his death). Wace makes a number of changes to his Latin account, adding ill-treatment received by Bernard at the hands of Richard's retainers, omitting Bernard's witty comparison of the reclusive duke to a wild animal who has to be sought out with bow and arrow, and replacing it with a statement that he had come from afar 'pur le los de sa bunté', 'because of his reputation for goodness' (2084). Wace also omits Bernard's warning to Richard against a heresy that had recently sprung up in Lisieux immediately prior to his death. As a result, the St Etienne interpolation becomes rather trite in Wace, who reduces it to a celebration of the duke's fame and piety.

These personal anecdotes are followed by just one further episode in the life of Richard II before the account of his death. Richard's son-in-law, Reginald Count of Burgundy, is captured and emprisoned by Hugh Count of Châlon. Richard's request that Reginald be released is refused, so he sends an army to Burgundy to his rescue under the command of his eldest son Richard. In order to secure the help of one of the counts of Peronne, adds Wace, Richard gave him the two manors of Elbeuf and Chanbois,[78] a piece of information of local interest, but which is presented as an instance of the wisdom of the duke, introduced with the proverb: 'Bien fait ki preste e mielz ki dune', 'He who lends does well and he who gives does better' (2161). The good relations between Richard II and King Robert the Pious of France are briefly mentioned by Wace at this stage: we are told that the king, 'en qui Richard out grant fiance', 'who was greatly trusted by Richard'

---

[78] This gift is also mentioned in Robert de Torigni (see Holden, note to lines 2162 ff.).

(2170), allowed the Normans to pass through his territories, and that the Normans in turn behaved in an exemplary manner, buying any food they needed at the local market price (2174–5). These additions to Wace's main source indicate a real interest in the practicalities of such a campaign and in the means by which necessary support could be won.[79] Needless to say, the campaign is a success. Hugh's lands are devastated; the extent of the destruction wrought by the Normans is vividly illustrated by Wace, who says that they left no plough working, no house standing and no cock crowing (2183–5), though he omits the statement (*Gesta Normannorum Ducum* v. 16) that they burnt down the fortress of Mimande with the men, women and children inside. Hugh has to beg for forgiveness, Reginald is released and young Richard returns home.

All of Wace's additions, omissions or modifications to his main source in this episode are readily explained as responding to the requirements of a specific narrative or political agenda, with one exception. When Richard sends his son Richard against Hugh of Chalon, Wace states: 'sun filz Richard esteit ja grant/ e Robert ert pruz e vaillant', 'his son Richard was already grown up, and Robert was a very brave and valiant man' (2159–60), thus giving the doubly misleading impression that both brothers went on this campaign together, and that Robert was somehow more experienced, with a fully established reputation. The deathbed instructions of Richard II to his barons (which Wace recounts in direct speech, 2217–32) make it quite clear that Robert owes obedience to his brother, but this early foregrounding of Robert at the expense of Richard prepares the reader for the tensions that will occur between the two brothers after their father's death and indicates where the poet's sympathies lie. The rule of Richard II ends in the usual manner, with the duke's burial place. In this case, there are no special monuments to remember him by, but the poet adds his eyewitness account of the reburial of his bones with those of his father (2241–6): an event which we know took place in presence of King Henry II, though Wace does not mention him.[80] The final note is suitably pious, with the mortal remains of the two dukes placed behind the main altar at Fécamp, where the monks treat them with great reverence.

Dukes Richard III and Robert I
The rule of Richard III was short, and Wace further lessens the impact of his rule by omitting any praise of the new duke at his accession (as opposed to *Gesta Normannorum Ducum* vi.1). We are told that he paid homage to the king of France for his fief and gave his brother Robert the territory his father had stipulated. Wace refuses to apportion blame for the ensuing conflict over the stronghold of Falaise (the *Gesta Normannorum Ducum* vi. 2 squarely sees the influence of the devil through the agency of malevolent advisers), and when Richard dies in suspicious circumstances shortly after being reconciled with his brother, the

---

[79] This makes the absence of such information in the final section of the *Troisième Partie* all the more noticeable; see below, Chapter 9, 'The Aftermath of Hastings'.
[80] J.-G. Gouttebroze suggests that this might indicate (or have caused) a rift between Wace and his patron ('Pourquoi congédier un historiographe', pp. 306–7). Henry II may have been trying to enhance the aura of saintliness of his ancestors through the ceremonial reburying of their bones by the main altar.

narrator resorts to his trademark 'ne sai' to avoid having to say too much on the matter. According to William of Jumièges, 'ut retulerunt plurimi, ueneno mortem obiit', 'as some people say, he died of poison' (*Gesta Normannorum Ducum* vi. 2); Wace concurs, adding that the duke's retinue was also victim of the poisoning, though he remains circumspect when it comes to apportioning blame (2269–74):

> Ne sai k'il manga ne k'il but,
> mais il engruta e murut,
> e plusurs de ses compaignuns
> e des meillurs de ses baruns.
> Ne sorent unkes ki reter
> ne ki haïr ne ki blasmer.[81]

William of Malmesbury is less cautious; he explicitly states in his *Gesta Regum Anglorum* (ii. 178) that some pointed the finger at Robert himself (though he qualifies the rumour as 'certe incerta', 'very doubtful'). It was clearly not in Wace's interest to cast a shadow over a direct ancestor of his patron; moreover, Robert was very promising material from a narrative point of view: a dashing young man of great generosity and prestige, who ended his life as a pilgrim in the Holy Land.[82] Richard III is therefore minimised in order to better celebrate his more glamorous brother; the only positive thing said of him (not by the narrator, one may note) is that if he had lived longer, there would not have been a lord to come up to him (2275–79). His only son, Nicholas, is a monk. His two-year rule appears as little more than a brief parenthesis.

By contrast, Robert is given the full treatment on his accession. He is said to take after his virtuous father, loving and honouring the Church and clerics, protecting the poor and caring for lepers (2291–6); he surpasses all his ancestors in generosity and nobility, doubling the number of his servants (2297–300). His piety is further proved by the foundation of an abbey at Cerisy, to which he gives full jurisdiction over its lands (2301–8). These details are all added by Wace to his source, which rather mentions as his salient characteristic his fierceness in dealing with rebels (*Gesta Normannorum Ducum* vi. 3; a feature not retained in the French poem). Wace integrates in his narrative a number of anecdotes relative to Robert, amongst which he interweaves stories concerning the conception and birth of his illegitimate son William, the Conqueror-to-be. The glittering depiction of Robert thus serves a dual purpose, enhancing his own stature as ruler on the one hand, whilst preparing for his arguably even greater successor, the first duke of Normandy also to be king. This process is effected through an extensive re-shaping of the source narrative, essentially by the strategic placing of strings of anecdotes between sections relating the duke's political or military deeds. Robert's founding of Cerisy is followed by three anecdotes illustrating the duke's generosity, which in the *Gesta Normannorum Ducum* occur only five chapters

---

[81] 'I do not know what he ate or what he drank, but he fell ill and died, as did a number of his companions and the finest of his barons. They never knew whom to accuse, whom to hate and whom to blame.'
[82] On the depiction of Duke Robert in medieval sources, see Jean Batany, 'Les trois bienfaits du duc Robert: un modèle historiographique du prince évergète au XIIe siècle', pp. 263–72 in *Clio. Actes du colloque Histoire et Historiographie*, ed. R. Chevalier (Paris, 1980).

later (vi. 8, Saint-Etienne interpolations). His dealings with the Bellême family (in a section where Wace conflates the material of *Gesta Normannorum Ducum* vi. 4 and vi. 7), his support of King Henry of France against his brother and mother (*Gesta Normannorum Ducum* vi. 7), and his problems with Alan of Brittany (*Gesta Normannorum Ducum* vi. 8, 9(10) and 10) are similarly followed by a series of anecdotes relating to Robert's son William; while the practical measures taken by Robert prior to his departure for Jerusalem (*Gesta Normannorum Ducum* vi. 11 (12)) give way to six anecdotes of Robert's regal behaviour in Constantinople. His death by poison in Jerusalem is also preceded by two striking stories, showing the extent of his wit, faith and generosity. Much of this material was present in Wace's copy of the *Gesta Normannorum Ducum*, in the interpolations by the monk of Saint-Etienne of Caen or by Orderic Vitalis; where it was not, Wace's account frequently agrees with William of Malmesbury's *Gesta Regum Anglorum*.[83] Uncongenial material is omitted, though only one episode directly involving the duke – the uprising of Baldwin of Flanders against his father, and his enforced reconciliation with him thanks to Robert's intervention (*Gesta Normannorum Ducum* vi. 6) – is eliminated entirely.[84]

The salient characteristic of Duke Robert is his extreme generosity and liberal spending, to which he owed to be called 'the Magnificent'. The initial cluster of anecdotes are chosen to illustrate this aspect of his personality. In the first story (2309–32), the duke notices during mass one feast day that a knight did not give anything at offertary, because he had no money. Robert gives one hundred pounds to the knight, who surprises everyone by giving the entire sum to the church. Asked why, he explains that the money was given to him for that purpose. Robert is so impressed that he gives the knight another hundred pounds for his own usage. In the second tale (2335–84), Robert hands over to a cleric a precious vase he has just received as a gift; the cleric, overcome by such generosity, dies of joy. The third anecdote is more interesting, inasmuch as Wace makes 'adjustments' to his source, the Saint-Etienne of Caen interpolation into the *Gesta Normannorum Ducum*, whereas the previous anecdotes had been very faithfully translated. In the Latin text (*Gesta Normannorum Ducum* vi. 8a) a blacksmith from Beauvais comes to present the duke with two knives, and is given one hundred Rouen pounds. Thereupon, two superb horses are presented to Robert, who hands them over to the bewildered blacksmith. Further gifts are given to Robert, who orders them also to be handed over to the blacksmith; but worried at this undeserved display of generosity, the man has already returned home. The duke regrets this early departure, declaring that he would have made him rich and powerful. Two years later, the blacksmith returns to Normandy with his two sons, both trained soldiers, offering their services to the duke. Wace follows the storyline, but omits the fact that the man is a blacksmith and replaces the ending, where the man returns with his sons, by a postscript explaining the duke's

---

[83] However, Wace's agreements with William of Malmesbury are not close enough for us to be sure that the Latin historian was a direct source.
[84] Wace also chooses (unsurprisingly) to omit the lengthy interpolation into William of Jumièges' material of the history of the foundation of the abbey of Le Bec and its abbots from Herluin to Lanfranc (*Gesta Normannorum Ducum* vi. 9).

behaviour in terms that bring to mind the customs of King Arthur's court in later romances (2413–26):

> Tele custume li ducs aveit,
> sa gent tote bien le saveit,
> quant hom present li aportout,
> se il a home le dunout,
> ja puis le jur present ne eüst,
> si ceo chose a mangier ne feust,
> ke cil ne l'eüst maintenant
> ke l'altre aveit eü devant.
> De tut se poeit saüler,
> ceo diseit il, fors de duner,
> ne ja si grant dun ne donast
> ke asez petit ne li semblast,
> ne si grant ne l'eüst duné
> ja puis fust par lui reprové.[85]

This much-needed explanation of Robert's somewhat eccentric behaviour appears at the beginning of the anecdote in the Latin (told on the authority of Isembert, Duke Robert's chaplain), Robert's need to be open-handed being an addition of Wace's, who in so doing completely changes the import of the tale. For Isembert, the episode showed not only how generous Robert was to those around him, but also the love he received in return: his gifts to the blacksmith earn him the loyalty of three well-trained men-at-arms. By contrast, Wace fails to mention the trade of the blacksmith, and the addition of these three low-born men to the duke's retinue is purposefully omitted – an indication, possibly, of disapproval at a story suggesting that Robert fell short of his father's high standards when it came to choosing members of his household. As a result, what seems to have been a conscious public relations ploy on the part of Robert, proving his political acumen, becomes a rather mindless exercise in asset-squandering.

The image of a 'nice-but-dim' Robert conjured up by Wace in these early anecdotes seems to have been intentional. The darker side to the duke is carefully excised by the French writer; as mentioned above, his fierceness towards rebels is passed over in silence, as is his conflict, early after his accession to the duchy, with Archbishop Robert of Evreux, and his blood-drenched punitive expedition against Baldwin of Flanders. The only instances of rebellious vassals recounted by Wace – the Bellême family and Alan of Brittany – are dealt with by the duke with surprising leniency. Despite having openly rebelled against Robert and being forced into submission after being besieged in Alençon, William of Bellême is forgiven and is reinstated in all his lands. A serious error, as Wace (like his source) makes abundantly clear; the siege of Alençon is followed by a short history of the family of Bellême where the poet repeatedly emphasises their

---

[85] 'The duke had a custom, as his men well knew, that when someone brought him a present, if he gave it to anyone, he would not receive another present that day, unless it was something to eat, without the same person who had had the earlier one immediately having this one. He could become satiated, he used to say, by anything apart from giving, and however great the gift it always seemed very small to him; he could never have given one so great that he would subsequently regret it.'

treacherous and evil nature, concluding with these words: 'Tuz tens furent malicius/ cil de Belesme e orguillus;/ de grant orguil les abati/ cil ki Belesme lur toli', 'The Bellême family was always evil and arrogant; the man who took Bellême from them rid them of this great arrogance' (2517–20). One might also discern a measure of naivety on Robert's part, when he apparently expected King Canute to restore their inheritance to Aethelred's sons Edward and Alfred, just for the asking (2731–44).

The highpoint of Robert's struggles against rebellious vassals, in Wace's work, is undeniably his campaign against his cousin Alan of Brittany, who claimed the title of king (2621–6), refused to pay him homage and laid waste the Avranchin in retaliation for Robert's burning of the city of Dol. Wace creates a vivid battle-scene, complete with pre-battle speech, battle cries and formulaic battle-clash, describing the Norman resistance to the Bretons and the eventual routing of Alan's men. Wace appears to have had information independently of the *Gesta Normannorum Ducum*, as he explains that Alan was disadvantaged because most of his troops had all dispersed gathering booty (2693–6); he also adds that the peasants of the area beat the countryside to cut down the fleeing Bretons and to kill the wounded (2715–20), thus explaining the extent of the massacre mentioned in the *Gesta Normannorum Ducum* and emphasised by Wace in a stylistically ornate passage (2721–6). This battle is the only one of Robert's rule to be described in any length; it also takes place without him. Wace seems unwilling to give full amplificatory treatment to episodes of warfare directly involving the duke; the punitive campaign against Brittany, for example, is described in just one line, 'Tute ert Bretaigne en grant tirpeil', 'the whole of Brittany was greatly agitated' (2801), something of an understatement in view of the ruthlessness with which it was conducted.[86] Robert's role is thus depicted as entirely positive, forgiving his cousin Alan (after he has paid homage to him) as he had William of Bellême; one might almost be deceived into thinking him innocent of the excesses of warfare.

Like his forebears, Robert the Magnificent is depicted as a king-maker, twice intervening in the succession of neighbouring countries. He first helps Henry, son of King Robert the Pious of France, establish his authority against his rebellious younger brother Robert of Burgundy and their mother Constance (*Gesta Normannorum Ducum* v. 7). Wace expands on his source's presentation of the conflict in terms reminiscent of his depiction of Queen Judon in the *Roman de Brut*, who had murdered her one son out of love for the other (2529–34):

> Mais Custance, ki fu lur mere,
> emprés la mort le rei lur pere
> haï Henri, sun filz l'ainzné
> e Robert ad forment amé;
> Henri haï comme marrastre
> heit et envie son fillastre.[87]

---

[86] *Gesta Normannorum Ducum* vi. 10 (11) makes it clear that this campaign was extremely brutal and destructive.

[87] 'But after the death of their father the king, Constance, who was their mother, hated her eldest son Henry and loved Robert greatly. She hated Henry as a stepmother hates and envies her stepson.'

The opposition to Henry I of France is thus presented as unnatural as well as contrary to the agreement made during Robert the Pious's lifetime, justifying Robert of Normandy's vigorous support of the new French king. Wace adds to the *Gesta Normannorum Ducum* the date of arrival of Henry at Robert's court to ask for help (the day before Palm Sunday, 2548), Henry's promise of the Vexin in exchange of the Norman help,[88] Robert's vow to assist him (2559–60) and a rhetorically ornate description of the lavish way in which the king was entertained (2561–70). At the same time, Wace omits all mention of Robert's uncle Maugier who assisted Robert and Henry in this matter, giving the impression that the re-establishment of Henry in his rights was achieved by Robert alone. This further justifies the gift to Robert of the Vexin, together with Pontoise and Chaumont, that Wace explicitly states took place after Henry's victory (2584–5). The twice-repeated reference to Robert's acquisition of the Vexin suggests that for Wace (or his immediate circle of readers and informants), this was a matter of greater importance than it had been for William of Jumièges. On an ethical level, Robert of Normandy is shown to be extending his domains, but through an act of mercy towards his beleaguered overlord rather than through offensive warfare; the Vexin is the reward for virtue. And in terms of Wace's overall agenda, the gift of Vexin becomes yet another cause for French antagonism towards Normandy, arousing 'grant envie' (2588).

The second instance where Robert the Magnificent is shown getting involved in matters of royal succession concerns his cousins princes Alfred and Edward, King Ethelred's sons who had been fostered by Robert's father, and with whom William of Jumièges hints Robert might have sworn brotherhood (*Gesta Normannorum Ducum* vi. 9 (10), note pp. 76–7). No motivation is retained for Robert's intervention by Wace, other than the fact that the two men were dispossessed 'a grant tort' (2734). King Canute, unsurprisingly, refuses to hand back their patrimony to Alfred and Edward, so Robert mounts a great fleet to impose their rights by force but bad weather prevents the boats from reaching England. Robert eventually gives up his plans and diverts part of his army on to Brittany instead. Both William of Jumièges and Wace interpret the storm that threw the ships back onto Jersey as due to divine providence; but whereas the older historian interprets the episode in relation to God's plans for the future Edward the Confessor, 'quem disponebat in futuro regnare sine sanguinis effusione', 'whom he meant to reign in the future without bloodshed', Wace omits all mention of Edward, thus giving the impression that the person preserved from having to partake in the wholesale massacre entailed by the conquest of England was Robert himself. The image of the virtuous, gentle duke is correspondingly strengthened.

The entire handling of the rule of Robert the Magnificent by Wace points to a wish to describe the duke as an admirable Christian prince, in a process which culminates with the anecdotes relating to Robert's pilgrimage to Jerusalem. The duke's serious intent is emphasised in the French text by the description of his penitential garb (2935) and the care with which he arranges his affairs before

---

[88] The gift of the Vexin in exchange for Robert's help is also mentioned by Orderic Vitalis in his *Historia Ecclesiastica*.

setting out. He has his young son William formally recognised as his heir by the Norman barons (2947–64) and by the king of France, who seizes the child of Normandy;[89] the fears of the Normans (to which Wace gives a prominent place, 2937–46) are further allayed by his appointing Alan of Brittany as regent of the land during his absence (though the narrator, in a proleptic comment, mentions that Alan did not live long after this, and was buried at Fécamp; 2977–86). The anecdotes relative to the pilgrimage itself show various facets of the duke's character: his humility (anecdote of the gatekeeper who whacked the duke on the back to make him hurry out of town, 2996–3036) and sense of humour (the gift of his cape to the 'underdressed' statue of Constantine in Rome, 3043–58, and his jest about his Saracen litter-bearers, 3121–50); the appropriateness of his behaviour (in the three anecdotes that take place at Constantinople) and his generous almsgiving (he pays the entry tax to Jerusalem for the poor pilgrims, 3151–210). Two of these anecdotes (in the Constantinople section) were already present in Wace's manuscript of the *Gesta Normannorum Ducum*, interpolated by the St Etienne of Caen redactor; the others were added by Wace from unidentified sources.

The munificence of Robert looms large in the stories relative to his pilgrimage, though Wace's interpretation of his actions does not necessarily coincide with that of the Saint-Etienne interpolator. The third of these anecdotes in the French poem, which relates Robert's orders to have his mule shod with gold, forbidding his followers to pick up any horseshoe he might lose, is explained by the Latin writer by the desire of the duke to counter the reputation for avarice the French had among the Greeks; and the emperor initially assumes that Robert is the king of France, because of his liberal spending. Neither of these points is retained by Wace, who thus attenuates Robert's ostentatiousness; the golden horseshoes remain unexplained and, coming immediately after the anecdote where Robert gave his mantle to the statue of Constantine to honour the emperor, they appear to be some form of recognition of the importance of Constantinople within the pilgrimage, or a way of giving alms to travellers following them. The fifth pilgrimage anecdote in the French text follows closely the story related in the Saint-Etienne interpolation: offended by the duke's refusal of all his gifts, the emperor of Constantinople forbids the selling of anything to the Normans in order to force them to accept his hospitality. However, Robert ingeniously has his men cook their meals with discarded nutshells instead of wood. The emperor relents and allows his subjects to sell goods to the Normans again. We are clearly dealing with a battle of wills between Robert and the emperor, and Robert comes out the winner; a point further emphasised in the French work by the embedding of this story within another anecdote, from an unknown source. On his arrival in Constantinople, Robert has an audience with the emperor; as was the custom, he spread his mantle on the floor to sit on it. He left it there as he departed, and to one of the Greeks who handed it back to him, he answered: 'Jeo ne port pas mun banc od mei', 'I do not carry my seat with me' (3080). All the other Normans followed

---

[89] This detail is not to be found in the *Gesta Normannorum Ducum*, but something similar is suggested by William of Malmesbury, *Gesta regum Anglorum* iii. 230, who states that King Henry of France was appointed as overseer of William's guardian.

his example. The conclusion to this story comes after the anecdote of the nutshells (3115–20):

> Pur la noblece des Normanz,
> qui de lur manteals firent bancz,
> fist l'enperere el paleis faire
> bancs e sieges envirun l'eire;
> ainz cel tens a terre seeient
> ki el paleis seeir voleient.[90]

Not only is Robert capable of holding his own against the all-powerful emperor of Constantinople, he also teaches him a lesson in civilised behaviour and is at the origin of an improvement in the quality of hospitality in the palace.

Most of Wace's account of Robert's deeds in the Holy Land are additions to the narrative of his main source and build up a saintly image in keeping with the duke's end, in full enjoyment of the indulgence that was connected with a pilgrimage to Jerusalem and without having had the opportunity for further sin. The *Gesta Normannorum Ducum* is very concise here: Robert spends 8 days at the Holy Sepulchre (vi. 11 (12), four lines of text), then sets back home; he falls ill in Nicaea, where he dies on 2 July 1035 and where he is buried by his men (vi. 12 (13), 15 lines of text). By contrast, the French poem devotes some 130 octosyllabic lines to this final phase of Robert's rule. Wace's first interpolation relates to the illness the duke develops, prompting him to hire local (Saracen) men to carry him to Jerusalem in a litter (3127–50). He meets a Norman pilgrim, whom he entrusts with a message for his friends (3143–8):

> "Dites," dist il, "a mes amis
> e a la gent de mun païs,
> ke as diables trestut vifs
> me faz porter en paraïs;
> paiens me unt en lur cols levé
> ki m'en portent a Damnedé."[91]

This witticism, which may have been interpreted by some of Wace's contemporaries as prophetic, shows the duke as a sort of peaceful crusader, gaining the goodwill of the Saracens through his munificence rather than by force. The crusading dimension comes to the fore in the anecdote immediately following, where the narrator describes the status of Christians in Jerusalem at the time of Robert's pilgrimage (3151–62):

> A cel terme e a cel tens
> ert Jerusalem as paiens,
> par tut le regne de Surie

---

[90] 'Because of the nobility of the Normans, who made benches out of their mantles, the emperor had benches and seats made in the palace, all round the hall; before that time, everyone who wanted to be seated in the palace sat on the floor.'

[91] 'Tell my friends', he said, 'and the people in my country, that, alive and well, I am having myself carried to paradise by devils; pagans, who are carrying me to the Lord God, have raised me up shoulder high.'

> ert as paiens la seignurie;
> tute esteit la terre as paiens,
> n'i aveit gueires crestïens,
> e cil qui lores i maneient
> as paiens tuit suget esteient.
> N'i poeit pelerin entrer
> en Jherusalem pur urer
> ki ainz ne dunast un besant
> u or u argent al vaillant.[92]

The viewpoint is that of someone for whom the reality of the Holy Land is now the Kingdom of Jerusalem and the Crusader States, where Christians no longer have to pay tribute in order to have access to the holy shrines; and while no overt support is expressed for the crusading movement that brought about this change, there is no doubt that Wace is describing 'bad old days' characterised by pagan oppression. The gates of Jerusalem are surrounded by crowds of poor pilgrims who have been denied entry in their thousands because they do not have the money. Duke Robert's compassion and charity impels him to pay for their entry; whereupon the lord of the city, impressed by such generosity, exempts the duke and all those who had entered with him of the tax, and hands over the day's takings to Duke Robert (who immediately distributes everything to the poor). In addition to its primary function of illustrating Duke Robert's qualities of generosity and Christian solidarity, this story is noteworthy for the positive depiction of the pagan ruler of Jerusalem, explicitly said to be 'de grant valur', 'of great worth' (3195), and who proves to be eager to emulate the example of the Norman duke. Robert does not need force of arms to incline the Saracens in favour of Christian ways.

Such virtue, however, was bound to meet with opposition, and Robert is murdered on his way back to Normandy. William of Jumièges ascribes Robert's death to illness, but Wace, in agreement with William of Malmesbury (ii. 178), makes it quite clear that the cause of death was poison; he furthermore states that Count Drogo died from drinking the same drink as the duke. The name of the poisoner is not given in the French work – he is simply referred to as 'un pautonier', 'a scoundrel' (3214) – though William of Malmesbury says it was a certain Ralph, surnamed Mowin, who had hopes of succeeding Robert to the dukedom. This could well be an instance of Wace trying to preserve the surviving relatives of the poisoner from the shame of widespread exposure; or influences may have been brought to bear. The death of Count Drogo is mentioned by Orderic Vitalis,[93] but not the cause of his death; the entrusting of the relics obtained in Jerusalem by Duke Robert to his chamberlain Turstin, who sent them to the abbey of Cerisy, is found in Wace alone. Wace seems to be aware that he is transmitting little-known facts here, as he makes a point of sketching out the

---

[92] 'At that time and in those days Jerusalem belonged to the pagans; throughout the entire kingdom of Syria the power lay in pagan hands. All the land was theirs and there were scarcely any Christians there; those who dwelt there at the time were totally subject to the pagans. No pilgrim could enter Jerusalem to pray without giving a besant or the equivalent in gold or silver before doing so.'

[93] *Historia Ecclesiastica* ii. 102; Chibnall, ed., vol. 2, pp. 116–17.

chain of transmission for his information, in the (unfortunately corrupt) line 3225: 'de par sa mere fu sis aives', literally, 'he was his grandfather through his mother', but now generally thought to be a scribal error for 'de par [m]a mere fu [m]is aives', 'he was my grandfather on my mother's side'. The mention of the relics allows Wace to end the rule of Duke Robert within the established pattern: his lasting achievements in Normandy (the abbey of Cerisy), the sadness at his death, and the length of his rule, before moving on to his successor, the child William.

The abundance of anecdotes in this section of the *Troisième Partie* suggests that Duke Robert the Magnificent was already turning into a semi-legendary character at the time Wace was writing. He may have been the inspiration for the character of Robert le Diable, the hero of the twelfth-century romance of the same title: the son of a duke of Normandy conceived through the help of the devil and who, after living up to his demonic beginnings, converts, fights to defend Christendom and dies in a state of grace.[94] Wace's depictions of Richard II and Robert the Magnificent appear to have provided a template of baronial excellence for later writers; they certainly seem to underlie, in an adapted and conflated form, the figure of Richart de Montivilliers, wise upholder of social balance through his respect for nobility, great warrior, good Christian and advisor to the emperor in the late twelfth-century romance *L'Escoufle*, by Jean Renart. Though Wace's Duke Robert is very much a historical character, in comparison with the *Gesta Normannorum Ducum*, Wace's Robert appears as more detached from the political realities of his time; we see relatively little of the duke as secular ruler and warleader, and what glimpses we do get are marginalised by the wealth of anecdotes introduced by Wace. Robert the Magnificent is well on the way to becoming the perfect romance hero. However, within the overall logic of the episode (and of the *Troisième Partie* in general), this idealising of Duke Robert is not an aim in itself but provides a suitable build-up towards the 'pièce de résistance' of the work: the future William the Conqueror.

All anecdotes in the *Troisième Partie* up to Robert the Magnificent have a more or less direct connection with the ruling duke (or, as we have seen, his consort); but in this section, we find an unexpected series of anecdotes relative to his son, which are inserted immediately after the account of Robert's failed invasion of England (2730–822) and have no equivalent in the *Gesta Normannorum Ducum*. The unborn child is aligned with the likes of Alexander or Arthur through a prophetic dream of his mother's describing him as a huge tree, and the midwife at the infant William's birth likewise interprets the newborn's seizing the straw of his bed as an omen of greatness (material derived from William of Malmesbury's *Gesta Regum* iii. 229). The parallel between Arthur and William is further reinforced by the fact that Duke Robert, like King Uther, is eventually murdered by poison. Wace also introduces a biblical flavour to the conception and birth of William in two further anecdotes. Young Arlot/Arlette tearing her shift from top to bottom before going to bed with Duke Robert, explained by the girl herself as a gesture of respect for the dignity of the duke (2823–46), also carries connotations

---

[94] See Alexandre Micha, *Robert le Diable* (Paris, 1996), pp. 7–19.

of the tearing of the veil of the Temple, thus lending dignity to what, in truth, was an instance of ducal fornication, and countering the potential taint on Arlette's character. Similarly, the episode where old William Talvas of Bellême, seeing William for the first time, prophecies that the child will do much harm to his lineage and curses him (2895–922) reads as an inversion of Simeon's prophecy at the Presentation of Christ at the Temple (Luke 2.25–35). As the Bellême family is consistently represented as treacherous and evil by Wace (see lines 2453–520), William appears as a providential child come to save his people from the likes of William Talvas. It is most unlikely that these anecdotes were made up by Wace himself; quite apart from the fact that total invention was not part of his methodology, it is fairly certain that the circulation of stories such as these would have been encouraged in William's lifetime, to compensate for his illegitimate birth. All of these anecdotes are connected with Falaise, where William's mother came from and where he was brought up; Wace could have heard of them through members of his own family (if his grandfather really was the duke's chamberlain, he would have been privy to many events that took place behind closed doors), or as gossip circulating in the ducal administration entrusted with the dissemination of such propaganda. Whatever their exact provenance, these stories have as consequence the overshadowing of Robert the Magnificent by his son, born to surpass his father in dignity and power.

8

William II of Normandy – the Conqueror

The rule of William II of Normandy takes up more than half of the *Troisième Partie*, covering some 6100 octosyllabic lines out of a total of 11440; in terms of length, this is therefore the most important episode in the work. The rule of his son and successor Duke Robert Curthose, at under 1800 lines in length, appears by comparison as a rather half-hearted postscript, thus echoing (whether by design or by accident) the impact of the Arthurian section and its aftermath in Geoffrey of Monmouth's *Historia Regum Britanniae* and in Wace's own *Roman de Brut*. However, William II of Normandy fails to attain the mythical stature of an Arthur, or even that of the more striking of his own forebears. The main reason for this lies in the fact that the material was too recent. From this point onwards, Wace has to tread carefully over what must have been a political minefield. He appears to have been under pressure from local families to include them in high-profile events such as the Battle of Hastings and omit them from accounts of unsuccessful rebellion; hence the presence of certain names in the *Gesta Normannorum Ducum* or other key sources unmentioned in Wace's narrative, and vice-versa. His favoured 'ne sai', which in the *Roman de Brut* and much of the preceding part of the *Rou* had been used as a device to set in greater relief the significance of what was being said through the very triviality of the information claimed not to be known, is increasingly used as a hedging device to avoid being drawn into taking sides. Of the hostility opposing Waukelin of Ferrières and Hugh of Montfort, at the beginning of the rule of young William, Wace coyly remarks: 'ne sai ki out dreit ne ki tort', 'I do not know who was in the right and who was in the wrong' (3256); and more forcibly, in the account of the battle of Val-ès-Dunes (4131–5):

> Ne vos voil dire, ne ne sai
> ne jeo escrit trové ne l'ai,
> ne jeo n'i fui, ne jeo nel vi,
> li quel d'els melz se combati,
> mais jeo sai que li reis venqui.[1]

Similarly, he sidesteps the thorny issue of the sincerity of Edward the Confessor's deathbed naming of Harold as his successor (5820, 'ne sai se par boen coer le fist'; 'I do not know whether he did so with a willing heart').

---

[1] 'I do not wish to tell you which of them fought better, nor can I, and I have not found it in writing; I was not there and did not see it, but I know that the king [i.e., of France] won the day.'

In terms of use of sources, Wace's main source, the *Gesta Normannorum Ducum*, had imperatively to be supplemented, as the account of William de Jumièges frequently becomes extremely terse from this stage; and those supplementary sources, depending on whether they were Norman or English, were likely to be in conflict. Once again, 'ne sai' becomes a useful way of signalling divergent traditions without rejecting any outright, as in the aside (quoted below) on the reasons for Harold's visit to Normandy.[2] Wace has just given an 'English' version of events, derived from the account of Eadmer in his *Historia Novorum*, whereby Harold had crossed the Channel in order to secure the release of relatives of his who had been sent to Normandy as hostages (5597–612):

> Issi l'ai jo trové escrit;
> e uns altres livres me dit
> que li reis le rova aler,
> por le realme asseürer
> al duc Guilliame, son cosin,
> que il l'eüst emprés sa fin;
> ne sai mie certe achaison,
> mais l'un e l'autre escrit trovon.
> Que que besoigne qu'il quesist
> e que que rien faire volsist,
> Heraut a la veie se mist,
> coment que pois li avenist;
> aventure qui estre dit
> ne poet remaindre qu'el ne seit,
> e chose qui deit avenir
> ne poet por nule chose faillir.[3]

The concluding allusion to divine providence is clearly meant to be conciliatory: the means by which things happen are secondary, what is important is that these things did happen, because they were intended to by God. However, as noted by Holden, it is striking that the version of events implicitly validated here by Wace is not the official Norman one, but that of a competing (even hostile) English tradition.[4] This is to be the hallmark of the section of the *Troisième Partie* relative to events that take place in England: English historians are repeatedly preferred to their Norman counterparts.

Wace clearly conducted painstaking research prior to composing the account of William's rule and deeds. In addition to the *Gesta Normannorum Ducum*, he

---

[2] Another striking use of 'ne sai' as a device to avoid having to choose between conflicting accounts is to be found in the passage relating Harold's death. The expression recurs three times in close succession: 'ne sai se de cel colp morut' (8827), 'jo ne sai qui l'ocist' (8834), and the emphatic 'Ne sai dire, ne jo nel di/ ne jo n'i fui, ne jo nel vi,/ ne a maistre dire n'oï/ qui le rei Heraut abati' (8851–4), which closely echoes lines 4131–5 quoted above.

[3] 'I have found this in writing, but another book has informed me that the king, to ensure that the kingdom passed to Duke William, his cousin, after his death, asked Harold to go to him. I do not know which is the correct explanation, but we can find both in writing. Whatever business he was pursuing and whatever he intended to do, Harold set out, no matter how things would turn out for him; an event which has to take place cannot be prevented, and something which has to happen cannot fail to do so for any reason.'

[4] Holden, *Le Roman de Rou*, Introduction (chapter VII: 'Sources'), p. 147.

makes full use of Orderic Vitalis's *Historia Ecclesiastica*, William of Malmesbury's *Gesta Regum Anglorum* and William of Poitiers' account of the Battle of Hastings, the *Gesta Guillelmi*, as well as of a number of minor sources such as the anonymous *Brevis relatio*, Guy of Amiens's *Carmen de Hastingae Proelio*, monastic archives (especially of the abbey of Cerisy) and family traditions. Where these sources clash, Wace chooses on a case-by-case basis; the degree of authority granted to his various sources by the poet does not always coincide with the views of modern historians, and he occasionally introduces factual errors. This typically happens when the information appears to have been derived from 'common knowledge' in the poet's circle; for example, Wace credits Roger of Montgomery with great feats of arms at Hastings (8281–90), something we know to be factually incorrect, as Montgomery was not present at the battle. As in previous sections, the errors can be of a genealogical nature, as when Wace states that William and Matilda had three sons and two daughters (4509–11), whereas they had four sons and at least five daughters.[5] But there is no doubt that Wace made a real effort to produce a history that would be as trustworthy as possible. The rare instances where he introduces factual errors into his work are overwhelmingly compensated for by the accuracy of most of the information he transmits. His informants might sometimes have misremembered, but the information given by the poet's father regarding the Norman fleet that set out to conquer England, for example, is certainly more credible than the exaggerated accounts of the Latin histories which otherwise would have been our only source of information.

Contrary to the view that held sway among historians during much of the twentieth century, Wace did not make up anything.[6] His list of the William's companions at Hastings, after having been deemed historically worthless, is now accepted as reflecting local and family traditions that can in certain cases be corroborated by external evidence. Elisabeth van Houts, in her groundbreaking study of this list, concludes

> The stories of the descendants of the Conqueror's companions might be piecemeal, slightly distorted or incomplete, but Wace nevertheless recognized their importance and included them in his history. Where he could he put them alongside written traditions as found in the Latin narratives or charters.[7]

Wace is therefore writing as a historian rather than as an adaptor of pre-existing historical writings. He has to select and make sense of his raw material himself, while his material in turn dictates the shape of his narrative. The constraint of historical truthfulness limits the historiographer's degree of control over the

---

[5] It is however possible that Wace was deliberately not counting children who did not live long enough to achieve anything of note. Another example of such a 'genealogical' error occurs in the final section of the *Roman de Rou*, where William, King Henry I's son, is said to have married Geoffrey of Anjou's sister, where in fact she was his aunt.

[6] See for example J. H. Round, *Feudal England: Historical Studies on the Eleventh and Twelfth Centuries* (London, 1895), pp. 258–321, or D. C. Douglas, 'Companions of the Conqueror', *History* 27 (1943): 129–47.

[7] E. M. C. van Houts, 'Wace as Historian', pp. 103–32 in *Family Trees and the Roots of Politics*, ed. K. S. B. Keats-Rohan (Woodbridge, 1997), quote p. 114.

structure, content and outlook of his work. Some inconvenient details might be passed over in silence (as we have seen in Wace's account of the rule of Robert the Magnificent), but key events would have to be mentioned, however potentially inimical to one's historiographical agenda.

Stylistically, the rule of William II follows the same pattern as the rest of the *Rou*, the main difference being in the prominence given to battle scenes in general and to the Battle of Hastings in particular. The depiction of William by Wace is very much that of a warrior duke, and the tone of this section of the work is markedly epic, with a recurrent use of 'Eis vos', 'Lo!', and 'lors/mult/dunc/ veïssiez ...', 'You would [then] have seen [great/many] ...'. Descriptive passages in high style, characterised by anaphora, isolocon and *enumeratio*, occur at some length, especially in the key battles of William's rule, chief among which is of course the Battle of Hastings. However, the very accumulation of such devices tends to weaken their effectiveness; modern readers frequently find their attention wavering. This is to some extent due to the fact that early twenty-first century readers have little exposure to – and therefore, reduced appreciation of – the epic as a literary genre; but it is also a consequence of the constraint of historical accuracy placed upon Wace at this stage. He was telling a story that was well known to his intended audience, and therefore he could not add 'ornamental' elements at will, or reshape the sequence of key events. The result is at times a certain feeling of *déjà vu*, particularly for the reader with little or no interest in the poem as historiography.

The tension between the celebratory, propagandist dimension to the *Roman de Rou* and Wace's obvious concern for historical 'truth' is a major challenge in this section of the work. Wace's response to this problem is threefold. First, he attempts to make the early rule of William conform to the pattern established in the accounts of previous dukes, through the remodelling of the sequence of certain events in his main source, the *Gesta Normannorum Ducum*. Secondly, he creates a nexus of thematic links between William and his ancestor Duke Richard I (whose deeds open the *Troisième Partie*) through the addition of anecdotes. The Arthurian dimension thus introduced allows Wace to present the build-up to the Battle of Hastings, and the Battle itself, in a stylised mode strongly reminiscent of Geoffrey of Monmouth's account of Arthur's Roman wars. Finally, Wace omits from his narrative any account of the actual conquest and pacifying of England after Hastings, where the celebratory stance would have been exceedingly difficult to maintain.

Subduing Normandy

The rules of the different dukes of the *Roman de Rou* in general, but more especially in the *Troisième Partie*, follow a loose pattern whereby the new ruler has to confront challenges to his authority among his own, Norman barons and then has to defend his lands from external interference, typically, though not by any means exclusively, by the king of France. Internal strife after the initial stage where the new duke establishes his command over Normandy tends to be underplayed, thus giving the impression of a (more or less) smooth progression from relative weakness to increasing strength, culminating in a review of the duke's cultural achievements – predominantly religious foundations – which in turn lead to the account of his death and succession. The difficulty with the career pattern of William II of Normandy is that it was anything but neat, with rebellious barons, aggressive Angevin neighbours, a hostile French king and complications in England messily intertwined throughout the earlier part of William's rule. The young duke spends his childhood and youth faced with a string of crises: internal feuding plunges Normandy into a situation of near-anarchy; the king of France takes advantage of the situation to humiliate the Normans, forcing them to hand over to him the fortress of Tillières and ravaging the land; William's uncle allies himself to the king of France in an unsuccessful attempt to usurp the dukedom; and his foster brother leads a coalition against him and plots his murder. William eventually has to seek the help of the king of France to quash the Norman opposition. His neighbour, Geoffrey Martel of Anjou, seizes Domfront and Alençon, which William has to reconquer; the king of France attacks Normandy and is routed in battle, but Geoffrey Martel resumes hostilities and the king of France mounts another, retaliatory (and unsuccessful) expedition.

Wace gives a semblance of order to events by creating implicit breaks between William's infancy, his youth and his maturity, forging a quasi-organic correlation between the person of the young duke and the authority he wields. William's infancy is thus placed under the shadow of anarchy and French strength. When William is old enough to act himself, he encounters his first successes, quashing the rebellion of his uncle William of Arques and defeating the French army supporting the Norman rebels (3399–560); however, the young duke remains very vulnerable, and has not yet attained his full potential. Wace adds two pieces of information (the sources for which are unknown) that emphasise this point. Alfred the Giant, one of his father's stalwarts, becomes a monk in Cerisy rather than helping William to defend himself (3561–84): a pious decision presented as praiseworthy by the narrator, but which suggests that the support given to the young duke by the Norman barons was at best lukewarm. William's isolation is further revealed in a striking anecdote connected with the rebellion of William of Arques's foster brother Guy the Burgundian, Nigel of the Cotentin and Ranulf of the Bessin. William has now been duke for 12 years, we are told (3585), but he clearly cannot trust his entourage. A fool wakes up William in the middle of the night, warning him of a plot to murder him; the young duke flees immediately, and seeks refuge with Hubert of Rie, who has him escorted to safety in Falaise, while he himself puts William's pursuers off the scent. The incident caused great unease in Normandy (3641–762).

At the root of the barons' hostility towards their young duke is clearly his bastardy: this is mentioned explicitly as the reason for the rebellion of William of Arques (3623–8), while young William's pursuers ask Hubert of Ryes if he has seen 'le bastart'. The future Conqueror therefore still has to establish the legitimacy of his rule among his own people. The anecdote of William's near-escape is the object of a degree of stylistic and rhetorical adornment, indicating that Wace considered it to be of some importance. The words of mad Goles appear in direct speech, with repetition, exclamation and rhetorical questions, giving the warning special impact (3655–62):

> "Ovrez," dist il, "ovrez, ovrez!
> Ja morreiz tuit, levez, levez!
> Ou giés Guilliame? por quei dorz?
> S'ateinz i es ja seras morz;
> ti enemi se vont armer,
> se ci te poent ja trover
> ja mais n'iestras de Costentin,
> ne ne vivras jusqu'al matin."[8]

A terrified William grabs a cloak to go over his breeches and shirt, jumps on a horse and hurries off as quickly as he can, a haste underscored by the narrator's 'ne sai s'il out nul eperon/ ne se il quist nul compaignon', 'I do not know whether he had any spurs or whether he sought any companion' (3671–2). This is a potentially comic scene, but the threat turns out to be a real one, and William's fear only too well founded. He has managed to get away from the assassins, but he does not know where to turn for help, 'ker ne se sout en qui fier', 'for he did not know whom to trust' (3682). This passage depicts a Guillaume reminiscent of his forebear Richard I in the *Deuxième Partie*, isolated, vulnerable and surrounded by enemies. Like Richard I, salvation comes from a faithful vassal who uses ruse to get his young duke to safety. Hubert of Ryes is the hero of this anecdote; he interacts with William, his three sons and the assassins in direct speech, showing himself to be loyal, assertive and wily – he insists on leading the way to William's pursuants, misleadingly claiming the first blow (3727–30). The overall picture is one of treachery among the great barons and the towns of Normandy, but of loyalty among the minor barons and the common people (represented by the fool Goles), thus reinforcing the reader's sympathy for the young duke. The assassination plot inserted by Wace into his narrative also has a political function, inasmuch as it provides additional motivation for William's decision to appeal to King Henry of France for help: an alliance that, within the moral outlook of the *Roman de Rou*, would appear to be somewhat against nature, France being the hereditary enemy, but which will lead to William's victory over the Norman rebels at Val-ès-Dunes in 1047. Thereafter starts what one may term William's maturity, culminating in the conquest of England.

In order to create a sense of progression in William's career, Wace modifies the sequence the events as recounted in his main source, the *Gesta Normannorum Ducum* – an uncharacteristic, and therefore noteworthy, departure from his usual procedure. In particular, the English narrative strand is excluded from the narrative prior to the battle of Val-ès-Dunes, whereas in the *Gesta Normannorum Ducum*, the death of King Canute and the ensuing bids for the English throne are mentioned before the account of the revolt led by Guy of Burgundy and Nigel of the Cotentin, and thus well before the battle of Val-ès-Dunes.[9] This battle, which

---

[8] 'Open up', he said, 'Open up! You will all be killed, get up, get up! Where are you lying, William? Why are you sleeping? If you are attacked here, you will soon be killed. Your enemies are arming themselves. If they can find you here, you will never get out of the Cotentin and not live till the morning.'

[9] The death of Canute, the unsuccessful attempt to conquer the throne by Alfred and Edward, and the rise of Earl Godwin, appear in *Gesta Normannorum Ducum* vii. 5 (8) – 6 (9); the revolt that led to Val-ès-Dunes is recounted in *Gesta Normannorum Ducum* vii. 7 (17).

was beyond dispute an important historical event, is depicted as a triumph over internal difficulties that will enable William to look beyond Normandy. The battle itself is described in great detail (3801–4194), with substantial additions found only in Wace's work and extensive borrowings from William of Poitiers and William of Malmesbury.[10] After gaining victory, William subdues his barons, reconquers the land wrongly taken from him (including by the count of Anjou, Geoffrey Martel), marries and has children. Then, and then only, does Wace allow the English connection to assert itself.

Something new in William's ducal career is announced through the addition of a lengthy anecdote relative to William's uncle, Archbishop Maugier. Maugier opposes William's marriage with Matilda on grounds of consanguinity and excommunicates them; William and Matilda have to give alms on a huge scale and build abbeys in atonement. The appropriateness of the match is implicitly vindicated in the French work through the mention of the children the couple had: three sons and two daughters, one of whom made a good marriage and continued the line, while the other became an abbess at Caen (4509–18).[11] Wace does not only appear to approve of the union; he also turns Maugier into an extraordinary and morally dubious character. Whereas Wace's sources merely mention Maugier's scandalous behaviour and subsequent exile in the isles off the Cotentin peninsula, Wace depicts the archbishop as a magician who has spirits and demons at his beck and call (4573–6):

> Plusors distrent por verité
> que un deiable aveit privé,
> ne sai s'esteit luitun ou non,
> ne sai nïent de sa façon.[12]

In addition to having a familiar (called Toret), Maugier has the gift of prophecy, though ironically he fails to realise that the death he foresees is his own. As in the opening anecdotes of the *Troisième Partie*, where the Normandy of Richard I takes on Arthurian overtones, Wace has created through the figure of the seer Maugier a parallel between William and King Arthur; this latter-day Merlin-figure is however a villain, plundering the churches of Rouen, and eventually going to live with a concubine after having taken his vows in Fécamp.

This anecdote brings to an end the 'enfances' (i.e., youthful exploits) part of William's rule; immediately following comes the account of Edward and Alfred's disastrous attempt to reconquer the throne of England following the death of King Canute, and Edward's eventual accession to the throne. Wace combines the material present in his copy of the *Gesta Normannorum Ducum* with extensive borrowings from William of Poitiers and, possibly, William of Malmesbury and Henry of Huntingdon, to create an extremely negative image of

---

[10] Wace's main additions (3841–4006 and 4051–112) have a strong focus on the deeds of Ralph Taisson, one of William's supporters, and his companions at arms. He may have been echoing accounts preserved by the families of these men.

[11] As noted above, Wace seems to have got his figures wrong here.

[12] 'Many people said in truth that he had a devil as familiar, I do not know whether or not it was a kind of goblin; I know nothing about it.'

the English and in particular of Earl Godwin, who is depicted as the arch-traitor (4679–90):

> Oez com faite deablie,
> grant traïson, grant felonie!
> Traïtre fu, traïson fist,
> qui en la lei Judas se mist;
> le filz son naturel seignor
> e qui esteit eir de l'enor,
> deçut li traïtre e traï
> come Judas qui Deu vendi;
> salué l'aveit e baisié
> e en s'escuële mangié,
> e bien l'aveit asseüré
> de porter fei e lealté.[13]

Not only is Godwin Judas-like in his dealings with Alfred, he and his king Harold Harefoot (an illegitimate son of King Canute) treat the unfortunate prince's companions with inhuman cruelty, cutting off the heads of nine out of ten men, then repeating the process once again (4705–12). Wace compounds Godwin's moral inadequacy by emphasising his ignoble origins, making his name ('Goïne') rhyme with 'de pute orine', 'of bad birth' (4669–70). This demonisation of Godwin prepares the reader/audience for the problems William will later encounter with his offspring.

Harold Harefoot dies and is succeeded by Edward's half-brother Harthacnut, who invites him to return to England; when Harthacnut dies a couple of years after having been made king, Edward succeeds him (4713–40). He marries a daughter of Earl Godwin, with whom, says Wace (following Orderic's interpolation in the *Gesta Normannorum Ducum*), he lived chastely and therefore had no children. However, we are told, 'le duc Guilliame ama tant/ comme son frere e son enfant', 'he loved Duke William just as much as he would his own brother and child' (4751–2). The king's lack of issue or surviving brothers, but with a strong bond with William, foreshadows the events to come, and adds verisimilitude to William's eventual claim to the English throne.

Though Wace concentrates all these events in one neat section, it is obvious that they take place over a number of years, and that in strictly chronological terms, they should have been mentioned sooner in the narrative (as in his sources). By placing these events after the settling of William's internal problems, Wace creates an impression of broadening perspectives for the young duke. England is established as a future area of legitimate expansion, with an impending succession crisis on the death of the childless Edward the Confessor. But first, William has to strengthen his position in relation to his French neighbours.

---

[13] 'Hear what devilry, great treason and great felony he committed! He was a traitor and committed treason, following in the footsteps of Judas. The traitor deceived and betrayed the son of his natural lord and the heir to the domain, as Judas had betrayed Jesus. He had greeted him and kissed him, eaten from his bowl and assured him he would bear him faith and loyalty.'

Confronting external threats

Having secured Normandy, William has to face threats from two immediate neighbours: the lord of Anjou, Geoffrey Martel, whom William expelled from usurped lands in the aftermath of Val-ès-Dunes (4227–495) and whose hostility remains unabated, and the king of France, who from ally at Val-ès-Dunes soon reverts to the role of antagonist. The theme of French ill-will and treachery towards the Normans is emphasised in a short passage in direct speech, in which the French king is convinced to wrest Normandy from the Normans (4757–66):

> Mult ont Franceis Normanz laidiz
> e de mesfaiz e de mesdiz,
> sovent lor dient reproviers
> e claiment bigoz e draschiers,
> sovent les ont meslez al rei,
> sovent dient: "Sire, por quei
> ne tolez la terre as bigoz?
> As voz ancestors e as noz
> la tolirent lor anceisor,
> qui par mer vindrent robeor."[14]

This resentment of the Normans in general adds itself to the contempt felt by the French for William himself because of his low-born mother. The besieged people of Alençon, during the reconquest of Normandy following Val-ès-Dunes, make a point of taunting William with his grandfather's trade: 'La pel, la pel al parmentier,/ ço apartient a son mestier', 'The hide, the tailor's hide, that is what belongs to his trade!' (4319–20). The perceived unworthiness of William may explain the surprisingly long list of allies supporting the king of France in this new campaign, ranging from Flanders to beyond the Seine (4779–805); as ever in the *Roman de Rou*, the Normans are blameless in this affair, which is motivated exclusively by French avarice and jealousy. William is shown to be fighting the same fight for survival as his ancestors, against the superior numbers of their French adversary.

During their campaign, the French are described as 'mult orgueillos, mult cruels e mult damagos', 'very arrogant, very cruel and very destructive' (4859–60), acting in a way similar to the pagan hordes of a Gurmund in the *Roman de Brut*, or those of the unconverted Vikings earlier in the *Roman de Rou*. They plunder, rape and destroy, indulging in carousing all night with the food and drink seized during the day: a fatal error, which will allow William and his men to massacre them at Mortemer, after having spread panic in the town by setting it on fire. The king of France has to retreat in humiliating conditions and promises not to support Geoffrey Martel against William in the future, in exchange for the release of the French prisoners. Geoffrey Martel figures here as a latter-day

---

[14] 'The French abused the Normans both through bad deeds and bad words. They often reproached them, calling them "bigoz" and eaters of pigswill and often setting the king against them, saying: "My lord, why do you not take the land away from the bigoz? Their ancestors, brigands who came by sea, took it away from your ancestors and from ourselves." '

version of Arnulf of Flanders, whose conflict with William Longsword eventually ended in the duke's murder. He is very much the enemy of William, determined not to lose the territories under his authority; and as with Arnulf of Flanders, Geoffrey Martel eventually manages to convince the king of France to renege on his settlement with the Normans, triggering off yet another campaign ending (once again) in disaster for France. At Varaville, the French troups, retreating from the Norman knights, archers and peasants defending the town, make a bridge collapse under their weight and are massacred. The king has to retreat and dies soon afterwards, leaving the crown to his son Philip, with whom Duke William is on friendly terms. The French threat is over. William can move on to greater things. It is the end of William's defensive wars.

That this is a major turning-point in the narrative is indicated by the presence of an autobiographical parenthesis, where Wace tells us all we know of him: his birth in Jersey, his studies in Caen, then in France; his literary activity in Caen; his prebend in Bayeux thanks to King Henry II of England. Whether Henry II would have appreciated this section of the *Troisième Partie* is doubtful. Wace has in effect taken sides against one of his father's forebears, in order to extol his maternal great-grandfather: Henry II was Angevin quite as much as he was Norman, and even though these events were well-known facts, Wace's presentation of them partakes more of the outlook of a Dudo than of an Anglo-Angevin courtier. However, the tensions that this account of hostility between Anjou and Normandy could have caused are carefully kept in check. William's victorious struggle against his French neighbours is dealt with relatively briefly (less than 600 lines) and the accent is placed mainly on the two battles of Mortemer and Varaville, thus diluting any political considerations in military and epic detail. Framed as it is by the brief account of Edward the Confessor's accession to the throne of England, then by William's campaign to secure that same throne himself, this section reads as something of a parenthesis in the duke's way to kingship. What might have been the high point in the rule of any other duke of Normandy is here only a preliminary to the big story of how William became king of England.

The claim to England

The third stage in William's progress, where he achieves the kingly status to which his lineage has been shown to be called since Rou, is briefly outlined by Wace (5320–2):

> Comme Guilliame reis devint
> e de l'enor qui(l) li avint,
> e qui sa terre enprés lui tint.[15]

This explicitly places William within a dynastic continuum, as befits the founder

---

[15] 'How William became king, about the domain which came to him and about who held his land after him.'

of a new royal line, and is an accurate description of the end of the *Troisième Partie*: William's obtaining the crown of England, the lands he ruled and his immediate successors. Wace's poem contains just that, and little more; in particular, he provides no account of the actual conquest of England beyond the Battle of Hastings. Moreover, one may note a degree of imprecision in Wace's description of his subject-matter. What successors are we talking about here? William's successors to the throne of England, or his successors to the duchy of Normandy? Or possibly both? At this stage, the reader/listener cannot tell, and Wace allows himself scope to be as selective or as complete as he wishes. This final phase in William's life begins in the same way as the end of other rulers, in the *Roman de Rou* as in the *Roman de Brut*: with an account of his achievements, and more especially his religious foundations (5323–95). We are thus told about the founding of the two abbeys of Saint-Etienne and Sainte Trinité in Caen, the relics placed there, and the establishment of the Trêve de Dieu in William's territories, ensuring a stay on all hostilities from Wednesday evening to Monday morning. But instead of leading on to his death and succession by one of his sons, as would be expected, the narrative takes a new turn, with the statement that (5397–400):

> Guilliame fu de grant bonté,
> mult l'ont estrange gent amé,
> mult fu gentilz e mult corteis
> e mult l'ama Ewart li reis.[16]

The English strand is reintroduced. From now on it will be at the forefront of events.

The English connection is not only in evidence in the narrative; it is also perceptible in the additional authorities Wace uses, which are now regularly insular rather than Norman. Before bringing up the question of Edward's succession, Wace takes pains to depict William as a genuine and caring friend to the English king, adding to his usual sources the account of a state visit of the Norman duke to England, cut short by problems with the Bretons (5401–12). Prior to Wace, this visit is mentioned only in English chronicles. Similarly, Wace's account of the exile of Godwin, the hostages he has to leave at Edward's court as guarantee against further treason and his death choking over food over which the king had made the sign of the Cross (5413–56), is derived from English sources rather than the *Gesta Normannorum Ducum* (with its various interpolations).[17] A number of details relative to Edward the Confessor, equally, were to be found only in insular sources.[18] Neither are Wace's English interests restricted to

---

[16] 'William was a man of great goodness. People from foreign parts loved him very much; he was very noble and courtly and King Edward cherished him.'

[17] On the sources for this section, see Holden, Introduction, pp. 147–61.

[18] Of the various accounts of the life of Edward the Confessor, the closest one to Wace's is that of Aelred of Rievaulx. Indebtedness is chronologically possible. Aelred's *vita* was completed in 1162; it was commissioned to support a second canonisation bid after the first one, in 1138–9, failed. See Joanna Huntington, 'Edward the Celibate, Edward the Saint: Virginity in the Construction of Edward the Confessor', pp. 119–39 in *Medieval Virginities*, ed. A. Bernau, R. Evans and S. Salih (Cardiff, 2003), esp. pp. 120–1. However, by this date, Wace had already started work on his *Rou*, so Aelred's work is unlikely to have shaped Wace's general view of the king and of his part in the events that unfolded after his death.

historical sources: he makes a point of showing off his personal knowledge of the English language, through a learned aside explaining the meaning of the name of the island of Zornee (Thorney), on which Westminster Abbey was built (5510–18):

> Zornee out nom, joste Tamise.
> Zornee por ço l'apelon
> que d'espines i out foison,
> e que l'eve alout environ.
> Ee en engleis isle apelon,
> ee est isle, zorn est espine,
> seit raim, seit arbre, seit racine;
> Zornee ço est en engleis
> isle d'espines en franceis.[19]

The striking feature of this passage is that the narrator's stance seems to be that of an Englishman: '*we* call it Thorney because it had lots of thorns' (5511–12); 'in English *we* call an island *ee*' (5515).[20] This is not conclusive proof that Wace mastered English; but it strongly suggests that by the time he was composing the *Roman de Rou*, he was familiar with the English language as well as with English historiographical tradition, and was not reluctant to advertise the fact.

The villain of this section of the work is, not unexpectedly, Harold Godwinson; but Wace's account betrays a degree of ambivalence on the issue of Edward's plans for his succession and on Harold's motivations at various stages of events. The conflict between the available authorities is acknowledged almost from the outset (5597–604):

> Issi l'ai jo trové escrit;
> e uns altres livres me dit
> que li reis le rova aler,
> por le realme asseürer
> al duc Guilliame, son cosin,
> que il l'eüst emprés sa fin;
> ne sai mie certe achaison,
> mais l'un e l'autre escrit trovon.[21]

The issue at stake here is why Harold set out on his ill-fated voyage to Normandy: was it to negotiate the freedom of his kinsmen, who had been handed over as hostages by his late father, or was it to hand over the realm to William? Was he going against the orders of King Edward who, we are told, distrusted William (5588–96),[22] or was he, on the contrary, sent by him, as stated by William of

---

[19] 'It was called Zornee [Thorney], near the Thames. We call it Zornee because there was an abundance of thorns there and because it was surrounded by water. *Ee* in English we call *isle*; *ee* is *isle*, *zorn* is *espine*, either branch or tree or root. Zornee in English is the *isle d'espines* in French.'

[20] Though in this latter case, it is also possible to translate the line as Burgess does (cf. note above), '*ee* in English, we call *isle*'.

[21] 'I have found this in writing, but another book has informed me that the king, in order to ensure that kingdom passed to Duke William, his cousin, after his death, asked Harold to go to him. I do not know which is the correst explanation, but we can find both in writing.'

[22] This follows the account in Eadmer's *Historia novorum*, Book I, p. 6 (ed. M. Rule (London, 1888))

Jumièges in his *Gesta Normannorum Ducum*? These represent two very different versions of events, neither of them apparently endorsed by Wace who falls back on divine providence as a means of avoiding having to take sides (5605–12), but with a revealing willingness to present at some length the 'pro-Harold' story. Harold's ship is thrown off course and he ends up being taken prisoner by Guy, Count of Ponthieu, who hands him over to William.

What follows corresponds in the main to the sequence in the Bayeux tapestry; indeed, both the tapestry and Wace's account gain from a simultaneous viewing and reading aloud of this section.[23] The French poem essentially follows the *Gesta Normannorum Ducum*, supplemented by William of Poitiers and on occasion Orderic Vitalis, with a handful of passages found only in Wace, drawn from unidentified sources. William keeps Harold at his side, taking him on his campaigns in Brittany and granting him his daughter Adela in exchange for his support in claiming the throne at the death of Edward (5665–80). William has a tub filled with his most precious relics, covers it with a cloth, and makes the unsuspecting Harold swear an oath over them, a trick not mentioned by the Norman historians (5695–8):

> Quant Heraut sus sa main tendi
> la main trembla, la char fremi;
> pois a juré e arami,
> si com uns hoem li eschari.[24]

This scene can be read either as proof of Harold's intention to commit perjury (his trembling indicating a guilty conscience), or of the fact that the oath was taken under duress (his trembling then suggesting fear and unwillingness to repeat the terms imposed on him). Only once he has taken his oath is he allowed to depart for England.

Whether or not the oath was valid (which technically it would not have been if taken under duress),[25] it is noteworthy that throughout the subsequent narrative, Harold is considered to be bound by it, not least by his brother Gyrth, who later pleads with him not to go to battle against William at Hastings (6905–18):

---

where Edward forbids Harold from going to Normandy, on the grounds that he would achieve nothing but damage the whole of the realm of England, and bring shame upon himself. When Harold returns to England, Eadmer also has Edward react to the news (p. 8), saying 'Nonne dixi tibi . . . me Willelmum nosse, et in illo itinere tuo plurima mala huic regno contingere posse?', 'Didn't I tell you that I knew William, and that many evils would befall this realm through your journey?'

[23] I tried the experience in Reading Museum, which has a Victorian copy of the Bayeux tapestry displayed in a more spacious room than the original, with suitable light for reading. Wace's text does not tally perfectly with the tapestry, but the similarities are striking and confirm the existence of twelfth-century alternative accounts, now lost, of these events. A full-colour reproduction of the entirety of the Bayeux tapestry and an overview of the scholarship relating to it may be found in Andrew Bridgeforth's recent *1066: The Hidden History of the Bayeux Tapestry* (London and New York, 2004).

[24] 'When Harold stretched out his hand, his hand trembled and his flesh quivered. Then he solemnly swore and affirmed according to the text someone dictated to him.'

[25] The question of Harold's free will in the matter appears to have been recognised as a real issue among the Norman historiographers as well as in English sources. William of Poitiers, in his account of the oath at Bonneville (*Gesta Guillelmi*, ed. R. H. C. Davis and M. Chibnall (Oxford, 1998), Part 1, ch. 42), takes pains to stress the fact that reputable witnesses have vouched for the fact that Harold took the oath 'libens', 'willingly'. As we can see, Wace is more circumspect.

> "Bel frere," dist il, "remanez,
> mais vos maisnies me livrez,
> en aventure me metrai,
> a Guillame me combatrai;
> n'ai od lui nule covenance
> par serement ne par fiance,
> ne jo ne sui od lui par fei
> ne jo serement ne li dei.
> Tel chose porreit avenir,
> n'i estovreit plus colp ferir.
> Jo criem, se vos vos combatez,
> ad ço que vos vos parjurez,
> que del parjure piés vos seit
> e que cil venque qui a dreit."[26]

This passage follows closely the account of the same scene interpolated by Orderic Vitalis in the *Gesta Normannorum Ducum* (vii. 14(35), pp. 166–9),[27] but the fears expressed by Harold's brother in Orderic's text are on behalf of the English themselves and relate to the fate of the land, rather than just to the person of Harold, 'ne clara libertas Anglorum pereat in tua pernicie', 'lest the liberty of the English should perish through your ruin' (pp. 168–9). In the French text the concern is firmly for Harold himself, and the fact that his oath was binding.[28] William's ruse is therefore decisive for the outcome of the element in the campaign to follow, ensuring that his main rival to the succession of Edward is morally ineligible. The background to the conquest of England has now been set.

With the return of Harold to England begins a new phase in the narrative, corresponding to the second part of William of Poitiers's *Gesta Guillelmi*, which is an important (if sporadic) source throughout the 'Conquest' part of the *Rou*. Wace opens this section with a deathbed scene, explaining why Edward named Harold as his successor. There are no known sources for this scene, which has been interpreted as reflecting a lost, pro-English account;[29] but the circumstances bear a striking resemblance with those surrounding the crowning of Henry I later on in the work, and could be an indirect comment on Wace's part on politically sensitive events closer to his own time. The entire scene is constructed around speeches that contain little of substance that is not to be found in Wace's surviving sources; we are therefore dealing with conventional amplificatory devices exploring a specific crisis where the demands of social stability appear to be in conflict with the rules of succession. Edward's preferred successor, we are

---

[26] 'My fair brother', he said, 'stay here, but let me have your troops. I will take the risk and do battle with William. I have no agreement with him, through oath or pledge. I am not his vassal through allegiance and do not owe him anything on oath. Things could turn out in such a way that there would no longer be any necessity for blows to be struck. I am afraid that, if you do battle with him, in view of the fact that you are perjuring yourself, worse will befall you as a result of your perjury and that he who is in the right will win.'

[27] Orderic repeats the same scene almost literally in his later *Historia Ecclesiastica*, Book III, ii. 145–6 (ed. Chibnall, vol. II, pp. 170–3).

[28] This view was shared by Eadmer, who (p. 9) ascribes the Norman victory to divine punishment for Harold's perjury. Wace is therefore echoing a widespread belief in this matter.

[29] Arnold, in his note on this passage, considers that 'il est évident qu'elle se rattache à la tradition anglaise' (p. 147).

told, was William (5729–30), but William is too far away and is taking too long to come (5731). Harold calls an assembly of the English leaders, who plead with the childless king to designate Harold as successor, for the good of the land: an unnamed Englishman, instructed by Harold, presents the case to the dying king (5743–88) and the entire assembly then supports his words (5793–4). Edward reminds the English that he had promised the land to the duke of Normandy, and that some of them had sworn William support (5797–802). Harold then asks for the crown directly and Edward relents, but with a chilling prophetic vision of what is to come (5809–14):

> "Heraut,", dist li reis, "tu l'avras,
> mais jo sai bien que tu morras;
> se jo onques le duc conui,
> e ses barons qui sunt od lui
> e la grant gent qu'il poet mander,
> rien ne t'en poet, fors Deus, garder."[30]

One may note that Harold's perjury is not mentioned, and that the key objection presented by Edward is William's strength and determination: a somewhat ambivalent view of the duke, particularly when read in the light of the openly negative opinion expressed by Edward before Harold's ill-fated voyage to Normandy (5593–4). Harold remains undaunted and Edward formally gives his assent to the English choosing themselves a king other than William: ' "Ore facent Engleis duc ou rei,/ Heraut ou altre, jo l'otrei" ', ' "Now let the English create a duke or a king, Harold or another, I grant this" ' (5821–2). This is a very lukewarm transmission of power, and the way Wace presents it, the English could have chosen as king someone other than Harold; which suggests that the succession in itself was valid, even though the person chosen to be king was not suitable. The needs of the land are paramount. The deathbed scene does indeed reflect English tradition to some extent – Eadmer (p. 8) writes that Edward designated Harold as his successor before his death – though Wace shrewdly counterbalances this apparent pro-English bias by having the narrator express some reservation as to the sincerity of Edward's assent (5820): 'ne sai se par boen coer le fist', 'I do not know whether he did so with a willing heart.' Wace's 'ne sai' does not only allow him to avoid taking sides; it also signals to the reader that this is not the true issue. As the narrator unequivocally states, summing up the situation: 'Rei a regne aveir estoveit,/ regne sainz rei ester ne deit', 'There had to be a king for the kingdom; a kingdom cannot be without a king' (5825–6). The same argument recurs almost verbatim at the death of William Rufus (10125–6), when it is decided to by-pass Duke Robert of Normandy who is absent on Crusade, in favour of the younger brother Henry.

William's reaction to the news of Harold's coronation is found only in Wace, and appears to have been derived from an eyewitness account. The duke was hunting in Rouen when a messenger informs him of Edward's death and Harold's

---

[30] 'Harold', said the king, 'you will have this, but I know that you will die. If I ever knew the duke and his barons who are with him and the great forces he can summon, nothing can protect you other than God.'

accession to the throne. William is angry, but remains silent, obsessively tying and untying his mantle (5841–64). He returns to his hall by boat, leans against a bench, his head on the armrest and fidgets, his face hidden by his cloak (5865–70). No one dares speak to him, until his seneschal arrives, humming a tune. The seneschal makes William break out of his black mood, making it quite clear that everyone knows the news anyway, so there is no point trying to suppress it (5871–900). William says that he is upset at Edward's death and Harold's perjury, but that he can't do anything about it: 'Ço peise mei ... mais n'en pois mie faire plus' (5901–2), at which William FitzOsbern intervenes to urge the dejected duke to avenge himself and take England by force, on the grounds that (5919–22):

> Prosdoen ne deit rien comencier
> ne esmover, por relaissier;
> ou comencier e a chief traire,
> ou tot laissier sainz noise faire.[31]

This image of a reluctant William is also found in Orderic Vitalis's *Historia Ecclesiastica* (Book III, ii. 120–1; vol. II, pp. 138–41), where Baldwin of Flanders rebukes the duke for having allowed his perjured vassal to seize the throne of England and offers his help. In the *Roman de Rou*, the impetus comes from the Norman retainers themselves whereas William's father-in-law, the count of Flanders, is later depicted as markedly unenthusiastic in his support for the proposed campaign; but William's reluctance to take up arms functions in both cases as evidence of his essentially peace-loving nature, and exonerates him from the charge of excessive ambition. Wace's apparently pro-English stance in the passages purporting to relate what happened in England is thus matched with a corresponding pro-Norman bias in describing the Norman point of view, leaving his readers to make up their minds as to the relative merits of each side.

The decision to invade England is shown to have been preceded by all possible preventative measures and safeguards. Wace follows the *Gesta Normannorum Ducum* (vii. 13(31)) and William of Malmesbury (*Gesta regum Anglorum*, iii. 238) in mentioning William's unsuccessful attempts to resolve the issue by diplomacy. He also gives William's *casus belli* more weight through Harold's expulsion from England of all the Normans who had settled there under King Edward. The personal slight to William (depriving him of a throne that was rightly his and jilting his daughter) is thus expanded into an attack on Norman interests as a whole, which the duke of Normandy cannot ignore. These Normans, stresses Wace, held their fiefs from King Edward himself, but Harold (5940–2)

> nen i volt nis un sol laissier;
> les peres chaça e les meres,
> filz e filles, serors e freres.[32]

---

[31] 'A worthy man must not begin anything or set anything in motion only to abandon it, either start something and bring it to fruition or leave everything without more ado.'

[32] 'He did not want to leave a single one there. He expelled fathers and mothers, sons and daughters, sisters and brothers.'

Harold's behaviour thus aligns him with the perfidious English who had massacred their Danish population on the feast of St Brice under King Ethelred (*Troisième Partie*, 1191–256) and mercilessly tortured to death the atheling Alfred after slaughtering his Norman followers (4663–712) in William's own day. Though Harold is not accused of actual bloodshed, he is clearly acting unjustly, and William's case is accordingly strengthened. The coronation of Harold at Christmas puts an end to the 'diplomacy' stage, leaving William with no hope of redress other than through open warfare: a bad decision on the part of the English king, as is stressed by the narrator who sums up the situation with proleptic hints as to the outcome, closing with the grim lines: 'mais malement le comperra/ il e la gent qu'il plus ama', 'but he paid for this wretchedly, he and the people he loved most' (5953–4). The prophetic warning of King Edward is about to be fulfilled.

Having failed to reach a peaceful solution, William has to prepare for war; and to do so, he has to secure the support of his barons. This takes place in two stages: William first has to ascertain whether his privy council is in agreement; then the matter has to be brought before the general assembly of barons. Wace supplements the account of the *Gesta Normannorum Ducum* with a list of the eight Norman nobles present at the privy council assembled for that purpose;[33] these barons fulfil a similar narrative function to Arthur's grandees in the Giant's Tower, when the decision is taken to wage war against Rome. The differences with the Arthurian war council, however, are significant. There is no lengthy oratory in direct speech rehearsing the case for war; and whereas Arthur waits for his barons to give their views before expressing his own opinion, William speaks first (in reported speech), explaining the slight Harold has inflicted on him. Interestingly, the plight of the exiled Normans is not mentioned. William's grandees grant him immediate and unconditional support (6019–32), but no firm commitments are made in terms of men or resources. The general assembly follows a similar pattern, with the duke presenting his case and requesting help (6035–44); but in sharp contrast with the wholehearted rallying around Arthur, the response is less than enthusiastic. The reticence described by William of Poitiers (II, 1) is depicted by Wace as a point-blank refusal on the part of many of the Normans to agree to support the campaign, and resolution is only achieved thanks to the intervention of William FitzOsbern.

If Harold was tricked into swearing allegiance to William, the Normans are no less deceived into supporting the English campaign. FitzOsbern convinces the barons to accept him as their representative, arguing that if William's plan failed he would blame them for their lack of support, so they should be more cooperative (6066–84). They accept to be bound by FitzOsbern's decisions, confident in the knowledge that he is fully aware of their unwillingness to serve overseas (6085–94), only to find that he goes on to promise William unreserved support on their part. FitzOsbern's speech to William systematically inverts the words of the assembled Normans. Whereas they tell FitzOsbern that 'la mer doton,/ oltre mer

---

[33] This list overlaps to a great extent (i.e., five out of Wace's eight) with the names given by Guillaume de Poitiers in his *Gesta Guillelmi*, Part II, ch. 1; Orderic Vitalis includes a similar list in his *Historia Ecclesiastica*, Book III, ii. 121–2 (ed. Chibnall, vol. II, pp. 140–1).

servir ne devon', 'We are afraid of the sea. We are not obliged to serve beyond the sea' (6085–6), FitzOsbern asserts to William (6103–22):

> Por vos, ço dient, avancier
> se larreient en mer neier
> ou en un feu ardant jeter,
> mult vos poez en els fier.
> Longuement vos ont ja servi
> e a grant cost vos ont suï,
> e volentiers vos serviront,
> se bien l'ont fait, mielz le feront;
> ensenble o vos mer passeront,
> vostre servise dobleront;
> qui selt mener vint chevaliers
> quarante en merra volentiers,
> e qui de trente servir selt
> de seisante servir vos velt,
> e cil qui selt servir de cent
> dous cenz en merra bonement;
> e jo merrai en bon amor
> en la besoigne mon seignor
> seisante nes apareillies,
> de combatanz homes chargies.[34]

The pledging of support to the utmost limit of one's resources echoes the Arthurian council scene, but the context in which it occurs makes FitzOsbern's words highly ironical and endows the entire episode with black humour. The Normans are outraged at having been so misrepresented and fear that FitzOsbern's promise will lead to the doubling of their feudal dues: the assembly degenerates into pandemonium (6123–38). William retires from court, calls each baron in individually to see him, gives reassurance than if they double their customary due this will not constitute a precedent, and has the exact numbers of men and ships pledged by each baron put down on paper.[35]

Having secured the reluctant support of the Normans, William approaches the neighbouring powers and gathers mercenaries. According to Wace, he attempts, unsuccessfully, to convince the king of France and the count of Flanders to join him in his venture. These negotiations with France and Flanders do not appear in other sources and contain a number of factual errors; but they further reinforce the impression of a campaign being launched under less-than-perfect auspices. The

---

[34] 'To further your cause, they say, they would let themselves be drowned at sea or thrown into a burning fire; you can trust them completely. They have already served you for a long time and followed you at great cost and will serve you gladly. If they have done this well, they will do so better. They will cross the sea with you and double their service to you. The man who is accustomed to bring twenty knights will voluntarily bring forty; he who normally serves with thirty will serve you with sixty, and he who normally serves with a hundred will gladly bring two hundred. As a sign of true affection, I will bring for my lord's hour of need sixty fully equipped ships laden with warriors.'

[35] If this anecdote is based on fact, it would account for the discrepancy in the number of ships said to have sailed from Normandy by Wace's father, and the figures given by William of Jumièges. One may safely assume that not all the pledges made under such circumstances would have been honoured, even if they were written down for posterity.

duke's attempt to convince the king of France to help him is a fiasco, and provides Wace with the opportunity to rehearse the charges against the French that recur throughout his *Roman de Rou*: William's offer to conquer England and hold it under the king of France is rejected out of fear that the Normans will become too powerful, and because of the trademark avarice of the French – they are not willing to part with money or men (6181–230). In strictly historical terms, Philip I of France was still a child at the time and was in no position to take such a decision, or to assess the arguments supposedly put forward by his French advisers; but the fact that William's campaign took place without the active support of his overlord lent itself well to a reassertion of the status of France as the hereditary enemy of Normandy, and gave justification to the claims of the Anglo-Norman kings that they did not owe allegiance to the crown of France for England. There were sound political reasons why Wace should have wished to include such an episode at this stage.

William's attempt to secure the support of the count of Flanders, though unattested by any other historian of the time, is entirely plausible, as William's wife Matilda was the daughter of the count (though Wace gets the relationship wrong, stating he was William's brother-in-law, 'serorge', 6251). As with the king of France, the negotiation flounders because of avarice: before he will commit himself, the count wants to know what part of England he could hope to gain in exchange for his help (6252–7). In response, William sends the count a sealed, folded blank sheet of parchment, with a note to the effect that the document contained a list of the English territories he would grant him. The count breaks the seal, and finding nothing written on the parchment, asks the messenger for enlightenment, only to receive this sharp rebuke (6281–90):

> "Nïent i a, nïent avreiz,
> e a nïent vos entendreiz.
> Li dus velt a vostre seror
> e a voz nevoz querre enor;
> s'il Engleterre aveir peüssent
> ja plus de vos seignor n'en fussent;
> de tot vos feïssent seignor,
> tote fust vostre e tote lor.
> Se Deu plaist, il la conquerra,
> ja vostre aïe nen avra."[36]

William's message to the count is designed to reveal his native wit, but also to establish him as a man who is acutely aware of the responsibilities that come with lineage, as opposed to the count whose outlook is narrowly self-centred. The duke emerges as a man of honour in a world where such values are a scarce commodity, and where the natural upholders of his rights renege on their duties. This anecdote may have been transmitted through the ducal administrative circle, to which the

---

[36] ' "There is nothing there. You will have nothing and should expect nothing. The duke wants to seek honour for your sister and your nephews. If they could have had England, they would have had no more control over it than you. They would have made you lord over everything; everything would have been yours and everything theirs. If this pleases God, he will conquer it and not have any help from you." '

messenger clearly belonged. Wace states that this servant of William's, in addition to being 'enloçoné', 'well-educated' (6271), had been with the duke for a long time ('longues', 6272); he was therefore an established and trusted member of the ducal household. The absence of any hint of doubt as to the veracity of the anecdote suggests that Wace considered his authority to be entirely reliable, to the extent of repeating what we know to be a glaring factual error, when Matilda is said to be the sister of the count of Flanders: the information could well have come from a direct descendant of the messenger himself. One thing may be considered certain: this anecdote is markedly Norman in flavour, and the message it relays is that William's eventual conquest of England was a specifically Norman accomplishment.

If William fails to secure the aid he could have expected from his overlord and his family, he does nevertheless receive support from an arguably far more important player: Pope Alexander II. Following William of Poitiers (II, 3) and most historians except William of Jumièges, Wace (6293–318) relates that the Pope gave his approval to William for the forthcoming campaign, bestowing upon him a banner so that he would march under the protection of St Peter and hold the conquered lands from him. Moreover, according to Wace (who is isolated in his relating of this fact), the Pope also sent William a ring with one of St Peter's teeth under the stone. The appearance of a precious relic at this stage of the narrative echoes the key role of relics in Harold's oath at Bonneville: on the eve of William's setting off to conquer England, a discreet gesture is thus made towards the event that gives the campaign its legitimacy. In addition, divine approval is signalled in the heavens by the appearance of a comet. Wace's description of the comet follows closely *Gesta Normannorum Ducum* vii. 13(31), where it is said to have been a star with a long three-forked tail stretching down south, that remained visible for a fortnight. But whereas the *Gesta Normannorum Ducum* states, in very general terms, that the comet was a portent of change, 'mutationem, ut assuerunt plurimi, designans alicuius regni', 'portending, according to many, a change in someone's kingdom',[37] Wace explicitly connects the appearance of the comet with William's campaign. The impression is given in the *Roman de Rou* (6319) that the portent appeared in the skies at the precise time fixed with the Pope's approval for the invasion, and it is said to announce a new king: 'Tele esteile selt l'en veeir/ quant novel rei deit regne aveir'.[38] The lukewarm response to William's plans by the secular lords is thus more than compensated for by the endorsement of the chief spiritual power of his time, and by evidence in the very skies of the providential nature of the campaign.

To this, one may add that a comet announcing a change of monarch had literary connotations of which Wace would have been acutely aware: a comet also appears in the *Roman de Brut* lines 8287–303, when King Aurelius dies leaving the throne to his brother Uther, future father of Arthur. This comet is said to have two rays which, Merlin explains to Uther (8325–44), signify his future offspring of one son and one daughter; one of these rays is subdivided into seven, signifying his descent from his daughter. Wace does not work up the Arthurian overtones of

---

[37] William of Jumièges, ed. van Houts, pp. 162–3.
[38] 'Such a star is accustomed to be seen when a new king is to have a kingdom', 6323–4.

the passage in the *Rou*, but the link between the dynasty that produced Arthur and that about to be founded by William himself becomes apparent less than fifty lines later, with the oft-quoted aside on Brocéliande (6373–98), added with studied light-heartedness at the end of a short section describing the building of the fleet (6329–42) and the gathering of the supporters of the duke at Saint-Valéry (6343–73). Wace's account of his disappointing trip to the fountain of Barenton has been discussed above; it creates a link with William's dashing forebear, Richard I of Normandy, and through him endows both the ducal dynasty and the Norman landscape with an Arthurian aura. It also has as effect of subtly undermining the importance of the Breton contingent in the army. Of the four barons mentioned by name in this passage, three are Breton lords; but in connecting their territory with his own avowed foolishness, Wace indirectly denigrates them – and whatever contribution to the campaign they eventually make. Their presence is noted, but in such a way as to hint at some inherent inferiority compared to the Norman contingent, whose resourcefulness and diligence were celebrated in the ship-building vignette. Equally, the placing of the debunking of Brocéliande within the narrative is not without significance. The preparations have now come to an end and William is about to conquer Arthur's insular realm.

The invasion and conquest of England

Wace's parenthetical account of his disappointment at Brocéliande is followed immediately by a description of the Norman fleet, its sailing from Saint-Valéry and the disembarking near Hastings. Mercenaries start flocking to William (a detail unique to Wace, 6399–416) and a miracle allows the fleet to sail away after a long period waiting for a suitable wind. The account in the *Roman de Rou* follows William of Poitiers in its main lines, supplemented by details and anecdotes from other sources, especially William of Malmesbury and, more contentiously, Wace's own father. By the time the *Rou* was being written, time had clearly had a distorting effect on memories, including those of the more 'respectable' historians, and Wace is reluctant to endorse all the information contained in his written sources (6417–32):

> Ne vos voil mie metre en letre,
> ne jo ne m'en voil entremetre,
> quels barons e quanz chevaliers,
> quanz vavasors, quanz soldeiers
> out li dus en sa compaignie
> quant il out prest tot son navie;
> mais jo oï dire a mon pere
> – bien m'en sovient, mais vaslet ere –
> que set cenz nes, quatre meins, furent
> quant de Saint Valeri s'esmurent,
> que nes, que batels, que esqueis,
> a porter armes e harneis;
> e jo ai en escrit trove
> – ne sai dire s'est verité –

> que il i out trei mile nes
> qui portoent veiles e tres.[39]

This passage is frequently quoted by modern historians of the Conquest; its testimony was long rejected as unreliable and J. H. Round took it as proof that Wace was not a suitable source for 'serious' historians, on the grounds that in 1066, Wace's father would not have been born.[40] In fact, it is far from impossible for a man born in, say, 1050, to father a child around 1110, particularly in a culture where wives were frequently much younger than their spouse, and to survive long enough to leave lasting memories to that child. The conflicting written source mentioned by Wace is the *Gesta Normannorum Ducum* vii. 14(34), whose figure of 3000 ships equally appears too neat to be entirely credible, and may well have been based on the list of 'virtual' crafts promised to William (one will recall that the duke had all this written down following his general assembly, according to Wace) rather than those that actually materialised. The issue has since been revisited by Elisabeth van Houts who has considerably tempered the scepticism prevalent among older scholars.[41]

What is omitted is as important in this passage as what has been included. William of Poitiers (II, 6), whose work Wace undeniably knew well, hints that a first attempt at setting off from Saint-Valéry had taken place, with grim consequences: 'Quin et consilio adversitatibus obvius, submersorum interitus, quantum poterat, occultavit, latentius tumulando', 'countering adversity with wisdom, he [i.e., William] hid as much as possible the deaths of those who had drowned, burying them in secret'.[42] This implies casualties before the campaign has properly started. By contrast, in the *Roman de Rou*, the absence of a favourable wind merely results in the barons becoming 'mult ennoié' (6437) – greatly upset. The accent is placed on the miracle performed for William by the relics of Saint Valéry, who granted the wishes of the army by sending a favourable wind (6438–46).[43] Wace does mention the loss of two ships, but only after the miracle, thus giving the impression that this occurred during the crossing itself (6461–4):

> De la flote, qui fu si grant,
> e de la gent, donc i out tant,
> n'i out que dous nes perillies,
> ne sai s'el furent trop chargies.[44]

---

[39] 'I do not wish to set down in writing for you, nor do I wish to expend any effort on this, how many barons and how many knights, how many vavassors and how many mercenaries the duke had in his company when all his ships were ready. But I hear my father say – I remember it well, though I was a young lad – that when they set off from Saint-Valéry there were seven hundred ships less four, either ships, boats or skiffs, carrying weapons or equipment. I have discovered in writing – I do not know if it is true – that there were three thousand ships under sail.'
[40] Round, *Feudal England*, pp. 407–8.
[41] See van Houts, 'The Ship List of William the Conqueror', *Anglo-Norman Studies* 10 (1987): 159–83.
[42] Translation my own.
[43] This miracle is mentioned in a number of Wace's sources, and appears to have been well known. See William of Poitiers II, 6 and 7, William of Malmesbury's *Historia Regum* iii. 238, and Orderic Vitalis, *Historia*, Book III, ii. 144–5. It is not mentioned, however, in the *Gesta Normannorum Ducum*.
[44] 'Of the fleet, which was so large, and the men, who were so numerous, only two ships perished; I do not know whether they were overloaded.'

What in William of Poitiers is a dangerously worrying event becomes in Wace a commonplace risk attached to all sea travel, and any blame is directed towards the sailors who may have overloaded the crafts. There is no mention of trying to suppress the news, or of surreptitiously burying drowned men; the tone is upbeat. Even the casualties are presented as almost miraculously few, and as evidence of a successful crossing.

The crossing and disembarking in England are given a heightened dimension through the use, as elsewhere in the *Roman de Rou*, of anecdotes relative to the duke. First comes the description of the ducal ship, a lantern on its mast, topped by a copper weather-vane, and with a copper child with a bow and arrow as prow figure (6447–60). A lavish vignette then depicts the disembarkation proper and the setting up of camp (6465–534). This scene has no parallel in any of Wace's sources and seems to draw on first-hand accounts of the practicalities of travelling by sea: thus, the lightly equipped archers disembark first and scout the area to make sure that it is safe; then the heavily armed knights on their horses leave the ships; and finally the craftsmen land with their tools and get down to building a fortified camp. Wace includes the striking detail that the count of Eu had arranged for all the necessary wood for the camp to be brought over with them, with all the wooden parts already shaped, pierced and trimmed (6517–26): a sort of flat-pack fortification that could be (and was) erected in less than a day, including the digging of a surrounding ditch. The technological and logistical achievement this implies is remarkable and points to the meticulous nature of William's preparations.[45]

The Norman landing is marked in the *Roman de Rou* by two anecdotes illustrating William's strength of mind and laudable freedom from superstition. On arrival, William enquires about his astrologer, who had predicted that the crossing would be a safe one and that Harold would submit to the duke without fighting. It turns out that the astrologer was in one of the ships that had sunk. William's reaction is to dismiss the man and his prophecies entirely (6561–6):

> "N'i poet," ço dit li dus, "chaleir,
> n'esteit mie de grant saveir,
> malement devinast de mei
> qui ne sout deviner de sei;
> s'il de tot seüst dire veir
> bien deüst sa mort porveeir."[46]

The parallel with William's uncle, Archbishop Maugier (4541–618), who like the court astrologer practised the black arts,[47] and like him met with a watery death, is

---

[45] Wace's interest in the craft of ship-builders and carpenters has been read as an indication that he came from a family of craftsmen himself (see Burgess, pp. xix–xx); but this fails to take account of the extraordinary circumstances being depicted.

[46] ' "This is not important", said the duke, "he was not a man of great learning. The man who could not prophesy with respect to himself would have prophesied badly with respect to me. If he had been able to tell the truth in everything, he should have predicted his own death." '

[47] The astrologer is explicitly said to practise 'nigromance', line 6538, while Maugier has a demonic familiar.

inescapable. Both episodes are added by Wace to his main source,[48] and in both cases the very principle of attempting to see in the future is condemned – an attitude which suggests that Wace's refusal to translate the Prophecies of Merlin in his *Roman de Brut* might have been prompted by moral considerations as well as interpretation issues and/or political self-preservation.

William's healthy scepticism towards astrology is of course vindicated by the fact that the astrologer's prediction was not entirely correct, something the narrator makes a point of noting (6551–2); but if this anecdote was based on a true event, the potential consequences for the morale of William's troops could have been disastrous. The death of the astrologer who had predicted that conquering England would be a military picnic would quite naturally be construed as meaning that the opposite of his prophecy was likely to happen, and that the invading army would be routed rather than victorious. William brazens out this setback, and the news of the astrologer's death appears to have been suppressed – the anecdote ends with the statement that 'issi est del devin remés/ e al sec sunt traites les nes' (6571–2);[49] but it is followed almost immediately by another bad omen, which is also recounted by William of Malmesbury in his *Gesta Regum Anglorum* (iii. 238). On disembarking, William loses his balance and falls face down, on his hands. This causes dismay in the army: 'sempres i out levé grant cri/ e distrent tuit: "Mal signe a ci!" '[50] William tries to give a positive gloss to the incident, stating that he has now taken possession of the land with both hands; and one of his followers, acting on cue, seizes a fistful of thatch from a nearby cottage and gives it to William as a sign of investiture (6578–92). This alternative reading of the omen is given further dignity and verisimilitude by two appeals to God by William (6578 and 6592); but tellingly, the duke felt the need to take special measures. According to Wace (whose source for this remains unknown), he immediately ordered for the ships to be dismantled, so that none would be tempted to flee (6593–8).

The destruction of the ships gives the campaign an aura of epic heroism, as the Normans now have no choice other than to fight to the death; and under cover of his limited knowledge, Wace reserves for himself the option of selectiveness in what he is going to recount, probably with the intention of enhancing the epic dimension to the events to follow (6599–604):

> Ne pois pas tot ensemble escrire
> ne tot ensemble ne pois dire,
> mais que que jo auge disant,
> primes arriere e pois avant,
> veritez est qu'a l'ariver
> fist li dus sa gent tote armer.[51]

---

[48] The anecdote of the astrologer draws on stories in the *Brevis relatio* (p. 31) and William of Poitiers, but is essentially proper to Wace.
[49] 'Nothing more was said about the prophet and the ships were drawn up on to dry land.'
[50] 'At once a loud cry arose and everyone said: "This is a bad sign!" ', 6575–6.
[51] 'I cannot write everything down at once or say everything at once, but whatever I do say, one way or the other, the truth is that, when he arrived, the duke made all his men arm themselves.'

Military action thus starts immediately, and the Normans meet with immediate success. They march on to Pevensey which they plunder, terrorising the local peasants (6613–16):

> Donc veïssiez Engleis foïr
> bestes chacier, maisons guerpir,
> as cimetieres tot atraient
> e encor la forment s'esmaient.[52]

One may note the 'donc veïssiez' which opens this description and marks the beginning of the hostilities on English soil: even stylistically, we are alerted to the fact that what is about to unfold is the stuff of *chansons de geste*.

Having described the landing of the Normans, Wace turns to the English. Drawing upon Guy of Amiens's *Carmen de Hastingae Proelio* (lines 149–56), he tells of an English knight who, having observed the arrival of the Normans from behind a mound, rushes to Northumbria to warn Harold of the invasion. The passage describing the disembarkation scene witnessed by the knight is worthy of comment, inasmuch as stylistically it closely echoes the episode in the *Roman de Brut* lines 1209–16, where Brutus surveys newly settled Britain, symbolically taking full possession of the land through his approving gaze. In both cases, we have a passage characterised by the repetition of the verb, 'vit', 'he saw', but the significance of the act of seeing is inverted for the English knight (6627–35):

> Vit les archiers des nes issir,
> les chevaliers emprés venir,
> vit charpentiers, vit lor coignies,
> vit les granz genz, vit les maisnies,
> vit les mairriens des nes jeter,
> vit le chastel faire e fermer,
> vit le fossé environ faire
> vit escuz e armes atraire.
> De quantqu'il vit out grant pesance.[53]

The parallel here is not between Brutus and the English knight, but between Brutus and William. Brutus's admiring of Britain leads to the founding of the first city of Britain, while the knight witnesses the building of a stronghold under William's orders. On a moral plane, Brutus has just cleansed Britain of the monstrous giants who inhabited the island, while William is about to confront a Harold depicted as unnatural and unjust. The English knight finds his king in Northumbria, where he has just killed his half-brother Tostig in battle at Pontefract.[54] Guy of Amiens, from whom Wace draws a number of details at this

---

[52] 'Then you would have seen the English fleeing, chasing their animals, abandoning their houses, all withdrawing to the cemeteries where they remained in terror.'

[53] 'He saw the archers emerging from the ships and afterwards the knights disembarking. He saw the carpenters, their axes, the large numbers of men, the knights, the building material thrown down from the ships, the construction and fortification of the castle and the ditch built all around it, the shields and the weapons brought forth. Everything he saw caused him great anguish.'

[54] Wace is isolated among historians of the period in placing Harold's battle at Pontefract ('Pontfrait'), rather than Stamford Bridge, where it actually happened. It is possible that the error indicates an oral source, which the poet or his informant misheard.

point, had a bias in favour of the Ponthieu and Boulogne families, and therefore depicted Tostig more positively than most sources: Tostig, Earl of Northumberland, had married Baldwin V's half-sister Judith while in exile in Flanders (1051).[55] Wace embraces his source's anti-Harold bias with alacrity. He represents Tostig's demand of their father's fief as being perfectly justified: 'ne quereit mie grant ultrage', 'he was not asking for anything unreasonable' (6658),[56] and condemns Harold for his brother's death in no uncertain terms: 'ocis fu Tosti vers Pontfrait/ e mult altre mal i out fait', 'Tostig was killed near Pontefract and Harold had many other evil deeds performed there' (6673–4). Harold may have won, but the implication is that he was fighting an unjust war.[57]

Harold's rejoicing at his victory, and therefore at the death of his own brother, is morally repugnant, and the narrator makes it quite clear that the proud English king is about to meet with his downfall (6677–82):

> Mais fols est qui se glorefie,
> tost est une joie faillie,
> male novele est tost venue,
> tost poet morir qui altre tue;
> sovent contre son destorbier
> se selt coer d'ome esleecier.[58]

Gnomic passages such as this one are not rare in Wace's work, functioning as proleptic asides.[59] In this case, it also provides reassurance that Harold's callous behaviour will not remain unpunished, any more than the fractricide Porrex was allowed to enjoy the throne in the *Roman de Brut* (2141–80). On a different level, we may discern in the relationship between Harold and Tostig, as depicted by Wace, an implicit parallel with the unjust treatment of the future Henry I of England by his brothers later in the work (*Rou 3*, 9449–656), exonerating Henry in advance of the acts of open warfare he will feel compelled to commit.

While Harold is clearly in the wrong in the *Roman de Rou*, Wace refrains from demonising him, contrary to William of Poitiers (II, 8) who calls him 'luxuria foedum, truculentum homicidam, divite rapina superbum, adversarium aequi et boni', 'soiled with luxuriousness, a cruel homicide, puffed up with the riches of theft, an enemy of justice and goodness'. Harold is flawed, but not to the extent of becoming grotesque. Once he is confronted with the new crisis, the English king reacts in a way that is lucid and dignified. He regrets not having granted Tostig his demand, as this prevented him from being able to deny William access to the land. Had he been there at the time, he says (6702–10),

---

[55] See the Introduction to F. Barlow, ed. and trans., *The Carmen de Hastingae Proelio of Guy Bishop of Amiens* (Oxford, 1999).

[56] It should however be noted that this passage echoes the message (in reported speech) of Tostig's envoys to Harold; the narrator does not comment on the issue directly.

[57] This is not the view of all the histories of the time, and Wace has clearly made a partisan choice in this instance. For example, the *Brevis relatio* (p. 6), which Wace knew of, states that Tostig wanted to conquer England from Harold: he therefore got killed in a war of aggression.

[58] 'But the man who gloats is a fool; one joy soon comes to an end. Bad news soon comes; he who kills another can soon die. A man's heart often rejoices at the approach of his own misfortune.'

[59] See Brosnahan, 'Wace's Use of Proverbs'.

"Bien defendisse le passage;
tant en feïsse en mer plungier
e tant en feïsse neier,
ja a la terre ne venissent,
ja rien del nostre ne preïssent,
ja de morir garant n'eüssent
se la mer tote ne beüssent.
Mais issi plot al rei celestre,
jo ne pois mie par tot estre."[60]

By contrast, in both the *Carmen de Hastingae Proelio* (lines 157–188) and the *Brevis relatio* (p. 6), an elated Harold is eager to fight with the invaders, prompting accusations by the narrator of the *Brevis relatio* of madness and hubris. Wace's Harold is an experienced war-leader who realises immediately that he is in an unfavourable position; he is also an unexpectedly pious man, whose fatalistic acceptance that his quandary is due to God's will suggests an altogether more complex character than Wace's sources allow. This passage could be interpreted as evidence that Harold was aware that he had incurred divine displeasure, but read in the light of what follows, it points to a king so focused on his duty to the realm that he is blind to the personal flaw condemning him to failure. He is a redoubtable adversary, with the makings of a tragic character.

As is proper, the encounter on the battlefield is preceded by a last-minute attempt at negotiation. Wace takes advantage of this stage in the narrative to rehearse the arguments of both sides, emphasising the miraculous dimension to William's coming victory and providing the occasional touch of light relief through the interweaving of anecdotes, negotiation scenes rich in direct speech and dialogue, and formal council proceedings allowing insights into the psychology of the main protagonists.

A total of four anecdotes punctuates the main phases in the run-up to battle: at the beginning of the negotiations, in the aftermath of William's first message to Harold, at the end of the negotiations and immediately before the battle itself. First (6711–40), a baron warns William that he will be facing overwhelming odds and advises him to return to Normandy. William refuses, stating he would still fight even if he only had ten thousand knights rather than some sixty thousand in his army (a passage translated almost literally from William of Poitiers, II, 10). The second anecdote, which occurs after William's first ultimatum has been rejected, relates how spies sent by Harold to the Norman camp are discovered, treated with courtesy, shown around the camp, then let free (7077–94). On their return, they speak very highly of the duke but are puzzled by the number of priests among the Normans. Harold has to explain to them that the clean-shaven men they saw were not priests but knights: ' "N'ont mie barbes ne guernons,"/ ço dist Heraut, "com nos avons" ', ' "They have neither beard nor whiskers", said Harold, "as we do" ' (7109–10). The implicit identification of the Normans with

---

[60] 'I would have protected this point of entry properly. I would have caused so many of them to dive into the water and so many of them to drown that they would never have come ashore and never taken anything of ours. They would have had no escape from death unless they had drunk the entire sea. But this is what pleased the Celestial King; I cannot be everywhere.'

the 'party' of God – they are taken for priests – is further reinforced by the anecdotal passage describing the behaviour of the two camps on the eve of the battle (7323–80). Wace, following William of Malmesbury (iii. 241–2), contrasts the drunken behaviour of the English with the prayer and fasting observed by the Normans; however, the impact is considerably stronger in the French text due to the inclusion of snippets of the English drinking songs juxtaposed by the Latin prayers said by the Normans:

> Bublie crient e weisseil
> e laticome e drincheheil,
> drinc hindrewart e drintome,
> drinc helf e drinc tome.[61]
>
> Junes font e afflictions
> e lor privees oreisons,
> salmes dient e misereles,
> litanies e kirieles,
> Deu requerent e merci crient,
> paternostres e messes dient,
> li uns Spiritus domini,
> li altre Salus populi,
> plusors Salve sancta parens
> qui aparteneit a cel tens.[62]

The Normans are characterised by their use of the language of liturgy and their behaviour aligns them with saints preparing for martyrdom. The English shouting out their profane ditties, on the other hand, are comparable to the pagan adversaries of Christian martyrs, the Saracen opponents of a Roland, or their own forebears, the Saxon enemies of a King Arthur.[63] Even though the English are clearly Christians, they are depicted as godless, giving the passage crusading undercurrents. In addition, the reference to the Virgin Mary in the final prayer, 'Salve sancta parens', recalls the devotion to Our Lady of King Arthur himself, who was said to have carried an icon of Mary in his shield.[64] The two sides are neatly polarised and the reader is left in no doubt as to who is worthy of victory.

The fourth and final anecdote (7487–530) occurs just after William's battle-speech to his men. In the hurry to get ready for the fight, William's servant presents him his hauberk back to front, to the dismay of his followers. As earlier in the campaign, the duke dismisses all omens as insignificant, stressing instead his faith in God (7515–21):

---

[61] 'Be happy', they cried, 'and let us drink together. Let the cup keep coming and let us drink. Drink this way and that; drink to my health. Drink an entire cup, then half a cup; drink to your health', 7331–4.

[62] 'They fasted and did penance, saying their own private prayers and reciting psalms, the *Miserere*, litanies and petitions; they beseeched God and begged for mercy, saying their *Paternosters* and Mass, one the *Spiritus domini*, the other *the Salus populi*, many of them *Salve sancta parens*, which was appropriate for that occasion', 7369–78.

[63] The English drinking song recalls the wassail scene in the *Roman de Brut*, lines 6948–80, where the Saxon Ronwen seduces King Vortigern.

[64] *Roman de Brut*, lines 9293–6. The description of Arthur's arms occurs just before the account of his first major battle against the pagan Saxons.

> Mais onques en sort ne creï
> ne ne cresrai, en Dieu me fi,
> ker il fait del tot son plaisir
> e ço qu'il velt fait avenir;
> onques n'amai sortiseors
> ne ne creï devineors,
> a Damledeu tot me commant.[65]

However, William also attempts to reassure his men by giving an alternative, more positive reading of the incident (7523–8):

> Li hauberc, qui fu trestornez
> e pois me rest a dreit donez
> senefie la trestornee
> de la chose qui iert muee;
> le non qui ert de ducheé
> verreiz de duc en rei torné.[66]

William's interpretation will of course prove to be the right one. This anecdote echoes those of the drowned astrologer and of William's tumble when disembarking, encapsulating the point made in both cases regarding omens. The battle is about to begin: the doggedly inauspicious conditions surrounding the Norman campaign have not weakened William's determination or his faith that right – and therefore God – is on his side.

The negotiations between William and Harold, related in three distinct phases, provide Wace with the opportunity to rehearse the arguments on the English side without needing to pass judgment himself. In an initial move, William sends a Fécamp monk called Hugh Margot to London, bearing an ultimatum: Harold has no legitimate claim to the throne, and he must relinquish it to the rightful king of the land, William, whom King Edward had designated as his successor, and was recognised as such on oath by Harold himself (6753–96). Harold reacts with anger and has to be restrained from assaulting the messenger by his brother Gyrth ('Guert' in the French). Wace at this point seems to be hinting that Harold's behaviour might be due to medical reasons: we are told that 'Heraut fu forment orgueillos/ ço dist qu'il vit qu'alques fu ros', 'Harold was very arrogant. Someone who saw him said he had reddish hair' (6797–8). This suggests that the English king had a choleric complexion, i.e., an excess of red bile in his physical makeup (indicated by the red hair) which led him to extreme and unconsidered actions. Where Wace got his information from is a mystery – no other sources mention the colour of Harold's hair – and it is striking that the episode is markedly different from what we find in William of Poitiers, where Harold's response to the Norman

---

[65] 'But I never believed in fate and I never will; I trust in God, for He does what He likes with everything and makes what He wants come about. I never liked soothsayers and never trusted diviners; I entrust myself fully to the Lord God.'
[66] 'The hauberk which was turned round and then given back to me the right way round signifies the turning round of things which will be altered. The name which was derived from "duchy" you will be seen turned from duke into king.'

envoy is one of quiet and icy dignity.[67] Wace's Harold, like Orderic Vitalis's and William of Malmesbury's,[68] is characterised by a streak of *démesure*. In his envoy to William, bearing the answer to Hugh Margot's message, Harold counters the arguments put forward by the duke, stating that his oath was made under duress (6815–28). He does not feel bound by it and denies William the moral high ground: 'se de rien mesfait li ai/ jo maïsmes m'en assoldrai', 'If I have done anything wrong by him, I will take it upon myself to procure absolution' (6829–30). Instead, he offers to buy William off with money, new ships and a safe-conduct (6831–4). If his offer should be refused, he will arrange a battle for the following Saturday (6835–8). These terms are of course refused by William, who further points out that he still has in his power the hostages handed over to him by Harold's father Godwin (6847–60); he nevertheless listens to the English messenger with courtesy and gives him a horse and clothes (6861–88). Like the Roman envoys who had carried the emperor's ultimatum to King Arthur, the messenger returns with only praises of William, much to Harold's discomfiture (6889–96).

The second attempt at a negotiated solution occurs shortly before the battle, with William now making three proposals: Harold could abdicate and marry William's daughter; or he could submit to the arbitration of the Pope; or he could settle the matter in single combat. These offers are rejected (7111–30). In a third and final attempt to come to a peaceful solution, on the day fixed for battle, William asks to meet with Harold in person. This request is blocked by Harold's brother Gyrth, who has cause to fear he might waver; but the duke's message is relayed in front of Harold and his council (7175–96). In it, William offers the whole of Northumberland to Harold, and to Gyrth he offers the lands that belonged to his father Earl Godwin. In the event of his terms being rejected, he threatens to sue Harold for perjury and warns the English that anyone supporting Harold will be excommunicate (7198–216). The threat of excommunication for anyone opposing William is something we find only in Wace. It is not entirely implausible, inasmuch as the duke is pursuing this campaign with papal approval and could therefore claim that those who bear arms against him are *de facto* attacking the Pope. This is William's trump card, kept to the end in order to isolate Harold from his barons, and it nearly works:

> D'icel escumeniement
> grondillierent Engleis forment,
> de l'escumenge ont grant poor
> e de la bataille graignor;
> mult les oïssiez grondillier

---

[67] In William of Poitiers II, 12, the (unnamed) monk is entrusted with offering Harold the option of single combat with William, to avoid bloodshed; Harold's cool refusal in II, 13 thus looks like cowardice compounded by a total absence of compassion for his people. Wace's Harold could not be more different.

[68] See for example the Orderic interpolation to the *Gesta Normannorum Ducum*, vii. 14 (35) and William of Malmesbury's account of the monk's mission to Harold, *Gesta Regum Anglorum* iii. 240. William of Malmesbury states that a number of proposals were put to Harold: abdication with conditions, continued rule but under William as suzerain, arbitration by the Holy See or single combat. Initially, Wace only mentions the first of these proposals. William of Poitiers mentions only the third.

> les uns as altres conseillier,
> n'i out tant proz qui ne volsist
> que la bataille remainsist.[69]

It takes a lengthy speech by Gyrth (7225–94), where he emphasises William's wily and untrustworthy nature and claims that the English fiefs had already been distributed by William among his followers, before the English barons overcome their reluctance.

The triplication of the negotiation motif by Wace allows him to present William as having done his utmost to avoid armed conflict, as is the duty of a good Christian prince. The duke appears to be determined but flexible, willing to make increasingly great concessions to Harold, while his rival is shown up as a man lacking in generosity and prudence, and afflicted by self-delusion regarding his own moral health. Until the last minute, the exchange of messages between the two camps also maintains a degree of suspense: we all know that the battle happened, but Wace hints that it could have taken relatively little to change the course of events. This gives a tragic aura to the episode and enhances its effectiveness in terms of narrative; it also gives scope for stylistic and amplificatory devices lending an epic dimension to what would otherwise have been mere charting of military events.

The character of Gyrth is central to Wace's narrative agenda. Harold's closest and most loyal adviser, with whom he also appears to have the strong bond uniting brothers-at-arms in the French *chanson de geste*, Gyrth functions to some extent as the wise Oliver to Harold's misguided and headstrong Roland. He has the lucidity to recognise from the outset that, whatever Harold might think on the matter, he is morally bound by the oath made to William over Normandy's holiest relics: a point explicitly made by Gyrth as the English are about to depart from London, in what may be considered the first council scene of the episode. As in William of Malmesbury (iii. 241) and Orderic Vitalis (interpolation to the *Gesta Normannorum Ducum*, vii. (35)), whose texts Wace follows here quite closely, he offers to take place at the head of the army instead of his brother, on the grounds that as he has sworn no oath, he may do so in all justice. Moreover, if he is defeated, Harold will still be able to restore the situation (6901–25). However, in Wace, this is not all. Gyrth continues with an outline of the strategy he thinks should be adopted: while he goes to battle, Harold should start a scorched earth campaign to starve the Normans out of the land (6927–38):

> Alez par cest païs ardant
> maisons e viles destruiant,
> pernez la robe e la vitaille
> pors e oeilles e aumaille,
> que Normant vitaille ne troissent
> ne nule rien donc vivre poissent;
> faites la vitaille esloignier,

---

[69] 'The English protested bitterly about this excommunication. They feared this greatly, even more than the battle. You would have heard them protesting greatly, each advising the other; no one was so brave that he did not want the battle to be called off', 7217–24.

> que il ne troissent que mangier,
> si les poez mult esmaier
> e faire arriere repairier;
> li dus meïsmes s'en ira
> quant la vitaille li faldra.[70]

This sound advice is not found in any of Wace's sources. Harold's response is also dissimilar to that mentioned by Wace's main Latin sources. Instead of reacting with anger, he explains why he will not do as Gyrth says. He cannot bring himself to make his people suffer by destroying their livelihood when he should be protecting them (6945–8):

> "Comment," dist il, "dei jo grever
> la gent que jo dei governer?
> Destruire ne grever ne dei
> la gent que deit garir soz mei."[71]

As for remaining behind leaving others to fight at the battle, he cannot do so out of fear that his absence will be attributed to cowardice (6951–8).

Harold's reasons for persisting in his resolve, though admirable in principle, are clearly misguided, and he belatedly comes to realise the fact. In an episode found only in Wace, on the morning of the encounter, Harold and Gyrth secretly go to a hill to survey the Norman army. Worried by what he sees, Harold proposes he return to London to raise more troops. Gyrth reacts with disgust (7019–34):

> "Heraut," dist Guert, "malvais coart!
> cist conseils est venuz trop tart,
> n'i a nïent del gopillier,
> avant vos estoet chevalchier.
> Malvais coart! Quant jol vos dis
> e as barons preier vos fis
> que a Londres remainsissiez
> e combatre me laissisiez,
> vos nel vosistes nïent faire,
> si vos en poet venir contraire;
> quant jol vos dis vos nel vosistes,
> ne mei ne altre n'en creïstes,
> or le volez e jo nel voil,
> trop tost avez perdu l'orgueil;
> d'iço que vos avez veü
> avez le hardement perdu."[72]

---

[70] 'Go through this land setting fire to everything, destroying houses and towns, capturing booty and food, swine, sheep an cattle, so that the Normans cannot find any food or anything off which they can live. Get the food a long way away so that they cannot find anything to eat; in this way you can frighten them greatly, and the duke himself will leave since his food will run out.'

[71] 'How', he said, 'could I harm the people it is my duty to govern? I must not destroy or harm the people to whom I owe protection.'

[72] 'Harold', said Gyrth, 'you wretched coward! That decision has come too late. This is not the time for cowardly action, you must ride forward. Wretched coward! When I told you and had your barons beseech you that you should remain in London and let me fight, you would not do anything of the sort.

This outburst is reminiscent that of Oliver in the *Song of Roland*, when Roland decides to blow his horn at Rencesvals (laisse 129, lines 1705–10):

> Dist Oliver: 'Vergoigne sereit grant
> E reprover a trestuz voz parenz;
> Iceste hunte dureit a lur vivant!
> Quant je l'vos dis, n'en feïstes nïent,
> Mais ne l'ferez par le men loëment.
> Se vos cornez, n'ert mie hardement.'[73]

The feelings expressed by Gyrth meet those of Oliver, even though the circumstances are not identical. Oliver objects to Roland calling for help during battle, while Gyrth points out to Harold that if he leaves at this stage, the entire army will disband, because the men will believe he is running away (7035–40). In both cases, however, the point made is essentially the same: it is too late to take the course of action in question. This echo of the *Song of Roland* was certainly meant by Wace to be picked up by his readers, inasmuch as the battle of Hastings as a whole was traditionally connected with the story of Rencesvals. William of Malmesbury tells us that the Normans found encouragement from the *Song of Roland* ('cantilena Rolandi') as they went to battle,[74] and it has been suggested that Guy of Amiens deliberately introduced echoes of the *Song of Roland* into his *Carmen*.[75] Wace himself provides us with a striking vignette firmly placing Roland within the sub-text to his account (8013–18):

> Taillefer, qui mult bien chantout,
> sor un cheval qui tost alout,
> devant le duc alout chantant
> de Karlemaigne e de Rollant,
> e d'Oliver e des vassals
> qui morurent en Rencevals.[76]

As noted by Dorothy Sayers, the allusion to Charlemagne, the upholder of Christianity against the Saracens, further legitimises William's claim during the battle;[77] but that is not the only function of the *Song of Roland* as a sub-text in Wace's account. The aligning of Gyrth with Oliver invites comparison of – and

---

Misfortune may come upon you as a result of this. When I said this to you, you refused to do it and did not believe me or anyone else. Now you want to do this and I do not; you have very soon lost your pride. As a result of what you have seen, you have lost your courage.'

[73] 'Oliver said: "It would be a great shame and an object of reproach to all your family; this shame would last their entire lifetime! When I told you to do it, you did nothing of the sort, but will not do it with my approval. If you blow your horn, it will not be an act of courage."' Text quoted from *La Chanson de Roland*, ed. I. Short (Paris, 1990); my translation.

[74] *Gesta regum Anglorum* iii. 242.

[75] See D. D. R. Owen, 'The Epic and History: *Chanson de Roland* and *Carmen de Hastingae Proelio*', *Medium Aevum* 11 (1982): 18–34.

[76] 'Taillefer, a very good singer, rode before the duke on a swift horse, singing of Charlemagne and Roland and of Oliver and the vassals who died at Rencesvals.' Taillefer is also mentioned in Guy of Amiens' *Carmen de Hastingae Proelio*, lines 391–408, Geffrei Gaimar's *Estoire des Engleis*, lines 5265–302 and Henry of Huntingdon, Book VI, chapter 30.

[77] 'The jongleur Taillefer at Hastings: Antecedents and Literary Fate', *Viator* 14 (1983): 79–88.

therefore, a contrast between – Harold and Roland. This comparison is not as incongruous as it might seem at the first glance. Like Roland, Harold is a doughty and successful warrior, beloved of his king (Charlemagne/the late King Edward) and who enjoys the loyal support of a valorous comrade. Like Roland he is impulsive and unwilling to listen to advice; and like Roland, he will be responsible for his own death and that of his followers in battle. On the other hand, contrary to Roland, Harold is fighting on the wrong side. Far from defending the Christian faith, he is (according to Wace) putting himself and his men under threat of excommunication; though unlike the Saracens at Rencesvals, who are aware that they are engaging in an act of treachery, Harold's moral blind spot prevents him from recognising the situation for what it is.[78] Harold also lacks the grim determination of a Roland, twice expressing misgivings to Gyrth who upbraids him harshly for this lapse.[79] However, these moments of weakness are transitory and private. Harold's honourable end in battle means that he is not entirely unworthy.

Nevertheless, Harold's true strength comes from his brother Gyrth, who may be said to be William's most redoubtable foe. The character is mentioned by a number of historians, including Orderic Vitalis, William of Malmesbury, William of Poitiers and Guy of Amiens, but Wace turns him into a hero in his own right, to the extent that it has been suggested that the poet might have been drawing on a lost English tradition.[80] This is possible. It may equally be the case that in order to prevent his narrative from becoming reductively Norman-orientated, Wace needed to find a credible focus on the English side. It was potentially dangerous to give too much weight to the character of Harold, but Gyrth, who had no part in the origins of the conflict with William and was acting purely out of loyalty to his king and countrymen, was the perfect foil. As his presence at Harold's side is attested by the Latin sources, he was a plausible mouthpiece through whom Wace could articulate the 'English' point of view, and his death in battle by the hand of William himself (a detail borrowed from Guy of Amiens) is rich in symbolical significance. The specific circumstances surrounding the appearances of Gyrth in the narrative are sufficiently formulaic in nature for Wace to have extrapolated them from cues in his sources, or transposed them from common situations in epic poems. With the exception of his death scene, they are passages rich in direct speech: his advice to Harold (6905–38); his rebuke of Harold when he thinks of leaving the army just hours before the battle (7019–40); his masterful speech to the fearful English barons (7225–94); and a lengthy exchange with Harold as they survey the advancing Norman troops (7849–928). This last passage is a 'hatchet job' on Harold's reputation by Wace. Harold is initially heartened to see how few men William has at his disposal

---

[78] In this respect, Harold is not unlike the traitor Ganelon as he is depicted in the *Song of Roland*: to the end, he remains convinced that he was justified in doing what he did (cf. laisse 273).

[79] These two passages occur just before the encounter: on their spying expedition, 7010–18, and just before the battle-clash, 7891–6. Neither passage has equivalents in Wace's extant Latin sources.

[80] See Holden, Introduction, vol. 1, p. 154: 'On est constamment frappé par le rôle presque héroïque attribué par Wace à ce personnage secondaire, pour lequel on ne trouve aucune justification dans les sources et qui pourrait remonter à quelque tradition anglaise disparue', 'One is constantly struck by the almost heroic role given by Wace to this secondary character, for which one finds no justification in the sources, and which could go back to some lost English tradition.'

(7855–63), but is immediately corrected by his brother, who points out that the English troops are made up mainly of 'vilanaille' (7866), whereas the Normans are well-trained and well-equipped. He prophetically expresses an especial fear of the Norman archers: 'les saetes sunt mult isneles,/ mult plus tost vont que arondeles', 'The arrows are very swift; they move much faster than swallows' (7877–8). As is well known, Wace, like William of Malmesbury (iii. 242) and the Bayeux Tapestry, has Harold wounded in the eye by one of these arrows (8161–74). As the Norman elite troops come into sight, Harold gets worried, prompting Gyrth to regret that Harold did not take his advice and stay in London, from where he could have organised an effective resistance to the invaders. On the contrary, the king fixed the day for the encounter himself (7897–902 and 7907–17). Harold then explains (7918–22):

> "Guert," dist Heraut, "por bien le fis,
> jo li assis a samedi
> por ço qu'a samedi nasqui;
> ma mere dire me soleit
> que a cel jor bien m'aviendrait."[81]

This admission casts Harold as a superstitious, effeminate being who allows old wives' lore to shape his policy. It is not known where Wace found the information relative to Harold's day of birth – this is not the sort of detail one would expect him to make up – but Gyrth's reaction is entirely in character (7923–8):

> "Fols est," dist Guert, "qui en sort creit,
> ja nul prosdoem creire n'i deit,
> nul prosdoem ne deit creire en sort,
> a son jor a chascun sa mort;
> tu dis qu'a samedi nasquis
> e a cel jor poz estre ocis."[82]

Such sentiment tallies perfectly with William's own views on the matter, illustrated in the anecdotes of the drowned astrologer and his tumble upon disembarking, and further confirmed by the incident of the hauberk that very morning. Harold's dialogue with Gyrth shows the English king as an anti-William, and the reasons for engaging in battle at that specific time are revealed to be disastrously wrong-headed. The English have superior numbers, but unsatisfactory leadership: a fact further emphasised by Harold's confession that he had not been as diligent in securing top-quality troops as he could have, because he had been lulled into a false sense of security by a letter from the count of Flanders.[83] Though William is not aware of it, his army will be fighting in relatively

---

[81] 'Gyrth', said Harold, 'I did it for the best. I fixed a day for it and made it Saturday because I was born on a Saturday. My mother used to tell me that things would go well for me on that day.'
[82] 'He who trusts fate is a fool', said Gyrth. 'No worthy man should ever trust in fate; each man has his own day on which to die. You say you were born on a Saturday and on that day you can be killed.'
[83] Cf. lines 7955–65. One may recall that according to Wace, the count of Flanders refused to support William's campaign without a firm promise of recompense in the form of English territories (6249–90); within the logic of the *Roman de Rou*, it is therefore relatively plausible that the count of Flanders gave sensitive military information to Harold.

favourable conditions. If Gyrth had been king rather than Harold, the reader is left in no doubt that this would not have been the case.

The Battle of Hastings

Wace's account of the battle proper is a highly reworked synthesis of all the written sources at his disposal, adorned with the occasional amplificatory passage (the detail of which is typically drawn from his own fund of literary motifs), and supplemented by information which may have been derived from oral family traditions. The core texts used by Wace appear to have been the *Gesta Guillelmi* by William of Poitiers and William of Malmesbury's *Gesta regum Anglorum*, with occasional details from the *Carmen de Hastingae Proelio* by Guy of Amiens; the main events and protagonists follow the authoritative texts, with little or no attempt to reshape them in the interests of effective story-telling. Historical accuracy is the priority in this section, probably in response to reader expectation. The account of the battle, from the preparations early that Saturday morning to the burying of the dead on the Sunday, cover some 1592 lines, over 980 lines of which are devoted to the actual fighting.

As is conventional in medieval historiography, the encounter is introduced by battle-speeches where the leaders of both sides encourage their men; they then set out their troops in the desired formation. Wace opens the episode with the Normans. William thanks his men for their support, promises them recompense (7391–402), and proceeds to pass in review the reasons for going to war. The claim to the throne is barely mentioned, the accent being put on the history of treachery of the English towards the kinsmen of the Normans, with the St Brice massacre (7415–22), the torture and death of the atheling Alfred at the hands of Earl Godwin and the massacre of his companions (7423–36). The battle is thus presented as an act of vengeance for these evil deeds, with the bonus of untold riches to be gained (7437–50). This rousing speech is rewarded by a spontaneous acclamation, where all vow to fight to the death for their leader (7451–4). William then continues, warning his men that no mercy is to be expected from the treacherous English and no retreat is possible:[84] they should choose an honourable death in battle rather than be cut down whilst fleeing. If they do so, he has no doubt that victory and glory will be theirs (7481–6). The speech is cut short by William FitzOsbern, William's steward, who is anxious to put on his armour; this haste leads to the incident of the hauberk put on the wrong way round (7487–530). The duke's speech is so effective that he has trouble finding someone who is willing to forfeit the chance of glory in battle in exchange of the honour of being the Norman standard bearer; two of his worthies decline the offer (Ralph of Conches and Walter Giffard), and the standard is eventually entrusted to Turstin son of Rollo the White from Bec-aux-Cauchois, who thus earns enduring privileges for his descendents (7575–644).[85] William then issues instructions to the barons

---

[84] This part of the speech (lines 7463–78) closely follows the corresponding passage in William of Poitiers (II, 15).

[85] The passage describing the choice of the standard-bearer is not found in Wace's sources, though

leading the different parts of the army, and Wace describes the equipment of the Norman troops and the battle formation (7645–98).

After the Normans, the focus moves to the English; and here, Wace was confronted with a dearth of information in his authorities, which imperatively had to be supplemented for the sake of narrative balance. The list of the counties that responded to Harold's summons (7707–44) is readily accounted for by Wace's knowledge of English geography, and the makeshift weapons of the English peasants (7703–6) were probably supplied by common sense.[86] Technical detail could have been derived from veterans' tales transmitted in Norman families; thus, the description of the makeshift shield wall favoured by the English (7791–808):

> Geldons engleis haches portoent
> e gisarmes qui bien trenchoent;
> fait orent devant els escuz
> de fenestres e d'altres fuz,
> devant els les orent levez,
> comme cleies joinz e serrez;
> fait en orent devant closture,
> n'i laissierent nule jointure
> par onc Normant entrels venist
> qui desconfire les volsist.
> D'escuz e d'ais s'avironerent,
> issi deffendre se quiderent;
> e s'il se fussent bien tenu
> ja ne fussent le jor vencu,
> ja Normant ne s'i enbatist
> que l'arme a honte n'i perdist,
> fust par hache, fust par gisarme
> ou par machue ou par altre arme.[87]

This shield wall is hinted at by William of Poitiers (ii, 16–17) and is roughly suggested on the Bayeux Tapestry, but the practicalities of its use and its effectiveness points to a source of information who had had the opportunity to observe the tactic closely.

The entire section devoted to the preliminaries of battle functions on a principle of opposition between the two sides. The improvised weaponry of the English soldiers is in sharp contrast with the high-quality, state-of-the-art

---

Orderic Vitalis also states that the person carrying the Norman banner was 'Turstinus filius Rollo' (Book III, ii. 147).

[86] Their 'machues' (cudgels), 'granz pels' (great pikes), 'forches ferees' (iron forks) and 'tinels' (clubs) are almost identical to the weapons of the rebellious peasants under Duke Richard II (*Troisième Partie*, 883–8).

[87] 'The English foot soldiers carried axes and pikes, which were very sharp; they had made shields for themselves out of shutters and other pieces of wood. They had them raised before them like hurdles, joined closely together; from them they had made a barrier in front of them. They left no gap through which a Norman, intent on discomfiting them, could penetrate them. They surrounded themselves with shields and small planks, thinking they could defend themselves in that way. If they had held firm, they would not have been beaten that day; no Norman would ever have broken through without losing his soul shamefully, whether from an axe or a pike or some other weapon.'

equipment of the Normans,[88] while the relatively small force supporting William is shown facing huge odds, with English troops coming from all the southern counties and as far north as Lincoln. William is an inspirational and enthusiastic orator, whereas in the equivalent passage on the English side, Harold is decidedly lacklustre, stressing the experience of the Norman troops and enjoining his men to be merciless with the enemy (7753–76). The scene describing William's impressive appearance when fully armed on horseback (7535–66) is matched by the terse statement that Harold 'out armes e ator/ qui conveneit a tel seignor', 'had weapons and equipment befitting such a lord' (7751–2), hinting that the English king was less personable than the Norman duke. Moreover, Harold's confession to Gyrth, just before the battle clash, that he had chosen that day for the encounter because of a superstitious belief, puts the finishing touches to Wace's constrasting of the two leaders. Finally, the arrangement of the English troops seems amateurish and haphazard compared to William's three divisions placed under specific war-leaders with clear orders: the men of Kent are placed in the front line, the Londoners defending the royal standard, their sole orders being not to break ranks.[89]

The situation prior to the battle-clash is that the Normans are fighting against huge odds, but have a distinct advantage in terms of experience, equipment and warfare technology. This is stressed by Wace (7777–90):

> Heraut out grant pople e estult,
> De totes parz en i vint mult,
> mais multitude petit valt
> se la vertu del ciel i falt.
> Plusor e plusor ont pois dit
> que Heraut aveit gent petit
> por ço que a lui meschaï,
> mais plusor dient e jel di,
> qui contre un home altre enveast
> la gent al duc poi foisonast;
> mais li dus aveit veirement
> plusors barons e meillor gent,
> plenté out de boens chevaliers
> e grant plenté de boens archiers.[90]

The statement that many people have questioned the odds faced by William's army is intriguing. This is the sort of comment one might expect from an English

---

[88] The quality of the equipment of the Normans, according to Wace, extends to horse armour; William FitzOsbern's horse is 'tot covert de fer', 'all covered in iron' (7490). This is surprising, as such metal horse protection did not become common practice before the thirteenth century (see Arnold, note to line 7490). The demands of rhyme ('fer' rhymes with 'Osber') probably explain much, though it is unlikely that Wace would have introduced an element that his audience could not recognise.

[89] It must be noted, however, that Wace probably did not have any information relative to the English battle plan, and thus could not include the sort of detail he provides for the Norman side.

[90] 'Harold had many bold men and they came in great numbers from all directions, but a multitude is not worth much if the favour of heaven is lacking. Then person after person said that Harold had few men because things had gone against him. But many people say, and so do I, that if pitted one to one against each other, the duke's men would not have been numerous. But the duke had in truth many courageous men and better men; he had plenty of good knights and a huge number of archers.'

perspective, but it is striking that Wace does not qualify this view in partisan terms, and it is equally possible that such 'revisionist' views were expressed by disgruntled French observers eager to belittle the achievement of an upstart Norman duke. One could easily imagine a youthful Wace being teased in this way during his studies in France, making the poet feel that the point needed to be made. The superior equipment enjoyed by the Normans is further noted by Gyrth as he observes the advancing of William's troops (7868–78), and the technological advantage offered by the cavalry is explicitly pointed out by the narrator in the course of the battle (8603–12):

> Engleis ne saveient joster
> ne a cheval armes porter,
> haches e gisarmes teneient,
> od tels armes se combateient;
> hoem qui od hace velt ferir
> od ses dous mains l'estoet tenir,
> ne poet entendre a sei covrir
> s'il velt ferir de grant aïr;
> bien ferir e covrir ensemble
> ne peot l'en faire, ço me semble.[91]

The dispassionate tone of this last passage is characteristic of the account of the actual fighting. The moral polarisation at work in the sections recounting the run-up to battle and the preliminaries to the battle-clash gives way to a more detached mode of narration where facts appear to be presented with surprisingly little propagandist slant. The English battle-cries show that the English are as Christian as the Normans, thus undermining the crusading overtones present in preceding passages, a fact underscored by Wace's pointed translation of these battle-cries for his non-English-speaking readership (7983–8):

> Alierot sovent crioent
> e Godemite reclamoent;
> Alierot est en engleis
> que Sainte Croiz est en franceis,
> e Godemite est altretant
> com en franceis Deu tot poissant.[92]

The bias is still in favour of the Normans, but not overwhelmingly so.

Ostensibly, the literary template for the battle of Hastings is the *Song of Roland*, which is recited by Taillefer before the first blow of the encounter (8013–18) and is mentioned again at the end of the fighting, where Duke William's prowess is likened to that of Roland and Oliver by his admiring retainers (8932–6). In actual fact, the amount of literary elaboration in this section

---

[91] 'The English were not skilled in jousting or in bearing arms on horseback. They held axes and pikes and did battle with such weapons; a man who intends to strike with an axe cannot give his mind to protecting himself, as he has to hold it with both hands to strike with great vigour. To strike well and protect oneself at the same time is impossible, it seems to me.'

[92] 'They often called out "Alierot" and called on "Godemite". Alierot [Holy Rood] in English is Sainte Croiz in French and Godemite is the same in French as Almighty God.'

of the work is limited and remains almost exclusively on a stylistic level. *Enumeratio*, isocolon, the repeated use of 'mult veïssiez' and its near-variations ensure an epic flavour to the account,[93] but these descriptive passages are mainly formulaic in nature and could have been found in any major battle scene elsewhere in the *Roman de Rou* or in the *Roman de Brut*. One might have expected the general mêlée to be punctuated by rousing descriptions of single combat between named heroes and especially redoubtable or prominent enemies, possibly with an element of gradation in the challenges the warriors have to face. This is the usual pattern in the *chanson de geste*, as indeed in Arthur's battles in the *Roman de Brut*. Wace was clearly aware of the convention, but he does not choose to follow it. The actual fight at Hastings is on the whole a faceless and anonymous butchery, with striking details tending to relate to groups of people, such as the English archers and their insect-like arrows (8149–60), rather than individuals. Duke William is given some prominence (in particular towards the end of the battle), but Wace was clearly reluctant to give even the Conqueror a markedly heroic stature. He thus omits entirely the moment in the battle where William takes off his helmet in order to put an end to rumours in the Norman ranks that he had been killed, a moment recounted by William of Poitiers (II,18) and Orderic Vitalis (*Historia Ecclesiastica* III, ii. 148) and depicted in the Bayeux Tapestry. Similarly, instead of working up Gyrth's death at the hand of William into a gripping confrontation with a final verbal exchange between the adversaries, Wace presents Gyrth's end as almost incidental. Harold's brother, realising how desperate the situation had become, tries to flee, but (8825–8):

> Atant poinst li dus, si l'ateinst,
> par grant aïr avant l'empeinst;
> ne sai se de cel colp morut,
> mais ço fu dit que pose jut.[94]

William has therefore struck a fleeing man, apparently in the back, and possibly without knowing who his victim was.[95] And the blow might not even have been the death blow: it is probable, but Wace refuses to state it categorically, hiding behind his trademark 'ne sai'. There is nothing heroic in all this. The handful of vignettes depicting scenes of single combat tend to be impersonal, mainly because none of the English protagonists are named; they thus become interchangeable ciphers characterised only by their weapons, whether battle-axe or pike.[96] On the Norman side, while we are given an abundance of names, many of

---

[93] The actual battle-clash thus starts with the epic 'Eis vos' (8041), while 'mult veïssiez' and its variations ('mult oïssiez'; 'lors veïssiez', 'dunc veïssiez', 'veïssiez') occurs some thirteen times, typically in clusters.
[94] 'Then the duke spurred his horse and reached him, pushing him forward very violently; I do not know whether this blow killed him, but it was said that he lay there for a long time.'
[95] By comparison, the Bayeux tapestry depicts Gyrth facing his attackers, rather than fleeing.
[96] There are three scenes where an English warrior wields an axe, typically to great effect: lines 8253–94, where the Englishman is killed by Roger of Montgomery; lines 8371–414, where the Norman combatants remain unnamed; and lines 8717–45, where an axe-wielding English soldier almost kills Duke William himself. English pikemen occur in only one single-combat scene, lines 8295–328, where an unnamed French mercenary kills two English soldiers armed with pikes and fighting as a unit.

whom are said to have fought valiantly, only a few of these are actually described engaging with the enemy: Roger of Montgomery, William Malet (who has to be rescued after his horse is killed), the lord of a place called Troisgots, Robert FitzErneis (who dies in his attempt to take the English standard), and the duke himself, whose prowess is described over some 120 lines (8669–788), thus towering over the other participants in the encounter.

The extreme restraint shown by Wace in attributing specific feats to specific men (other than William) in this battle may partly be ascribed to caution. The people mentioned in his work would have had descendants eager to see their ancestor depicted in as positive a light as possible: a feat attributed to an unnamed knight could be claimed by a number of families for their own forebear, without causing too much friction. One suspects that the more obscure names mentioned in the lists of participants reflect local power dynamics that Wace as a Bayeux canon could not easily afford to ignore. This dimension is explicitly acknowledged in the passage relating to Roger of Beaumont (8331–6):

> Merveillos priés eü i ont
> ço pert as eirs qui riches sunt.
> Bien poet l'en saveir as plusors
> que il orent boens anceisors,
> e furent bien de lors seignors,
> qui lor donerent tels enors.[97]

The potential for offence to sensitive family pride must have been great, hence the poet's careful statement that he had to leave many names out of his narrative because of constraints of space (8653–62):

> Altres barons i out assez
> que jo n'ai mie encor nomez,
> mais nus ne poet a toz entendre
> ne de toz ne poet raison rendre.
> Ne pois de toz les cols retraire
> ne jo ne voil longue ovre faire;
> ne sai nomer toz les barons
> ne de toz dire les sornons,
> de Normendie e de Bretaigne
> que li dus out en sa compaigne.[98]

Moreover, it is certainly no chance that Wace refrains from attributing the key events of the battle – the deaths of Harold and his brothers – to anyone specific,

---

[97] 'Remarkable fame accrued to him from this, as is apparent from his heirs, who are rich; many people will tell one that they had good ancestors and that these men were on good terms with their lords who gave them such domains.'

[98] 'There were many other barons there, whom I have not yet named, but no one can deal with each one or give an account of each one. I cannot recount all the blows and do not want to compose a long work. I cannot name all the barons and do not know the full names of all the men from Normandy and Brittany whom the duke had in his company.' This is not just an excuse: a number of the men mentioned by Wace are difficult to identify precisely because the name he gives for them does not coincide with the full, 'official' name they might have had in, say, legal documents.

hiding behind his trademark 'ne sai'. As we have seen, the poet refuses to state categorically that Gyrth died as a result of William's blow; similarly, regarding Harold, we are told that 'jo ne sai qui l'ocist dire', 'I cannot say who killed him' (8834), a point laboured at some length a few lines later (8851–8):

> Ne sai dire, ne jo nel di,
> ne jo n'i fui, ne jo nel vi,
> ne a maistre dire n'oï
> qui le rei Heraut abati
> ne de quel arme il fu nafrez,
> mais od les morz fu morz trovez;
> mort fu trové entre les morz,
> nel pout garir ses granz esforz.[99]

The reference to authorities in this quote raises the question of Wace's attitude towards his sources. His refusal to make any statement regarding the nature of Harold's death-wound suggests that he did not consider any of the accounts at his disposal to be entirely reliable. Yet the works of William of Poitiers and Guy of Amiens are as close to eyewitness accounts as one can reasonably expect, and in the Middle Ages as nowadays, first-hand information was considered to be especially trustworthy. Wace may have viewed with some scepticism sources written with an overtly partisan agenda. Equally, he may have secured additional sources of information which he trusted more.

The possibility that Wace might have drawn upon narratives of the battle of Hastings that no longer exist is supported by the somewhat unusual sequence of events in the *Roman de Rou* at the beginning of the encounter. The Normans, we are told, meet with a first reverse when the English make them fall into a hidden ditch, leading to considerable loss of life (8093–6):

> En tot le jor n'out mie tanz
> en la bataille ocis Normanz
> com el fossé dedenz perirent,
> ço distrent cil qui les morz virent.[100]

This does not correspond to the events as recounted by William of Poitiers or Guy of Amiens; a hidden wall or ditch is mentioned by the extant written sources, but later on in the battle, and incidentally to the description of a feigned retreat by the Normans. However, the event was not made up by Wace: the Chronicle of Battle Abbey mentions a 'Malfosse' that certainly refers to the same thing.[101] The information is said to come, not from a combatant directly, but from 'those who saw the dead', that is, in all probability, the clerics whose duty it was to give a Christian burial to the victims of Hastings. The clerical origin of this particular story

---

99 'I cannot say, and do not say, nor was I there and did not see it, nor have I heard any authority say who felled King Harold or with which weapon he was wounded. But he was found dead along with the other dead bodies. He was found dead amongst the dead; his great efforts could not save him.'
100 'During the entire day the English had not killed as many Normans as perished in the ditch; this is what those who saw the dead bodies said.'
101 *The Chronicle of Battle Abbey*, ed. and trans. Eleanor Searle (Oxford, 1980), pp. 38–9.

may further be inferred from the fact that the hero of the hour is not William or one of his knights, but a bishop. The servants who were supposed to guard the equipment are so horrified by what they see that they are on the point of abandoning the equipment and running away (8097–105); but Odo of Bayeux calms them down and rushes into battle himself, armed with a club (8106–28). Once again, Odo's part in the battle is not mentioned by Wace's written sources, though the Tapestry of Bayeux depicts a scene very similar to that recounted in the *Roman de Rou*.[102] The search for additional sources for important events would be consistent with Wace's working methods for the entirety of his *Roman de Rou*, and indeed for all of his preserved work.

A final reason for Wace's apparently half-hearted depiction of the Battle of Hastings could simply be that by the second half of the twelfth century, it was no longer a straightforward issue. The descendants of many of the conquerors had married into English aristocratic families and settled down in England sufficiently for them to feel a measure of discomfort with regard to the more violent aspects of the Conquest. It is perhaps significant that Wace's conclusion to Hastings (8875–7):

> Comment que chascun le feïst
> qui que morust ne qui vesquist
> veirs est que Guillame venqui.[103]

echoes that to the other key victory in the life of William, the battle of Val-ès-Dunes (4131–5):

> Ne vos voil dire, ne ne sai,
> ne jeo escrit trové ne l'ai,
> ne jeo n'i fui, ne jeo nel vi,
> li quel d'els melz se combati,
> mais jeo sai que li reis venqui.[104]

In the case of Val-ès-Dunes, William wins a battle fought against his own barons, with the support of the king of France. This is not really a cause for celebration; William's victory is also a Norman defeat. The narrator therefore avoids taking sides, concentrating on the end result: a strategy repeated with regards to Hastings. The Conquest is a highpoint in William's life, but Wace does not describe it as a moment of unadulterated glory. Not content with toning down the heroic gloss given to the battle by his Norman sources, the poet gives a final image of Hastings that is decidedly grisly, and not altogether complimentary to William himself. In a final act to defiance to the dead Harold, the duke has his standard raised where the English banner had been, and has his tent set up among the dead (8887–90):

---

[102] The main difference between the scene where Odo reassures the squires in the tapestry and Wace's version of events is that Odo's horse on the tapestry is black, whereas Wace states that he rode 'un cheval tot blanc', 'an all-white horse' (8121).
[103] 'However each man performed, whoever died and whoever lived, it is true that William won the day.'
[104] 'I do not wish to tell you which of them fought better, nor can I, and I have not found it in writing; I was not there and did not see it, but I know that the king won the day.'

> Entre les morz fist son tref tendre
> e la rova son hostel prendre,
> la fist son maingier aporter
> e apareillier son souper.[105]

On the face of things, this anecdote (which is found in Wace alone) seems to indicate William's faith in God's protection – as Walter Giffard points out to him, among the dead there could be survivors faking death, who might take advantage of the opportunity to avenge themselves on the Norman leader (8891–914). However, there are overtones of vindictiveness in this decision to feast, literally, over the dead bodies of his adversaries; the Conqueror does not come through as a likeable person, and he seems to have scant respect for the huge loss of human life around him.

Wace's account of the Battle of Hastings is unsettling, and designedly so. The final word on the rights and wrongs of the English campaign is put into William's own mouth, on his deathbed (9141–4):

> Engleterre conquis a tort,
> a tort i out maint home mort,
> les eirs en ai a tort ocis
> e a tort ai le regne pris.[106]

It is not Wace's purpose to describe the negative effects of this wrongful behaviour on the English – he summarily dismisses William's coronation and the subduing of England in just over 40 lines (8973–9014). However, the Conquest marks the beginning of the decline of the Normans, a painful process charted in the final section of the *Troisième Partie* of the *Roman de Rou*, recounting William's death and the chequered lives of his successors. Retribution cannot be avoided, and the new regal dignity acquired by William will prove to be something of a poisoned gift to his successors.

---

[105] 'He had his tent set up amongst the dead, ordered his lodgings to be taken there; he had his food brought there and his supper prepared.'
[106] 'I conquered England wrongfully and many men there were killed wrongfully; I killed their heirs wrongfully and took over the kingdom wrongfully.'

9

The Aftermath of Hastings

If William the Conqueror is to the *Roman de Rou* what Arthur is to the *Roman de Brut*, we would expect his highpoint to be followed by a pattern of decline. This is indeed what happens, but in such a different way to what we find in the *Roman de Brut* that the comparison is barely valid. Contrary to Arthur, William is a deeply flawed character, from whom much of the darkness in the ensuing narrative originates; his failure to follow in the footsteps of his wiser forebears and forego the royal dignity results in an identity crisis in the ducal family and leads to internecine warfare. The narrative ends with the demise of the last duke of Normandy (as opposed to duke-king), Robert Curthose, at the hands of his younger brother, King Henry I of England. There is more to this final section of the *Roman de Rou* than meets the eye. While Wace refrains from overtly commenting on the issues that arise in the wake of the merger of England and Normandy, we find echoes from earlier episodes in the work that give strong indications as to the poet's views. The final 1600-odd lines of the work are thus highly politicised, albeit in a relatively discreet way.

The aftermath of Hastings is both violent and unpleasant in the *Roman de Rou*, with Normandy apparently treated in a way not dissimilar to England by the victorious duke (9011–18):

> Maint travail out e mainte guerre
> ainz qu'il eüst en pais la terre,
> mais comment que il li fust grief
> de tote traist il bien a chief;
> en Normendie trespassa
> e quant il i vint tant ala
> pais fist deça, pais fist dela,
> larrons destruist, felons greva.[1]

The impression given by these lines is that William's grasp over Normandy is as insecure as it is over England, with the stress put on the punitive aspect of his visit. Whilst the quelling of robbery and thieving ('larrons') is entirely laudable,[2]

---

[1] 'William suffered much hardship and much fighting before he held the land [i.e., England] in peace, but, however distressing it was to him, he dealt with everything very successfully. He crossed over to Normandy; when he arrived there, he came and went as he pleased, making peace here and peace there, destroying thieves and punishing evil-doers.'

[2] The more positive view that William was an effective ruler able to impose law and order is the angle taken by Orderic Vitalis in the closest equivalent passage of his *Historia Ecclesiastica* (Book IV, ii. 165 and 167–8; ed. Chibnall, vol. II, pp. 192–9); but his interpolation to the Epilogue of William of

the mention of 'felons', which can mean 'traitors' as well as 'criminals', suggests an undercurrent of feudal revolt by nobles trying to take advantage of their lord's protracted absence, and therefore a breakdown in law and order due directly to the English campaign. This is in stark contrast with the way William of Poitiers (II, 45) describes the duke's return to Normandy in 1067:

> Aestiva illa, et autumnum partemque hiemis citra mare transegit, tempus hoc patriae amori omne donans; quae neque hac mora, neque superioris anni expeditione suas opes attenuatas fuisse dolebat.[3]

A terse, two-line mention of the foundation of an abbey on the site of 'the battle' (i.e., of Hastings) just after this passage relative to Normandy further increases the feeling of confusion in the *Rou* between William's two domains, and immediately gives way to the duke-king's problems with the king of France.

In practical terms, post-Hastings is depicted as being remarkably similar to pre-Hastings for William in that he still has to defend his duchy against external threats. Despite the fact that the king of France had forfeited any right to suzerainty over William's English territories by refusing to support him in his claim, Wace shows King Philip I of France attempting to capitalise on his vassal's good fortune and trying to extract service out of him for England (9021–43). In truth, the situation as presented by the poet is a considerable simplification of the events as recounted by other medieval historians, and obliterates the history of rebellion that opposed Robert Curthose to his father; but it allows a reiteration of the arguments in favour of the independence of the English crown from France, an issue which was still live at the time of Wace's writing. The *Roman de Rou* replaces family dissension by a vision of endemic warfare with a hostile neighbouring power (9047–54):

> Franceis sovent le guerreioent
> e mult sovent le laidengoent;
> Guilleme bien se deffendi,
> cels de France sovent laidi
> e mainte feiz li meschaï,
> ier gaaigna e hui perdi;
> de guerre faire vait issi,
> qui out perdu pois retoli.[4]

The way this passage is phrased recalls the stalemate that forced Rou and his companions to leave Denmark at the beginning of the *Deuxième Partie* (141–2):

Jumièges' *Gesta Normannorum Ducum* (vii. 44) mentions 'multiplices expeditiones', numerous expeditions, in Normandy, Brittany and Maine as well as in England (pp. 192–5).

[3] 'He spent that summer and autumn and part of the winter on this side of the sea, devoting all this time to his beloved homeland, which could not complain of having had its resources diminished by this sojourn or by the expedition of the previous year' (my translation).

[4] 'The French often waged war against him and very often caused him harm. William defended himself well and often damaged the French; many a time things turned out badly for him; one day he won and the next he lost. This is the way it goes in warfare; the man who had lost then gets things back.'

> Ainz dura la guerre, que onques ne faille,
> chescun y gaaigna e chascun y perdi.[5]

Whilst it is possible to read too much in this parallel (Leger Brosnahan lists some twelve passages in the *Roman de Rou* echoing a similar sentiment),[6] there is no doubt that it casts a shadow over the latter years of the Conqueror's rule. The acquisition of a crown has not given Normandy additional stability; on the contrary, it would seem.

William's death is presented as an indirect consequence of the state of semi-permanent conflict with France. The duke, we are told, was ill in Rouen and remained bedridden for a period of time (9055–60). The French king hears of this, and, poking fun at William's corpulence, makes a particularly bad joke (9064–8):

> Mandé li a par mal respiet
> que longues geseit en gesine
> comme feme fait en cortine,
> bien deüst des or mais lever,
> trop poeit longues reposer.[7]

William's reaction to this insult is extreme. He sends back an answer in the same vein. Referring to the thanksgiving ceremony that women underwent after childbirth, William states that when he is recovered, he will go to Mass in the king's lands with an offering of a thousand wooden candles with iron flames at their tip (9071–6). True to his word, as soon as he is able to do so, he mounts an expedition and sets fire to the French countryside. He burns down the town of Mantes, showing no regard for places of worship (9084–6):

> La vile mist tote en charbon,
> les bors arstrent e les citez
> e les mostiers ont alumez.[8]

Wace's account follows that of William of Malmesbury (*Gesta Regum Anglorum* iii. 281–2), though in a slightly abridged form, omitting in particular the mention of a recluse who was burnt to death in her cell. But even without the stigma of having caused the death of a female religious, William has clearly gone too far, and he is punished through the very fire he ordered to be lit (9087–94):

> Parmié la vile trespassout
> sor un cheval que mult amout,
> en un arsiz mist ses dous piez,
> mais tost les out a sei sachiez,
> par grant aïr avant sailli;
> li reis se tint qu'il ne chaï,

---

[5] 'Thus the war continued relentlessly; each man gained from it and each man lost.'
[6] See Brosnahan, 'Wace's Use of Proverbs', pp. 468–9.
[7] 'He sent him word as an unpleasant joke that he was lying in childbed for a long time, just as a woman does when she has a baby; from now on he ought to get up, as he could be resting for too long.'
[8] '[He] burnt the whole town to a cinder, setting fire to the burgs and the cities and setting the churches aflame.'

> e neporoc mult se bleça
> a son arçon ou il hurta.⁹

The wound will prove to be mortal. This very apt ending, one may note, is not in Orderic Vitalis (Wace's main source for this section alongside William of Malmesbury), and even William of Malmesbury presents the story as not necessarily entirely reliable, prefacing his account with the words 'dicunt quidam', 'some say'.[10] No such doubts in the *Roman de Rou*: William has met with retribution as a result of his own deeds.

William's deathbed speech further reveals the disturbing fact that he has scant respect for his own people. He acknowledges the warlike qualities of the Normans (9113–16), but then depicts them as unreliable and requiring a harsh and repressive leader (9119–30):

> Se il nen ont de seignor crieme,
> qui les destreignë e aprieme,
> tost en avra malveis servise,
> Normant ne sunt proz sainz justise,
> foler e plaisier les covient;
> se reis soz piez toz tens les tient,
> e qui bien les defolt e poigne,
> d'els porra faire sa besoigne.
> Orgueillos sunt Normant e fier
> e vanteor e boubancier,
> toz tens les devreit l'en plaisier,
> ker mult sunt fort a justisier.[11]

Admittedly, Wace is closely following Orderic Vitalis here; but William's deathbed speech in the *Historia Ecclesiastica*,[12] which is much longer than that in the *Rou*, does not give the same impression of unrelenting contempt for the Norman people. Moralising comments on the weaknesses of the Normans are not unusual in Orderic, who tends to use this device to avoid introducing a note of triumphalism when recounting past victories;[13] with Wace (who on the contrary has hitherto depicted the Normans in an entirely favourable manner) these words put in the mouth of one of the greatest of all of Rou's descendents have a very different impact.

While it could be argued that William's views of his own people are justified by his personal experience of almost continuous rebellion on their part, what is

---

9 'William rode through the town on a horse of which he was very fond; it set two of its feet down on a burnt part, but swiftly withdrew them and darted forward very violently. The king prevented himself from falling, yet he was severely wounded by his saddle-bows with which he collided.'

10 *Gesta regum Anglorum* iii. 282. 2.

11 'If they [i.e., the Normans] have no fear of a lord who constrains and represses them, they will begin to give bad service. The Normans are not brave without discipline; it is appropriate to oppress and subdue them. If a king constantly keeps them down and is someone who represses and subdues them well, he will be able to conduct his affairs with them. The Normans are arrogant and proud, boastful and overweening; they should be repressed the whole time, for they are very hard to discipline.'

12 The Conqueror's deathbed scene is in Book VII, 15–16 of Orderic Vitalis's *Historia Ecclesiastica* (ed. Chibnall, vol. 4, pp. 80–101).

13 See Marjorie Chibnall, *The Ecclesiastical History of Orderic Vitalis* (Oxford, 1980), vol. 1, pp. 77–84.

striking in the *Rou* is the extent of his alienation from them. There is no hint of affection in his words, and the treatment he advocates towards the Normans is closer to that meted out to an unstable conquered population than to one's own kinsmen. Depending on one's viewpoint, these instructions to Robert Curthose, his successor to the duchy, are either prophetic – Robert will indeed fail to maintain his authority over the Norman barons – or the direct cause of the troubles to come, as he instils into his son governing principles that seem designed to cause uprisings. William's perspective as an outsider is further indicated by the fact that he speaks of a king ('reis', 9124) keeping the unruly Normans 'soz piez', literally, 'underfoot', rather than of a duke. Once again, this could be seen as prophetic – the crown of England and the duchy of Normandy will not remain in separate hands for very long – but it could equally be construed as an encouragement to his more favoured son William (and after him, Henry) to view Normandy as an appendage to England, thus sowing the seeds of brotherly strife.

England, on the other hand, is viewed by William with remorse. In sharp contrast with the unwavering certainty he displayed throughout his life, he now confesses that he had no right over England, and therefore does not feel able to grant the English crown to his son William Rufus (9141–8):

> Engleterre conquis a tort,
> a tort i out maint home mort,
> les eirs en ai a tort ocis
> e a tort ai le regne pris;
> e ço que j'ai a tort toleit,
> ou jo nen aveie nul dreit,
> ne dei mie a mon filz doner
> ne a tort nel dei eriter.[14]

This follows what we find in Orderic Vitalis, but the almost obsessive repetition of 'a tort' gives special prominence to the point. This last-minute realisation on William's part is not entirely convincing in the *Rou*, any more than it is in the *Historia Ecclesiastica*, and smacks more of a pious pose than of heartfelt contrition. It is also politically astute: William arranges for the archbishop of Canterbury to offer his son the throne (9149–54), thus giving the illusion of a freely chosen succession by the English. However, though belatedly, the legitimacy of Harold's elevation to the throne of England is now implicitly validated, and with it the legitimacy of the eventual accession to Henry I to the English crown in comparable circumstances. In addition, the reticence of the Normans to lend William their support and the obvious distrust with which the barons viewed their duke is retrospectively justified, as his moral judgment is now revealed to have been flawed.

The extent of William's personal inadequacy is encapsulated in the account of his funeral. Even though his death is that of a good Christian king, having received the sacraments (9165–70) and entrusting his soul with his dying breath

---

[14] 'I conquered England wrongfully and many men there were killed wrongfully; I killed their heirs wrongfully and took over the kingdom wrongfully. What I stole wrongfully and had no right to I ought not to give to my son, neither should I endow him with it wrongfully.'

to God and Our Lady in full lucidity (9228–32), he immediately reaps the reward for his lack of respect towards his people. His retainers steal all they can and leave his dead body unattended (9241–8):

> Veïssiez mult servanz errer
> e cels issir e cels entrer,
> velos e covertos embler
> e quanqu'il porent trestorner.
> Une loee prof entiere
> ainz que le cors fust mis en biere,
> laissierent sol le rei gesant
> que l'en soleit criendre vivant.[15]

There is no emotional bond between William and those surrounding him, and as a result there is no mourning at his passing, just a joyful plunder of the spoils left behind. The contrast made by Wace between past fear and present disrespect is not just a moralising comment on the fall of the mighty,[16] but a hint as to the underlying cause for the undignified treatment of the dead Conqueror: he had relied too heavily on fear. The state funeral is then disrupted not once, but twice. A fire alert just as the coffin was about to enter the church results in the instant disbanding of the procession; the body remains stranded outside the church doors with only the monks in attendance (9249–72). Only when the fire has died down can the ceremony be resumed. A second interruption occurs as the body is about to be placed in its final resting-place. A certain Ascelin son of Arthur claims property of the land, stating that William had unlawfully dispossessed him of the ground on which the church was built: 'par sa force le me toli/ onques pois dreit ne m'en offri', 'he took it away from me by force and never afterwards offered to compensate me' (9307–8). On investigation, it is established that Ascelin's claim is entirely founded. He eventually releases the tomb in exchange for sixty shillings (given by the bishops) and assurances from the barons (9325–38). The narrator notes the irony that a king who had been so powerful 'nen a de terre quite tant/ ou sis cors giese al moriant', 'did not have any land free of claim in which his body could lie in death' (9323–4): once again, an apparently conventional sentiment, but which could also be read as a reiteration of the underlying theme of William's moral inadequacy.[17] Wace implies that the Conqueror did not despoil just the English of what was rightfully theirs; the Normans were equally his victims. Worse: even William's pious gestures have been tainted by theft.[18] His was not a good rule.

---

[15] 'You would have seen many servants moving about, coming and going, taking away velvet and coverlets and whatever they could remove. It took almost the time needed to cover a full league before they placed the body on a bier; they left the king, whom people were accustomed to fear when he was alive, to lie alone.'

[16] Wace draws this scene from Orderic Vitalis, *Historia Ecclesiastica* vii. 16 (ed. Chibnall, vol. 4, pp. 110–13); the moralising comment, however, is his own.

[17] Wace does not make any overt connection between William's illegitimate birth and his shortcomings as a ruler, but the recurrent mention of his bastardy and his low-born maternal grandfather in the section of the *Rou* recounting his youth may have been intended to point in that direction, in the light of the events surrounding his death.

[18] While Wace had no compunction in including in his narrative anecdotes illustrating the absence of love

William's succession arrangements, whereby his eldest son receives Normandy, his second son England and his youngest son just a sum of money (albeit a hefty one), prove to be disastrous. Warning of forthcoming brotherly strife is given with the account of William's conflict with his own brother Odo of Bayeux, inserted by Wace after the mention of the general amnesty proclaimed by the dying Conqueror.[19] Whereas, according to William of Malmesbury, Odo was trying to buy himself the papacy, in Wace his ambitions make him a potential rival to William (9185–92):

> Priveement aveit enquis
> e demandé a ses amis,
> se ja evesque reis sereit
> ne se ja reis estre porreit;
> reis esperout qu'il devendreit
> se li reis ainz de lui morreit,
> en son grant aveir se fiout
> e es granz genz que il menout.[20]

Odo's secular ambitions eventually lead to his being treated like a secular lord and imprisoned in Rouen for four years.[21] With such an example set to William's elder sons, it was unlikely that either would take the risk of making Henry 'riche e manant/ plus que home de lui tenant', 'rich and wealthy, more than any man holding land from him' (9161–2), as their father enjoined them to do. Such a course of action would have been tantamount to encouraging their young brother to aspire to their own dignities. But the fact remains that according to Wace's account, an injustice has been committed.[22] A king's son should not be landless, as Henry is. No good can come of it.

The final section of the *Roman de Rou* is very much Wace's own, with a number of details and anecdotes not found elsewhere and a focus that is quite different to that of Orderic Vitalis,[23] William of Malmesbury or Robert of Torigni's Continuation to the *Gesta Normannorum Ducum*, where the emphasis moves towards England. The subject-matter of the work for Wace remains Normandy and her dukes: England and the Anglo-Norman kings are only of

---

between the Normans and their dead duke, one may note that he refrains from mentioning details that relate exclusively to William's person, as opposed to his place in society. He thus omits the final indignity related by Orderic Vitalis, the stench which pervades the church as the hastily prepared body of the duke-king bursts: this purely physiological accident does not interest him.

[19] This explanatory parenthesis is also noteworthy in that departures from chronological sequence are rare in Wace's narratives.

[20] 'In secret he had enquired and asked of his friends whether a bishop could ever become king or whether he would ever become king; he hoped he would become king if the king died before him. He put his trust in his great wealth and in the large number of men he led.'

[21] In Orderic (Book vii. 8) and William of Malmesbury (iv. 277), William's refusal to allow Odo episcopal prerogatives, stating that he was arresting the count of Kent, not the bishop of Bayeux, reads more like a glib answer than the quite apt response to a case of overweening political ambition, as in the *Rou, Troisième Partie*, 9179–214.

[22] William of Malmesbury, *Gesta regum Anglorum* iii. 282, tells us that Henry was given his mother's lands; Wace chooses to follow Orderic Vitalis.

[23] Even Orderic Vitalis, who strives to be even-handed, betrays a bias in favour of Henry I. See Chibnall, *The Ecclesiastical History of Orderic Vitalis*, vol. 1, pp. 43–4 and 81–4.

peripheral interest, and are granted space in his narrative only when their actions and decisions impinge on Normandy. As in the earlier parts of the *Roman de Rou*, Wace therefore does his utmost to give a positive image of the new duke, Robert Curthose, whitewashing through omission where possible and including suitable material garnered, one assumes, from local family traditions. As elsewhere in the *Rou*, this information does not always prove to be entirely accurate, suggesting reliance on fallible human memories rather than written sources.

Initially, all seems to be well. After their father's funeral, Robert, we are told, remained in Normandy; his nickname of 'Curthose' is summarily explained as due to his short legs (9341–8). William Rufus goes to England and is crowned king by Archbishop Lanfranc; he rules for thirteen years (9349–8). As for Henry, he invested his money wisely (9349–64). In England, William Rufus attracts many valorous knights, in a manner not unlike King Arthur, and displays a generosity aligning him with his grandfather Robert the Magnificent (9365–70):

> Li reis Ros fu de grant noblesce,
> proz fu e de mult grant largesce;
> n'oïst de chevalier parler
> que de proeise oïst loer,
> qui en son brief escrit ne fust
> e qui par an del soen n'eüst.[24]

The point made by Wace here, once these lines are stripped of their formulaic gloss, is that William Rufus has built up the base for a strong and loyal army. When Robert, jealous at the fact that his younger brother has been made king, decides to invade England to seize the throne for himself, the reader immediately knows that the duke is taking on more than he thinks. Henry's canny handling of his money is also of prime importance in this matter, as Robert borrows it to fund the campaign.

At this stage, Henry appears to be on good terms with Robert Curthose, if not actually close. He lends him his money, receiving the Cotentin in return as pledge, to enjoy until the loan is refunded (9380–96). Similarly, in an anecdote found only in the *Rou*, Robert generously 'gives' Henry one of his vassals, Richard of Reviers, at Henry's request. Richard is not consulted on the matter, nor, apparently, is he best pleased with this enforced career move, which is very much a demotion;[25] this prompts the duke to recommend Henry to the reluctant knight with what seems to be genuine brotherly affection (9413–20):

> "Richart," dist li dus, "si fereiz,
> Henri mon frere servireiz,
> vostre fieu e vos li otrei;
> n'est pas mains gentilz hoem de mei.
> Sis hoem seiez, jel vos comant,

---

[24] 'King Rufus was a man of great nobility; he was brave and very generous. He did not hear of any knight whose prowess he heard praised and then fail to mention him in his register and give him some annual reward.'

[25] The narrator hedges the issue somewhat: 'jo ne sai que Richart pensa/ mais semblant fist qu'il li pesa/ que il deveit du duc partir', 'I do not know what Richard thought about this, but he gave the impression of being very upset that he was to leave the duke' (9409–11).

> servez le bien d'ore en avant,
> vos n'avreiz ja de lui hontage,
> nos somes andui d'un parage."[26]

Wace's depiction of the relationship between Henry and Robert is overwhelmingly to the advantage of Robert. Whereas Henry is prepared to back a fratricidal war with his money rather than trying to advise against it, Robert's trust in Henry is such that he willingly divests himself of an outstanding retainer out of sheer generosity of spirit. In this he is being imprudent, alienating the loyalties of men who are treated like pawns and weakening himself on the eve of a major campaign. Such imprudence, and an ill-advised indulgence of Henry, will be the hallmarks of Robert's rule.

At the heart of the relationship between the three brothers is the issue of money. Robert's campaign against William Rufus (the details of which are entirely omitted by Wace)[27] is eventually settled without bloodshed, by an agreement on the part of the king to make a yearly payment to his older brother of five thousand pounds, for the rest of his life. This settlement changes the patterns of alliance with the brothers. William Rufus resents Henry for having lent Robert his money, while Robert resents owing the money to him. The duke reclaims the Cotentin, but does not refund Henry, who finally seeks refuge in Brittany and defies his brother from his stronghold on the Mont St Michel. The poet's sympathies at this stage seem to be with Henry, on bad terms with both his brothers and left virtually destitute as a result of his loan to Robert. The decision to wage war from the Mont St Michel comes from despair and Henry acts on the advice of Count Hugh of Avranches, who in a vignette found only in Wace praises the site as an excellent base for military activities, concluding (9515–18):

> "Jo ne te rois ne ne comant,
> ne tu, ço crei, ne vals pas tant
> que tu faces ço que jo di,
> mais jo l'eüsse fait issi."[28]

Hugh of Avranches, in this little speech, as good as dares Henry to defy his brother in open warfare, and in the absence of any obvious alternatives, that is exactly what he does (9519–23):

> Jo ne sai se li quens plus dist
> ne quel semblant a Henri fist,
> mais Henri est sempres montez
> e el Mont est sempres alez.[29]

---

[26] ' "Richard", said the duke, "you will do this and serve my brother Henry. I grant him your fief and yourself as well; he is no less noble a man than I. Be his vassal, I command you, serve him well from now on and you will never be shamed by him. We are from the same family." '

[27] One may note that Wace is alone in saying that Robert and his army actually landed in England (9426–7). However, the three pages devoted by Orderic to the debate as whether to buy off Robert dwindle to a mere six lines outlining the final decision (9435–40).

[28] 'I do not ask you or command you, nor, I believe, do you have it in you to do what I say, but I would have done it in that way.'

[29] 'I do not know whether the count said any more or what impression he gave Henry, but Henry mounted his horse at once and went straight to the Mount.'

Henry comes over as an inexperienced and isolated young man taken over by events, forced into rebellion rather than naturally fractious.

Henry's first military experience, harrying the Cotentin and the Avranchin from his stronghold with the support of Breton troops, proves to be so much of a success that his brothers decide to join forces and besiege the Mont St Michel. This campaign is recounted by Wace in a light-hearted manner at odds with the gravity of the situation. The fighting has a stylised quality, reminiscent of chivalric romances where wandering knights seek jousting partners (9541–6):

> Mult veïssiez joster sovent
> e torneier espessement
> entre le Mont e Ardevon
> e la riviere de Coisnon;
> chascun jor al flo retraiant
> vont chevaliers jostes querant.[30]

While the terms 'jostes', 'joster' and 'torneier' are found in battle descriptions, they also belong to the more recreational register of tournaments. The two anecdotes provided by Wace relative to this campaign, drawn from Orderic Vitalis and William of Malmesbury respectively, further reinforce the impression that this is not a war conducted in earnest. The first of these concerns William Rufus. Knocked off his horse, he falls with his saddle. Rather than abandon the saddle, he fights hampered by it until reinforcements come and rescue him. Later, he is teased about it (9567–72):

> E li reis diseit en riant
> qu'il deveit estre al soen garant,
> honte est del soen perdre e guerpir
> tant com l'en le poet garantir;
> pesast li que Brez s'en ventast
> de sa sele qu'il enportast.[31]

After William Rufus's quirky attachment to his saddle, we are told of Robert Curthose's gift to his besieged opponents who had run out of drink. Henry quietly ('soëf', 9580) makes it known to Robert that he would really like some wine: he had plenty of everything, but not of that. As a besieged stronghold cannot last long without drink, one would have expected Robert to sit back and wait for his brother's surrender; but his response is quite different (9583–94):

> E Robert li a enveié
> – ne sai se il en ot pitié –
> un tonel plein de vin mult tost,
> del meillor qu'il trova en l'ost;
> e tot le jor a otreié

---

[30] 'You would have seen a great deal of jousting and intense fighting between the Mount and Ardevon and the river Couesnon. Each day, when the tide ebbed, the knights went forth in search of jousts.'
[31] 'The king said with a laugh that he had to be the protector of what was his; it is shameful to lose and abandon one's belongings as long as one can protect them. It would have upset him that a Breton could boast of having taken away his saddle.'

> e par trieues doné congié
> que cil del Mont eve preïssent
> e le Mont d'eve garnesissent,
> ou qu'il volsissent la preïssent
> seürement, rien ne cremissent.
> Donc veïssiez servanz errer
> e a veissels eve aporter.[32]

This is a disastrous decision, in military terms – the opposite of what a besieger is supposed to do – and Robert is sharply rebuked by William Rufus as a result. The duke justifies his action in terms of moral duty (9609–12):

> Torné me fust a felonie,
> e jo feïsse vilanie
> de neer li beivre e viande
> quant il meïsme le demande.[33]

Beyond the strong sense of honour and the admirable generosity evidenced here by Robert, one senses that this war, as depicted by Wace, is in part a game between Henry and his brother. The fact that Robert sent the drink to Henry is surprising enough; the fact that Henry quietly asked for it in the first place is even more so. William of Malmesbury iv. 310 states that Henry had sent envoys to Robert to discuss the need of water on the Mount – a public gesture – and Robert as a result ordered his men to slacken their watch, so that the water could be smuggled through the lines – an unofficial response. His generosity was therefore less flamboyant than is the case in Wace, but arguably greater, as the besieged could not have known that Robert was helping them. The appearances of warfare are maintained in William of Malmesbury as they are not in Wace's account.

The Mont St Michel siege in Wace brings out personality traits in the three brothers that will explain much of further events. William Rufus's refusal to abandon any property of his, even a saddle, foreshadows his eagerness to defend the territories under his control and reveals his sense of responsibility. Robert's gallantry, generosity and good nature are complemented with piety as he goes on Crusade to Jerusalem, but also foreshadow the lack of forethought that will characterise him on his return from the Holy Land. As for Henry, his barefaced cheek shows a man prepared to take risks and unencumbered by excessive scruples. Wace hints at a continuing history of confrontation between Robert and Henry, mentioning that Henry was imprisoned in Rouen for a period but managed to escape to Paris, was recognised by one of his retainers in disguise, and went on to take possession of Domfront. However, the reasons for the antagonism between the two brothers and the hard facts of warfare are pointedly left aside, with the narrator repeatedly refusing to broach the topic: 'Ne voil avant conter ne dire . . .',

---

[32] 'Robert sent him at once – I do not know if he felt pity for him – a barrel full of wine, the best he could find in the army. He granted the whole day and gave permission through a truce for the inhabitants of the Mount to be provided with water; they could take it wherever they wanted it in security, fearing nothing. Then you would have seen servants moving about and bringing water in vessels.'

[33] 'I would have been accused of felony and would have acted basely to deny him food and drink when he himself asked for it.'

'I do not wish to recount or say any more ...' (9629); 'Ne voil dire par quel saveir ...', 'I do not wish to say how cleverly ...' (9641); 'Ne voil dire coment li dus ...', 'I do not wish to relate how the duke ...' (9649). Robert does not appear to be very successful in his struggles with his brother (we are told that he had to leave all his equipment at Domfront, where he tried to besiege Henry there; 9647–56), while Henry has a touch of the romance character about him, escaping from towers and helped by a master of disguise.[34] He is predestined for great things, as we see from the prophetic words uttered (in Wace only) by the old peasant woman just before the death of William Rufus in a hunting accident: 'Or sai, or sai,/ une novele te dirai:/ Henris ieirt reis hastivement/ se mis augures ne me ment', 'I know, I know. I will give you a piece of news. Henry will soon be king if my ability to see into the future does not let me down' (10091–4).

It has been said of the final section of the *Roman de Rou* that it is somewhat confused,[35] and it must be admitted that the time-frame is hazy, while the relation between events is not always perspicuous. Indeed, when one looks more closely at the text, there are remarkably few 'facts' among the various anecdotes. One reason for this is that Wace was attempting to recount a genuinely confusing period in the history of Normandy, where internal strife probably gave rise to conflicting traditions as to what happened. A detailed account may well have carried too much of a risk of factual inaccuracy. Moreover, this is not a glorious moment in the history of Normandy, and too much information would inevitably have detracted from the stature of the narrative's avowed hero: the duke of Normandy. Hence, the wealth of asides by the narrator allowing him to skim over certain events, in particular the military campaigns opposing Duke Robert to his brother during the six years before his defeat and capture at Tinchebray,[36] where Wace attempts to give the impression of a stalemate between opponents of equal valour.[37] On a structural level, the unifying narrative principle of the work – the focus on the person of the duke – comes close to breakdown as the actual status of the protagonists changes with events. William Rufus, in addition to being king of England, is thus *de facto* ruler of Normandy and Maine while his brother Robert is on Crusade;[38] as for Henry, by the end of the work, he has moved from being a bitter enemy of the duke of Normandy to becoming the duke of Normandy himself. A crudely partisan approach is not possible, despite the fact that Robert Curthose is the first Norman duke to be defeated on his own territory. The solution adopted by Wace is to give even more prominence to anecdotes, drawn from a variety of sources (some of them lost) which allow the reader to compare and analyse characters and situations at various points in the narrative.

Wace's enhanced use of colourful anecdotes is readily perceptible in

---

[34] We are told (9637–40) that 'Haschier' – a character identified by Marjorie Chibnall (*The Ecclesiastical History of Orderic Vitalis*, vol. 4, p. 258) as Henry's tutor Richard Achard – had one of his eyes covered with a plaster in order not to be recognised.

[35] See for example Holden, *Le Roman de Rou*, Introduction, p. 163.

[36] See especially lines 11147–51 and 11345–52.

[37] See line 11143, 'Forz est li reis, forz est li dus', 'the king was strong and the due was strong'. Fluctuations in the balance of power are acknowledged through the inclusion of proverbial expressions on the unpredictability of war (see lines 11153–4) and an indirect reference to Fortune's wheel (11155–8).

[38] Robert mortgages his lands to his brother in exchange for the funds needed to go on Crusade (9666–78).

William's campaign of pacification against the citizens of Le Mans and their rebellious leader Helias while his brother is away crusading.[39] The story of William's decision to bypass two rivers because their names – the Cul, i.e., 'arse' and the Con, i.e., 'cunt' – would have given rise to too much teasing had he crossed them (9873–86, an anecdote found only in Wace) is clearly included to provide some light relief. The house he has demolished because, having vowed that he would take the most direct route to Le Mans, he found it barred his way (9819–32), gives insights into the king's character, illustrating unwavering determination. A third category of anecdotes give hints prefiguring future events, such as when William Rufus refuses to listen to the fears of the sailors, who are reluctant to set sail because of the weather conditions (9843–4):

> "Onques," dist il, "n'oï parler
> de rei qui fust neié en mer."[40]

This is a profoundly ironic statement in view of the death at sea of Henry's only son some years later, recounted by Wace in some detail (10173–94),[41] with a touching emphasis on the distress of the bereaved father and the faithfulness of his daughter-in-law to the memory of her deceased husband. When the White Ship sinks, it takes with it its royal passenger, but a mere butcher survives, proving William Rufus to be tragically wrong. Another anecdote announcing things to come, found only in Wace, relates to the siege of Mayet, sabotaged by the treacherous Robert of Bellême who passes off a joke by the king for an order, with the result that the besiegers fear for their lives at the hands of their own side and flee (9923–53). The same Robert of Bellême will be partly responsible for the demise of his duke, withholding his support at the crucial battle of Tinchebray (11391–4). The prominence given to the campaign against Helias of Le Mans, with a wealth of direct speech and descriptive passages, probably reflects its relatively straightforward nature, which allowed the poet more scope for elaboration. It was certainly an important event, but one may also note that it is one of the rare episodes in the final part of the *Roman de Rou* that does not oppose two members of the ducal family.

The death of William Rufus brings up once again the issue of the succession to the throne of England, as Robert Curthose finds himself passed over for the second time. With the account of the hunting accident of William Rufus, Wace treads on delicate ground. He scrupulously presents all the versions of the event at his disposal, carefully refraining from personal comment, with expressions such as 'si com l'on dist', 'so people say' (10048), 'plusors dient', 'many people say' (10061) and 'alquanz dient', 'some say' (10065). Even though both Orderic Vitalis and William of Malmesbury name the accidental slayer of the king as one Walter Tirel, Wace appears to be unconvinced (10057–60):

---

[39] This campaign covers over 330 lines (9699–10030); the material is drawn essentially from Orderic Vitalis's *Historia Ecclesiastica* (mainly from Book x. 8; ed. Chibnall, vol. 5, pp. 228–51) and William of Malmesbury's *Gesta regum Anglorum* iv. 320.
[40] ' "I have never heard of a king", he said, "who was drowned at sea." '
[41] Wace follows essentially the account of Orderic Vitalis here (*Historia Ecclesiastica* Book xii. 26; ed. Chibnall, vol. 6, pp. 295–307), in an abridged form.

> Ne sai qui traist ne qui laissa
> ne qui feri ne qui bersa,
> mais ço dist l'en, ne sai sel fist,
> que Tirel traist, le rei ocist.[42]

Such reluctance on the poet's part strongly suggests that Tirel was not universally believed to have been responsible for William Rufus's death;[43] and since Henry was present on that hunting expedition, it would have been surprising had he not been suspected of having a hand in such an opportune accident. Wace's inclusion of the otherwise unreported anecdote of the old crone may have been designed to counter such suspicions: at the time of the accident, Henry is given an alibi – he is with the peasants, well away from the scene of death. The large number of squires accompanying him (10101–2) could have vouched for this. Moreover, he could not have shot the king, since the string on his bow had snapped (10077–82). This solicitude for Henry's reputation reappears in the scene where he is offered his brother's throne. Wace, in marked contrast to Orderic Vitalis in this respect, states that Henry was very reluctant to accept the crown (10127–30):

> Henri s'en fist assez preier
> ainz qu'il le volsist otreier,
> son frere, ço dist, atendreit
> qui de Jerusalem vendreit.[44]

Henry's reticence in assuming a dignity that should by rights be his brother's could be interpreted as another argument against his having been in any way responsible for William Rufus's death; it is also a way of exonerating him from the charge of taking advantage of the absence of a man fighting for Christianity.

The deeds of Robert Curthose in the Holy Land are recounted relatively briefly by Wace (9685–98), but no doubt is allowed but that the duke was an important element in the success of the Crusade, bringing back as trophy a standard which he donated to Sainte Trinité, the abbey founded by his mother in Caen. We appear to have here an instance of divided loyalty on Wace's part: his subject-matter as he understood it dictated a pro-Robert bias, but he seems to have a powerful motive for giving a more positive image of Henry I than events really warrant. The need to placate Henry II was probably a consideration; but if one accepts Wace's claim that he was personally acquainted with Henry I, it could also reflect a measure of respect and admiration on the poet's part for the older king. In the event, the arguments put forward by the barons are powerful (10121–6):

> Ne voldrent pas Robert atendre,
> qui a Jerusalem ert prendre,

---

[42] 'I do not know who shot arrows and who did not, nor who made the hit and who stretched the bow, but people say, I do not know if he did it, that Tirel shot and killed the king.'

[43] These alternative versions could well have come from Tirel himself, of whom Wace seems to know more than his sources. He thus states that exiled Tirel lived for a long time in Chaumont (10115–16).

[44] 'Henry had to be begged a great deal before he was willing to accept it, saying that he would wait for his brother to return from Jerusalem.' The corresponding passage in Orderic Vitalis is *Historia Ecclesiastica*, Book x.15 (ed. Chibnall, vol. 5, pp. 290–5).

> n'il ne saveient qu'il fereit
> ne se ja mais repairereit;
> e al realme rei estoet
> ker sainz rei pas estre ne poet.[45]

As mentioned above in the discussion of the circumstances surrounding Harold's accession to the throne, this final argument echoes the justification for bypassing William, the Conqueror-to-be. In this case, however, the point was especially valid. Not only was Jerusalem far away, Robert was involved in an extremely dangerous military campaign against an unpredictable enemy; if he was not killed by the Saracens, he could be felled by some strange illness on the way home. The suggestion that Robert might not be willing to accept the throne (line 10123) could be a hint that he might choose to become king of Jerusalem instead.[46] It would indeed have been unwise to wait for him; though not unexpectedly, Robert will not see things in that way on his return to Normandy.

The events that unfold when Robert realises that the English throne has slipped through his fingers a second time initially parallel what had happened under William Rufus. Robert gathers an army, crosses the Channel, and prepares to fight for his rights. This second campaign is recounted at some length, and in much greater detail than the first expedition against William Rufus. Robert chivalrously refrains from attacking Winchester because the Queen is there in childbirth he marches in the direction of London and stops outside Alton Wood, having been told that Henry's troops are awaiting him on the other side. Negotiation then starts in earnest, as none of the barons wish to engage in a battle that would oppose them to their kinsmen (10369–74):

> D'ambes dous parz out filz e peres,
> oncles, nevoz, cosins ou freres,
> nus nen osout avant aler
> por ses parenz qu'il crient tuer;
> nus ne velt ferir son cosin
> ne son parent ne son veisin.[47]

They realise that if they do nothing, they will be forced to kill their own relatives (10390–2):

> que parent tuast son parent,
> cosin cosin e frere frere,
> parent parent e filz son pere.[48]

---

[45] '[They did not want] to wait for Robert, who was involved in the capture of Jerusalem. They did not know what he would do or if he would ever return. It is necessary for a kingdom to have a king, for it cannot exist without a king.'

[46] William of Malmesbury, *Gesta regum Anglorum* iv. 389, states that Robert refused the kingdom of Jerusalem, 'non reuerentiae, ut fertur, contuitu sed laborum inextricabilium metu', 'not from any consideration of modesty, it is supposed, but through fear of its insoluble difficulties'.

[47] 'On both sides there were sons and fathers, uncles, nephews, cousins or brothers, and no one dared advance for fear of killing his relatives. No one wanted to strike his cousin, his relative or his neighbour.'

[48] 'That relative would be killing relative, cousin cousin and brother brother, relative relative and a son his father.'

The efforts of the envoys, Robert of Bellême and Robert FitzHaimo, meet with success, mainly because Henry and Robert are equally perturbed by this situation (10381–4):

> Dote li reis, dote li dus,
> mais jo ne sai qui dota plus,
> por ço dotoent e cremeient
> qu'a lor parenz se combatreient.[49]

The arguments put forward by the envoys, foremost among whom are Robert of Bellême and Robert FitzHaimo, appeal to the opponents' sense of honour, dignity and, of course, family feeling (10421–5):

> Ne deit mie son frere abatre
> ne si grant gent faire combatre;
> de totes parz ad filz e peres
> e d'ambes parz nevoz e freres.[50]

In addition, Robert Curthose is reminded of his duty to set an example to those around him, having just returned from the Holy Sepulchre, and is subtly warned that the situation might turn against him (10435–8):

> Ensorquetot al comencier
> tel quide veintre e se fait fier,
> qui a la fin s'en part vilment
> e mult le fait hontosement.[51]

The warring brothers eventually come to an agreement; Henry undertakes to give Robert 3000 marks of silver every year for the rest of his life, and both formally pledge military support to the other in case of need (10451–62). Somewhat unwillingly, Henry also relinquishes Domfront and the Cotentin, which he had in his possession (10463–8).

Wace's account of this episode is noteworthy on three counts. First, he includes important information that is not found in his sources. In particular, Robert's gallant decision not to besiege Winchester is not related by Orderic Vitalis, William of Malmesbury or Robert of Torigni; the reluctance of the two armies outside Alton forest, which is a major factor in the outcome of the quarrel in the *Roman de Rou*, is likewise attested only by Wace.[52] Secondly, the prominence given to the theme of the bonds of kinship provides a moral yardstick with which to judge coming events. This in-fighting among brothers is clearly presented as unnatural as well as unseemly, and while the issue is not raised explicitly, under such strain, the loyalties of the barons are in danger of wavering.

---

[49] 'The king was afraid and the duke was afraid, but I do not know which was more so; they were afraid and fearful that they would be fighting their relatives.'
[50] 'A brother should not do this to his brother or make so many men fight each other; on both sides there were sons and fathers and on both sides nephews and brothers.'
[51] 'Moreover, a man who from the start expects to win and is ready for action can end up departing wretchedly and doing so in great shame.'
[52] To this, one may add that according to Wace, Robert lands at Portchester rather than Portsmouth.

The deceptively innocuous warning to Robert of the unpredictability of war, put in the mouth of the future traitor Robert of Bellême, foreshadows the choice that the Norman barons will eventually make. Finally, the personality of the two brothers is shown to be increasingly incompatible. Robert retains the generosity and sense of honour he displayed during the siege of Mont St Michel, considerate towards ladies (the queen in Winchester) and responsive to appeals to his sense of duty, whereas Henry comes across as somewhat ungracious. The financial settlement he offers Robert is not as generous as that offered by William Rufus before him, and he makes the territorial concessions grudgingly.[53] In addition, his subsequent dispossessing of their English estates of all the barons who had supported Robert smacks of vindictiveness.

Duke Robert's open-handedness and forgiving character soon proves to be counterbalanced by lack of forethought. Prompted by indignation at the injustice done to the barons dispossessed by Henry, he crosses the Channel with a small force, with the intention of confronting his brother. This expedition occurs 'sodeement', 'suddenly' (10569), without any prior negotiations, apparently, and with a woefully inadequate retinue (just twelve knights including himself, 10571). The duke had clearly failed to think things out properly. Moreover, hints Wace, he may have been manipulated, encouraged to act rashly by people carrying out Henry's instructions. The finger is pointed at William of Warenne, who fled to Normandy after being dispossessed of his English estates. Henry had a long-standing hatred for William of Warenne, we are told, because he used to tease him when he was young, calling him 'stag foot' due to his love of hunting (10513–54; this detail is found only in the *Rou*). But this could just have been a front (10555–62):

> Plusors dient, que que jo die,
> que par engien e par veisdie,
> par fause e par feinte haïne
> fu faite ceste dessaisine,
> e que li cuens fu enveiez
> por ço que il fu vezïez
> en Normendie al duc parler,
> ker mult saveit mal enarter.[54]

Wace is opposing a duke who is a paragon of honour to a king who is cunning rather than chivalric; and while Henry is never condemned directly by the narrator (who puts the blame on bad advisers, 10843–5), Robert is presented as a victim of deviousness.

Robert's second expedition to England is, of course, a disaster. The only reason Henry does not summarily capture and imprison him is that his retainer Robert of Meulan points out to him that there might be financial gain in not doing

---

[53] In fact, these concessions appear to have been a matter for debate; Orderic for example (Book x. 19; ed. Chibnall, vol. 5, pp. 318–19) states that Henry kept Domfront, and only ceded the Cotentin to his brother.

[54] 'Many people say, whatever I myself say, that this dispossession was the product of cunning and deviousness and of false and feigned hatred, and that, because the count was so cunning, he was sent to Normandy to speak to the duke, for he was very skilled at plotting to do harm.'

so (10585–94). Robert of Meulan thus manages to panic the duke (who does not seem to have realised that his presence in England could be construed as an act of aggression) into seeking refuge with the queen, and the queen in turn talks him into releasing Henry from the yearly sum he had undertaken to give his brother. Duke Robert endeavours to present this to Henry as a freely granted token of his brotherly love (10679–82):

> D'un pere e d'une mere fumes,
> un pere e une mere eümes,
> fraternité garder vos dei,
> ausi a vos com vos a mei.[55]

In a passage echoing his words to Richard of Reviers when ordering him to leave his service to join Henry, he also stresses their equal dignity, underplaying the importance of his seniority (10683–6):

> Altresi gentil, ço savez,
> comme jo sui, estre devez,
> n'a entre nos nul avantage,
> ço m'est avis, fors d'ainznaage.[56]

Even that advantage, he continues, compounding his humiliation, became Henry's when he was crowned king. He gives his brother a cue to match his generosity, inviting him to repay him with 'bels aveirs', 'fine things', rather than money (10702), but his hint apparently falls on deaf ears. This is the last appeal to brotherly love in the *Roman de Rou*; hereafter, Robert knows that Henry feels none for him and ceases to expect it from him.

Though the narrator's sympathy is firmly on the side of Duke Robert, the conflict with his brother revives as a direct consequence of his own unreasonable behaviour. In a retaliatory gesture for Henry's dispossessing of those barons who had chosen to support his brother, Robert harries Domfront and the Cotentin. When Henry decides to take up weapons on the issue, Robert tries to secure the loyalty of his barons by outlawing vassalage to both the king of England and himself, on the grounds that no one could serve two lords equally; a view endorsed by the narrator (10819–38). The reference to serving two lords is of course a biblical echo, the lords in question being God and Mammon;[57] and aptly, the entire end of the *Roman de Rou* is dominated by the power of money. Henry, who is described early on in the narrative as knowing how to invest his capital, shows in his maturity that he also knows how to spend it judiciously. He brings huge amounts of cash with him to Normandy, literally by the cartful (10857), to buy the duke's barons, and employ huge numbers of mercenaries (10875–82). By contrast, Robert does not know how to handle money; he squanders his resources (10884–8) and alienates the burgesses of Caen (the fortifications of which he has

---

[55] 'We were born of one father and mother; we have the same father and mother. I must maintain my brotherly relationship with you, I to you just as you to me.'
[56] 'As you are aware, you should be just as noble as I am, and between us there is no advantage, it seems to me, other than seniority of birth.'
[57] See Matthew VI.24 and Luke XVI.13.

strengthened) by his unreasonable demands when he runs out of funds to pay his mercenaries himself (10899–912), thus paving the way for their eventual treason. Duke Robert may well be a template of chivalric honour, but he is also signally divorced from reality and has none of the political acumen of his brother. Despite a gesture in the direction of a positive 'spin', Wace describes the duke as someone as feckless as he is unreliable (10923–34):

> N'ert mie mult encïentos
> e si esteit mult pereços;
> por pereços fu mult tenuz
> pois qu'il fu d'oltre mer venuz;
> peresce semble malvaistïé,
> plusor l'en orent chastïé,
> mais por nul boen chastiement
> ne pout aveir amendement.
> Quant li dus doner ne poeit,
> ou ne poeit ou ne voleit,
> par pramesses se delivrout,
> mult prameteit e poi donout.[58]

This is mild criticism compared to what we find said of Robert Curthose by Orderic Vitalis, and is closer to the more generous estimate of the duke's character by William of Malmesbury;[59] nevertheless, one senses a hint that Robert might not have returned from the Crusade with all his faculties intact, making him an incompetent leader of men.

However, despite his shortcomings, Robert Curthose remains the rightful ruler of Normandy and is faithfully served by outstanding men such as Gohier of Aunay (10935–43), whose defence of the town of Bayeux will be so successful that Henry resorts to burning it down (11103–28), and Robert of Arches, whose killing of Brun (one of Henry's mercenaries) in a joust eventually leads to his exile, to avoid the king's vindictiveness (10945–11060).[60] Loyalty to the duke also remains strong among the Norman people, as is shown by the extreme anger directed against the captured turncoat by the population of Bayeux, who almost lynch him for having 'guerpi son droit seignor', 'abandoned his rightful lord' (11102). Wace makes no effort to disguise his disapproval of those who left Robert to fight alongside Henry.[61] Robert FitzHaimo, who had changed camps

---

[58] 'He was not very prudent and indeed was very negligent; people had considered him to be negligent since his return from the Holy Land. Negligence seems like cowardice and many people admonished him for it, but in spite of being thoroughly admonished he showed no improvement. When the duke had nothing to give, being either unable to give or not wanting to do so, he evaded any difficulty with promises; he promised much and gave little.'

[59] See especially *Gesta regum Anglorum* iv. 389. 8, where William of Malmesbury ascribes many of Robert's problems to his 'morum dulcedine', his gentleness of character.

[60] The lively account of the tournament outside the battlements of Bayeux is found only in Wace. Holden, in his discussion of the sources to this section of the *Roman de Rou* (p. 168) suggests that it was included because of Wace's personal connection with Bayeux; while this may explain the origin of the episode, I would argue that its primary function in the narrative is to lend some much-needed chivalric glamour to a basically unedifying tale.

[61] The strongest condemnation of such behaviour occurs in the passage immediately following the defeat of Tinchebray (11383–9): 'Grant honte fait, ne poet graignor/ qui traïst son lige seignor;/ nus hoem a

and was rewarded for his services by the wardenship of the town of Caen, thus goes from being 'de grant non', 'of great renown' (11202) to being of very bad reputation, 'mult malvais cri' (11242). Tensions from that period of civil war may still have been live in Normandy in the second half of the twelfth-century, to judge from Wace's cautious refusal to name names in connection with the conspiracy that led to the betrayal of the town of Caen (11281–84):

> Plusors a ceste over partirent
> e ceste chose consentirent
> donc jo ne vos sai les nons dire,
> ne jo n'en voil mençonge escrire.[62]

Indeed, it would seem that Henry's eventual victory led to widespread resentment in Normandy towards those who had made it possible (11377–80):

> Lor seignor al besoig guerpirent,
> e por la honte que il firent
> del rei reçurent tels loiers
> donc il orent mal reproviers.[63]

This statement, made in relation to the battle of Tinchebray, makes it clear that from the Norman viewpoint mediated by Wace, these people have dishonoured themselves, and the rewards they have received merely emphasise the fact that they are traitors.

The ultimate proof that Duke Robert's demise was engineered by the forces of evil is provided in the *Roman de Rou* by the anecdote of the garden of Caen. The conspirators planning to hand over the town to the king meet in a garden, where they formally agree to abandon the cause of Duke Robert; but their treason has an unexpected effect (11304–8):

> Oïr poez miracle apert!
> Ker onques pois cel parlement
> – ço pois dire veraiement –
> li gardin ne fructefia,
> pome ne altre fruit ne porta.[64]

Beyond the moral message contained in the sudden barrenness of this garden, one may note that Wace vouches for the truthfulness of this story; he specifies where in the town the garden is to be found (between the church of Saint Martin and the wall next to the Porte Arthur, 11299–300), implying that the site could still be

---

seignor terrïen/ ne deit faillir por nule rien,/ menbre e vie li deit salver/ e terrïen enor garder./ Mal fist qui son seignor guerpi', 'He acts very shamefully, no one could do worse, who betrays his liege lord. No man, for any reason, should fail his earthly lord; he should protect his life and limb and uphold his earthly honour. He who abandoned his lord did wrong.'

[62] 'Many men, whose names I cannot tell you, and I do not wish to write down lies, were involved in this affair and consented to what happened.'

[63] '[They] abandoned their lord at this time of need; as a result of their shameful actions, they received rewards from the king, for which they were severely reproached.'

[64] 'You can now hear what is clearly a miracle! For never since this meeting – I can say this in truth – has the garden borne fruit; it has produced neither apples nor any other fruit.'

visited and was locally held to be a place blighted by the iniquity that took place there. The refusal of the earth to bear fruit for these people is also a form of poetic justice, referring to the motivation behind their treason: greed. The renegade barons at Tinchebray do so for the rewards promised by the king, but the plotters at Caen are depicted as little better than common thieves. When the duke eventually retreats from the town, a most undignified scene occurs (11321–32):

> Un barrier, qui out non Taisson
> – ne sai s'il aveit altre non –
> un chamberlenc a encontré,
> d'une male l'a destrossé;
> e li dus s'en ala avant,
> ne volt retorner par itant;
> jo ne sai se pois li rendi,
> mais jo sai bien qu'il li toli.
> Li pautonier qui içò virent
> ço que Taisson out fait si firent,
> les escuiers ont destrossez
> e abatuz e destorbez.[65]

The anecdote of the robbed chamberlain counteracts any sympathy the reader might have had for the burgesses of Caen, under constant pressure for money and so little valued by the duke that any defections on their part are dismissed with a 'Laissiez aler, laissiez venir! Ne poon pas toz retenir', 'Let them come, let them go! We cannot retain everyone' (10921–2). The duke is obviously at fault here, as he cannot be bothered to intervene – a marked contrast with his brother William Rufus, who had endangered his life for a mere saddle – but it is equally obvious that the desire for riches has overcome all other considerations among the townsfolk. And covetousness, stresses the narrator, is the root of all evils (11285–8).

The final note to the *Rou* is one of shame. Besieged in Tinchebray, Duke Robert and his men fight valiantly, but too many of his vassals have defected to the king. The Normans have turned traitor to their natural lord: the battle does not last long, and there are few casualties (11365–9). The duke is taken prisoner, and he dies after a long period of imprisonment in Cardiff, under the guard of Robert Count of Gloucester; he is eventually buried in Gloucester (11407–14). His faithful vassal, the count of Mortain, also remains imprisoned until Henry's death. This is the end of an era; from now on, Normandy will no longer be the sole concern of its ruler, competing with the responsibilities attendant on the throne of England. It is also the beginning of Wace's own lifespan, as he indicates in his Epilogue (11431–8):

> Treis reis Henris ai coneüz,
> en Normendie toz veüz;

---

[65] 'A gate-keeper by the name of Taisson – I do not know if he had any other name – encountered a chamberlain and robbed him of a bag; the duke moved forward, not wanting to go back for such matters. I do not know whether the latter returned it to him, but I do know he took it from him. The rascals who saw what Taisson had done did the same and robbed the squires, knocking them down and manhandling them.'

> d'Engletere e de Normendie
> orent truit trei la seignorie.
> Li secont Henri que jo di
> fu niés al premerain Henri,
> né de Mahelt, l'empereriz,
> e li tierz fu al segont filz.[66]

This passage is very close to that found in the Prologue to the *Troisième Partie* of the *Roman de Rou* (177–84), echoing it sufficiently to signal to the reader that the work is finished, but with one revealing difference. In the Prologue we are told that these three Henrys were both duke and king: 'Rei de Engleterre la guarnie/ e duc furent de Normendie', 'they were kings of England the Rich and dukes of Normandy' (183–4); in the Epilogue, the title specific to the Norman rulers is obliterated. Rou's successors have lost their identity.

---

[66] 'I have known three King Henrys and seen them all in Normandy; all three had lordship over Normandy and England.'

Part III CONCLUSION: THE EPILOGUE

It is customary to consider the *Roman de Rou* as an unfinished work, abandoned by its author before its completion because Henry II decided to entrust the project to someone else (11419–24):

> Die en avant qui dire deit;
> j'ai dit por Maistre Beneeit,
> qui cest'ovre a dire a emprise
> com li reis l'a desor lui mise;
> quant li reis li a rové faire
> laissier la dei, si m'en dei taire.[1]

This is certainly the impression derived from a first reading of these lines, and it must be admitted that the *Roman de Rou* ends rather abruptly. On the other hand, abruptness is the hallmark of the final section of the *Troisième Partie*, partly due to the increasingly present (and increasingly censorious) narrator. Moreover, from the battle of Val-ès-Dunes onwards – that is, in the part of the *Rou* where Wace writes as a historian rather than a historiographer – one senses a reticence, if not outright ambivalence, towards the material treated. Secure in his Bayeux prebend, Wace could easily have continued his work had he wished to do so; but there is nothing in the last 6000 lines of the *Rou* suggesting that he had ever contemplated going beyond Tinchebray. Bowing to the king's wishes reads as a convenient, non-controversial way of justifying this breaking point beyond which the subject-matter of the poem becomes subsumed under the history of the kings of England.

To this, one must add Wace's apparent disaffection towards Henry II himself. The warmth of the Prologue, where the king is lauded as a worthy scion of Rou, gives way in the Epilogue to an openly critical tone (11425–30):

> Li reis jadis maint bien me fist,
> mult me dona, plus me pramist,
> e se il tot doné m'eüst
> ço qu'il me pramist, mielz me fust;
> nel poi aveir, ne plout al rei,
> mais n'est mie remés en mei.[2]

---

[1] 'Let he whose business it is continue the story. I am referring to Master Beneeit, who has undertaken to tell of this affair, as the king has assigned the task to him; since the king asked him to do it, I must abandon it and fall silent.'

[2] 'The king in the past was very good to me; he gave me a great deal and promised me more, and if he had given me everything he promised me things would have gone better for me. I could not have it, it did not please the king; but it is not my fault.'

This unflattering image of the king reneging on his promises is not unlike that of Robert Curthose, who, like Henry II, was generous with his promises but less forthcoming when it came to keeping them. The nature of the promises made to Wace can only be guessed at, but the depth of the rift with Henry II may be inferred from his absence from the text at points where you would have expected the king to be mentioned. Most strikingly, Wace proudly states he was present at the reburial ceremony of the bones of Duke Richard II (2242) but fails to mention that the king was there too: an omission interpreted by Jean-Guy Gouttebroze as a deliberate slight on the part of the poet. Less glaring, but perhaps more significant, is the fact that in the lengthy parenthesis where Wace provides information regarding the marriage and offspring of Henry I, no mention is made of Henry II, or of his mother's second marriage. In sharp contrast with the attention devoted to Henry's son and daughter-in-law, Matilda is tersely dismissed (10144–8):

> Par le conseil Henri son pere
> fu en Alemaigne menee
> e a l'empereor donee,
> pois fu al regne coronee,
> empereriz fu apelee.[3]

This deliberate refusal on the part of the poet to introduce some little compliment to the king is all the more intriguing as Geoffrey Plantagenet is actually named a few lines later – but only as the brother of Prince William's widow.[4] Was the poet alienated by Henry's behaviour towards the Church, as suggested by Gouttebroze, and could the rift with Henry II have been caused by Wace's siding with Thomas Becket in the investiture crisis?[5] It has also been suggested that the poet might have lost his protector at court: Rita Lejeune connects Henry II's decision to withdraw his patronage from Wace with Eleanor of Aquitaine's estrangement from her husband after she had supported her sons' rebellion against their father.[6] This link with Eleanor is not entirely convincing, but the death of Henry of Blois in 1171 might well have damaged Wace's standing at court. Jean Blacker further considers the possibility that Henry II was offended by the relatively positive depiction of Robert Curthose in the *Roman de Brut*.[7] However, the key issue could have been one of scholarly integrity.

There is a real possibility that, when he undertook the *Roman de Rou*, Wace had misunderstood the brief entrusted to him by Henry, who in turn had seriously misjudged the poet's character and working methods. Henry's goal was a glorification of his ancestors leading up to a duly flattering account of his own reign. Wace's understanding of the commission was that it was to be a work of history with a celebratory stance. Jean Blacker, in her *The Faces of Time* (p. 44) notes

---

[3] 'Through the advice of her father, Henry, she was taken to Germany and given in marriage to the emperor; then she was crowned in that realm and called empress.'
[4] In fact, she was his aunt; one of Wace's occasional factual errors.
[5] 'Pourquoi congédier un historiographe', esp. pp. 302–8.
[6] R. Lejeune, 'Le role littéraire de la famille d'Aliénor d'Aquitaine', *Cahiers de Civilisation Médiévale* 3 (1958): 319–37.
[7] Jean Blacker-Knight, 'Wace's Craft and his Audience: Historical Truth, Bias and Patronage in the *Roman de Rou*', *Kentucky Romance Quarterly* 31 (1984): 355–62.

Conclusion: The Epilogue

Wace's persistence in grappling with difficult material and his 'zeal for accuracy': these very virtues may have caused his fall from favour. As long as the sources used by the poet conformed to the propagandist model Henry had in mind, this 'disjunction between intended and actual function'[8] was not perceptible; once Wace had to create his own historical discourse from a variety of sources, only a minority of which had a eulogistic intent, the misunderstanding would have become obvious. As we have seen, Wace's only real concession to propaganda is his willingness to omit material; he does not actively distort facts or misrepresent characters to make them fit into the propagandist mould. His account of the war opposing Henry I and Robert Curthose makes no secret of the fact that it was a disastrous episode in the history of Normandy, characterised by the breakdown of law and order and the ensuing paralysis of the economy.[9] It is fair to say that Wace's stance in the *Troisième Partie* of the *Roman de Rou* is increasingly similar to that of a monastic historian. This, on the one hand, is not unexpected: the poet was by now a senior ecclesiastic, and was writing in a manner befitting his new status. On the other hand, it could have come as a nasty surprise to Henry II, who probably did not foresee that the financial independence that came with Wace's prebend allowed him to free himself of the constraints placed on a court poet. Wace no longer could be considered a safe pair of hands; moreover, he was Norman, an insider with privileged access to sources that would not necessarily have corroborated Henry's preferred version of events. To make things worse, the poet was himself an eyewitness for much that had happened in Normandy (and possibly England) for over a half-century: his work would have held real authority. One can readily imagine the damage to Henry's image that the poet's seemingly artless mentioning of varying versions of the same incident could cause in (for example) the account of the ten-year campaign in Normandy of Henry's father Geoffrey of Anjou, as he was trying to reconquer the duchy for his son. Ultimately, Henry's reason for entrusting the project to Benoît de Sainte-Maure may well have been that he was not Norman, and therefore unlikely to become as personally involved in the material as Wace.

It would be interesting to know when the rift occurred between Wace and Henry II, and whether that estrangement really made a significant difference to the *Roman de Rou* as it has come down to us. It will certainly have cut short the time that Wace intended to devote to the work, but in terms of scope, the *Rou* starts with the first duke of Normandy, charts the undefeated sequence of his successors, and ends with the defeat in battle, capture and death of Robert Curthose, the last ruler Normandy did not have to share with a foreign power. Tinchebray is a logical place to end, and the fact that Benoît de Sainte-Maure did not take the narrative much further than Wace could suggest that it marked at the very least the conclusion of a major section, the sequel of which was at best hazy and undefined, and possibly unintended. On the other hand, the negative colouring given by Wace to the Norman rulers after William the Conqueror's

---

[8] Blacker, *The Faces of Time*, p. 193. Blacker uses the expression in relation to the poet, but it applies equally well to his patron.

[9] *Roman de Rou*, *Troisième Partie*, esp. lines 11135–42. We are even told (lines 11137–8) that the peasants no longer dared to till their land.

English campaign could have been a direct result of a perceived breach of contract on Henry's part. Broken promises are repaid by a narrative that is more abrupt and candid than had hitherto been the case; to the extent, indeed, that one suspects the final section of the *Roman de Rou* might have been composed after Henry removed his patronage from Wace, rather than before.

Wace's final line to his Epilogue, 'quin velt avant faire sin face', 'anyone who wishes to do more, let him do it', is generally read as betraying the elderly poet's bitterness at the humiliation of seeing someone else entrusted with his own work.[10] In fact, it is a gesture of defiance. This invitation to continue his *Rou* is a conscious echo of the Epilogue to the *Gesta Normannorum Ducum*:

> Que uero eius nobilissima gesta probissimaque merita letifica spe iam tenemus, latera illius ambientibus sapientia et eloquentia preminentibus uiris honestam materiam honestis edendam factis relinquo.[11]

Like William of Jumièges, Wace implicitly draws a line at relating contemporary events, and places the work within a continuum of scholarly endeavour. It is in the nature of histories to be unfinished and to require updating by each generation: but that Wace conceives of his work as being continued at all constitutes a claim to authority, rather than a dejected admission of incompleteness. Whatever the reasons for Henry's decision, no fault can be attached to Wace: it is his work that will be the reference, the base text that future historians will complete as time goes on – not the revised version that Henry II has commissioned from Benoît de Sainte-Maure. One senses a hint of condescension towards Benoît, who has taken on the unenviable job of reshaping the past to conform to the king's political agenda.

The initial expectations of Henry II when he entrusted the *Roman de Rou* to Wace were probably based on a serious misapprehension of the poet's previous works. He may have assumed that Wace was a more 'imaginative writer' than he actually was, and hoped that he would reshape the image of his Norman ancestors to conform to hagiographical conventions, whilst endowing them with a quasi-Arthurian prestige through a judicious chivalric gloss to their deeds. In other words, he thought he had commissioned a highly fictionalised form of historiography, and that is what Wace seemed to be delivering in the *Première Partie* and *Deuxième Partie* of his *Roman de Rou*. In fact, Wace was first and foremost a scholar, whose narratives were accurate adaptations of his Latin sources. Instead of propaganda, Henry II got history.

---

[10] However, Blacker (*The Faces of Time*, pp. 44–5) reads the Epilogue more positively as a 'gesture of generosity', with Wace refusing to adopt a proprietorial attitude toward his work.

[11] 'However, I leave the composition of an honest account, based on true facts of his most noble and excellent merits we joyfully may expect from him in the future, to the men, most eminent in wisdom and eloquence who are surrounding him.'

Conclusion

Having come to an end of our survey of Wace's surviving works, it may be concluded that the most salient feature of his oeuvre is the consistency of his approach. The five characteristics of the poet's religious works listed in the conclusion to Part I apply equally to both the *Roman de Brut* and virtually all of the *Roman de Rou*. These characteristics were:

1. The use of more than one source.

In the case of the hagiographical poems, it could be argued that the plurality of sources used by Wace was dictated by the agenda his patron(s) wished him to fulfil. His brief was never merely to transpose into French a Latin original, it would seem, but to produce an up-to-date version of the legends or Lives, taking account of all the information scattered in all available sources. In the simplest case, *La Vie de sainte Marguerite*, this led to a narrative based on one main source, into which relevant elements from a second version of the legend were seamlessly woven. With *La Vie de saint Nicolas*, which is essentially a compendium of miracles, the approach is more compilatory, but with a discrimination and selectiveness not usually connected with compilation. Wace used more than two sources here, showing that his work was intended to be an entirely new redaction of the Life of the saint. Finally, *La Conception Nostre Dame* is a highly complex piece of writing, gathering together an impressive number of sources in what is a completely new, independently thought-out account of the Life of the Virgin.

The evidence of the *Roman de Brut*, where such research would not seem to have been necessary, shows that the gathering of material related to the subject to be treated was a routine stage in Wace's preparation. He thus studied both the text authored by Geoffrey of Monmouth, known as the vulgate version of the *Historia Regum Britanniae*, and its revised (or Variant) version, by an anonymous redactor. Contrary to what may have been expected, the anonymous Variant was chosen to provide the base of his work, possibly because it corresponded more to the historical conventions of the time. Geoffrey of Monmouth's text becomes a fund of supplementary information, like the saints' lives and the oral tales that Wace had gathered for their relevance to the early history of England. This indicates that the *Roman de Brut* was not conceived of by its author as the translation of one author's masterpiece, but like his saint's lives, as an up-to-date synthesis of all that was known of the history of Celtic Britain. The reason it ends up reading like a translation is due to the fact that the *Historia Regum Britanniae* was the final word on the subject, and very little was to be found to complement or contradict it.

Finally, in the *Roman de Rou*, the plurality of sources is evident. As in the

Roman de Brut, even where the main source, William of Jumièges's *Gesta Normannorum Ducum*, would have been amply sufficient to produce a lively and authoritative narrative, Wace double-checks his source against its own sources (notably, Dudo of St Quentin). Where the *Gesta Normannorum Ducum* is unduly terse (typically from the rule of Duke William II, better known as William the Conqueror), Wace's indebtedness to a wide range of sources of various origins and, frequently, of varying ideological slant, becomes obvious. The second half of the *Troisième Partie* of the *Roman de Rou* stands out from the rest of Wace's work by the extent to which the poet has to take personal responsibility for his interpretation of the past in the absence of a coherent master-narrative he could follow. However, the underlying *modus operandi*, involving the gathering of as many texts and testimonials as possible in order to build up an accurate synthesis, remains the same in principle as that used for his other poems.

2. Efforts are made to give central characters a more attractive image than the one they have in the main sources.

The Latin Lives used by Wace for his hagiographical work frequently depicted their heroes in a way better suited to appeal to monks than to lay people. The Latin Margarita's constant harping on her purity, Nicholas's aversion to the slightest contact with women, the Virgin Mary's apparent detachment from the reality of everyday life, these are features that detracted from the emotional response Wace wished to elicit from his readers/audience. Mary thus becomes the head of a recognisable household, where the apostles laugh as well as pray. Stripped of his extreme asceticism, Nicholas is turned into little more than a cipher, with no recognisable personality traits beyond his extreme piety and goodness. Margaret is recast as a vulnerable young girl whose inner strength is celebrated only after she has successfully undergone the grimmest of tests, allowing the reader/audience to pity her before coming to admire (and indeed, venerate) her.

The *Roman de Brut* did not present the same problem in that it was not crucial that the successive kings should be either admirable or likeable. Wace does nevertheless ensure that the focus of the narrative remain firmly on the ruling monarch; a good example of this is found in the Brutus episode. Of the central characters, the most prominent one is of course King Arthur, and he is depicted in an enthusiastically glamorous way. This probably reflects the fact that Wace was integrating into his characterisation of the once-and-future king features found in the Arthurian tales he mentions, and which would have shaped the expectations of his readers/audience. Other kings do not fare so well: when Caesar invades Britain, it is the Roman general, not King Cassibelan, whose image is enhanced. This, as in the case of Arthur, certainly reflects the bias of Wace's 'marginal' authorities. The true hero, in the *Roman de Brut*, is the nation, and Wace regularly attenuates the atrocities committed by the favoured ethnic group: the Trojans, chosen by higher powers to govern the isle of Britain; the British, culminating in Arthur; and eventually, the Christianised Saxons, the new Chosen People who are to take over the dominion of Britain. However, this softening of the collective image is discreet.

The *Roman de Rou*, with its celebratory intent, had a vested interest in giving as positive a depiction of the dukes of Normandy as possible. Wace does this in a manner reminiscent of his *Vie de saint Nicolas*: through the omission of uncongenial material in his sources, and through an enhanced reliance on anecdotes (miracles, in the case of Nicholas) in order to project a flattering image of his hero. The treatment of the character of Duke Robert the Magnificent is an especially good example of a successful use of this whitewashing strategy. After the battle of Hastings, however, the combination of the editing out of certain facts and the inclusion of anecdotes no longer suffices to mask the essential nastiness of the situations and people at the heart of the narrative. This could be due to the fact that Wace simply could not find any anecdotes that could be construed as positive; or that collective memory in Normandy viewed this period so negatively that he felt that endowing it with prestige and glamour would have violated the truth. Alternatively, this section might have been composed after his rift with Henry II, in which case Wace may well have felt released from the propagandist agenda of his patron, and allowed himself the luxury of unaccustomed candour. Certainly, his depiction of Robert Curthose as a negligent leader who failed to keep his promises jars with the consistently positive (if sometimes trite) gloss on the earlier Norman dukes, up to William the Conqueror. Yet even this, one may note, is considerably gentler than what Wace could find in Orderic Vitalis or William of Malmesbury. It is only striking with regards to the *Roman de Rou* itself; put in a wider context, Robert Curthose is depicted quite favourably. Indeed, the drive to omit facts that might have shown him up in a negative light results in a latter section of the *Roman de Rou* almost void of 'hard facts' relating to the rule of this duke.[1]

3. A marked didactic intent.

The simple fact that Wace was writing in French rather than Latin meant that his target audience was non-clerical, non-Latinate, and probably non-literate. This had an impact on the way he presented his material. The poet was acutely aware of the gap between his own well-educated self and the people he was addressing through his works. This awareness is given its clearest expression in the religious works, and in particular the *Vie de saint Nicolas*, where the poet shows a real pride in his scholarly clerical status whilst at the same time acknowledging the responsibilities it entails. That Wace thought of himself as a teacher may be seen from the fact that throughout his active life as a writer, he consciously avoided including details that might not be understood by a lay audience, and added where necessary parenthetical explanations of 'difficult' passages. The Latin book cited by the demon Belgibus in Wace's sources is thus omitted from the *Vie de sainte Marguerite*, and the Gnostic overtones of the dialogue between the demon and the saint in her prison are attenuated. In the *Conception Nostre Dame*, symbolism requiring knowledge of biblical exegesis is explained by the narrator, so that the

---

[1] Jean Blacker (*The Faces of Time*, p. 133) sees this loss of practical information as a characteristic of twelfth-century French historical writing: 'Despite the differences in approach between the Latin and the French historians, the French tend to repeat many of the personality assessments they found in the Latin histories while leaving many of the "raw data" aside.' This trait is readily explained by the fact that works in French were by definition popularisations, which therefore tended to leave aside details that would have been perceived as too scholarly. However, the final section of the *Roman de Rou* is rather extreme in this respect.

reader/audience is aware when certain things should not be taken literally. In the *Roman de Brut*, any Latin words or expressions other than what a reasonably pious person might be expected to know are translated; similarly, both in the *Roman de Brut* and the *Roman de Rou*, English words are systematically glossed for a French-speaking readership. Cultural references that the average layman could not be expected to be familiar with (for example, the sirens in the *Roman de Brut*) are similarly accompanied by a clear and concise explanation.

4. A controlled use of rhetorical and stylistic effects.

Wace's use of rhetoric and stylistics is the one area where a certain evolution may be discerned in his oeuvre. However, in this respect as in others, there is on the whole a greater sense of continuity from one text to the other than there is of change. *La Vie de sainte Marguerite* stands out because of the poet's restraint when it comes to amplificatory devices or rhetorical adornment; but one has no sense of writerly insecurity in this work, and it could be argued that such a degree of narrative control is the mark of an experienced poet. The alternation in the *Vie de saint Nicolas* between streamlined narrative and lively episodes adorned with descriptions, narrator's asides and dialogue suggests that we are dealing with two narrative modes manipulated with equal ease by the poet. Wace's skilful use of dialogue and direct discourse will remain the hallmark of his style. The descriptive passages of his *Vie de saint Nicolas* show that for all his self-restraint in other parts of the work, the poet enjoyed verbal pyrotechnics, especially lists involving the repetition of key words, typically within a repeated syntactical construction. This combination of *enumeratio*, anaphora and isolocon remains typical of Wace's high style throughout his literary output; however, this high style is only rarely used in a sustained manner, and then typically to mark out particularly important events (for example, key battles).

5. Wace re-appropriates the structure of his sources.

Even though Wace's preferred method is to select a main source and follow its general structure, it is clear that he is prepared to modify that structure to make it more compatible with his interpretation of his material. The *Vie de sainte Marguerite* is a case in point, as is the Arthurian section of the *Roman de Brut*. This is not surprising, as Wace clearly had experience in producing 'hybrid' works, for which there was no single source that could be followed: the *Conception Nostre Dame* and, to a great extent, the *Roman de Rou*, fall into this category. If Wace produced a poem that was a faithful translation of just the one Latin text, it has not survived; on the evidence of his surviving work, it is unlikely that such a poem ever existed. This has implications for the way in which the works are read: each poem has to be taken as a unit, an organic whole, in order to discern Wace's discourse behind that of his sources. Because all the material required to make sense of the topic to be treated had been studied and digested before the poet set about his work, and because the structure of the resulting poem bears the mark of Wace's personal interpretation of his sources, a piecemeal approach (isolating for example the reign of Arthur from those of his predecessors and successors, in the *Roman de Brut*) can seriously distort one's perception of his work. Wace's longer poems are criss-crossed with narrative and verbal echoes inviting comparison between characters, events and situations: he clearly intended the more discerning of his readers to consider each event within its wider narrative context before proceeding to its interpretation. Such willingness to reshape source narratives indicates a great deal of self-confidence on the poet's part, both in the validity of his interpretation of his sources and in his skill at story-telling.

Beyond these initial categories, the fuller picture including the *Roman de Brut* and the *Roman de Rou* also reveals two further enduring characteristics to Wace's work. First is the poet's continuing interest in hagiography: the move to historiography of a more secular variety does not prevent him from taking special note of the activity of saints or their miracles, expanding on cues offered by his Latin sources or adding the material independently. The *Roman de Brut* provides us with a detailed account of St Augustine of Canterbury's mission among the English, and the *Roman de Rou* makes a point of mentioning St Edmund's punishment of King Canute, with an explicit reference to Edmund's Life.[2] The viewpoint always remains that of a cleric; even without any comment by the narrator, we know that a character who burns down churches is a reprobate, while references to acts of piety (such as the Normans fasting and praying before Hastings) tend to be given especial prominence.

The second salient feature to come out from our study is Wace's poetical skill. This is not something we could take for granted; there are plenty of medieval French works written in verse, but that cannot be called poetry. All of Wace's surviving works are works of scholarship, the result of painstaking research and a rigorous intellectual commitment; from his own testimony in his *Vie de saint Nicolas*, he thought of himself primarily as someone whose work it was to make important knowledge accessible to a wide audience. This involved presenting his material in an attractive manner and producing 'serious entertainment'.[3] Wace was not the only cleric doing this, but the talent he brought to the job must have made him stand out from an early stage. One needs only to compare his *Vie de sainte Marguerite* with the *Vie de saint George* once attributed to him, or his *Roman de Brut* with Gaimar's somewhat plodding *Estoire des Engleis*, to realise that Wace was in a different league. This is all the more significant because Wace kept his poetical impulse under stringent control when composing his 'scholarly' works, prioritising clarity, effectiveness and narrative economy. Such self-discipline does not come naturally and testifies to the quality of his education. One senses that Wace had special relish for the epic; his account of the adventures of the Viking Hasting is one of the neglected masterpieces of the Middle Ages and is worthy of inclusion in any anthology, if only for its quirky comedy. His fondness for scenes full of busy activity leads to remarkably effective battle scenes, despite the fact that they are essentially formulaic in nature and often virtually interchangeable, both in the *Roman de Brut* and the *Roman de Rou*. Such scenes come to life when read aloud,

---

[2] *Troisième Partie*, lines 1313–16.
[3] The phrase is Nancy Partner's (*Serious Entertainments: the Writing of History in Twelfth-Century England*), whose book, though focused on Latin historical writing, remains essential reading for anyone interested in medieval historiography.

evidencing the poet's delight in sound and rhythm, but also indicating that Wace the 'clerc lisant' was writing with oral delivery in mind right up to the end. This ties in with the tendency we have observed for the poet to impose a chronological sequence on any events he recounts, making his narrative easier to follow for an audience at public readings.

Wace's obvious pleasure in writing begs the question concerning his lost works: the 'romanz' mentioned in the Prologue to the *Troisième Partie* of the *Roman de Rou*. This passage, where the poet laments the niggardliness of his patrons, hints at intensive literary activity: 'Mais ore puis jeo lunges penser/ livres escrire e translater,/ faire romanz e serventeis . . .', 'But now I can put in a great deal of effort, write and translate books and compose romanz and *serventeis* . . .' (151–3). We seem to have an implicit distinction here between scholarly translation and more freely composed pieces of writing. If such is the case, it would appear that his more light-hearted work did not meet with the same degree of success, as it was not sufficiently copied for it to have survived; it could be that Wace, though an outstanding scholar, populariser and poet, was rather less proficient as an independent story-teller who had to construct his own plots. On the other hand, it is possible that these 'romanz' are none other than his hagiographical works, and may have included his *Roman de Brut*.

In conclusion, the overriding impression derived from this study is that Wace, for all his having obtained royal patronage at the height of his career, probably had more in common with an Orderic Vitalis or a William of Malmesbury than a Chrétien de Troyes. He made his name by producing adaptations of Latin works in a pleasant and entertaining style, but the intellectual rigour underlying his work does not seem to have been widely recognised, least of all by Henry II. In this respect, there may have been an evolution within Wace's own lifetime. The ecclesiastical patron who commissioned (or facilitated) the *Conception Nostre Dame* clearly entrusted Wace with the work because of his scholarly integrity, and this must have been a decisive factor in the poem's success. Later in life, what had been a major asset could have become a handicap, as accuracy is often inimical to flattery. Wace may be seen as the product of a society in a state of flux. His training prepared him to be a good cleric in the monastic mould; the world he encountered demanded that he write as a courtier. A thirst for vernacular narrative was developing, but there was as yet no intermediate status between the lowly *jongleur* and the scholar. It is noteworthy that Wace felt he had to resort to both personas in his *Roman de Rou*.

Wace is widely seen as a precursor to writers of romance proper, and in particular to Chrétien de Troyes. This is mainly due to the fact that both men wrote about King Arthur, though one senses at times echoes of Wace's style in some of his successors. On a deeper level, the Norman poet's scholarly rigour, linked to his literary excellence, will have lent respectability to writing in the vernacular, and paved the way for professional writers who were not primarily scholars. However, his status remains ambiguous to this day, as may be seen from the varying ways in which modern scholars have referred to him: from 'trouvère' (Mancel and Trébutien) and 'historiographe' (Gouttebroze) to the more recent (if somewhat cumbersome) 'poet-translator-historian' (Blacker, p. 36). It has also prompted erroneous assumptions as to the nature of Wace's work, particularly up to the mid-twentieth century, with critics talking about his 'imagination',[4] whereas, as we have seen, Wace's methodology did not draw extensively on that faculty. The fact is that we have no handy label for someone who translates, adapts, reshapes and synthesises at the same time as producing great literature. Neither are the conceptual tools elaborated for works of fiction entirely suitable to approach Wace's work: his omissions are often as revealing as that which he includes, and this is something that only his sources can reveal. But in complexity lies richness. And rare is the writer who is as satisfying to the scholar as (s)he is enjoyable to the general reader.

---

[4] See for example Pierre Gallais, 'La *Variant Version* de l'*Historia Regum Britanniae* et le *Brut* de Wace', *Romania* 87 (1966): 1–7. It must be said that these earlier critics were writing at a time when the textual history of Wace's sources had not yet been studied in depth.

Select Bibliography

Primary sources

Aelred of Rievaulx, *Aelred. Life of St Edward the Confessor*, trans. J. Bertram (Southampton, 1997)
The Anglo-Saxon Chronicle, ed. and trans. M. Swanton (London, 1996)
Anselm of Canterbury, *S. Anselmi, ex Beccensi abbate Cantuarensis archiepiscopi Opera Omnia necnon Eadmeri Monachi Historia Novotum et alia opuscula*, ed. D. G. Gerberon, vol. 2: Appendix (spuria): 'Miraculum de conceptione Beatae Mariae', cols. 325–6; 'Tractatus de conceptione Beatae Mariae Virginis', cols. 301–18. *PL* 159 (Paris, 1865)
Apocalypses apocryphae Mosis, Esdrae, Pauli, Johannis, item Mariae Dormitio, ed. C. de Tischendorf (Leipzig, 1866)
The Apocryphal New Testament. A Collection of Apocryphal Christian Literature in an English Translation, trans. J. K. Elliott (Oxford, 1993)
Benedeit, *The Anglo-Norman Voyage of St Brendan by Benedeit*, ed. E. G. R. Waters (Oxford, 1928)
Benoît de Sainte-Maure, *Chronique des ducs de Normandie*, ed. C. Fahlin (Uppsala, 1951–4; Bibliotheca Ekmaniana 56 and 60)
Bernard of Clairvaux, *Opera Omnia. PL* 182 (Paris, 1862)
Bernard of Clairvaux, *S. Bernardi Opera, VII: Epistulae I*, ed. J. Leclercq and H. Rochais (Rome, 1974)
Brevis relatio de origine Willelmi Conquestoris, ed. I. A. Giles, pp. 1–21 in *Scriptores Rerum Gestarum Willelmi Conquestoris* (London, 1855)
'The *Brevis relatio de Guillelmo nobilissimo comite Normannorum* written by a Monk of Battle Abbey', ed. E. M. C. van Houts, pp. 1–48 in *Chronology, Conquest and Conflict in Medieval England*, ed. E. M. C. van Houts (London, 1997)
La Chanson de Roland, ed. and trans. I. Short (Paris, 1990)
Le Charroi de Nîmes: chanson de geste du XIIe siècle éditée d'après la redaction AB, ed. D. Macmillan (Paris, 1978)
The Chronicle of Battle Abbey, ed. and trans. E. Searle (Oxford, 1980)
Le Couronnement de Louis, ed. E. Langlois (Paris, 1925; Classiques Français du Moyen-Age 22)
De nativitate Mariae: Kritische Voorstudie en Tekstuitgave, ed. R. Beyers (PhD Leuven; Antwerp, 1980)
De probates Sanctorum histories, ed. L. Surius (Coloniae Agrippinae, 1581 and 1618)
Dudo of St Quentin, *De moribus et actis primorum Normanniae ducum auctore Dudone Sancti Quentini decano*, ed. J. Lair (Caen, 1865)
Dudo of St Quentin. History of the Normans, trans. E. Christiansen (Woodbridge, 1998)
Eadmer, *Eadmeri Historia Novorum in Anglia et opuscula duo de vita sancti Anselmi et quibusdam miraculis ejus*, ed. M. Rule (London, 1884)
Evangelia Apocrypha, ed. C. de Tischendorf (Leipzig, 1876)
Geffrei Gaimar, *L'Estoire des Engleis, by Geffrei Gaimar*, ed. A. Bell (Oxford, 1960; Anglo-Norman Texts Society 14–16)

Geoffrey of Monmouth, *The Historia Regum Britanniae of Geoffrey of Monmouth with Contributions to the Study of its Place in Early British History*, ed. A. Griscom and R. E. Jones (New York, 1929)

Geoffrey of Monmouth, *The Historia Regum Britannie of Geoffrey of Monmouth, I: Bern, Burgerbibliothek MS 568*, ed. N. Wright (Cambridge, 1985)

Geoffrey of Monmouth, *The Historia Regum Britannie of Geoffrey of Monmouth, II: The First Variant Version*, ed. N. Wright (Cambridge, 1988)

Geoffrey of Monmouth, *The Historia Regum Britanniae, a Variant Version*, ed. J. Hammer (Cambridge, Mass., 1951)

Geoffrey of Monmouth, *The History of the Kings of Britain*, trans. L. Thorpe (Harmondsworth, 1966)

Geoffrey of Monmouth, *Life of Merlin. Geoffrey of Monmouth, Vita Merlini*, ed. and trans. B. Clarke (Cardiff, 1973)

Gormont et Isembart, ed. A. Bayot (Paris, 1921; Classiques Français du Moyen-Age 14)

Goscelin of Saint Bertin, *Vita sancti Augustini*, in *PL* 80 (Paris, 1863), cols. 43–94

Guy of Amiens, *The Carmen de Hastingae Proelio of Guy, Bishop of Amiens*, ed. and trans. F. Barlow (Oxford, 1999)

'The Harley Brut: an Early French Translation of Geoffrey's *Historia Regum Britanniae*', ed. B. Blakey, *Romania* 82 (1961): 44–70

Henry of Huntingdon, *Historia Anglorum: the History of the English People*, ed. D. Greenway (Oxford, 1996)

Jacobus de Voragine, *Legenda Aurea, vulgo historia Lombardica dicta*, ed. T. Graesse (Dresden and Leipzig, 1846)

Jean Bodel, *Le Jeu de saint Nicolas*, ed. A. Henry (Geneva, 1981)

Jean Renart, *L'Escoufle: roman d'aventure. Nouvelle edition d'après le manuscript 6565 de la Bibliothèque de l'Arsenal*, ed. F. Sweetser (Geneva, 1974; Textes Littéraires Français 211)

Jordan Fantosme, *Jordan Fantosme's Chronicle*, ed. R. C. Johnston (Oxford, 1981)

Laȝamon, *Brut, edited from British Museum MS Cotton Caligula A ix and British Museum Cotton Otho C xiii*, ed. G. L. Brook and R. F. Stanley, 2 vols. (London, 1963 and 1978; Early English Texts Society 250)

Brut: Lawman, trans. R. Allen (London, 1992)

Libellus de nativitate sanctae Mariae, ed. R. Beyers (Turnhout, 1997; Corpus Christianorum. Series apocryphorum 10)

The Life of King Edward Who Rests at Westminster, attributed to a monk of Saint-Bertin, trans. F. Barlow (London, 1962)

Le Livre de Catun, ed. T. Hunt (London, 1994; Anglo-Norman Texts Society, PTS 11)

Le Moniage Guillaume: Chanson de geste du XIIe siècle, ed. N. Andrieux-Reix (Paris, 2003)

Der Münchener Brut. Gottfried von Monmouth in französischen Versen des XII. Jahrhunderts, ed. K. Hoffmann and K. Vollmöller (Halle, 1877)

'Nennius', *Historia Brittonum*, ed. D. Dumville (Cambridge, 1985)

Nivard, *Ysengrimus*, ed. and trans. J. Mann (Leiden, 1987; Mittellateinische Studien und Texte 12)

Orderic Vitalis, *The Ecclesiastical History of Orderic Vitalis*, ed. M. Chibnall, 6 vols. (Oxford, 1969–80)

Osbert of Clare, 'La Vie de S. Edouard le Confesseur par Osbert de Clare', ed. M. Bloch, *Analecta Bollandiana* 41 (1923): 5–31

'A Hitherto Unprinted Version of the *Passio Sanctae Margaritae* with Some Observations on Vernacular Derivatives', ed. E. A. Francis, *PMLA* 42 (1927): 87–105

Quintilianus, M. Fabius, *Institutio oratoria*, ed. M. Winterbottom, 2 vols. (Oxford, 1970)

Raoul de Cambrai, ed. S. Kay (Oxford, 1992)
Robert le Diable, ed. E. Loseth (Paris, 1903; Société des Anciens Textes Francais 48)
Robert le Diable. Roman du XIIe siècle, trans. A. Micha (Paris, 1996)
Sancti Confessoris Pontificis et celeberrimi Thaumaturgi Nicolai Acta Primigenia nuper detecta per Nicolaum Carminium Falconium ecclesiae Sanctae Severinae in Brutiis Ulterioribus, ed. N. C. Falconius (Naples, 1751)
Sanctuarium seu Vitae Sanctorum, ed. B. Mombritius, 2 vols. (Milan, 1479; new ed., Paris, 1910)
Symeon of Durham, *Symeonis monachi opera omnia*, ed. T. A. Arnold, 2 vols. (London, 1882–5)
Trioedd Ynys Prydein: the Welsh Triads, ed. and trans. R. Bromwich (Cardiff, 1978; first ed., 1961)
Wace, *L'Établissement de la fête de la Conception Nostre Dame dite la fête des Normands par Wace trouvère anglo-normand du XIIe siècle publié pour la première fois d'après les manuscrits de la Bibliothèque du Roi*, ed. G. Mancel and G.-S. Trébutien (Caen, 1842)
Wace, *The Conception Nostre Dame de Wace*, ed. W. R. Ashford (microfilm; doctoral dissertation Chicago, 1933)
Wace, *Le Roman de Brut de Wace*, ed. I. Arnold, 2 vols. (Paris, 1938–40)
Wace, *Wace's Roman de Brut. A History of the British. Text and Translation*, trans. J. Weiss (Exeter, 1999)
Wace, *Le Roman de Rou de Wace*, ed. A. J. Holden, 3 vols. (Paris, 1970–3)
Wace, *The Roman de Rou*, trans. G. S. Burgess (St Helier, 2002)
The History of the Norman People – Wace's Roman de Rou, trans. G. S. Burgess (Woodbridge, 2004)
Wace, *La Vie de sainte Marguerite, poème inédit de Wace*, ed. A. Joly (Paris, 1879)
Wace, *La Vie de sainte Marguerite*, ed. E. A. Francis (Paris, 1932; Classiques Français du Moyen Age 71)
Wace, *La Vie de sainte Marguerite*, ed. H. E. Keller (Tübingen, 1990; Beihefte zur Zeitschrift für romanische Philologie 229)
Wace, *La Vie de saint Nicolas par Wace, poème. Poème religieux du XIIe siècle publié d'après tous les manuscrits*, ed. E. Ronsjö (Lund and Copenhagen, 1942; Etudes romanes de Lund 5)
William of Jumièges, *The Gesta Normannorum Ducum of William of Jumièges, Orderic Vitalis and Robert de Torigni*, ed. E. M. C. van Houts, 2 vols. (Oxford, 1992–5)
William of Malmesbury, *The Early History of Glastonbury. An Edition, Translation and Study of William of Malmesbury's De Antiquitate Glastonie Ecclesie*, ed. and trans. J. Scott (Woodbridge, 1981)
William of Malmesbury, *Gesta regum Anglorum. The History of the English Kings. William of Malmesbury*, ed. and trans. R. A. B. Mynors, R. A. Thomson and W. Winterbottom, 2 vols. (Oxford, 1998–9)
William of Newburgh, *Historia rerum Anglicarum. The History of English Affairs*, ed. and trans. P. G. Walsh and M. J. Kennedy (Warminster, 1988)
William of Poitiers, *Gesta Guillelmi*, ed. R. H.C. Davis and M. Chibnall (Oxford, 1998)
William of Poitiers, *Guillaume de Poitiers. Histoire de Guillaume le Conquérant*, ed. and trans. R. Foreville (Paris, 1952; Classiques Français du Moyen-Age 23)

Studies

Albu, E., 'The Normans and their Myths', *Haskins Society Journal* 11 (2001): 123–35
Albu, E., *The Normans in their Histories: Propaganda, Myth and Subversion* (Woodbridge, 2001)
Amman, E., *Le Protévangile de Jacques et ses remaniements latins* (Paris, 1910)
Anderson, C. B., 'Wace's *Roman de Rou* and Henry II's Court: Character and Power', *Romance Quarterly* 47 (2000): 67–82
Aurell, M., 'La Cour Plantagenêt (1154–1204): entourage, savoir et civilité', pp. 9–46 in *La Cour Plantagenêt (1154–1204). Actes du colloque tenu à Thouars du 30 avril au 2 mai 1999*, ed. M. Aurell (Poitiers, 2000)
Barber, R., *Henry Plantagenet* (Woodbridge, 2001)
Barlow, F., *Edward the Confessor* (New Haven, 1997)
Barré, H., 'Immaculée Conception et Assomption au XIIe siècle', *Virgo Immaculata* 5 (1955): 151–80
Barron, W. R. J., ed., *The Arthur of the English: the Arthurian Legend in Medieval English Life and Literature* (Cardiff, 2001)
Batany, J., 'Les trois bienfaits du duc Robert: un modèle historiographique du prince évergète au XII siècle', pp. 263–72 in *Clio. Actes du colloque Histoire et Historiographie*, ed. R. Chevalier (Paris, 1980)
Bates, D., 'The Rise and Fall of Normandy, c. 911–1204', pp. 19–35 in *England and Normandy in the Middle Ages*, ed. D. Bates and A. Curry (London, 1994)
Bates, D., *Normandy before 1066* (London, 1982)
Baumgartner, E., ' "Écrire disent-ils." À propos de Wace et de Benoît de Sainte-Maure', pp. 37–47 in *Figures de l'écrivain au Moyen Age. Actes du Colloque du Centre d'Études Médiévales de l'Université de Picardie, Amiens 18–20 mars 1985*, ed. D. Buschinger (Göppingen, 1991)
Baumgartner, E., 'Jeux de rimes et roman arthurien', *Romania* 103 (1982): 550–60
Becker, M., 'Der gepaarte Achtsilber in der französischen Dichtung', *Abhandlungen der sächsichen Akademie der Wissenschaften, phil.-hist. Klasse* 43 (1934): 1–117
Becker, P. A., 'Die Normannenchroniken: Wace und seine Bearbeiter', *Zeitchscrift für romanische Philologie* 63 (1943): 481–519
Bédier, J., 'Richart de Normandie dans les chansons de geste', *Romanic Review* 1 (1910): 113–42
Beer, J., *Narrative Conventions of Truth in the Middle Ages* (Geneva, 1981)
Bennett, P. E., 'Poetry as History? The *Roman de Rou* as a Source for the Norman Conquest', *Anglo-Norman Studies* 5 (1983): 21–39
Beyers, R., '*La Conception Nostre Dame* de Wace: premier poème narratif sur la Vierge en ancien français', pp. 359–400 in *Serta Devota in memoriam Guillelmi Lourdaux, II: Cultura medievalis*, ed. W. Verbecke, M. Haverals et al. (Louvain, 1995)
Bezzola, R. R., *Les Origines et la formation de la littérature courtoise en Occident (500–1200)*. 3 vols. (Paris, 1958–63)
Biller, G., *Étude sur le style des premiers romans français en vers 1150–1175* (Göteborg, 1916)
Blacker, J., *The Faces of Time: Portrayal of the Past in Old French and Latin Historical Narrative of the Anglo-Norman regnum* (Austin, 1994)
Blacker, J., ' "Ne vuil sun livre translater": Wace's Omission of Merlin's Prophecies from the *Roman de Brut*', pp. 49–59 in *Anglo-Norman Anniversary Essays*, ed. I. Short (London, 1993; Anglo-Norman Texts Society, OPS 2)

Blacker, J., 'La geste est grande, longue et grieve a translater: History for Henry II', *Romance Quarterly* 37 (1990): 387–96
Blacker-Knight, J., 'Wace's Craft and his Audience: Historical Truth, Bias and Patronage in the *Roman de Rou*', *Kentucky Romance Quarterly* 31 (1984): 355–62
Bolton, W. F., *A History of Anglo-Latin Literature, 597–1066* (Princeton, 1967)
Bourgain, P., 'Les Prologues des texts narratifs', pp. 245–73 in *Les Prologues médiévaux. Actes du colloque international organisé par l'Accademia Belgica et l'École Française de Rome avec le concours de la F.I.D.E.M. (Rome, 26–28 mars 1998)*, ed. J. Hamesse (Turnhout, 2000)
Boutet, D., *Formes littéraires et conscience historique aux origines de la littérature française (1100–1250)* (Paris, 1999)
Bridgeford, A., *1066. The Hidden History of the Bayeux Tapestry* (London and New York, 2004)
Broadhurst, K., 'Henry II of England and Eleanor of Aquitaine: Patrons of Literature in French', *Viator* 27 (1996): 53–8
Brooke, C. N. L., *The Twelfth-Century Renaissance* (London, 1976)
Brosnahan, L., 'Wace's Use of Proverbs', *Speculum* 39 (1964): 444–73
Brusegan, R., 'Culte de la Vierge et origine des puys et confréries en France au Moyen Age', *Revue de Langues Romanes* 95 (1991): 31–58
Bryan, E. J., 'The Afterlife of Armoriche', pp. 117–55 in *Laȝamon: Contexts, Language, and Interpretation*, ed. R. Allen, L. Perry and J. Roberts (London, 2002; King's College London Medieval Studies 19)
Bullock-Davies, C., 'Expectare Arturum: Arthur and the Messianic Hope', *Bulletin of the Board of Celtic Studies* 29 (1981/2): 432–40
Bullock-Davies, C., *Professional Interpreters and the Matter of Britain* (Cardiff, 1966)
Burger, M., *Recherches sur la structure et l'origine des vers romans* (Geneva, 1957)
Burgess, G. S., *Chrétien de Troyes. Erec et Enide* (London, 1984)
Buridant, C., '*Translatio medievalis*: théorie et pratique de la traduction médiévale', *Travaux de Linguistique et de Littérature* 21 (1983): 81–136
Burridge, A. W., 'L'Immaculée Conception dans la théologie de l'Angleterre médiévale', *Revue d'Histoire Ecclésiastique* 32 (1936): 570–97
Busby, K., *Gauvain in Old French Literature* (Amsterdam, 1980)
Buttry, D. J., 'Contempt or Empathy? Master Wace's Depiction of a Peasant Revolt', *Romance Notes* 37 (1996): 31–8
Cabassut, A., 'Eadmer', cols. 1–5 in *Dictionnaire de spiritualité ascétique et mystique. Doctrine et histoire* (Paris, 1960), vol. 4, part 1
Caldwell, R. A., 'Wace's *Roman de Brut* and the *Variant Version* of Geoffrey of Monmouth's *Historia Regum Britanniae*', *Speculum* 31 (1956): 675–82
Calin, W., *The Old French Epic of Revolt: Raoul de Cambrai, Renaud de Montauban, Gormond et Isembard* (Geneva, 1962)
Carr, G. F., 'The Prologue to Wace's *Vie de Saint Nicolas*: a Structural Analysis', *Philological Quarterly* 47 (1968): 1–7
Carruthers, M., *The Book of Memory: a Study of Memory in Medieval Culture* (Cambridge, 1990)
Cazauran, N., 'Richard sans Peur: un personnage en quête d'auteur', *Travaux de Littérature* 4 (1991): 21–43
Chibnall, M., 'Charter and Chronicle: the Use of Archive Sources by Norman Historians', pp. 1–17 in *Church and Government in the Middle Ages*, ed. C. Brooke (Cambridge, 1976)
Chibnall, M., 'Monastic Foundations in England and Normandy, 1066–1189', pp. 37–49

in *England and Normandy in the Middle Ages*, ed. D. Bates and A. Curry (London, 1994)

Chibnall, M., *The World of Orderic Vitalis: Norman Monks and Norman Knights* (Oxford, 1984)

Cingolani, S. M., 'Filologia e miti storiografici: Enrico II, la corte plantageneta e la letteratura', *Studi Medievali* 32 (1991): 814–32

Cingolani, S. M., 'Wace agiografo: considerazioni sulle tecniche poetiche delle origini (X–XIIe sec.)', *Romanistische Jahrbuch* 42 (1991): 121–35

Clayton, M., *The Apocryphal Gospels of Mary in Anglo-Saxon England* (Cambridge, 1998)

Clayton, M., *The Cult of the Virgin in Anglo-Saxon England* (Cambridge, 1990)

Collet, C., Leroux, P., and Marin, J.-Y., *Caen, cité médiévale. Bilan d'archéologie et d'histoire* (Caen, 1996)

Copeland, R., *Rhetoric, Hermeneutics and Translation in the Middle Ages: Academic Traditions and Vernacular Texts* (Cambridge, 1991)

Crick, J. C., *The Historia Regum Britannie of Geoffrey of Monmouth, III. A Summary Catalogue of the Manuscripts* (Cambridge, 1989)

Crick, J. C., *The Historia Regum Britannie of Geoffrey of Monmouth, IV. Dissemination and Reception in the Later Middle Ages* (Cambridge, 1991)

Crouch, D., 'Normans and Anglo-Normans: A Divided Aristocracy?', pp. 51–67 in *England and Normandy in the Middle Ages*, ed. D. Bates and A. Curry (London, 1994)

Curtius, E. R., *Europäische Literatur und lateinisches Mittelalter* (Bern, 1948)

D'Alessandro, D., 'Analisi del descrittivo nell'opera romanzesca di Wace', *Annali dell'Istituto Universitario Orientale, Sez. Romanza* 33 (1991): 205–16

D'Alessandro, D., '*Historia Regum Britannie* et *Roman de Brut*: une comparaison formelle', *Medioevo romanzo* 19 (1994): 37–52

Damian-Grint, P., '*Estoire* as Word and Genre: Meaning and Literary Usage in the Twelfth Century', *Medium Aevum* 66 (1997): 188–205

Damian-Grint, P., *The New Historians of the Twelfth-Century Renaissance* (Woodbridge, 1999)

Damian-Grint, P., 'Translation as *enarratio* and Hermeneutic Theory in Twelfth-Century Vernacular Literature', *Neophilologus* 83 (1999): 349–67

Davis, H. W. C., *England under the Normans and the Angevins, 1066–1272* (London, 1905)

Dean, R. J., *Anglo-Norman Literature. A Guide to Texts and Manuscripts* (London, 1999)

Delbouille, M., 'Le témoignage de Wace sur la légende arthurienne', *Romania* 74 (1953): 172–99

Dolbeau, F., 'Les Hagiographes au travail: collecte et traitement des documents écrits (IXe–XIIe siècles)', pp. 49–76 in *Manuscrits hagiographiques et travail des hagiographes*, ed. M. Heinzelmann (Sigmaringen, 1992)

Douglas, D. C., 'Companions of the Conqueror', *History* 27 (1943): 129–47

Dubuis, D. J., and Lemaître, J.-L., *Sources et méthodes de l'hagiographie médiévale* (Paris, 1993)

Durling, N. V., 'Translation and Innovation in the *Roman de Brut*', pp. 9–41 in *Medieval Translators and their Craft*, ed. J. Beer (Kalamazoo, 1989)

Eley, P., and Bennett, P. E., 'The Battle of Hastings According to Gaimar, Wace and Benoît: Rhetoric and Politics', *Nottingham Medieval Studies* 43 (1999): 47–78

Fahlin, C., *Étude sur le manuscrit de Tours de la Chronique des Ducs de Normandie par Benoit* (Uppsala, 1937)

Faral, E., *Les Arts poétiques du XIIe et du XIIIe siècles: Recherches et documents sur la*

technique littéraire du moyen âge (Paris, 1924; Bibliothèque de l'Ecole des Hautes Etudes 238)
Fleischmann, S., 'On the Representation of History and Fiction in the Middle Ages', *History and Theory* 22 (1983): 278–310
Flint, V., 'The *Historia Regum Britanniae* of Geoffrey of Monmouth: Parody and its Purpose. A Suggestion', *Speculum* 54 (1979): 447–68
Foulon, C., 'Two Additions by Wace', *Bibliographical Bulletin of the International Arthurian Society* 24 (1972): 191
Gallais, P., 'La *Variant Version* de l'*Historia Regum Britanniae* et le *Brut* de Wace', *Romania* 87 (1966): 1–7
Gérold, T., *Le Manuscrit de Bayeux* (Strasbourg, 1921)
Gijsel, J., 'Die unmittelbare Textüberlieferung des sogenannten Pseudo-Matthäus', *Verhandlungen van de koninklijke Academie voor Wetenschappen, Letteren en schone Kunsten van België, Klasse der Letteren* 43 (1981)
Gillingham, J., 'The Context and Purposes of Geoffrey of Monmouth's *History of the Kings of Britain*', *Anglo-Norman Studies* 13 (1990): 99–118
Gossen, C. T., *Französische Skriptastudien. Untersuchungen zu den nordfranzösischen Urkundensprachen des Mittelalters* (Wien, 1967; Österreichische Akademie der Wissenschaften, Philosophisch-Historische Klasse, Sitzungsberichte 253)
Gouttebroze, J.-G., 'Entre les historiographes d'expression latine et le jongleurs, le clerc lisant', pp. 215–30 in *Le clerc au Moyen Age* (Aix-en-Provence, 1995)
Gouttebroze, J.-G., 'Henry II Plantagenêt, patron des historiographes anglo-normands de langue d'oïl', pp. 91–105 in *La Littérature angevine médiévale* (Angers and Paris, 1981)
Gouttebroze, J.-G., 'Pourquoi congédier un historiographe, Henry II Plantagenêt et Wace (1155–1174)', *Romania* 112 (1991): 289–311
Gransden, A., 'The Growth of Glastonbury Traditions and Legends in the Twelfth Century', *The Journal of Ecclesiastical History* 27 (1976): 337–58
Holden, A. J., 'L'Authenticité des premières parties du *Roman de Rou*', *Romania* 75 (1954): 22–53
Hollister, C. W., *Monarchy, Magnates and Institutions in the Anglo-Norman World* (London, 1986)
Holmes, U. T., Jr, 'Norman Literature and Wace', pp. 46–67 in *Medieval Secular Literature: Four Essays*, ed. W. Matthews (Berkeley and Los Angeles, 1967)
Houck, M., *Sources of the* Roman de Brut *of Wace* (Berkeley and Los Angeles, 1941)
Huntington, J., 'Edward the Celibate, Edward the Saint: Virginity in the Construction of Edward the Confessor', pp. 119–39 in *Medieval Virginities*, ed. A. Bernau, R. Evans and S. Salih (Cardiff, 2003)
Huws, D., and Roberts, B. F., 'Another Manuscript of the Variant Version of the *Historia Regum Britanniae*', *Bulletin of the Board of Celtic Studies* 25 (1973): 147–52
Jean-Marie, L., *Caen aux XIe et XIIe siècles. Espace urbain, pouvoirs et société* (Caen, 2000)
Jirmounsky, M. M., 'Essai d'analyse des procédés littéraires de Wace', *Revue de Linguistique Romane* 63 (1925–6): 261–96
Keller, H.-E., *Etude descriptive sur le vocabulaire de Wace* (Berlin, 1953)
Keller, H.-E., 'Le mirage Robert Wace', *Zeitschrift für Romanische Philologie* 106 (1990): 465–5
Keller, H.-E., 'Wace et Geoffrey de Monmouth: problème de la chronologie des sources', *Romania* 98 (1977): 1–14
Kusaba, Y., 'Henry of Blois, Winchester and the 12th-century Renaissance', pp. 69–80 in

Winchester Cathedral. Nine Hundred Years, 1093–1993, ed. J. Crook (Chichester, 1993)
Lamy, M., *L'Immaculée Conception. Étapes et enjeux d'une controverse au moyen-âge (XIIe–XVe siècle)* (Paris, 2000)
Lapidge, M., *Anglo-Latin Literature 600–899* (London, 1996)
Lapidge, M., *Anglo-Latin Literature 900–1066* (London, 1993)
Le Patourel, J., *The Norman Empire* (Oxford, 1976)
Le Saux, F. H. M., 'Du temps mythique au temps historique dans le *Roman de Brut*', pp. 137–43 in *Temps et histoire dans le roman arthurien*, ed. J.-P. Faucon (Toulouse, 1999)
Le Saux, F. H. M., 'Mais où sont les fenêtres? De l'*Historia Regum Britanniae* de Geoffroy de Monmouth au *Roman de Brut* de Wace et au *Brut* de Layamon', pp. 295–305 in *La fenêtre au Moyen-Age*, ed. C. Connochie-Bourgne (Aix-en-Provence, 2003)
Le Saux, F. H. M., 'On Capitalisation in Some Early Manuscripts of Wace's *Roman de Brut*', pp. 29–47 in *Arthurian Studies in Honour of P. J. C. Field*, ed. B. Wheeler (Cambridge, 2004)
Le Saux, F. H. M., 'The Reception of the Matter of Britain in Thirteenth-Century England: a Study of Some Anglo-Norman Manuscripts of Wace's *Roman de Brut*', forthcoming in *Thirteenth-Century England*, ed. R. Frame (Woodbridge, 2005)
Leckie, R. W., Jr, *The Passage of Dominion: Geoffrey of Monmouth and the Periodization of Insular History in the Twelfth Century* (Toronto, Buffalo and London, 1981)
Legge, M. D., *Anglo-Norman Literature and its Background* (Oxford, 1963)
Legge, M. D., ' "Clerc lisant" ', *Modern Language Review* 47 (1952): 554–6
Lejeune, R., 'Le rôle littéraire de la famille d'Aliénor d'Aquitaine', *Cahiers de Civilisation Médiévale* 3 (1958): 319–37
Letellier, C., ed., *Le Roman de Brut entre mythe et histoire. Actes du colloque, Bagnoles de l'Orne, septembre 2001* (Orléans, 2003; Medievalia 47)
Lindley, P., 'The Medieval Sculpture of Winchester Cathedral', pp. 97–122 in *Winchester Cathedral. Nine Hundred Years, 1093–1993*, ed. J. Crook (Chichester, 1993)
Marchello-Nizia, C., 'L'historien et son prologue: forme littéraire et stratégies discursives', pp. 13–25 in *La chronique et l'histoire au moyen âge*, ed. D. Poirion (Paris, 1984; Cahiers de Civilisation Médiévale 2)
Mathey-Maille, L., 'Traduction et création: de l'*Historia Regum Britanniae* de Geoffrey of Monmouth au *Roman de Brut* de Wace', pp. 187–93 in *Ecritures et modes de pensée au moyen âge*, ed. D. Boutet and L. Harf-Lancner (Paris, 1993)
Meisen, N., *Nikolauskult und Nikolausbrauch im Abendlande. Eine kultgeographisch-volkskundliche Untersuchung* (Düsseldorf, 1931)
Meneghetti, M. L., *I fatti di Bretagna. Croniche genealogishe anglo-normanne dal XII al XIV secolo* (Padova, 1979)
Meyer, P., 'Le Couplet de deux vers', *Romania* 23 (1894): 1–35
Meyer, P., 'Les Manuscrits français de Cambridge, I. Saint John's College', *Romania* 8 (1879): 305–42
Meyer, P., 'Notice du MS 1137 de Grenoble renfermant divers poèmes sur saint Fanuel, sainte Anne, Marie et Jésus', *Romania* 16 (1887): 214–31
Meyer, P., 'Notice sur un manuscrit interpolé de la *Conception* de Wace (Musée Britannique, Add.15606)', *Romania* 16 (1887): 232–47
Meyer, P., 'Notice sur un MS Bourguignon (Musée britannique addit. 15606) suivie de pièces inédites', *Romania* 6 (1877): 1–46 and 600–4
Minnis, A. J., *The Medieval Theory of Authorship* (London, 1984)

Morse, R., *Truth and Convention in the Middle Ages: Rhetoric, Representation and Reality* (Cambridge, 1991)
O'Carroll, M., ed., *Theotokos. A Theological Encyclopedia of the Blessed Virgin Mary* (Wilmington, Delaware, 1986)
Owen, D. D. R., 'The Epic and History: *Chanson de Roland* and *Carmen de Hastingae Proelio*', *Medium Aevum* 11 (1982): 18–34
Paradisi, G., '«Par muement de languages». Il tempo, la memoria e il volgare in Wace', *Francofonia* 45 (2003): 27–45
Paradisi, G., *Le passioni della storia. Scrittura e memoria nell'opera di Wace* (Rome, 2002)
Paris, G., Review of the edition of the *Roman de Rou* by Hugo Andresen, *Romania* 9 (1880): 592–614
Partner, N., *Serious Entertainments: the Writing of History in Twelfth-Century England* (Chicago and London, 1977)
Payen, J.-C., 'Le Livre de Philosophie et de Moralité d'Alard de Cambrai', *Romania* 87 (1966): 145–50
Pelan, M. M., *L'influence du «Brut» de Wace sur les romanciers de son temps* (Strasbourg, 1931)
Philpot, J. H., *Maistre Wace. A Pioneer in Two Literatures* (London, 1925)
Round, J. H., *Feudal England. Historical Studies on the Eleventh and Twelfth Centuries* (London, 1895)
Rychner, J., *La chanson de geste: essai sur l'art épique des jongleurs* (Lille, 1955)
Sayers, D., 'The jongleur Taillefer at Hastings: Antecedents and Literary Fate', *Viator* 14 (1983): 79–88
Scheidegger, J., *Le Roman de Renart ou le texte de la derision* (Geneva, 1989)
Schultz, J., 'Classical Rhetoric, Medieval Poetics and the Medieval Vernacular Prologue', *Speculum* 59 (1984): 1–15
Schultze-Busacker, E., *Proverbes et expressions proverbiales dans la littérature narrative du moyen âge français* (Geneva and Paris, 1985)
Tatlock, J. S. P., *The Legendary History of Britain* (Berkeley and Los Angeles, 1950)
Uitti, K., 'The Clerkly Narrator Figure', *Medioevo Romanzo* 2 (1975): 394–408
van Emden, W., *La Chanson de Roland* (London, 1995)
van Houts, E. M. C., 'The Adaptation of the *Gesta Normannorum Ducum* by Wace and Benoît', pp. 115–24 in *Non nova sed nove: Mélanges de civilisation médiévale dédiés à Willem Noomen*, ed. M. Gosman and J. van Os (Groningen, 1984)
van Houts, E. M. C., 'Genre Aspects of the Use of Oral Material in Medieval Historiography', pp. 297–311 in *Gattungen mittelalterlicher Schriftlichkeit*, ed. B. Frank, T. Haye and D. Tophinke (Tübingen, 1998)
van Houts, E. M. C., *Memory and Gender in Medieval Europe, 900–1200* (London, 1999)
van Houts, E. M. C., 'The Ship List of William the Conqueror', *Anglo-Norman Studies* 10 (1987): 159–83
van Houts, E. M. C., 'Wace as Historian', pp. 103–32 in *Family Trees and the Roots of Politics*, ed. K. S. B. Keats-Rohan (Woodbridge, 1997)
Warner, M., *Alone of All her Sex: the Myth and Cult of the Virgin Mary* (London, 1989)
Weiss, J., 'Two Fragments from a Newly Discovered Manuscript of Wace's *Brut*', *Medium Aevum* 68 (1999): 268–77
Wright, C. E., *English Vernacular Hands from the Twelfth to the Fifteenth Centuries* (Oxford, 1960)
Zink, M., *La Prédication en langue vulgaire romane avant 1300* (Paris, 1966)

Index

Abbaye aux Femmes: see Sainte Trinité
Abbaye aux Hommes: see Saint-Etienne
Abraham: 47
Adela (daughter of William the Conqueror: 221
Ælfsige: see Helsin
Aelred of Rievaulx: 219
Afaitement Catun: see Elie of Winchester
Agag: 92–3
Aganippus of France: 124
Alain Fergant (Duke of Brittany): 188
Alan of Brittany: 200–2, 204
Alard of Cambrai, *Le Livre de Philosophie et de Moralité*: 13n
Alba: 109
Albany: 184–5
Albion: 163, 184
Aldeberd of Kent: 149
Alderney / Auremen: 165
Aldroen of Brittany: 92, 107n, 121
Alemaigne: see Germany
Alençon: 201, 213, 217
Aleth: 146
Alexander the Great: 162, 183, 207
Alexander II (Pope): 228
Alfred atheling: 192, 202, 203, 214n, 216, 225, 244
Alfred the Giant: 213
Alton Wood: 267, 268
Anacletus: 102
anaphora: 16, 24, 41, 104–5, 166, 282
Androgeus: 107, 115
anecdote(s): 147, 178, 181–2, 185–9, 190–1, 197, 200–2, 204–6, 207–8, 215, 223–4, 227–8, 232, 235–7, 243, 252, 255, 259, 260, 262–3, 264–5, 269, 272–3, 281
Angevin: 218
Angles: 110
Anglo-Norman: 155
Anglo-Saxon Chronicle: 192
Angusel of Scotland: 96–8, 107n, 137
Anjou: 213
Anne (St): 34, 39, 42, 46–8
Annunciation: 38, 47
Anquetil / Anscytel: 171–2, 176
Anselm of Canterbury (St): 31, 34, 36, 117
Antioch: 16, 17
apocrypha: 31; see also *Conception Nostre Dame*, sources of –
Aquitaine: 163, 185; see also Eleanor of Aquitaine
archers: 231, 233, 243, 246, 248
Ardevon: 262

Arlette: 191, 207–8
Armene/Armoenia: 25, 26
Armorica/Armoriche: 120, 163; see also Brittany
Arnulf of Flanders (Count): 177–9, 218
Arthur: 40, 81, 86, 87, 89, 90, 95, 98, 107, 109, 110, 112, 118, 122–44, 149, 151, 189, 196, 201, 207, 215, 225, 228–9, 236, 238, 248, 253, 260, 280, 282, 284; his armour: 125–6, 236; his death: 143–4
Arthurian overtones/themes: 4, 155, 167n, 184–9, 190, 209, 215, 225–6, 228–9, 238, 278, 280
Artois: 13
Arviragus: 95, 109n
Ascelin son of Arthur: 258
Aschanius: 102n, 108, 109, 110
Aschil of Denmark: 131n
Assaracus: 101–2
Assumption of Our Lady: 38, 40, 42, 49
astrologer(s)/astrology: 147, 149, 231–2, 243
Athelstan: 145, 173, 177
Augustine of Canterbury (St): 98, 99, 118, 141n, 145, 283; his mission in England: 148–9
Aurelius: 93, 106, 108, 121n, 122, 228
authority: 22, 25, 82, 86, 87, 91, 139, 146, 173, 182–4, 220, 280
Avalon: 143, 144
Avranchin: 202, 262

Babylon: 162
Baldulf: 125
Baldwin of Flanders: 200, 201, 224, 234
Balzo: 171, 177, 178
Bangor: 145n; Bangor massacre: 149
baptism: 19, 75–8, 79, 167, 196
Barenton (fountain): 188, 229
Barfleur: 97–8, 138
Bari: 51, 64
Bassian and Geta: 110
Bath: 111
Bath, battle of: 103, 125
Bathsheba: 124
Bayeux: 2, 4, 6, 9–10, 53, 156, 218, 249, 271, 275
Bayeux manuscript (Paris, Bibliothèque nationale fonds fr. 9346): 5
Bayeux tapestry: 221, 243, 245, 248, 251
Bec-Hellouin (abbey): 157
Bede: 89, 93
Belgibus: 21–2, 27, 281
Belgium: 76
Belin: 90, 92, 95, 110, 112–14
Bellême: 200, 201–2
Benedeit, *The Voyage of St Brendan*: 33n

Benoît de Sainte-Maure: 10, 87, 156, 275, 277–8
Berkeley (witch of –): 186n
Bernard of Clairvaux (St): 8, 31, 35–6
Bernard the Dane: 174, 179
Bernard the Philosopher: 197
Biblical references/echoes: 55, 92–3, 182n, 207–8, 270
Björn / Bïer: 164–6, 168
Bladud: 111
Bonneville: 221n, 228
Borel: 132
Boso of Oxford: 139
Boulogne: 131, 155, 234
Brennes: 90, 92, 95, 110, 112–14
Breton: 219, 229; language: 89; 110
Brevis relatio de origine Willelmi Conquestoris: 179n, 211, 232n, 234n, 235
Brian: 95, 143, 145–7, 149
Britain: 86, 87, 94, 96–8, 104, 105, 108–50, 279, 280
Brittany: 105, 107, 108, 119–21, 146, 149, 163, 174–5, 187–9, 196, 202, 221, 249, 254n, 261
Brocéliande: 187–9, 194, 229
Bruges: 76
Brun: 271
Bruno (Archbishop): 175
Brutus: 89, 95, 101, 105, 108–9, 110, 149, 233, 280
Burgundy: 112, 192, 197

Cador of Cornwall: 127, 135–6
Cadwallader: 95, 107–8, 145, 150
Cadwallan: 95, 107, 145–50
Cadwan: 149
Caen: 1–2, 8–9, 11, 51–3, 157, 161, 164, 215, 218, 266, 270, 272–3
Caerleon: 112, 114, 125, 132
Cambridge: 33, 54
Camlan (battle of –): 129, 143
Canterbury: 145, 257
Canute (King): 202, 203, 214, 215, 216, 283
Caradoc of Llancarfan: 6
Cardiff: 273
Cariz: 148
Carmen de Hastingae proelio: see Guy of Amiens
Carolingians: 184
Carpentras: 33
Cassibelan: 107, 114–15, 280
Celidon forest: 125
Celtic Church: 148–9
Cerisy: 199, 206–7, 211, 213
Cernel: 102n, 111–12, 145
Chanbois: 197
Channel: 210, 267, 269
chanson de geste: 3, 4, 6, 9, 14, 79, 81, 86, 131, 16, 160–2, 174–6, 178–9, 181, 184, 239, 248
Charlemagne: 165, 189, 242
Charles of Bourbon: 5n
Charroi de Nîmes: 179n
Chartres: 3, 83, 174, 180
Chaumont: 203, 266n
Cherbourg: 197

Cherin: 92
cheval fust: 23
Chrétien de Troyes: 6, 87, 186, 284
Christ: 9, 33, 35, 37n, 38–9, 42, 43, 45, 47–9, 95, 116, 117, 161, 208
Christianity: 18, 29, 73, 108, 116–20, 122, 125, 126, 172, 180, 203, 236, 247, 266, 280; conversion to –: 63, 95, 117, 148, 164–5, 174, 176, 180–1
Chronicle of Battle Abbey: 250
Chronique Ascendante: see *Roman de Rou*
Cirencester: 99, 146
Claudius: 95
clerc lisant: 1–4, 9, 80, 166, 284
Cologne: 92, 118, 120
Cluny: 6
comet: 228–9
Con (river): 265
Conan (founder of Brittany): 92, 105, 118–20
Conan (pre-Arthurian king): 145, 147
Conan (post-Arthurian king): 170
Conception Nostre Dame: 7–9, 11, 12, 13, 29, 30–50, 52, 57, 65, 79, 80, 82, 155, 170, 279, 280, 281, 282, 284; direct speech in –: 44–9; manuscripts of –: 32–3; narrator's interventions in –: 38–41; prologue to –: 34–8; sources of –: 30–1, 34–44, structure: 38
conquest of England: 36, 157, 173, 203, 214, 229–52, 277–8
Constant: 109, 116n
Constance (Queen of Robert the Pious of France): 202
Constance (King): 121–2, 141
Constantine(Emperor); 51, 62, 68, 90, 118–19, 204
Constantine (King): 108–9, 121–2
Constantine of Cornwall: 144, 147, 148
Constantinople: 14n, 52, 68–9, 163, 185, 204
contemptus mundi: 185
Corcers: 186
Cordeille / Cordelia: 100, 124
Corineus: 92, 149
Cornish language: 89
Cornwall: 145
corruption (linguistic): 110–12, 184–5
Cotentin: 196, 214, 215, 260, 261, 262, 268, 270,
Couesnon (river): 262
Couronnement Louis: 179n
Creusa: 102n, 109
Cross of Christ: 17, 39; Invention of –: 92; sign of the Cross: 219
Crusade: 223, 236, 263, 264–5, 266, 271
Crusader States: 206
Cul (river): 265

Danes: 36, 37, 164; 168, 179, 180–1, 191–2, 196, 225
Dacia: 172
Danas of Troy: 164
Danube: 166
David: 124
degeneracy: 162

Index 299

Demetia: 184–5
demon/devil(s): 17, 18, 19, 20–3, 29, 42, 43, 58, 60, 61, 62, 73–4, 76, 78, 122, 124, 190, 205, 215, 281
De nativitate Mariae: 30, 31n, 42n
Denmark: 37, 112, 130–1, 192, 254
Diana: 60, 95
Dieppe: 180
Dieudonné: 71–3
Dinan: 146
Dinoot (abbot): 149
Distichs of Cato: 154
Dionot of Cornwall: 118–19
Dive: 195
Dol: 202
Doldani of Gotland: 128, 131
Domesday Book: 35
Domfront: 213, 263–4, 268, 270
Dorchester: 99, 145
Dormition of Our Lady: 38–40
dream: see omen; also see prophecy
Dreux: 196
Drogo, Count: 206
Duchesne, André: 155
Dudo of St Quentin, *De moribus et actis primorum Normanniae ducum*: 157, 165, 169–73, 174, 181–2, 183, 185, 189, 190, 218, 280
Dunian: 117
Durham: 53, 85, 86, 87, 88

Eadmer of Canterbury: 31, 35–6; *Historia novorum*: 190, 210, 220n, 221n, 222n, 223
Eagle (Auguries of the –): 150n
Ebissa: 102, 122
Ebrauc: 109, 119
Edmund (St): 196, 283
Edward the Confessor: 35, 192, 202, 203, 214n, 215, 218–20, 221n, 224, 225, 237, 242; his succession: 209, 216, 219–21, 222–3
Edward I: 87
Edwin: 145, 147, 149
Elbeuf: 197
Eldad: 93
Eldolf: 103
Eleanor of Aquitaine: 7, 82–4, 169, 276
Elfrid / Ethelfrid: 149
Elidur: 102n
Elie of Winchester, *L'Afaitement Catun*: 154
Eleutherius (Pope): 117
Emma (wife of Duke Richard I): 191
Emma (sister of Duke Richard II): 192
Eneas: 108, 109
England: 3, 8, 9, 14, 31, 32, 36, 38, 49, 51, 79, 86, 87, 117, 163, 195, 210–12, 215, 216, 219, 224, 227–52, 253–4, 257, 259–60, 274, 275, 279
English: 10, 110, 148–9, 164, 192, 196, 216, 225, 257, 267, 283; language: 9, 111, 163–4, 220, 236, 282; battle-cries: 247; sources: 164, 210, 219–20, 222–3, 242
enjambement: 16, 47–9, 65, 104, 160
enumeratio: 41, 48, 104, 166, 248, 282

Eparc: 68, 69
epic of revolt: 178
Escorande: 73
L'Escoufle: see Jean Renart
Essex: 101
Ester: see Danube
Estoire des Engleis: see Gaimar
Estorie de Joseph d'Arimathie: 87
Ethelred (King of England): 191, 192, 193, 195–6, 202, 225
etymologies: 163–4, 173, 183, 185
Eucharist: 76
Euphrosine: 70, 71, 73
Eustace (son of King Stephen of England): 7, 82
Eustachius: 68
Evelin: 115
Everwic: see York
Evreux: 180
Exeter: 149

factual errors: 9, 116–17, 195, 211, 215n, 226, 228, 276n
Fagan: 117
Falaise: 198, 208
Falconius, Nicolaus Carminius –: 52, 59–61, 62, 63, 67, 73
Family traditions: 211
Fanuel (St): 34n
Fécamp: 31, 165, 171–2, 176, 191, 193, 198, 204, 215, 237
Ferrex and Porrex: 110, 234
Flanders: 131, 165, 191, 226–7, 234, 243,
font (baptismal): 8n, 76–7
Fortune's wheel: 114, 115, 133, 264n
France: 14, 51, 55, 114, 125, 131–2, 133–4, 161, 176, 180, 185, 192, 213, 214, 217–18, 226–7, 247, 251
Franche-Comté: 13
Franco of Rouen (Archbishop): 174
French: 111, 112, 161–2, 174–6, 203, 216–18; language: 4, 5, 13, 56, 64, 79, 94, 164
Frolle / Frollo: 131–2, 134

Gaimar, *Estoire des Engleis*: 86, 103, 241n, 283
Ganelon: 242n
Garin (Rou's brother): 172
Garin of Chartres: 139
Gascony: 165
Gaul: 130–1
Gawain / Gauvain: 118, 131, 135–6, 137, 149
Geffrei Gaimar: see Gaimar
Geoffrey of Anjou: 7, 14, 53, 82, 211, 276, 277
Geoffrey Martel, count of Anjou: 213, 215, 217–18
Geoffrey of Brittany: 192, 197
Geoffrey of Monmouth: 6, 8, 15, 83–4, 89–102, 109, 114, 116, 123, 151, 155, 157, 209, 212, 279; *Vita Merlini*: 117; see also *Historia Regum Britanniae*
Geoffroi of Paris, *La Bible qui est compillee des .vii. estaz du monde*: 32
Germany: 51, 96, 97, 163, 185

Gesta Guillelmi Ducis: see William of Poitiers
Gesta Normannorum Ducum: see William of Jumièges
Gesta Regum Anglorum: see William of Malmesbury
Getro: 70, 71
giant(s): 92, 138, 140, 233
Giants' Circle: 123, 137n; also see Stonehenge
Giant's Tower: 225
Gildas: 89
Gildas (St): 4
Giles (St): 180
Gillomar of Ireland: 128
Glastonbury: 6, 9, 87
Gloucester: 273
Godwin (Earl): 214n, 216, 219, 238, 244
Gogmagog: 92
Gohier of Aunay: 271
Goles: 213–14
Gonvais of Orchenie: 128, 131
Gormond et Isembard: 178n
Goscelin of Saint Bertin, *Vita Sancti Augustini*: 90, 145n, 151
Gospel of Pseudo-Matthew: 31
Gospel of Pseudo-Melito: 31
Gratian: 120
Greece: 107, 108, 163, 185; Greeks: 36, 204
Gregory the Great (Pope): 99
Grenoble: 34
Gudlac of Denmark: 92, 113
Guernsey: 165
Guillaume d'Angleterre: 155
Guillaume d'Orange: 174, 178, 179n
Guincelin (lat. Guithelinus): 92, 101n, 107n, 121
Guinevere: 87, 96–8, 127, 141–3
Guiot: 87
Gunnor (Duchess): 185n., 190–1
Gurguint: 101n
Gurmund: 9, 95–6, 98–9, 110, 114, 118, 141n, 145, 148, 217
Guy of Amiens, *Carmen de Hastingae proelio*: 190, 211, 233, 234n, 235, 241–2, 244, 250
Guy of Burgundy/ the Burgundian: 213, 214
Guy of Ponthieu (Count): 221
Gwynedd: 128n
Gyrth: 221, 237–44, 248

Harold of Denmark (King): 180
Harold Godwinson (King): 35–6, 130, 209, 210, 220–5, 228, 233–44, 246, 250, 257, 267; his hair colour: 237; his superstition: 243, 246; his death: 249–51
Harold Harefoot (King): 216
Haschier / Richard Achard: 274 n
Hasting: 153, 157, 164–8, 169, 172–4, 283
Hastings (battle of –): 188, 209, 211, 212, 219, 221, 229, 244–52, 253–4, 281, 283; battle formation: 244–6
Harthacnut (King): 216
Hawise: 192
Heavenfield (battle of –): 145
Hebrew: 111

Helen (St): 90, 92, 118–19
Helias: 88
Helias of Le Mans: 265
Hellequin's hunt: 186
Helsin (Abbot): 32n, 34–5, 37, 42n
Hengist: 92, 101, 106, 122, 124,
Henry I (King of England): 1–3, 7, 8, 11, 14, 32, 49, 50, 84, 117–18, 153–4, 159, 184, 211n, 222, 234, 253, 257, 259, 260–74, 274, 276
Henry I of France: 200, 202–3, 204, 214
Henry I of Germany: 177
Henry II (King of England): 2, 3, 7, 9–11, 14, 53, 82, 84, 86, 88, 117–18, 153, 155, 159, 161, 169, 185, 198, 218, 266, 274, 275–8
Henry II of Bayeux (Bishop): 2
Henry the Young King: 3, 14, 274
Henry of Blois: 6–9, 50, 76–7, 79, 276
Henry of Huntingdon: 215, 241n
Hercules (columns of –): 92
Herluin: 177, 200n
Herm: 165
Hesdin: 13
Hestrild: 109
Hirelgas: 115
Historia Brittonum: 89, 116–17
Historia Ecclesiastica: see Orderic Vitalis
Historia novorum: see Eadmer of Canterbury
Historia Regum Britanniae (vulgate version and First Variant version): 6, 15, 83–4, 89–102, 104 n, 107, 109, 116, 118, 123, 124, 125–50, 151, 152, 153, 155, 156, 157, 279–80, 282, 283, 284, 285n
Hoel of Brittany: 96–8, 103, 108, 127, 131, 136–9
Holdin: 132
Holy Land: 185, 199, 205–6, 263, 266, 271
Holy Sepulchre: 205, 268
Holy Trinity: see Fécamp
homiletic style: 41, 48, 59, 65, 103
Hôtel Dieu (Caen): 52
Hubert of Ryes: 213–14
Hugh of Avranches (Count): 261
Hugh of Châlon (Count): 197–8
Hugh, Bishop of Lisieux: 195
Hugh Margot: 237–8
Hugh of Montfort: 209
Hugh (the Great) of Paris: 174, 177, 179
Hugh Capet (King of France): 184, 191
hunting: 102, 180, 187, 223, 264, 265–6
Humber estuary: 92
humour: 44, 166, 193–4, 226, 283

Iceland: 127
Immaculate Conception of Our Lady: 8, 31, 35, 38, 41, 44, 79
Innocent III (Pope): 52n
intercession: 23, 24, 28, 43–4, 47
Ireland: 106, 127–8
Isaac: 46
Isacar: 45
Isembard: 146
Isembert (Duke Robert I's chaplain): 201

isocolon: 16, 24, 104–5, 166, 282
Israelites: 93
Italy: 119, 163, 185

Jamnee et Jambree (Liber-): 22n
Janus: 100
Jean Renart, *L'Escoufle*: 207
Jeanne of Burgundy: 13
Jehan Bodel, *Le Jeu de saint Nicolas*: 55n
Jerome (St): 155
Jersey: 1, 164, 165, 218
Jerusalem: 2, 200, 203–4, 205–6, 263, 266–7; Kingdom of –: 206
Jeu d'Adam: 13, 32
Jeu de saint Nicolas: see Jehan Bodel
Jeufosse (treaty of –): 154, 180
Jew: 58, 63
Joachim (St): 39, 42, 45–7
Job: 46
John the Evangelist (St): 31, 38, 39, 42n
Johannes Diaconus: 52, 59
John Archdeacon of Bari: 59
jongleur(s): 4n, 6, 170–2, 174n, 176, 181–2, 284
Jordan Fantosme: 86, 154
Joseph: 47
Joseph, St: 31, 47
Joseph of Arimathea: 87
Judas: 216
Judea: 109
Judith: 234
Judon: 102n, 202
Julius Caesar: 70, 95, 107, 110, 114–15, 144n, 162, 183, 280
Jumièges: 165, 174, 177; see also William of Jumièges

Kaerlu: 110
Kaerusk: see Caerleon
Kent: 259n
Kimbelin: 116

Lacman of Sweden (King): 196
laisses similaires: 174–5
Landolfus Sagax: 90, 94
Lanfranc (Archbishop): 31, 36, 117, 200n, 260
Langres: 139
Laon: 178
latimer: 4
Latin (language): 4, 13, 55–6, 94, 103, 121, 164, 189, 236, 280, 281, 282
Latium: 109
Lavinia: 101, 109
Laʒamon: 82, 86
Le Bec (abbey): 158, 200n,
Le Mans: 265
Legenda Aurea: 61–3
Leicester: 100, 112n
Leir: 100, 106, 107n, 124, 151
Lieceline: 195
Life of Saint Edmund: 192
Ligier: 132
Lincoln: 86, 246

lineage: 218–19
Lisieux: 197
Livre Noir de Bayeux: 53
Llydaw / Letavia: 120n; also see Brittany
Locrin: 109
Lombardy: 109
London: 33, 110–11, 146, 163, 184, 192, 240, 267
Lorraine: 33, 97
Loth: 130–1
Lothar of France (King): 179–80, 184, 191
Louis IV of France (King): 174, 177, 178–9
Louis VIII of France (King): 155
Luces: 117
Lucifer: 22
Lucius Hiberus: 96–7, 107, 118, 134, 138
Lud: 110
Luke (Evangelist): 208, 270n
Luni: 165–8, 169
Lutece: see Paris
Lycia: 68
Lyons: 33, 35n

magic: 166, 215, 231; see also supernatural
Maine: 83, 254n
Malcolm Canmore of Scotland: 14
Malfosse: 250–1
Malgo: 148
Malin and Malan: 110
Mammon: 270
Mantes: 255
Marcel: 139
Margadud: 107
Margaret of Antioch (St): 4, 7, 13–29, 79–80, 280
Margaret of Scotland (St): 7, 14, 15
Marie de France: 186
Matthew (Evangelist): 47, 55, 270n
manuscripts: see under individual texts
Marie de France: 5
Mary, Blessed Virgin –: 13, 30–50, 79–80, 138, 161, 236, 258, 280
Matilda (Richard II's sister): 192, 196
Matilda (William I's queen): 3, 211, 215, 227
Matilda (Empress): 7, 14, 162, 191, 274, 276
Maugier (Archbishop): 197, 203, 215, 231
Maximianus: 118
Maximien (lat. Maximianus): 109, 115, 119
Mayet: 265
Melga: see Wanis and Melga
Melun: 192
Membriz: 102
Menbricius: 107
Mercia: 95
Merlin: 84, 88, 91, 100, 106, 117, 122–4, 137n, 143, 145, 150, 215, 228; see also prophecies
Methodius (Patriarch of Constantinople): 52
Middlesex: 101
Mimande: 198
mirabilia: 114
miracle(s): 17, 19, 23, 47, 54, 56–78, 79, 229, 230, 235, 272, 281, 283
Miraculum de conceptione sanctae Mariae: 34–7
Modena cathedral: 167

Modred: 96–7, 106, 107, 110, 125, 137–8, 139n, 141–3; his sons: 146–7
Mombrizio, Bonino: 16, 52, 59–61, 62–3, 67, 72
money: 6, 62, 66, 67, 71, 73, 75, 96, 97, 113–14, 179, 195, 197, 200, 206, 227, 259–61, 264n, 268, 269–70, 273
Moniage Guillaume: 176
du Monstier, Arthur: 155
Montreuil: 177
Mont St Michel: 138, 140, 191, 261–3, 269
Montefalcone: 14
Morcar (Earl): 2
Mortain: 273
Mortemer: 217
mutability topos: 162–3, 183, 185; see also *contemptus mundi*
Myra: 51, 52

name change: 163–4, 184–5; see also corruption (linguistic)
Nebuchadnezzar: 162
Neustria: 185; see also Normandy
Nicea: 205
Nicholas of Myra (St): 51–78, 79, 280, 281
Nicholas of Pinara (St): 52
Nicholas (son of Duke Richard III): 190, 199
Nigel of the Cotentin: 213, 214
Ninevah: 162
Nivard: see *Ysengrimus*
Normans: 2n, 84, 111, 153, 160–74, 190–274, 277, 283
Normandy: 2, 3, 9–10, 14, 32, 51, 53, 79, 83, 96, 151, 153–85, 189, 191–6, 200, 203, 205–8, 209–10, 212–15, 217–18, 224, 235, 239, 253–5, 257, 260, 264, 267, 270, 272–4, 277, 280, 281
Norse (language): 164
Northumberland: 107, 238
Northumbria: 233
Norway: 112, 125, 130–1, 137n, 196
Novele cirurgerie: 103

Octa: 102, 122
Octave (king of Britain): 119
octosyllabic couplet: 15–16, 47–9, 65, 79–80, 94, 103–4, 152, 155, 160, 162, 175, 181, 185, 205
Odo of Bayeux: 251, 259
Odo of Chartres: 191, 192, 196
Odyssey, Homer's: 128
Olaf II of Norway (King and St): 196
Oliver: 239, 241, 247
Olybrius (lat. Olimbrius): 17, 19–27, 28, 29
omens: 69, 91, 96–7, 138, 166, 172, 207, 228, 231–2, 236–7
oral sources/tales: 117, 129, 138, 146, 151, 157, 171–2, 182, 186–7, 195, 223, 229, 245, 260, 280
Orderic Vitalis: 2, 4, 9, 157, 164, 186n, 189–90, 200, 203n, 206, 211, 216, 221–2, 224, 225n, 238n, 239, 242, 245n, 248, 254n, 256–7, 258n, 259, 261n, 262, 264n, 265–6, 268, 269n, 271, 281, 284

Ordres: 114
origins: 108, 109, 110, 113, 157, 164
Osmund (rebel against Duke William I): 171
Osmund (Duke Richard I's tutor and bodyguard): 178
Oswald: 145
Oswi: 95, 107, 145
Othloh of St Emmeram: 52n
Otto the Great (Emperor): 179
Ovid: 124
Oxford: 162

pagans: 58, 60, 61, 70, 118, 126, 164–5, 168, 180, 191, 196, 206, 217, 236
Palm Sunday: 203
Pandrasus of Greece: 102
papacy/pope: 117–18, 238, 259
parable: 55 (Talents)
Paris: 10n, 13, 32, 53, 54, 64, 85–6, 131–2, 133, 163, 185
Passio Sanctae Margaritae: 16n, 18–29
patronage: 4, 5–9, 11–12, 31, 79, 80, 88
peasants: 128, 168, 188, 202, 243, 245, 266; revolt: 192–5
Pellit: 149
Penda: 95, 107, 147, 149
perjury: 221–2, 223, 224
Peronne: 197
Peter (St): 117, 228
Peter's Pence: 145
Petreius: 139
Pevensey: 233
Philippe Auguste of France (King): 155
Philip I of France (King): 218, 227, 254
Picard dialect: 13, 32, 33, 53, 54, 55, 155
Picts: 125
pilgrimage / pilgrims: 14, 63, 165, 199, 203–6
poison: 199, 200, 206, 207, 252
Ponthieu: 234
Pontoise: 203
Pontefract: 233–4
Porrex: see Ferrex
Portchester: 268n
Portsmouth: 268n
proleptic comments: 113
propaganda: 208, 212, 247, 277
prophecy: 116, 150, 157, 175, 208, 215, 223, 225, 257; see also Prophecies of Merlin
Prophecies of Merlin: 88, 95, 117, 122, 144, 232
Protevangelium Iacobi Minoris: 31
proverbs: 164, 182, 196, 197, 224, 234, 254–5
providence, divine –: 210
Pseudo-Melito Transitus: 42, 44
Pseudo-Turpin chronicle: 155
Pyrrhus: 101

Quintilian, *Institutio oratoria*: 104

Rachel: 47
Ralph of Conches: 244
Ralph Mowin: 206
Ralph Taisson: 215n

Ramsey Abbey: 35
Ranulf of Briquessart (Vicomte of the Bessin): 213
Ralph ('of Evreux', Duke Richard II's uncle): 194–5
Ralph Torta: 179
Raoul de Cambrai: 178
Reading Museum: 221n
rebellion: 178, 191–2, 193–5, 196, 198–9, 201–2, 213, 254, 265
Reginald I of Burgundy (Count): 197–8
Reginold of Eichstaett (Bishop): 52n
Regnier of Hainault (Count): 173
relics: 14, 64, 70, 71, 168, 174, 206, 207, 221, 228, 230
Rembaut of Frisia: 172
Renaud de Montauban: 178n
Rencesvals: 241–2
Rennes: 34
repetitio cum variatio: 63
resurrection (miraculous): 60–3, 73–4, 76
Reynard the Fox: 167–8
Richard I of Normandy: 154, 160, 169, 174n, 177, 178–91, 214, 215, 229, 276
Richard II of Normandy: 10, 191–8, 207; his generosity: 197–8
Richard III of Normandy: 189–90, 197–9
Richart de Montivilliers: 207
Richard of Reviers: 260–2, 270
Richier: 132
Ritho: 138
Riulf: 171, 176–7
Robert of Arques: 271
Robert II of Bellême: 265, 268, 269
Robert of Burgundy: 202
Robert le Diable: 207
Robert of Evreux (Archbishop): 201
Robert FitzErneis: 249
Robert FitzHaimo: 268, 271
Robert of Gloucester (Count): 273
Robert de Meulan: 269–70
Robert I of Normandy (the Magnificent): 157, 190, 191, 193, 198–208, 281; his piety: 199–200, 205–6, 260; his generosity: 200–2, 204–6, 212
Robert II of Normandy (Curthose): 14, 156, 157, 159, 184, 190, 209, 223, 253, 254, 257, 260–73, 276–7, 281; his shortcomings: 271
Robert the Pious of France (King): 192, 196, 197, 202, 203
Robert Theoldi / Tioudi/ le fiz Tiout: 52, 77, 78; his sons Robert and Roger: 52–3
Robert de Torigni: 157–9, 170, 197n, 259, 268
Roger of Beaumont-le-Roger: 249
Roger of Montgomery: 211, 248n, 249
Roland: 236, 239, 241–2, 247
roman antique: 87, 155
Roman de Brut: 7, 9, 10, 12, 16, 30, 32, 40, 50, 79, 81–152, 118, 153, 166, 170, 172, 176, 184, 185, 189, 191, 196, 209, 217, 219, 233, 234, 248, 253, 279, 280, 282, 283, 284; courtliness in –: 81, 83, 133–4; descriptive technique: 104–6, 132–3; intended audience: 82–4; importance of Gawain: 135–40; manuscripts: 85–9; manuscript layout: 86–88; narrator in –: 6, 102–3, 166; parody in –: 84; passage of dominion theme in –: 145–50; Prologue: 81–2; reception: 86–7; sources: 89–94; speeches in –: 88n, 100, 106, 113, 134–7, 140, 225; structure: 94–102; stylistic features: 102–7
Roman d'Eneas: 87
Roman de Renart: 167
Roman de Rou: 1, 5, 6, 9, 10, 12, 15, 32, 50, 65, 88, 118, 153–284, 280–1, 282, 283–4; *Chronique Ascendante*: 153–4, 160–2, 173, 181, 189; *Première Partie*: 153–4, 160, 162–8, 173, 278n; *Deuxième Partie*: 5, 9, 154, 160, 168–84, 190, 214, 254, 278n; *Troisième Partie*: 3, 5, 9, 154, 160, 182–274, 275, 277n, 280; Epilogue: 159, 274, 275–8; Prologues: 162–4, 173, 184–5, 274, 275; adaptation principles: 170, 209–12, 280; Arthurian overtones: 184–9; descriptions: 167; epic phraseology: 175; manuscripts: 155–6; metre and rhythm: 154, 160, 162, 169, 181; narrator's stance: 5, 166, 170–2, 176, 181–4, 189, 209–10, 229–50, 263–4, 265–6; rhetorical/stylistic effects: 166, 212, 213–14, 233, 248, 267; sources: 156–9, 169–72, 181–2, 189–90, 210–11, 215–16, 221–2, 229–30, 233–5, 244, 279; speeches in –: 217, 225, 239, 244; structure: 160, 189–91, 212–13, 214
Roman de Troie: 87
Rome: 33, 89, 90, 96–8, 100, 106, 107, 108–24, 125, 131, 132, 133, 165, 166, 196, 238; sack of –: 114; Arthur's campaign against –: 134–41, 212, 225
Ronwen: 110, 122, 236n
Rou, first duke of Normandy: 153, 161, 162, 165, 168–70, 172–6, 177, 196, 218, 254, 275
Rouen: 165, 176, 178, 191, 192, 196, 215, 223, 259, 263, 274; 1174; siege of –: 156, 162
Round Table: 81, 90, 125, 128–30, 133, 143, 146, 151, 187
Rufo (dragon): 21
Rummaret of Wenelande: 128

Saint Albans (battle): 124
Saint Brice's Day massacre: 196, 225, 244
Saint-Etienne: 3, 4, 51, 197, 200, 204, 219
Saint-Evroult: 4, 157, 164
Saint-Ouen: 157, 181, 186
Saint-Valéry: 229, 230
Sainte Trinité de Caen: 3, 51n, 52, 219, 266
Sara: 47
Samson: 47
Samuel: 47, 93
Santa Claus: 51
Saracens: 205–6, 236, 242, 267; see also pagans
Satan: 42
Saul (King): 92–3
Saussy (battle of –): 139, 140
Saxons: 95, 99, 107, 110, 114, 118, 124, 122, 125–8, 141, 142, 147–9, 236, 280

Scandinavia / Scandinavians: 35, 128, 180, 191
Scotland: 14, 96, 126–7, 154, 163, 184–5
Senate (of Rome): 100, 134
Sermo de conceptione Beatae Mariae: 34
sermo humilis: 63
serventeis: 180
Sever: 109
Severn: 92, 101, 133
Shrewsbury: 9
Ship List of William the Conqueror: 230
Sibyll: 136, 150
Sichelin of Norway: 130
Sicily: 51
Silvius Postumus: 109
Simeon: 208
Simeon Theophrastes: 52n
sirens: 92, 282
social issues: 188, 191, 193–6
Solomon: 21, 22
Song of Roland: 241–2, 247
Southampton: 138
Spain: 170, 181
Sparatin: 104n
Stamford Bridge: 233n
Statutes of Edward I: 87
Stephen of Blois (King of England): 7, 14, 76, 82
Stonehenge: 93, 101, 103, 106
Stour river: 92
supernatural: 143–4, 185–7, 190
Sussex: 101
Svein of Denmark (King): 36–7
Svein I of Denmark and England (King): 191–2, 196
Sweden: 196

Taillefer: 241, 247
Taisson (gate-keeper): 273
Taliesin/Teleusin/Telgesinus: 9, 116–17
Thames: 114
Tapestry of Bayeux: see Bayeux Tapestry
Thebes: 162
Theobald of Bec (Archbishop of Canterbury): 3
Theotimus: 16, 18, 25
Thibaut (adviser to King Lothar): 180
Thomas (St): 191
Thomas: see *Tristan*
Thomas Becket: 3, 118, 155, 276
Thor / Tur: 164
Thorney Island: 220
Three Estates: 56
Tillières: 196, 213
Tinchebray (battle of –): 2, 10, 154, 264, 265, 271n, 272, 273, 275, 277
Tintagel: 123
Tonuenne: 107n, 112, 113
Toret: 215
Torigni: see Robert de Torigni
Tostig, Earl of Northumberland: 233–4
Tour Gigantine (Giant's Tower): 135
Touraine: 13
Tournai marble: 76
Tours: 13–14, 15, 32

Toutain of Hiémois: 157
Tractatus de conceptione sanctae Mariae: 31
transfer of remains/relics: 14, 198
'Transitus' texts: 42; 44 (Latin)
translatio: 25, 82, 185, 189
treachery: 121–2, 130, 141, 143, 161–2, 166–8, 177–9, 201–2, 208, 214, 216, 217–18, 242, 269, 271–3
Trêve de Dieu: 219
tribute: 97
Trinity: 66, 67
Trinovant / Troie Noeve: 110, 163, 184–5
Trinubium Annae: 31, 39
Tristan: 112
Troisgots: 249
Trojan(s): 89, 101–2, 104, 109, 110, 280
Troy: 89, 102n, 109, 162, 164
Troyes: 13, 15
Turnus: 101
Turstin (Robert I's chamberlain): 206
Turstin from Bec-aux-Cauchois (William the Conqueror's standard-bearer): 244

Ulfin: 123–4
Ursula: 92, 118–20
Usk river: 133
Uten: 45, 93
Uther Pendragon: 102, 108, 110, 121n, 122–4, 126, 137n, 207, 228

Valéry (St): 230
Val-ès-Dunes (battle of –): 209, 214, 217–18, 251, 275
Varaville (battle of –): 218
Venedocia: 184–5
Vergil: 109
verisimilitude: 39, 131, 138, 146–7, 232
Vexin: 203
Vie de saint Georges: 283
Vie de sainte Marguerite: 7, 8, 11, 12, 13–29, 31–3, 40, 44–5, 47, 50, 52, 54, 59, 79, 80, 82, 151, 279, 280, 281, 282, 283; authorship of –: 15; humour in –: 21; sources of –: 15–18; speeches in –: 19–20, 23–28; structure: 18–25; style of –: 15–16
Vie de saint Nicolas: 7, 8, 11, 12, 13, 30, 33, 48n, 51–80, 151, 279, 280, 281, 282; adaptation technique: 65–75; baptismal symbolism in –: 75–6, 78; characterisation: 78–9, 82; clercs in –: 71–5, 163; direct speech in –: 67–8; manuscripts of –: 53–5; miracles: 60–1 (list of –), 66–7 (the girls saved from prostitution), 68–70 (the three counts), 75–6 (miracle of the cup), 70–3 (the abducted child), 73–4 (the strangled child); narrator's stance: 55–9; Prologue to –: 55–6, 74, 163; sources of –: 52, 59–63; structure: 59–63
Viking(s): 153, 157, 164, 168, 170, 172, 217, 283
Vita per Michaelem: 52
Vita Sancti Augustini: see Goscelin of Saint Bertin
Vita Merlini: see Geoffrey of Monmouth

Index

Vortigern: 92, 100, 101, 106, 108–9, 114, 121–2, 142, 236n
Vortimer: 122
Vortiporius: 148
Vosges: 13
Voyage of St Brendan: see Benedeit
virginity: 17, 18, 20, 25, 42n, 219n

Wales: 4, 9, 83, 84, 92, 100, 101, 112
Walter Archdeacon of Oxford: 89
Walter Giffard: 244
Walter Tirel: 265–6
Wanis and Melga: 118, 120
wassail: 236
Waukelin of Ferrières: 209
Welsh: 89 (language); 9n, 112, 149 (people)
Wenelande: 128
Westminster Abbey: 220
White Ship: 14, 265
Whitsun festivities: 125, 132–3
William (illegitimate brother of Duke Richard II): 191, 195
William (son of King Henry I): 211n
William of Arques: 213
William of Bellême: 201
William Talvas of Bellême: 208
William Clito: 14
William of Conches: 3, 83
William the Conqueror: 3, 6, 32n, 34–7, 76, 130, 157–9, 187, 189, 191, 195, 199, 200, 204, 207–8, 209–60, 267, 277, 280, 281; his youth, 213–18; defensive wars: 217–18; his claim to England: 216, 218–29; the English campaign: 229–52; his religious foundations: 219; rejection of superstition: 231–2, 237–8, 243; his marriage: 215; his offspring: 211, 215; his death: 252, 256, 257–8; his burial; 258
William II of England (Rufus): 2, 117–18, 223, 257, 260–7
William FitzOsbern: 224–5, 244, 246n
William of Jumièges, *Gesta Normannorum Ducum*: 156–9, 165, 169–70, 172, 183, 185, 189–229, 230, 238n, 239, 253–4n, 259, 278, 280
William of Malmesbury, *Gesta Regum Anglorum*: 2, 6, 158, 174, 176, 177, 183, 186n, 189, 192, 199, 200, 204n, 206, 207, 211, 215, 224, 229, 230n, 232, 236, 238–9, 241–2, 244, 255–6, 259, 262–3, 265, 267n, 268, 271, 281, 284; *De Antiquitate Glastonie Ecclesie*: 6n
William Malet: 249
William of Newburgh: 90
William I of Normandy (Longsword): 169–72, 174, 176–8, 218
William of Poitiers, *Gesta Guillelmi Ducis*: 158, 190, 211, 215, 221–2, 225, 228, 229, 230–1, 234–5, 238n, 242, 244–5, 248, 250, 254
William of Taillou (Count): 197
William of Warenne: 269
Winchester: 8, 36, 50, 142, 146, 267, 268, 269; Winchester cathedral font: 8n, 76–7; treaty of Winchester: 93

Yder: 139
Ygerne: 110, 123–4
York: 143, 184–5
Ysengrimus (Nivard's): 167
Yvor and Yni: 150

Zedelghem: 76

www.ingramcontent.com/pod-product-compliance
Lightning Source LLC
Chambersburg PA
CBHW071233230426
43668CB00011B/1414